Wittgenstein and Levinas

Ludwig Wittgenstein and ...nuel Levinas are two of the most influential and challenging thinkers of the twentieth century. Despite this, their writings are seen as coming from opposed philosophical camps and as a result little work has been done comparing the two philosophers. This book explores the hitherto neglected affinities and tensions between their philosophies, and the often antagonistic intellectual traditions each represents.

The two competing philosophical accounts of the ethical are juxtaposed in order to allow the reader to deepen their understanding of one by means of the other. The two systems of thought are brought to bear on each other in the areas of faith, guilt and vulnerability, concepts central to the discussion of ethics, and in doing so a surprising amount of commonality is highlighted. The central focus of the book is the complex, yet mutually illuminating, interplay of a number of ethical-religious themes in both Wittgenstein's mature thinking on religious belief and suffering, and Levinas's distinctive account of ethical responsibility.

This unique book demonstrates how a critical engagement with Wittgenstein and Levinas facilitates a rethinking of some of the most pressing religious, ethical and political problems facing the twenty-first century. As such, the book will be of use to postgraduate students of Continental and Analytic philosophy, as well as those interested in contemporary theology.

Bob Plant completed his Ph.D. in Philosophy and French at the University of Aberdeen in 2001. He has published widely on philosophers from both 'Analytic' and 'Continental' traditions, most recently in *Philosophy and Literature, Philosophical Investigations, Philosophy and Social Criticism, International Journal for Philosophy of Religion, Modern Theology, Journal of Scottish Philosophy* and *Journal of Religious Ethics*.

Routledge studies in twentieth-century philosophy

1. **The Story of Analytic Philosophy**
   Plot and heroes
   Edited by Anat Biletzki and Anat Matar

2. **Donald Davidson**
   Truth, meaning and knowledge
   Edited by Urszula M. Żegleń

3. **Philosophy and Ordinary Language**
   The bent and genius of our tongue
   Oswald Hanfling

4. **The Subject in Question**
   Sartre's critique of Husserl in *The Transcendence of the Ego*
   Stephen Priest

5. **Aesthetic Order**
   A philosophy of order, beauty and art
   Ruth Lorland

6. **Naturalism**
   A critical analysis
   Edited by William Lane Craig and J.P. Moreland

7. **Grammar in Early Twentieth-Century Philosophy**
   Richard Gaskin

8. **Rules, Magic and Instrumental Reason**
   A critical interpretation of Peter Winch's philosophy of the social sciences
   Berel Dov Lerner

9 **Gaston Bachelard**
Critic of science and the imagination
Cristina Chimisso

10 **Hilary Putnam**
Pragmatism and realism
Edited by James Conant and Urszula Zegleń

11 **Karl Jaspers**
Politics and metaphysics
Chris Thornhill

12 **From Kant to Davidson**
The idea of the transcendental in twentieth-century philosophy
Edited by Jeff Malpas

13 **Collingwood and the Metaphysics of Experience**
A reinterpretation
Giuseppina D'Oro

14 **The Logic of Liberal Rights**
A study in the formal analysis of legal discourse
Eric Heinze

15 **Real Metaphysics**
Edited by Hallvard Lillehammer and Gonzalo Rodriguez-Pereyra

16 **Philosophy After Postmodernism**
Civilized values and the scope of knowledge
Paul Crowther

17 **Phenomenology and Imagination in Husserl and Heidegger**
Brian Elliott

18 **Laws in Nature**
Stephen Mumford

19 **Trust and Toleration**
Richard H. Dees

20 **The Metaphysics of Perception**
Wilfrid Sellars, critical realism and the nature of experience
Paul Coates

21 **Wittgenstein, Austrian Economics, and the Logic of Action**
   Praxeological investigations
   Roderick T. Long

22 **Ineffability and Philosophy**
   André Kukla

23 **Kant, Cognitive Metaphor and Continental Philosophy**
   Clive Cazeaux

24 **Wittgenstein and Levinas**
   Ethical and religious thought
   Bob Plant

25 **Philosophy of Time**
   Time before times
   Roger McClure

Wittgenstein and Levinas

Ethical and religious thought

Bob Plant

LONDON AND NEW YORK

First published 2005
by Routledge
2 Park Square, Milton Park, Abingdon, Oxon OX14 4RN

Simultaneously published in the USA and Canada
by Routledge
270 Madison Ave, New York, NY 10016

Routledge is an imprint of the Taylor & Francis Group

Transferred to Digital Printing 2006

© 2005 Bob Plant

Typeset in Baskerville by Wearset Ltd, Boldon, Tyne and Wear

All rights reserved. No part of this book may be reprinted or reproduced or utilised in any form or by any electronic, mechanical, or other means, now known or hereafter invented, including photocopying and recording, or in any information storage or retrieval system, without permission in writing from the publishers.

British Library Cataloguing in Publication Data
A catalogue record for this book is available from the British Library

Library of Congress Cataloging in Publication Data
A catalog record for this book has been requested

ISBN10: 0-415-34995-8 (hbk)
ISBN10: 0-415-42593-X (pbk)

ISBN13: 978-0-415-34995-6 (hbk)
ISBN13: 978-0-415-42593-3 (pbk)

For Joy and John Wharton

This ribald laughter clawed at my heart. How could they laugh like that when somewhere someone was groaning in despair, suffering boundless torments?

Stefan Zweig, *Beware of Pity*

The question is not: How much are you going to get out of it? Nor is it How much are you going to put into it? But rather: How immediately are you going to say Yes to no matter what unpredictability, even when what happens seems to have no relation to what one thought was one's commitment?

John Cage, *A Year from Monday*

Contents

Preface xii
Acknowledgments xiv

Introduction 1
Hauntings 1
Wittgenstein: radical pluralism and the natural 3
Levinas: the guilt of the survivor 7
Saintliness and Levinas's anti-naturalism 8
A note on 'radical otherness' 9

1 **Peaceful thoughts: philosophy as therapy in Pyrrhonism and Wittgenstein** 12
Introduction 12
The abandonment of belief: Pyrrhonian naturalism 13
The social chameleon: ethical-political implications of Pyrrhonism 18
Wittgenstein's grammatical therapy and the sources of disease 21
Seeing the world aright: Wittgenstein's rhetoric 28
Wittgenstein and Pyrrhonian conservatism 37

2 **Trusting in a world-picture: knowledge, faith and ethics after *On Certainty*** 41
Introduction 41
Echoes of Pyrrhonism: doubt, knowledge and the groundlessness of belief 42
Rock and sand: fundamental propositions and blasphemy 52
Fools, heretics and dogmatism: the question of religious fundamentalism 57
Persuasion, conversion and judging others: ethical-political implications of On Certainty *63*

3 Pluralism, justice and vulnerability: politicizing Wittgenstein 70
Introduction 70
Politics, religion and the rhetoric of pluralism 71
Totalitarianism and Lyotard's politics of dissensus 77
Body, soul, suffering and the specter of amoralism 82
The primitive and the modern: Wittgenstein on Frazer's Golden Bough *90*
Reconsidering Lyotard's pagan justice 94

4 Interlude: on preferring peace to war 96

5 Wretchedness without recompense: Wittgenstein on religion, ethics and guilt 101
Introduction 101
The consequences of belief: understanding Wittgenstein's hesitancy 102
Immortality and ethical responsibility 109
Sin, wretchedness and bad conscience 113
Guilt, being judged and Dostoyevsky's imperative: religion without recompense 116

6 Trespassing: guilt and sacrifice in Heidegger, Levinas and ordinary life 122
Introduction 122
Conscience and guilt in Heidegger's Being and Time *123*
Levinas's ghosts: trespassing and the violence of being 128
Guilt and the grammar of the face 131
Confessions: the singularity of guilt and ordinary experience 138

7 The unreasonableness of ethics: Levinas and the limits of responsibility 148
Introduction 148
Thanking God for the third party: the haunting of the political/Levinas's prayer 149
The unreasonableness of ethics: Levinas's anti-naturalism 159
Versions of the natural: Levinas, Nietzsche and Wittgenstein 166
The bark of a dog: the other (as) animal 171
Something animal 177

8 Contaminations: Levinas, Wittgenstein and Derrida   180
Introduction 180
Haunted houses: Levinas's phenomenology of home 181
The perils of hospitality 183
From the law of iterability to the confessional 186
Skepticism, trust and violence 188
(Deciding) On the impossible 193
Enduring faith 196

Synopsis	199
Notes	201
Bibliography	269
Index	286

Preface

This book is a revised version of my doctoral thesis, written under the supervision of Dr. Jonathan Friday and Dr. Ian Maclachlan at the University of Aberdeen between 1997 and 2001. That is the abridged account. The slightly longer version goes something like this: I began studying philosophy (of a broadly 'Analytic' type) in 1992, and soon became preoccupied with the significance of Wittgenstein's later work for ethics and the philosophy of religion. Then, between 1995 and 1997, I studied for a postgraduate degree in modern 'Continental' philosophy. My reasons for taking this route were entirely circumstantial, but it was here that I first encountered Levinas. I will not pretend that my initial reaction to his philosophy was anything other than hostile. Nevertheless, by working through selected essays and interviews I gradually found myself warming to certain aspects of Levinas's thinking. (As the reader will discover, I am not wholly persuaded by Levinas's distinctive oeuvre.) To the dismay of some of my tutors, throughout this period my interest in Wittgenstein persisted, and it was here that I first read *On Certainty* – a text that continues to preoccupy me more than any other of his writings. All this eventually culminated in a Masters dissertation on the question of religious apologetics in Wittgenstein and Levinas. It was on the basis of this piece that I began my doctoral work in 1997.

Throughout the following chapters I draw on the work of a number of philosophers from both so-called 'Analytic' and 'Continental' traditions. However, in all this a rather special place is reserved for Derrida. Given the explicit focus of this book I should therefore say something about my interest in him.

I came to Derrida's voluminous writings very late. In fact, prior to beginning my doctorate I had conscientiously avoided him. The image I then had of Derrida (an image that continues to dominate much 'Analytic' philosophy) was of an insidious – albeit playful – 'postmodern' skeptic. After reading his work on a variety of ethical-political questions, I was therefore surprised to discover that Derrida was not only a deeply humane thinker but anti-skeptical in a not dissimilar way to Wittgenstein. Moreover, in his recent articulation and development of a number of Levinasian themes, Derrida's work fed naturally into many of my most persistent philosophical interests. It therefore seemed (and still seems) to me entirely appropriate that he should be allowed to 'haunt' the following analysis of Wittgenstein and Levinas.

It is customary at this juncture to force a neat, linear narrative out of such biographical details. But that would give a false impression of how this book came about. Instead, I would like to cite a few passages from Wittgenstein's last notebooks *On Certainty*, for these encapsulate the central themes of the following chapters.

Toward the end of *On Certainty* Wittgenstein imagines someone whose beliefs and practices seem 'radically' different from his own. He there writes:

> Is it wrong for me to be guided in my actions by the propositions of physics? Am I to say I have no good ground for doing so? Isn't precisely this what we call a 'good ground'? ... Supposing we met people who did not regard that as a telling reason. Now, how do we imagine this? Instead of the physicist, they consult an oracle. (And for that we consider them primitive.) Is it wrong for them to consult an oracle and be guided by it? – If we call this 'wrong' aren't we using our language-game as a base from which to *combat* theirs? ... And are we right or wrong to combat it? Of course there are all sorts of slogans which will be used to support our proceedings ... Where two principles really do meet which cannot be reconciled with one another, then each man declares the other a fool and heretic ... I said I would 'combat' the other man, – but wouldn't I give him *reasons*? Certainly; but how far do they go? At the end of reasons comes *persuasion*. (Think what happens when missionaries convert natives.)
>
> (1999: §§608–12)

In these few brief remarks Wittgenstein raises a host of troubling questions concerning rhetoric, conflict and the limits of rational justification. Since first reading *On Certainty* I have found myself continually drawn back to these specific passages. But it seemed to me then, as now, that the questions Wittgenstein here poses call for an ethical, as well as the more customary epistemological response. It is my hope that the present book goes some way toward providing this.

A final word. Throughout the book I have indulged in what some will judge an excessive amount of cross-referencing. In my defense I would like to say two things. First, many of the texts I refer to are either not indexed at all (Derrida's publishers are especially guilty of this), or insufficiently detailed on this score. This, it seems to me, is a deeply frustrating practice with no discernible rationale. And second, this book represents the first detailed discussion of Wittgenstein *and* Levinas. As such, I felt it was important to bring as much relevant material to bear on the themes in question.

Bob Plant
Sheffield, 2004

Acknowledgments

This book would not have been possible without the encouragement, philosophical rigor and therapeutic laughter of Jonathan Friday and Ian Maclachlan. It is also due to their friendship that my time spent under their supervision at the University of Aberdeen has left me with only the happiest of memories. I would also like to thank Simon Glendinning for his support and, not least, for setting the precedent in openly ignoring the so-called 'Analytic/Continental divide.' Sincere gratitude to the departments of Philosophy and French at the University of Aberdeen for providing such a hospitable environment in which to work, and to Paul Tomassi and Gordon Graham in particular for their comments on early drafts of Chapters 2 and 3 (respectively). Thanks also to Eric Matthews for his perceptive remarks on my doctoral thesis, and to Peter Baumann for so many stimulating conversations that sharpened my awareness of (to borrow Derrida's formulation) 'the production of the extraordinary *within* the ordinary.' For their friendship and generosity a special thank you to Jackie Rattray and Audrey Small.

Sections of this book have appeared (in condensed form) in a number of journals. I am grateful to them for granting me permission to reproduce some of the material here. A version of Chapter 1 was published as 'The End(s) of Philosophy: Rhetoric, Therapy and Wittgenstein's Pyrrhonism', in *Philosophical Investigations*, Vol. 27, No. 3 (July 2004), 222–57. Parts of Chapter 2 were published as 'Our Natural Constitution: Wolterstorff on Reid and Wittgenstein', in *Journal of Scottish Philosophy*, Vol. 1, No. 2 (Autumn 2003), 157–70. Parts of Chapters 2 and 3 appeared as 'Blasphemy, Dogmatism and Injustice: The Rough Edges of *On Certainty*', in *International Journal for Philosophy of Religion*, Vol. 54, No. 2 (October 2003), 101–35. Parts of Chapters 5 and 6 were published as 'Ethics without Exit: Levinas and Murdoch', in *Philosophy and Literature*, Vol. 27, No. 2 (October 2003), 456–70. Parts of Chapters 5 and 7 were published as 'Doing Justice to the Derrida–Levinas Connection: A Response to Mark Dooley', in *Philosophy & Social Criticism*, Vol. 29, No. 4 (July 2003), 427–50. I would also like to thank three anonymous readers for their remarks on an earlier draft of this book, and Joe Whiting, Amrit Bangard, Terry Clague and Yeliz Ali at Routledge and Gail Welsh and Alan Fidler at Wearset for their help and encouragement in this project.

Introduction

> This life of ours is a hospital, in which all the patients are obsessed with a desire to change beds. One would prefer to suffer near the stove, and another thinks he would soon recover near the window. I always have the feeling that I would be better anywhere except where I actually am, and the idea of a removal is one which I am constantly discussing with my Soul.
>
> C. Baudelaire, *The Poems in Prose*

> If our condition were truly happy, we should not have to divert our thoughts from it in order to be happy.
>
> B. Pascal, *The Pensées*

Hauntings

Levinas was once asked whether, contrary to structuralism, his work represented 'an attempt to preserve subjectivity in some form?' His response was unequivocal: 'My thinking on this matter goes in the opposite direction to structuralism.' Levinas's commitment is not, of course, to the Cartesian 'self-sufficient *cogito*' (1984: 63) but rather to an ethically constituted subject. For the 'other haunts our ontological existence and keeps the psyche awake ... Even though we are ontologically free to refuse the other, we remain forever accused, with a bad conscience' (ibid.: 63–4). Although the philosophical grounding and implications of these remarks are hardly self-evident, there are two reasons for my beginning with them. First, part of my objective is to show that the sentiments expressed here form the nucleus of Levinas's philosophy. That the other 'haunts our ontological existence' is the guiding thread running throughout Levinas's writings, and it is in this sense that his work constitutes an extended meditation on existential 'guilt.' The second reason for citing these passages is that they foreground the central themes of my argument more broadly. I will now explain how.

That the human subject cannot adequately be understood abstracted from its relation to others is a broad enough claim to raise little philosophical interest. What is significant is how Levinas's specific understanding of this relationship renders a distinctly ethical account of subjectivity. It is the aforementioned notion of 'being haunted' that I will therefore explore within a number of ethical, political and religious contexts. But posing the question of subjectivity in this way simultaneously moves us within the orbit of certain aspects of Wittgenstein's thinking. This may seem a surprising claim given that Wittgenstein's later work appears to lack a 'developed notion of the self' (Werhane 1995: 62). While this may be true if one means by 'self' something akin to the Cartesian *res cogitans*,[1] there is nevertheless a sense of ethical subjectivity in Wittgenstein's work that is easily overlooked in the routine excavation of his writings for epistemological theses. Of course, elucidating this ethical dimension requires considerable textual reconstruction. It also necessitates discretion regarding some of Wittgenstein's more often quoted remarks. I do not want to suggest that Wittgenstein provides a systematic account of ethical subjectivity. Nevertheless, I will argue that he provides important indications of how such an account should be conceived. It is at this point that Levinas's thinking becomes extremely pertinent.

Levinas's work is often as bewildering as it is insightful. Indeed, his general textual practice frequently resembles a '*poetic composition*' (Wittgenstein 1994a: 24) rather than anything traditionally 'philosophical.' But Levinas's thinking is nevertheless rich in philosophical content. As I will explain, for those unfamiliar with Levinas (or for those, like myself, who find him continually able to disrupt their sense of familiarity), his writings might usefully be read as a sustained attempt to 'say' what, according to the early (and arguably later[2]) Wittgenstein, can only be 'shown.' That is, Levinas's incessant running 'against the boundaries of language' (Wittgenstein 1993: 44) represents his endeavor to write 'the book on Ethics which really was a book on Ethics' (ibid.: 40) that Wittgenstein thought to be both 'absolutely hopeless' (ibid.: 44) *and* the most 'important' (1996b: 94) task.[3] These aspects of Wittgenstein's early thinking provide an initial route into Levinas's work. However, my principal concern is to show that there are more interesting correlations between Levinas and the later Wittgenstein. For, while the orientation of each philosopher may seem very different, Wittgenstein nevertheless has valuable things to say on a number of 'Levinasian' themes. Not only are both philosophers concerned with the relationship between the 'grammar' of the ethical and religious, so too does each focus attention on (for example) the human face, vulnerability and guilt.

Although within the proceeding chapters I draw on the work of a number of philosophers from both 'Analytic' and 'Continental' traditions, a special place is reserved for Derrida, whose thinking provides a continual point of reference. It should be noted, however, that my primary interest in Derrida lies with his more recent writings on ethical, political and religious matters.[4] What specifically concerns me is how Derrida both problematizes and recasts a number of Levinasian motifs in his reflections on the aporias of the gift, hospitality and home, the sacrificial structure of ethical life, and the manifold ruses of 'good conscience.' While there is a substantial secondary literature available concerning the relationship between Derrida and Levinas[5] (and some interest in Derrida and Wittgenstein[6]), there is currently no detailed work available on Wittgenstein and Levinas.[7] I would therefore like to say something about each philosopher in turn, and thereby contextualize my own project.

Wittgenstein: radical pluralism and the natural

While Wittgenstein is not a systematic thinker, his later writings have been extensively quarried and their central 'arguments' extracted. But this general philosophical appropriation has been undertaken with little regard for the broader therapeutic-naturalistic vision therein.[8] Due to his recurrent emphasis on 'language-games' (1958: §24), '*forms of life*' (ibid.: p. 226) and 'world-picture[s]' (1999: §167), Wittgenstein's later work is often seen to be fundamentally concerned with linguistic-conceptual 'plurality.' This is perhaps unsurprising given that his avowed 'interest is in shewing that things which look the same are really different' (Drury 1981: 171).[9] Nevertheless, two important questions need to be raised here: (1) What are the philosophical motives for Wittgenstein's concern with these 'differences'?[10] And (2) how deep do such 'differences' actually go? I will now briefly indicate what is at stake in these two questions, and the role each plays in my argument.

What are the philosophical motives for Wittgenstein's concern with 'differences'?

In Chapter 1 I argue that this question can only be answered by considering Wittgenstein's broader therapeutic aspirations. A crucial part of what motivates his aforementioned preoccupation with 'differences' is his desire for a life liberated from theoretical bewilderment. These perplexities arise because language 'seduces us into thinking' (1958: §93) that – as Wittgenstein himself had once thought – philosophical questions can only be answered by discovering the 'a priori ... *utterly simple*' (ibid.: §97) essence of things, and specifically 'the *essence* of language' (ibid.: §91). The later Wittgenstein attempts to demonstrate how this supposition actually exacerbates those perplexities we seek liberation from. If we resist the lures of abstract theorizing (and the '*preconceived idea* of crystalline purity' guiding it) and instead concern ourselves with describing the multifarious ways language actually functions 'in ordinary life' (ibid.: §108) we find that different language-games are governed by different, more-or-less interwoven 'rules.' Only by acknowledging and respecting this 'given' (ibid.: p. 226) multiplicity[11] can we eschew both our obsession with 'essences' and the philosophical anxieties this generates.

4 *Introduction*

Wittgenstein's preoccupation with conceptual vulnerabilities is not, however, unprecedented. Thus, a number of striking similarities emerge between his work and Pyrrhonian Skepticism. Both Wittgenstein and Sextus Empiricus cast their respective projects in overtly therapeutic terms, and similarly share the ideal of the non-philosophical life liberated from conceptual anxieties. But what also needs to be recognized here is the ethical-political terrain of each philosophy. For Sextus this relates directly to the rejection of the life of theoretical speculation and inculcation of a natural 'ataraxia' (unperturbedness). Recovering our 'animal' nature is therefore ethically significant insofar as it liberates us also from the burdens of ethical-political commitment. Only by taking our guidance from momentary 'appearances' (1996: 1:19), and passively conforming to the 'handed down laws and customs' (ibid.: 1:24) of our immediate community, can we both procure and maintain 'ataraxia.' These implications of Pyrrhonism are both troubling and problematic. Nevertheless, they are extremely useful for negotiating the somewhat less obvious ethical-political terrain of Wittgenstein's later work. Given both Wittgenstein's preoccupation with multiplicity and plurality, and commitment to only describe the 'actual use of language' (1958: §124), his work has often been suspected of quasi-Pyrrhonian 'conservatism' and/or relativism. This brings us to the second question.

How deep do the aforementioned 'differences' actually go?

In order to answer this question attention must be given to the minimal naturalism underpinning Wittgenstein's later thinking. If within the multiplicity of language-games, forms of life and world-pictures we discover *radical* 'differences' at play, then the social realm could legitimately be characterized as one of interminable conflict or (in Lyotard's terms) 'dissensus.' As Wittgenstein remarks: 'Where two principles ... meet which cannot be reconciled with one another, then each man declares the other a fool and heretic' (1999: §611). On this account, the prospects for non-coercive communication between such parties look increasingly bleak, not least because '[a]t the end of reasons comes *persuasion*. (Think what happens when missionaries convert natives.)' (ibid.: §612). Such sentiments are common in *On Certainty*, and it is therefore unsurprising that this text has been identified as Wittgenstein's most conservative and relativistic work. But while those making such accusations correctly identify *On Certainty* as having *some* ethical-political import, they underestimate its internal complexities. For a thorough investigation reveals that the depth of those 'differences' and conflicts between world-pictures here remains undetermined. Not only does Wittgenstein allude to 'something universal' (ibid.: §440), his reflections on 'man ... as an animal; as a primitive being' (ibid.: §475) and the ineliminable role of 'trust' (ibid.: §509)[12] in all language-games suggests that the social realm is not *fundamentally* fragmented. Rather, as he suggests elsewhere, the 'common behavior of mankind' (1958: §206) provides the natural background against which human life has meaning.[13] (As I argue later, this point is substantiated both in Wittgenstein's remarks on the derivative nature of linguistic behavior from '*pre-linguistic*' (1990: §541), 'primitive behavior' (ibid.: §545), and his numerous reflections on the human body, face and soul.) I have intentionally referred to Wittgenstein's naturalism as 'minimal' – or what might be called a 'naturalism of surfaces' (Gaita 2003: 194). This is not willful equivocation, for the sort of naturalism I attribute to Wittgenstein is – as I argue in Chapter 3 – necessarily presupposed by even the most radically anti-naturalistic, anti-foundationalist thinkers. This minimal naturalism is therefore neither reductive nor insensitive to the genuine 'differences' between human beings, cultures, historical epochs and indeed human and non-human animals. But perhaps the best way of expressing this point is to recall Wittgenstein's own allusion to the relationship 'between concepts and very general facts of nature' (1958: p. 230). For I similarly want to supply 'remarks on the natural history of human beings,' and thereby make 'observations which no one has doubted, but which have [often] escaped remark ... because they are always before our eyes' (ibid.: §415).

As intimated above, Wittgenstein's naturalism is not immediately obvious in *On Certainty*. Nevertheless, if one reads this text alongside others (as I do in Chapter 3), then a clearer picture emerges of how Wittgenstein's naturalism fits into his broader therapeutic project. Moreover, identifying this dimension of Wittgenstein's later work enables us to respond to a closely related accusation made against his thinking on specifically religious matters; namely, Wittgenstein's apparent anti-apologetic 'fideism.'[14] As Smart pithily remarks, Wittgenstein's approach to religion (or at least a certain interpretation of this[15]) is problematic 'because it would put me out of a job, or at least out of half a job, since it would make the study of religions other than one's own ... [a] waste of time' (Smart 1971: 173). The problem of 'Wittgensteinian fideism' provides a useful test case for examination in the light of Wittgenstein's naturalism, and in Chapter 5 I argue that the problem of fideism only arises if one disregards this important aspect of Wittgenstein's thinking. On a fairly common, quasi-communitarian reading of his later work[16] many of his remarks do seem to lead to fideistic conclusions.[17] Thus, when Wittgenstein claims that the believer and non-believer each employ an 'entirely different kind of reasoning' (1994b: 58) and remain on an 'entirely different plane' (ibid.: 56), it appears that he is committed to a radical incommensurability thesis. However, when in 'Remarks on Frazer's *Golden Bough*' Wittgenstein criticizes Frazer's anthropology of 'primitive'[18] religious and magical practices, he emphasizes 'the importance of finding *connecting links*' (1996a: 69) between these allegedly 'superstitious' practices and 'any genuinely

6 *Introduction*

religious action of today' (ibid.: 64). What Frazer fails to take into account is how the rituals he describes reflect a 'general inclination' (ibid.: 78), 'kinship' (ibid.: 70) or 'common spirit' (ibid.: 80) of human beings.[19] Thus, in those specific 'phenomena' connected with 'death, birth, and sexual life' (ibid.: 66–7)[20] we discover the most elementary features which unify human life *despite* its immense socio-historical diversity. But such remarks are of more general ethical-political interest beyond questions of religious belief. This can be seen in Greisch's recent remarks concerning the difference between the later Wittgenstein and Werner Marx's work on the 'unifying principle' (Greisch 1999: 50) of sympathy. Greisch thus laments how

> anyone who is familiar with the thought of the later Wittgenstein will have difficulty sharing the optimism of [Werner Marx] who calculates that an ethics of compassion appears capable of surmounting the heterogeneity of language games and the corresponding forms of life.
>
> (1999: 58)

Although both Greisch and Smart express the same general misgiving about Wittgenstein's later work (namely, that it divides human life into fundamentally incommensurable 'forms of life'),[21] Greisch puts a distinctly ethical-political twist on the matter. This emphasis is correct, not least because the question of religious 'fideism' is already an ethical-political question of how to engage justly with a 'world picture' other than one's own.[22] However, what is striking about Greisch's remarks is how he overlooks the role of 'primitive' behaviors (including those of 'sympathy' (Wittgenstein 1993: 381)) in Wittgenstein's own thinking – behaviors upon which ethical-political life is hinged.

This is how the first few chapters of the book are oriented. In Chapter 5, however, I focus on Wittgenstein's ethicalization of certain 'religious' themes. Specifically what interest me here are his suggestions concerning the relationship between the notion of 'immortality' and 'ethical ideas of responsibility,' and how the latter are connected with an experience of guilt 'that even death couldn't stop' (1994b: 70).[23] The sentiments expressed here are not uncommon in Wittgenstein's work, for the intimated fissure between the ethical 'ought' and ontological 'can' is a recurrent feature of his account of genuine religiosity.[24] Toward the end of Chapter 5 I therefore argue that, rather than reading Wittgenstein's antiapologetics as essentially fideistic, we might instead read him as gesturing toward an ethicalized conception of religiosity where the believer is promised nothing 'in return' for their commitment. The possibility of faith without eschatological assurance is, I believe, a more philosophically interesting way of understanding Wittgenstein's claim that the 'man who stated … [his religious convictions] categorically was more intelligent than the man who was apologetic about it' (ibid.: 62–3). It also helps us to elucidate the relationship between religious belief and ethical responsibility. Yet despite these tantalizing possibilities, Wittgenstein never systematically worked out his views on religion and ethics. What is beyond serious dispute, however, is that he firmly believed that the religious and ethical dimensions of human life are intimately connected – so much so that no real sense could be made of the former without reference to the latter. Wittgenstein's fragmentary reflections on religion thus call for supplementation, and – as I argue in Chapters 6 and 7 – Levinas provides this.

Levinas: the guilt of the survivor

Like Wittgenstein, Levinas considers religion and ethics to be inseparable. But he goes further than Wittgenstein and describes the 'relation with the other' *as* 'religion' (1996a: 7). That is, we must seek 'a non-ontological notion of God,' and this is only possible 'starting from the relationship with the other [human being]' (2000: 180). Still, a number of important parallels emerge between Levinas and Wittgenstein. Both, for example, see vulnerability and suffering as fundamental in one's relations with others. Moreover, Levinas's reflections on the ethical significance of the 'face' (which constitutes 'a summons and a demand' in its silent '"Thou shalt not kill"' (1998b: 186)) usefully extends Wittgenstein's own remarks on the body and face. I highlight these correlations in Chapters 6 and 7. But there is one facet of Levinas's work that enables us to sharpen some of Wittgenstein's thoughts on religious and ethical themes. Though it is rarely designated as such, Levinas's ethics is haunted by a very particular notion of guilt; the guilt 'of the survivor' (2000: 12). Briefly stated, Levinas maintains that simply in virtue of my being-in-the-world I live *at the expense of another*. 'What is an individual, if not a usurper?' he rhetorically inquires, '[w]hat is signified by the advent of conscience ... if not the discovery of corpses beside me and my horror of existing by assassination?' (1997a: 100). Challenging Heidegger's preoccupation with ontology, Levinas therefore claims that 'my being calls for justification: being-there, is that not already occupying another's place? The *Da* of *Dasein* is already an ethical problem' (1993: 48). As such, the first question is not '"Why is there being rather than nothingness?"' but rather '"Is it just to be?"' (ibid.: 92). These are shocking themes, not least because Levinas repudiates the suggestion that such guilt can be assuaged. Rather, one's relation to the other is 'an exposure without shelter, as under a leaden sun without protective shade' (2000: 196), for responsibility actually 'increases as one responds to it; it is an impossibility of acquitting the debt' (ibid.: 195). Concerning the other 'our accounts are never settled' (1993: 125), not only because one could always have done more for *this* other but also because even the most ethical of responses to *this* other is always at the expense of *another* other. Levinas's deeply non-teleological conception of ethics is why religiosity needs to be thought 'independently of the Happy

8 *Introduction*

End' (1988a: 175) promised by specific religious world-pictures. I therefore argue in Chapter 6 that a proper understanding of Levinas's conception of guilt can only be attained if we recognize its dual source in: (1) the Nazi death camps of the 1940s, and (2) Heidegger's *Being and Time*. I will briefly explain this twofold approach.

By his own admission, Levinas's thinking is 'dominated' by the 'memory of the Nazi horror' (1997a: 291). Indeed, his work constitutes a sustained attempt to respond to the question: 'can we speak of an absolute commandment after Auschwitz? Can we speak of morality after the failure of morality?' (1988a: 175). Not only does Levinas's rhetoric parallel that of more 'confessional' Holocaust writers, his concern with the 'nakedness' (1993: 102), 'exposure' (1998b: 145) and 'vulnerability' (1996a: 102) of the other necessarily leads us to reflect on the daily realities of the death camps. Yet, it is in Levinas's remarks on the 'shame of surviving' (1998b: 169) that the philosophical force of the Holocaust on his writings truly emerges.

Relating Levinas's ethics to Heidegger's ontology is a more precarious enterprise, given the former's suspicions concerning the ethical-political implications of the Heideggerian project. Although Levinas considers *Being and Time* to be 'one of the finest books in the history of philosophy' (1992: 37), he remains unsure that Heidegger's notorious affiliation with the Nazis (and specifically his 'silence concerning ... the Holocaust' (1989: 487)) can be entirely dissociated from the central themes of that 'extraordinary book' (ibid.: 488). Nevertheless, in Chapter 6 I argue that §§54–60 of *Being and Time* (regarding the 'call of conscience' and ontological 'guilt') are crucial for understanding both Levinas's ethics and Derrida's subsequent articulation of many of the former's central themes. (I turn explicitly to Derrida in Chapter 8.) Although these themes are intimately connected to Heidegger's analysis of Dasein as that 'entity which in its Being has this very Being as an issue' (1999: p. 68) which Levinas rejects, they nevertheless provide the latter with the raw philosophical material from which to assemble his own ethicalized account of subjectivity – that is, a subject who is haunted not by its own 'potentiality-for-Being' (ibid.: p. 276) but by the *other* who calls its murderous being-in-the-world into question.

Saintliness and Levinas's anti-naturalism

If commentators have underestimated Wittgenstein's naturalism, then Levinas's anti-naturalism has received even less attention. In Chapter 7 I address this omission by considering: (1) why Levinas casts his ethics in an overtly 'religious' vocabulary, and (2) how his ethics feeds off a distinctly bleak conception of 'the natural.' The central issue here is Levinas's claim that in sacrificing one's own interests and welfare for the sake of another (and our persistent belief that 'saintliness' (1988a: 172) or 'love without reward is valuable' (ibid.: 176–7)) the realm of 'the human breaks with pure being.' In short, the human is an 'unreasonable animal' because it 'cannot not admire saintliness ... that is, the person who in his being is more attached to the being of the other than to his own' (ibid.: 172). This claim not only lies at the heart of Levinas's conception of religiosity, it is also what founds his anti-naturalism. For he maintains that 'the first truth of ontology [is] the struggle to *be*' and it is this principle that governs the natural realm. Contrary to the laws of being, ethics is '*against nature* because it forbids the murderousness of my natural will to put my own existence first' (1984: 60).

One outcome of Levinas's anti-naturalism is that his purportedly 'radical' rethinking of ethics simply reiterates traditional anthropocentric assumptions. He therefore insists that, although '[o]ne cannot entirely refuse the face of an animal ... the priority here is not found in the animal, but in the human face' (1988a: 169); ethical concern for non-human animals 'arises from the transference to animals of the idea of suffering' (ibid.: 172). According to Levinas, genuine concern for others marks a *radical* break, not only from the animal component of human being, but also from what is 'reasonable.' On this latter point Wittgenstein would agree: the ethical is indeed not founded upon 'reason.' However, Levinas's conclusion that ethics is therefore 'unreasonable' must be questioned. Here, I argue, it would be better to borrow Wittgenstein's terms and say that ethical life 'is not reasonable (or unreasonable)' (1999: §559), for talking of 'reason' here diverts attention away from those natural, primitive phenomena '[w]e are used ... to "dismissing" ... as irrational [or] as corresponding to a low state of intelligence, etc.' (1993: 389). Levinas misrepresents the natural realm insofar as he neglects the possibility that 'it is a primitive reaction to tend, to treat, the part that hurts when someone else is in pain; and not merely when oneself is' (Wittgenstein 1990: §540). In short, Levinas's bleak vision of the natural simultaneously excludes those primitive reactions upon which ethical life (including 'saintliness') is founded; natural behaviors we share with many non-human animals.

A note on 'radical otherness'

Attention to Levinas's writings remains somewhat uneven in contemporary philosophy. His work is embraced more-or-less critically by those casting themselves as rigorously (sometimes exclusively) 'Continental.' Often Levinas seems more at home in departments of religious studies, literature or cultural theory, and in many academic institutions his work receives no attention at all. The reasons for this are doubtless complex,[25] but the lack of secondary literature currently available that attempts to present Levinas's thought to those working outside 'Continental' circles can only exacerbate this situation. Still, while Levinas's conceptual vocabulary may not have captured the imagination of many philosophers, notions of the 'absolute singularity' and 'radical otherness of the "other"' have become dominant in many other disciplines.[26] Clearly the value of this terminology should be assessed within the particular context of its application. However, it is equally apparent that such tropes are frequently used without any explanation or justification[27] – what Bernstein rightly condemns as 'the facile "postmodern" temptation to lump together all differences under the general rubric of *the* "Other"' (1991: 219).[28] Too much philosophical mischief has been done with this terminology, and yet it is routinely assumed that 'radical otherness' makes perfectly good sense. Although I focus on this in Chapters 3 and 5, the hazard with such notions can be easily summarized. Even if one accepts that the other *is* 'radically other' (and this is far from unproblematic), nothing of any *ethical* consequence necessarily follows; one might just as well talk of the 'relation' with the other in terms of wonder, astonishment or simple befuddlement.[29] If the other is indeed *radically* 'other' then how could one ever know that there had been an encounter with the other, for *as such* the other 'would not even show up' (Derrida 1992a: 68)?[30] A second question emerges at this juncture that relates specifically to Levinas's work. By stressing the relation between self and the singular 'other,' Levinas must account for the passage between the ethical relation and the political relation concerning those *other* 'others' outside the intimacy of the face-to-face relation. So, something substantive needs to be said in order to: (1) account for the very notion of 'radical otherness,' and (2) bridge the gap between the mere encounter with this 'radically other' and the demands of ethical-political responsibility. Although Levinas does attempt to explain this movement from ethics to justice, his recurrent emphasis on the *absolute* singularity of the 'other' inevitably makes the realm of the political appear as a 'betrayal' (1994a: 158) of the ethical relation. Without simply rejecting the notion of 'otherness,' I want to temper its purported radicality by reference to Wittgenstein's minimal naturalism.[31] My contention is that critically negotiating between Levinas and Wittgenstein in this way not only brings their respective philosophical projects into close (though not always comfortable) proximity, but also enables us to address matters of ethical, political and religious importance.

Before substantiating these claims, there is one further point I would like to make concerning the assumed 'otherness' of so-called 'Continental' philosophy in 'Analytic' circles (and vice versa). While I recognize that it is possible to maintain the distinction between these 'traditions,' in this book I do not do so. It is not that I have deliberately avoided this relatively recent demarcation, but rather that it simply does not interest me. Likewise, I do not think that those in the Continental camp are inherently 'difficult' while those on the Analytic side are blessed with innate 'clarity' – philosophers are 'difficult' in many different ways. I make no apologies for all this, although some will doubtless think a justification is necessary.

To those readers all I can say is that if there is any value in the proceeding analyses (and, as always, that is for others to judge) then it is due to my experiencing a quasi-Pyrrhonian indifference when faced with the routine antagonisms haunting contemporary philosophy. The practice of philosophy always involves tacit meta-philosophical decisions concerning what counts – and what *should* count – as 'philosophy.'[32] So, for example, in the UK Continental philosophy has pulled ranks against a wider philosophical establishment that often simply refuses to acknowledge the former as 'seriously philosophical.' But it would be mistaken to think that Continental philosophers are wholly innocent on this score. Philosophical sectarianism and questionable intellectual 'good consciences' plague both sides of the so-called 'Analytic/Continental divide.' The situation has perhaps begun to change in recent years, but this remains both piecemeal and often cynical in its motivation. While the need for a critical hospitality between these enclaves remains, in the interim perhaps a strategic indifference will have to suffice.

1 Peaceful thoughts
Philosophy as therapy in Pyrrhonism and Wittgenstein

> I have noticed that children are rarely afraid of thunder unless the claps are terrible and actually hurt the ear. Otherwise this fear only affects them when they know that the thunder sometimes hurts or kills. When reason brings fear, reassurance comes through habit.
>
> Rousseau, Emile

> A philosopher is always someone for whom philosophy is not *given*, someone who in essence must question the self about the essence and destination of philosophy.
>
> Derrida, Ethics, Institutions, and the Right to Philosophy

Introduction

Wittgenstein once remarked that he had 'reached a resting place' insofar as he knew that his method was 'right.'[1] He proceeded: 'My father was a business man, and I am a business man: I want my philosophy to be business-like, to get something done, to get something settled' (Drury 1981: 125–6). Despite Wittgenstein's awareness of his 'special' philosophical 'ability' (ibid.: 91), for most of his life he was nevertheless 'making plans to forsake this work and to live an entirely different mode of existence to that of the academic philosopher.' Drury concludes:

> Now we may indeed be glad that nothing final came of these various plans, and that he continued to work at his philosophical writings up to a few days before his death. But I am certain that we will not understand Wittgenstein unless we feel some sympathy and comprehension for his persistent intention to change his whole manner of life.
>
> (1981: 92)

In short, Wittgenstein's plans to change his life 'were not just a transitory impatience but a conviction that persisted for years until the time came when he realized that such a change was no longer a possibility' (ibid.). These reflections of one of Wittgenstein's few close friends[2] are of both biographical and philosophical interest. Drury was right to emphasize that

Wittgenstein's desire to abandon philosophy was no mere psychological idiosyncrasy, but rather central to his conception of good philosophic practice.[3] Moreover, in his insistence that we will misunderstand Wittgenstein's work if we ignore this motivation – or overlook that his work *had* 'a real goal' (ibid.: 96) – Drury identifies the risks involved in ignoring Wittgenstein's craving for the non-philosophical life.

Of course, conceding this does not eliminate the suspicion that it is Wittgenstein's anti-philosophical conception of philosophy that betrays something deeply idiosyncratic. But such a judgement would be hasty. For although Wittgenstein rarely showed much interest in his philosophical predecessors,[4] this should not be conflated with the claim that his approach to philosophy shares nothing with other philosophers. In this chapter I will argue that Wittgenstein's 'therapeutic' conception of philosophy can be aligned with Pyrrhonian Skepticism – a deeply provocative mode of Greek thought revived in the sixteenth century.[5] My reasons for pursuing this connection are threefold. First, because the Pyrrhonist's own therapeutic framework provides a way of understanding the *philosophical* significance of Wittgenstein's 'persistent intention' to abandon philosophy for something more pedestrian, insofar as both Pyrrhonism and Wittgenstein are guided by a philosophical ideal that aims at philosophy's own undoing. Second, because Pyrrhonism raises a number of substantive questions (regarding, for example, the aporetic nature of judgement criteria, the existential stakes of belief, and the place of 'the natural' in philosophical practice) that not only parallel many of Wittgenstein's concerns but also provide a touchstone for my subsequent engagement with ethical, political and religious themes. And third, because it is the significance of Wittgenstein's later work for ethical-political questions that ultimately interests me, and specifically whether the philosophical ideal of 'unperturbedness' (advocated by both the Pyrrhonists and Wittgenstein) can be transformed into a broader existential ideal encompassing the ethical-political realm. In later chapters we will see how attempts to 'politicize' Wittgenstein have relied upon highly selective readings of his later work which neglect its underlying naturalism. Although Wittgenstein's thought does have ethical-political significance,[6] my contention is that these implications can only be understood if we take into account where his work relates to – and ultimately diverges from – Pyrrhonism. Before this can be substantiated, however, some of Pyrrhonism's central motifs require elucidation.

The abandonment of belief: Pyrrhonian naturalism

Therapeutic techniques played a role in a number of Greco-Roman philosophies, but it is in Pyrrhonism that we find their most radical application.[7] For the Pyrrhonist it is the human tendency toward belief *per se* that constitutes the malady requiring philosophical 'treatment.'[8] Only by eliminating this craving are we released from superfluous existential burdens and can thereby attain the requisite state of *ataraxia* – an 'untroubled and tranquil condition of the soul' (Sextus 1996: 1:10).[9] It remains contentious whether Pyrrhonism should not be thought of as a technique to be mastered (but rather as a 'disposition' (ibid.: 1:8) to be inculcated) is ultimately cogent. Nevertheless, one can appreciate the motivation behind this demarcation. For what Sextus wants to emphasize is both the non-theoretical orientation of the Pyrrhonian attitude, and that no single methodology should dominate here.[10] Rather, just as 'doctors who treat physical symptoms have remedies that differ in strength ... so too the Skeptic sets forth arguments differing in strength' (ibid.: 3:280).[11] It is therefore unsurprising that the Pyrrhonist's attitude toward reasoned argumentation is extremely pragmatic. Rational procedures are to be valued only insofar as they facilitate the attainment of existential health.[12] Taking these curative aspirations into account it is necessary to determine what, according to the Pyrrhonian therapist, constitutes a 'healthy' state of being. In order to answer this question, however, we must first understand both Pyrrhonism's characterization of traditional philosophic practice and how it understands itself in relation to that heritage.

While Sextus divides traditional philosophy into the 'dogmatic,' 'academic' and 'skeptical,' his principal concern is with the latter – the others supplying a strategic point of contrast.[13] Indeed, Sextus immediately problematizes this typography by charging both dogmatist and academic with holding equally bold beliefs concerning truth.[14] For while dogmatists assert 'that they have found it,' academics claim that 'it cannot be apprehended' (ibid.: 1:4). Despite their surface differences, a closer inspection thus reveals a telling congruity between these philosophies insofar as truth retains a pivotal position in both.[15] For Pyrrhonism, however, it is this most elementary of beliefs – and the haughty assertiveness accompanying it – that requires therapeutic dissolution. As such, the Pyrrhonist expunges all explicit reference to 'truth' from her conceptual vocabulary,[16] replacing 'it is' with the more phenomenological 'it appears to me to be.'[17] This eliminative strategy is crucial because by emphasizing only what *appears* to be the case Sextus hopes to circumvent the aporias of truth-criteria.[18] After all:

> [I]n order to decide the dispute that has arisen about the criterion [of competing truth-claims], we have need of an agreed-upon criterion by means of which we shall decide it; and in order to have an agreed-upon criterion it is necessary first to have decided the dispute about the criterion. Thus, with the reasoning falling into circularity mode, finding a criterion becomes aporetic.
> (Sextus 1996: 2:20–5)[19]

But 'nobody ... disputes about whether the external object appears this way or that, but rather about whether it is such as it appears to be' (ibid.:

1:23–7).[20] The failure of traditional philosophy thus lies in its encouragement of a certain cognitive inflexibility in the face of natural forces. In their respective claims to have provided the necessary foundations upon which to live, philosophers fail to appreciate that their theories simply compound the problems they aim to resolve.[21] Engagement with any such philosophy requires numerous epistemic and normative commitments, but it is precisely these that augment[22] existential disease by hampering natural instinct.[23] What is needed to attain *ataraxia* is not dogma but the inculcation of a natural pliancy in the face of life's unpredictabilities.[24] In short, the Pyrrhonist wants to extract the normative from her life and thereby emphasize that 'we can just go on living as nature takes us, without a . . . view about how things *ought* to go on' (Nussbaum 1991: 531).

What therefore underpins the Pyrrhonian attitude is an appeal to the realm of animality. Indeed:

> When [Pyrrho's] fellow-passengers on board a ship were all unnerved by a storm, he kept calm and confident, pointing to a little pig in the ship that went on eating, and telling them that such was the unperturbed state in which the wise man should keep himself.
>
> (Diogenes 1925: 481)

Leaving aside for the moment its problematic normativity, this model clearly sits uncomfortably alongside the dominant tendency of Western thought to elevate the human realm far above that of the animal. But for the Pyrrhonist humanity has much to learn from its bestial neighbors if the desire for *ataraxia* is to be satisfied.[25] After all:

> What creature escapes being wrecked in the tempest? The creature who goes through life only as natural instinct prompts it, without ambitious enterprises, without oppositional structure . . . Not builders of fortresses, but nomads, who move along grazing here and there as natural need dictates.
>
> (Nussbaum 1991: 523)

Supplementing his suggestion that a deep congruity exists between dogmatic and academic philosophies, Sextus proceeds to delineate another point of contact, this time between these positions and Pyrrhonism. For academic, dogmatist and skeptic are all said to share the goal of *ataraxia* – thereby providing the Pyrrhonist with a practical measure against which to assert her superiority. As mentioned above, the divergence between Pyrrhonism and dogmatic philosophy emerges in the latter's mistaken assumption that the attainment of objective truth is prerequisite to securing this shared liberatory end.[26] According to the Pyrrhonist, however, *ataraxia* can only be achieved through the substitution of the pursuit of truth for the life of momentary phenomenological

16 *Philosophy as therapy*

experience: 'Not anything that lies beyond this, no, *this* – the way life actually goes in nature – *this* is the end' (ibid.: 532). Pyrrhonism thus questions not merely the possibility of attaining truth but, more radically, the benefit of even trying to do so. Abandoning this obsessive commitment one is freed from theoretical speculation to follow 'natural animal impulse' (ibid.: 546).[27] Thus, according to Diogenes, Pyrrho himself 'led a life consistent with this doctrine, going out of his way for nothing, taking no precaution but facing all risks as they came' (1925: 475). Released from the burdens of commitment one is – like the wild beast – left only with fleeting 'appearances' (Sextus 1996: 1:19) and the guidance of instinct.[28] The changing world simply 'strikes' the Pyrrhonist who, in turn, maintains a state of passive acquiescence, allowing herself to be 'swayed' (Nussbaum 1991: 533).

But what is it about *belief* that impedes the 'untroubled and tranquil . . . soul'? Sextus explains:

> [T]he person who believes that something is by nature good or bad is constantly upset; when he does not possess the things that seem to be good, he thinks he is being tormented by things that are by nature bad, and he chases after the things he supposes to be good; then, when he gets these, he falls into still more torments because of irrational and immoderate exultation, and, fearing any change, he does absolutely everything in order not to lose the things that seem to him good. But the person who takes no position as to what is by nature good or bad neither avoids nor pursues intensely. As a result, he achieves *ataraxia*.
>
> (1996: 1:27–8)[29]

> [H]aving in addition a belief [that something is by nature good or bad] is worse than the actual experience itself, just as sometimes people undergoing surgery or some other such experience bear up under it while bystanders faint because of their belief that what is going on is bad.
>
> (1996: 3:235–6)[30]

Disquiet, pain and suffering are an inextricable feature of natural life. Sextus' point is that while these cannot be eliminated, one can nevertheless avoid aggravating them unnecessarily.[31] The Pyrrhonist's aspirations are not therefore naively utopian, for although *ataraxia* is indeed his aim regarding matters of superfluous belief, he does not think the same degree of unperturbedness is possible in all areas of life. Certainly 'sometimes he is cold and thirsty and has various feelings like those,' but

> whereas ordinary people are affected by two circumstances – namely by the *pathe* [states of the soul] themselves and not less by its seeming

that these conditions are by nature bad – the Skeptic, by eliminating the additional belief that all these things are naturally bad, gets off more moderately ... [W]e say that as regards belief the Skeptic's goal is *ataraxia*, but in regard to things unavoidable it is having moderate *pathe*.

(1996: 1:29–30)[32]

Physical and psychological suffering is naturally unpleasant and often best avoided,[33] but believing them to be 'by nature' evil or a sign of divine castigation simply compounds one's anguish.[34] To attain *ataraxia* we do not therefore require theoretical explanations but rather the ability to resist supplementing unavoidable torments with superfluous speculation. Insofar as the 'goal of the Skeptic Way' (ibid.: 1:25) is *ataraxia*, Pyrrhonism therefore maintains its impetus in a fundamental trust in both the possibility of liberation from dogmatism and the subsequent ability to 'live rightly' (ibid.: 1:17).[35] It thus remains questionable whether the Pyrrhonist can purge herself of all traces of dogmatism.[36] For in at least one thing she must have a little faith; that *ataraxia* is itself a goal worth pursuing – and not only for herself.[37] Indeed, without this commitment there would be no basis upon which to either adopt or advocate the Pyrrhonian attitude.[38] In short, Pyrrhonism necessarily involves a normative – and to that extent minimally dogmatic – dimension.[39]

This brings us to questions of methodology. For how, given the aforementioned teleology, does the Pyrrhonist actually go about undermining philosophical dogmatism? Sextus explains:

We oppose phenomena to phenomena or noumena to noumena ... For instance, we oppose phenomena to phenomena when we say that the same tower appears round from a distance but square from close up; and noumena to noumena when, in reply to one who infers the existence of divine providence from the order of the heavenly bodies, we oppose the fact that often the good fare ill and the bad fare well.

(1996: 1:31–2)[40]

Having persuaded the dogmatist of the equal plausibility ('equipollence' (ibid.: 1:8)) of his assertion(s) being either true or false, the point of this quasi-dialectical[41] move is to promote a radical 'agnosticism' (Diogenes 1925: 475).[42] Persuasion is crucial here, for given the Pyrrhonist's non-theoretical, non-dogmatic aspirations, she cannot risk getting 'infected' by the dogmatist's discourse. All she can legitimately say is 'this is what my experiences cause me quite naturally to do; and this is what I have so far observed to result from these doings. See what happens in your own case' (Nussbaum 1991: 540).[43] As noted earlier, rational debate is of purely therapeutic concern to the Pyrrhonist, for she will happily employ the same line of argument in one situation which, elsewhere, she would subvert.[44] The primary value of argumentation is therefore '[p]ersuasiveness here and now to the pupil'; rhetoric 'simply replaces logical validity and soundness as the desideratum.'[45] Any number of 'logical sins' (ibid.: 548) may be committed, so long as they prove effective in undermining dogmatism and bringing about *ataraxia*.[46] What the Pyrrhonist hopes to inaugurate by demonstrating the *equipollence* of the dogmatist's assertions is an experience of indecision where any judgement in favor of the initial assertion being either true or false seems arbitrary. This methodological point is significant, for the Pyrrhonist's intention is not to bring about *doubt* in the patient. The experience of indecision is rather to be understood as an aporetic state of 'being-at-a-loss.'[47] What distinguishes this sort of hesitancy from doubt – and thus what separates Pyrrhonism from other forms of skepticism – is that while doubt implies understanding, being-at-a-loss does not.[48] One can only 'doubt' the cogency of an assertion if one already understands what that assertion (and its denial) might mean. One cannot, for example, doubt the truth of the claim 'Wednesday is green, but Tuesday is only four feet long' unless one possesses some idea of what the truth of the claim might entail.[49] Presented with such a case one would indeed 'be-at-a-loss' as to how to respond. (This is perhaps the major difficulty facing the would-be Pyrrhonist; namely, of representing *all* truth-claims as though they were nonsensical.[50]) It is precisely this state of hesitancy ('epoche,'[51] or what Sextus discusses under the rubric of the 'perhaps' and 'maybe' (1996: 1:194–5)[52]) that the Pyrrhonist seeks to inculcate in her patient.[53]

To summarize: The route from philosophical sickness to full health begins with the demonstration that mutually incompatible views are equally plausible (*equipollence*). Subsequently, a state of indecision is brought about where the choice between either view seems arbitrary (*epoche*). Finally, having thus paralyzed reason, unperturbedness (*ataraxia*) follows 'like [a] shadow' (Diogenes 1925: 519).[54] Having outlined the epistemological terrain of Pyrrhonism, we can now turn to questions of a more social nature. I am not overly concerned with the practicalities of the Pyrrhonian life,[55] but rather with the likely ethical-political consequences of the Pyrrhonist's broader philosophical outlook. For the moment I will therefore assume that the life Sextus advocates is at least minimally practicable.

The social chameleon: ethical-political implications of Pyrrhonism

Having extricated belief and surrendered to the life of 'apparent facts' (Diogenes 1925: 517), the Pyrrhonian convert will, according to Nussbaum, 'come to lack all attitudes such as anger, fear, jealousy, grief, envy, passionate love ... because these all rest ... upon belief; and she will have no beliefs.'[56] Nussbaum continues:

> [T]he removal of belief removes arrogance and irascibility ... Dogmatists, they insist, are self-loving, rash, puffed-up ... skeptics, by contrast, are calm and gentle ... dogmatists are imagined as interfering with others, imposing their own way on others; the skeptic, by contrast, is tolerant.
>
> (1991: 553)

This synopsis presents Pyrrhonism in an overly favorable light, for other features of the Pyrrhonian life present a far more troubling image.[57] This can best be explored by drawing attention to Nussbaum's additional point: that in keeping 'himself to himself' and letting 'others go their way' the Pyrrhonist is not 'a slave to social prejudices' (ibid.).[58] Given the quietistic form of 'conservatism' (Popkin 1979: 49) the Pyrrhonist favors,[59] this claim should be treated with caution. Thus, earlier in her exposition, Nussbaum rightly suggests of the Pyrrhonian convert that

> as [she] becomes more and more used to the skeptic way she will, quite possibly, come to hold all of her convictions more and more lightly; so she will need, progressively, weaker and weaker arguments. Argument gradually effects its own removal from her life. At the end, I imagine that the bare posing of a question will already induce a shrug of indifference, and further argument will prove unnecessary.
>
> (1991: 540)

The critical point here is that there is nothing within the Pyrrhonian framework to ensure that this 'shrug of indifference' would not also manifest itself in the social-political realm.[60] Indeed, in Sextus' own description of the Pyrrhonian life we are explicitly told that, given the *equipollence* of different lifestyles,[61] accepting the prevailing 'laws and customs' provide the Pyrrhonist with the criteria of what is good and bad 'in the conduct of life' (1996: 1:23–4). That is, the Pyrrhonist follows 'a certain rationale that, in accord with appearances, points [her] toward a life in conformity with the customs of [her] country and its laws and institutions' (ibid.: 1:17).[62] These passages do not merely suggest that prevalent '[c]ustoms of friendly and marital loyalty will be observed' (Nussbaum 1991: 554). Taking into account that: (1) the normative dimension of the pre-Pyrrhonian (dogmatic) life is, during conversion, extricated along with belief,[63] and (2) the Pyrrhonist prides herself on her ability to conform to the prevailing social-cultural milieu,[64] the suggestion that she would remain unaffected by 'social prejudices' is untenable. For if the Pyrrhonist finds herself in a cultural setting ingrained with (what we, including Nussbaum, would consider to be[65]) 'social prejudices,' then on what grounds could she legitimately avoid indulging in such practices? After all, to shun these activities would be conducive neither to the attainment nor maintenance of *ataraxia*. In her defense one might argue that here the

Pyrrhonist could attain *ataraxia* because she would not adopt the *beliefs* fuelling such 'prejudices.'[66] The Pyrrhonist would not *believe* Jews to be fit only for extermination, or homosexuality to be an abomination before God. Nor would she *believe* that women are naturally subordinate to men. She would, however, follow others and engage in racist, homophobic and/or sexist activities if doing otherwise would jeopardize her attaining *ataraxia*.[67] Could the Pyrrhonist here propose *ataraxia* as an alternative to such customs? Could she, for example, advocate to her fellow citizens an attitude of racial, sexual and gender 'blindness'? Presumably not, for there is no reason within the Pyrrhonian framework to engage in such burdensome (and normative) counter-cultural activities. Indeed, the general motivation to help others cure themselves of dogmatism seems peculiarly supererogatory, if not incompatible with the maintenance of one's own *ataraxia*.[68]

This dimension of Pyrrhonism is nicely dramatized in the following passage from *Catch-22*:

> 'I don't believe anything you tell me,' Nately replied, with a bashful mitigating smile. 'The only thing I do believe is that America is going to win the war.'
>
> 'You put so much stock in winning wars,' the grubby iniquitous old man scoffed. 'The real trick lies in losing wars, in knowing which wars can be lost. Italy has been losing wars for centuries, and just see how splendidly we've done nonetheless . . .'
>
> Nately gaped at him in undisguised befuddlement. 'Now I really don't understand what you're saying. You talk like a madman.'
>
> 'But I live like a sane one. I was a fascist when Mussolini was on top, and I am an anti-fascist now that he has been deposed. I was fanatically pro-German when the Germans were here to protect us against the Americans, and now that the Americans are here to protect us against the Germans I am fanatically pro-American . . .'
>
> 'But,' Nately cried out in disbelief, 'you're a turncoat! A time-server! A shameful, unscrupulous opportunist!'
>
> 'I am a hundred and seven years old,' the old man reminded him suavely.
>
> 'Don't you have any principles?'
> 'Of course not.'
>
> (Heller 1961: 261–2)

This passage usefully highlights the paradoxical nature of the Pyrrhonian attitude. For what remains problematic for the Pyrrhonist is that, in her desire to be noncommittal in ethical-political matters, she thereby holds a substantive ethical-political position.[69] To refrain from (explicitly) making ethical-political choices is already to be (implicitly) engaged in making one very important ethical-political decision: to refrain from making (explicit) ethical-political decisions.[70] Here, the Pyrrhonist has *committed* herself to non-commitment – or, as Derrida might put it, she says 'yes' to saying 'no' (or to saying neither 'yes' *nor* 'no'[71]) – thus rendering her 'indecision' a chimera.[72] Moreover, it is unclear that this decision (in favor of indecision) can itself be justified even on Pyrrhonian-pragmatic grounds. For if the Pyrrhonist finds herself in a social-cultural setting which both values the ability of individuals to make their own ethical-political decisions (and which thereby condemns the sort of quietism she favors), then she will be forced by the teleology of her own position to engage in further ethical-political decisions and actions – or at least *appear to others* to be doing so. It is not even clear that simply emulating the decisions of others will be possible – let alone conducive – to the unperturbed life. For one must first choose *who* and *what* to emulate (and thus exclude), thereby involving another crucial ethical-political judgement.[73] In short, the thoroughgoing Pyrrhonist must here sacrifice her parasitism to preserve the liberatory objectives of the very Pyrrhonism she espouses. Even assuming she can successfully mimic those around her and therefore *appear* to be a morally respectable, autonomous individual – and not, like Heller's old man, a 'shameful, unscrupulous opportunist' – the resultant fissure between her public and private life[74] would itself likely prove detrimental to the attainment and maintenance of *ataraxia*. The desire to become a social chameleon and maintain a state of indecisive non-commitment is not therefore merely troubling, it is perhaps fatally paradoxical.

I will return to some of these questions in later chapters. But I would now like to develop the previous analysis by identifying some important correlations between the respective philosophical therapies offered by Sextus and Wittgenstein. Although I will draw attention to a number of methodological similarities between these philosophers, my objective here is to identify – and later critique – the influential 'conservative' interpretation of Wittgenstein's later work.

Wittgenstein's grammatical therapy and the sources of disease

Rhees suggests that there was something categorical about Wittgenstein's instruction for the philosopher to 'Go the bloody *hard* way.'[75] Wittgenstein, he claims, 'was not saying, "Whatever you seek, you will have to accept the drudgery on the way to it" ... As though the drudgery or the struggle were a special misfortune' (1969: 169). Rather, going 'the bloody *hard* way' was something worth doing for its own sake:

> Unless one understands this, then I do not think one can understand Wittgenstein's conviction that philosophy is important. For he did not think that philosophy is important in the way in which therapy is

important to the patient ... Philosophy, as he practiced it, was 'the bloody hard way' in the sense of being opposed to looking for consolation ... And it was not only a way of thinking and working, but a way of living as well. And the '*hardness*' was really a criterion of the sort of life that was worthwhile. Perhaps I should add 'for him.'

(Rhees 1969: 169–70)

Although it is correct to highlight both the 'hardness' of philosophy advocated by Wittgenstein and the broader existential ambitions of those procedures,[76] due either to a misunderstanding or simple distaste for the therapeutic-curative analogy, Rhees erroneously conflates 'consolation' with something like 'going the *easy* way.' This is mistaken because there is nothing necessarily 'easy' about philosophy practiced as a curative therapy. Indeed, philosophy-as-therapy will often be a prolonged and arduous process, where a '*slow* cure is all important' (Wittgenstein 1990: §382).[77] But what perhaps underlies Rhees's suspicion is the equally unfounded assumption that the therapeutic analogy *trivializes* the philosophical enterprise – however that may be construed.[78] From this perspective the correlation of Wittgenstein with such a radically therapeutic approach as Pyrrhonism not only neglects the intense seriousness with which Wittgenstein approached his work,[79] it also undermines the philosophical stature of his writings. If this is indeed Rhees's suspicion he is not alone in harboring it.[80] But we must not confuse Wittgenstein's seeking to bring an end to philosophical perplexity with the claim that he viewed philosophy as 'trivial.' These are quite separate issues, as the former objective remains entirely compatible with a 'serious' philosophical attitude. (A dentist presumably wants to cure her patient's toothache, but she does not thereby judge dentistry – or toothache – to be 'trivial.') What Rhees fails to address is *why* Wittgenstein thought philosophizing to be so important; to what *end* did Wittgenstein practice philosophy in his own inimitable way?[81] In the remainder of this chapter I will argue, not only that the correlation between Wittgenstein and Pyrrhonism is justifiable but, further, that by explicating this relationship one can most adequately respond to these questions in terms which both retain the importance of philosophy for Wittgenstein and simultaneously show the guiding telos of such philosophizing to be the *non*-philosophical life. On my account, Rhees's suggestion that Wittgenstein thought philosophy (at least as *he* practiced it) to be intrinsically connected to the 'worthwhile' life becomes highly questionable. For we should remember that Wittgenstein never attempted to lure non-philosophers into the philosophical fold, although he found some success in persuading students to abandon philosophy for something more pedestrian and, in his eyes, 'worthwhile' (though not necessarily because they lacked the moral fiber required for going 'the bloody *hard* way').[82] Contrary to Rhees's suggestion, Wittgenstein's injunction to go 'the bloody *hard* way' should in fact be understood as *hypothetical*. His point is that *if* one is determined to do philosophy *then* one should do it properly and 'go the bloody *hard* way,' but there is no value in doing philosophy in the first place – indeed, if you can live without it, then so much the better. The categorical force of Wittgenstein's attitude thus transpires only after one has finally decided – against his own advice – to 'do philosophy'; it makes no demand of the non-philosopher. Moreover (again contrary to Rhees), philosophy is important for Wittgenstein precisely because philosophical *perplexity* is a source of human suffering. Philosophy, like medicine or any other therapy, is valuable only to the extent that we seek to attain, improve and then retain our state of 'health' – however the latter is construed. Like all therapies, philosophy is not *intrinsically* valuable, but rather parasitic upon the depth of bewilderment from which we seek liberation.[83] While the world would doubtless be 'better' were medicine *not needed*, so too would it be 'better' were philosophy *not needed* (which is distinct from the claim that the world would be 'better' were medicine and/or philosophy simply *no longer practiced*).[84] What ultimately concerns Wittgenstein here is therefore something broadly ethical – namely, the conceptual vulnerabilities of human beings:

> When we ask on what occasions people use a word, what they say about it, what they are right to substitute for it, and in reply try to describe its use, we do so only insofar as it seems helpful in getting rid of certain philosophical troubles ... We are interested in language only insofar as it gives us trouble. I only describe the actual use of a word if this is necessary to remove some trouble we want to get rid of ... Sometimes I have to lay down new rules because new rules are less liable to produce confusion or because we have perhaps not thought of looking at the language we have in this light.
> (Wittgenstein 1979b: 97)[85]

False pictures of language, seductive[86] philosophical presuppositions and an 'urge to misunderstand' (1958: §109) are what generate the problems; careful, linguistic-descriptive philosophical practice renders those problems unproblematic. There is nothing 'trivial' about this. Indeed, the emancipatory-Pyrrhonian model of philosophy previously outlined suggests the opposite, for what could be more painstaking, serious and worthy a goal than attaining existential health? With these general points in mind I will now explain how Wittgenstein's work follows this Pyrrhonian route.

It is widely acknowledged, if not always adequately understood, that Wittgenstein characterized his work as a therapeutic strategy oriented toward the 'treatment' (ibid.: §255) of 'philosophical disease' (ibid.: §593). Indeed, that he considered training for both the medical and psychoanalytic professions is perhaps not as incidental to his philosophical work as he protested.[87] Such biographical facts are worth noting, but I would here like to focus on some specific passages that parallel the

24 *Philosophy as therapy*

Pyrrhonian therapy already discussed. In *Philosophical Investigations* Wittgenstein describes his manner of philosophizing as follows:

> It is not our aim to refine or complete the system of rules for the use of our words in unheard-of ways.
>
> For the clarity that we are aiming at is indeed *complete* clarity. But this simply means that the philosophical problems should *completely* disappear.
>
> The real discovery is the one that makes me capable of stopping doing philosophy when I want to. – The one that gives philosophy peace, so that it is no longer tormented by questions which bring *itself* in question. – Instead, we now demonstrate a method, by example; and the series of examples can be broken off. – Problems are solved (difficulties eliminated), not a *single* problem.
>
> There is not *a* philosophical method, though there are indeed methods, like different therapies.
>
> (1958: §133)

This passage echoes a number of Pyrrhonian themes. For example, the philosophical 'clarity' Wittgenstein is 'aiming at' is here equated with the disappearance of the problem, not its theoretical solution. Moreover, this 'clarity' emerges at the precise moment when philosophy finds 'peace,' and thought is freed from being 'tormented.' Finally, in order to stress both his own anti-theoretical stance and the medical-therapeutic analogy, Wittgenstein (like Sextus[88]) denies that philosophy possesses a single method. Rather, the internal diversity of the new therapy simply mirrors the multitude of diseases it treats.[89] Let us examine each of these themes.

In passages from the so-called 'Big Typescript' Wittgenstein refers to the 'particular peace of mind that occurs when we can place other similar cases next to a case that we thought was unique' (1993: 175). He proceeds: 'If I say: here we are at the limits of language, then it always seems ... as if resignation were necessary, whereas on the contrary complete satisfaction comes, since no question remains.' In other words, the 'problems are dissolved in the actual sense of the word – like a lump of sugar in water' (ibid.: 183).[90] Likewise, the 'new' philosopher is characterized as the one who 'strives to find the liberating word ... that finally permits us to grasp what up until now has intangibly weighed down on our consciousness.' That is, the Wittgensteinian therapist 'delivers the word to us with which one ... can express the thing and render it harmless' (ibid.: 165). Finally, this time in *Culture and Value*, Wittgenstein summarizes: 'My ideal is a certain coolness. A temple providing a setting for the passions without meddling with them' (1994a: 2); 'Thoughts that are at peace. That's what someone who philosophizes yearns for' (ibid.: 43). The Pyrrhonian overtones of such passages are striking: Philosophy, if practiced correctly, will enable the dissolution of specific perplexities and lead to a state of unperturbedness.[91] The same point is expressed slightly differently in *Zettel*, where the most 'remarkable and characteristic phenomenon in philosophical investigation' is identified as 'the difficulty ... of recognising as the solution something that looks as if it were only a preliminary to it.' For 'the difficulty here' is knowing when 'to stop.' Wittgenstein then warns us: ' "We have already said everything. – Not anything that follows from this, no, *this* itself is the solution!" ' (1990: §314). This latter formulation is interesting because it is echoed in Nussbaum's summary of the Pyrrhonist's naturalism ('Not anything that lies beyond this, no, *this* – the way life actually goes in nature [and custom] – *this* is the end' (1991: 532)). On this striking similarity Nussbaum has nothing to say. Yet through this distinctly Wittgensteinian formulation she highlights an important feature of Wittgenstein's own philosophical project. For although he is less explicit than Sextus regarding the non-philosophical life, Wittgenstein nevertheless shares something of Pyrrhonism's yearning for a more unaffected (and for him rather Tolstoyan) kind of existence. Indeed, as I will argue in Chapter 3, Wittgenstein's injunction: 'Don't take the example of others as your guide, but nature!' (1994a: 41) receives considerable philosophical grounding in both his emphasis on the derivative nature of the linguistic from the pre-linguistic,[92] and his critique of Frazer's anthropology.[93] But it is to Wittgenstein's own understanding of the sources of philosophical 'disease' that I first want to turn.

According to the Pyrrhonist, it is the propensity toward belief that generates unnecessary anxiety. Given that human life inevitably involves a degree of suffering, *believing* such things to be inherently evil or of divine orchestration simply compounds one's misery. To evade such burdens one must abandon belief, adopt an ethos of non-resistance and thereby learn to bend with the flux of the world. In the Pyrrhonian schema the source of anxiety is thus spawned from certain natural tendencies, and yet the key to overcoming such anxieties is also located in the animal submission to natural (and to some extent cultural) forces. In short, nature is here both curse and cure. As I said before, I am not overly concerned with the internal coherence of this picture – of how, for example, the Pyrrhonist can legitimately favor one aspect of the natural order (primitive human drives) over another (the natural tendency toward belief). What interests me is that a similar pattern emerges in Wittgenstein's work. Where then, according to him, do we find the source of philosophical 'disquietudes' (1958: §111)? Wittgenstein insists that the root of the problem lies in our being 'bewitched' (1999: §31)[94] or fascinated by certain 'forms of expression' (1969: 27) or 'grammatical illusions' (1958: §110). The new descriptive philosophy is therefore characterized as a 'fight' (1969: 27) and 'battle' (1958: §109) against these tendencies.[95] But why are the latter so irresistible? It is here tempting to read Wittgenstein as laying the blame solely at the feet of traditional philosophy, and there are indeed numerous passages that support this hypothesis. To choose two particularly striking examples, he employs the following analogies:

26 *Philosophy as therapy*

> Philosophers often behave like little children who scribble some marks on a piece of paper at random and then ask the grown-up 'What's that?' – It happened like this: the grown-up had drawn pictures for the child several times and said: 'this is a man', 'this is a house', etc. And then the child makes some marks too and asks: what's *this* then?
>
> (1994a: 17)

> I am sitting with a philosopher in the garden; he says again and again 'I know that that's a tree', pointing to a tree that is near us. Someone else arrives and hears this, and I tell him: 'This fellow isn't insane. We are only doing philosophy . . . '
>
> (1999: §467)[96]

There is an obvious sense in which traditional philosophy is here portrayed as something distinctly idiotic; in the former the philosopher behaves like a confused child,[97] while in the latter his activities have to be excused in the presence of a third party. Wittgenstein is not claiming that the philosopher is just going about his philosophic business or that this is simply what philosophy actually (and rightly) entails. For these portraits remain deeply sardonic. In any case, this is but one part of the overall picture Wittgenstein presents. For although traditional philosophic practice is frequently accused of *compounding* the problems, the problems themselves are not essentially of philosophy's *making*.[98] Rather, Wittgenstein maintains that what holds us 'captive' lies deep 'in our language' (1958: §115). Philosophy thus exacerbates confusions, the 'roots' of which 'are as deep in us as the forms of our language' (ibid.: §111). Most notable in this regard are the misleading similarities between different regions of discourse.[99] For although Wittgenstein claims that 'everything lies open to view' and thus 'what is hidden . . . is of no interest' (ibid.: §126),[100] he nevertheless distinguishes between 'surface' and 'depth grammar' (ibid.: §664).[101] The form this distinction takes is unfortunate insofar as it suggests a clandestine reality below the surface of language usage requiring excavation. But such a Tractarian picture is precisely not what Wittgenstein has in mind. Rather:

> The aspects of things that are most important . . . are hidden because of their simplicity and familiarity. (One is unable to notice something – because it is always before one's eyes.) . . . we fail to be struck by what, once seen, is most striking and most powerful.
>
> (1958: §129)[102]

It is therefore not wholly accurate for Wittgenstein to say that *nothing* is hidden; there *is* something 'hidden,' but not in a subterranean or esoteric sense. Rather, what prevents us from commanding '*a clear view* of the use of our words' (ibid.: §122) is their *overfamiliarity*. Such 'grammatical problems' are difficult to dissolve precisely because 'they are connected with the oldest thought habits, i.e., with the oldest images that are engraved into our language itself' (1993: 183–4):[103]

> As long as there is a verb 'to be' which seems to function like 'to eat' and 'to drink', as long as one talks about a flow of time and an expanse of space, etc., etc., humans will continue to bump up against the same mysterious difficulties, and stare at something that no explanation seems able to remove.
>
> (1993: 185–7)[104]

Wittgenstein thus sees language itself as the villain insofar as it imposes misleading trains of thought upon us.[105] 'Ordinary language' is both the place to which philosophic language must be relocated and the scene of our seduction.[106] In other words, Wittgenstein presents ordinary language as simultaneously 'home' (1958: §116) and a site of estrangement or exile. The upshot of this is that philosophical perplexity is a quite natural phenomenon. It is not the philosopher's language that creates such a 'mythology,' rather, philosophy itself draws its life force both from language's own latent 'forms' (1993: 199) and a 'certain instinct' (Moore 1993: 114) or 'urge' on our part to 'misunderstand them' (Wittgenstein 1958: §109).[107] Such urges provoke 'a constant battle and uneasiness' (1993: 163),[108] not least because these are difficulties 'not ... of the intellect, but of the will' (ibid.: 161).[109] Indeed, just 'as it is difficult to hold back tears, or an outburst of anger,' so is it often difficult 'not to use an expression' (ibid.: 161) that confuses us.[110]

Although Wittgenstein says relatively little about the nature and origins of such 'confusions,'[111] the previous passages clearly suggest that they are not artificially constructed, but rather as natural as our disposition to cry at the death of a loved one or stamp our feet in rage. But just as the medical doctor need not offer hypotheses concerning the genetic basis of the illnesses she treats, so too is it inessential for Wittgenstein to provide analogous speculations on the underlying causes of conceptual disease. While 'very general facts of nature' are relevant to his therapeutic project (as I will argue in later chapters, they are absolutely central to its ethical dimension), Wittgenstein insists that he is neither doing 'natural science' nor 'natural history' (1958: p. 230). Thus for both medical and Wittgensteinian therapists it is sufficient that they be able to point out the ways such illnesses are transmitted and what can be done to combat them. This is not to say that such therapists require no understanding of the underlying causes, but rather that this knowledge need not be especially deep.[112] The general point I have wanted to highlight here is how both Sextus and Wittgenstein maintain that the origin and (potential) cure of such diseases are located within the *natural* realm – that is, in primitive tendencies or urges, and the turn to a more peaceable state of non-philosophical life.

Seeing the world aright: Wittgenstein's rhetoric

The following question arises here: Is Wittgenstein's claim that 'peaceful thoughts' are 'what someone who philosophizes yearns for' (1994a: 43) itself descriptive or normative?[113] Another way of formulating this is to ask precisely *whom* the various appeals to 'we' refer to in remarks such as: 'We are struggling with language. We are engaged in a struggle with language' (ibid.: 11), and 'we may not advance any kind of theory. There must not be anything hypothetical in our considerations. We must do away with all *explanation*, and description alone must take its place' (1958: §109)? On reflection it is clear that such passages are not descriptions of orthodox philosophic practice. Rather, they are both descriptions of Wittgenstein's own methodology and condemnations of traditional philosophy; as he puts it in more judicial terms: 'Our only task is to be just. That is, we must only point out and resolve the injustices of philosophy, and not posit new parties – and creeds' (1993: 181).[114] Although commentators tend to underestimate the significance of Wittgenstein's normativity here, such reticence is unsurprising insofar as it seems difficult to square with his numerous injunctions to 'only *describe*' (1996a: 63) and leave 'everything as it is' (1958: §124).[115] But this is precisely my point, for these are indeed *injunctions* for the philosopher to proceed in a certain way or '"Look at things like this!"' (1994a: 61). To borrow Derrida's terms, Wittgenstein tacitly appeals to us: '"believe me" . . . "I promise you that I am speaking the truth"' (Derrida 1996b: 82), or 'choose my solution, prefer my solution, take my solution, love my solution; you will be in the truth if you do not resist my solution' (Derrida 1998a: 9).[116] Here then an additional correlation emerges between Wittgenstein's implicit normativity and Pyrrhonism's own minimal dogmatism. For, we will recall, given that the 'goal of the Skeptic Way . . . for the sake of which everything is done' is '*ataraxia*' (Sextus 1996: 1:25), the Pyrrhonist cannot rid herself of all traces of belief – or, by implication, dogmatism.[117] Analogously, we might ask how Wittgenstein can legitimately prescribe his methodology when that very methodology seeks to inaugurate an entirely new[118] and 'just' (1993: 181) philosophical practice of descriptivity? This clearly raises questions regarding the meta-philosophical status of Wittgenstein's writings – questions that usually arise in relation to the *Tractatus*. Although there is a broadly Pyrrhonian response to this in his later writings, I would first like to turn to the Pyrrhonian treatment of such methodological-rhetorical problems in Wittgenstein's earlier work.

In the penultimate section of the *Tractatus* Wittgenstein famously cautions:

> My propositions serve as elucidations in the following way: anyone who understands me eventually recognises them as nonsensical, when he has used them – as steps – to climb up beyond them. (He must, so

to speak, throw away the ladder after he has climbed up it.) ... He must transcend these propositions, and then he will see the world aright.

(1995: 6.54)

Although Wittgenstein likely borrowed this metaphor from Mauthner,[119] it derives from Sextus' comparison of his own position to 'the person who has climbed to a high place with the help of a ladder' and then 'kick[s] over the ladder after the ascent' (Mates 1996: p. 258). Wittgenstein employs this image to 'show' the sense of the *Tractatus*'s demarcation between what can and cannot be meaningfully 'said.'[120] That is, within the boundaries of meaning established in the 'picture theory,' Wittgenstein must account for his own text which is neither logical (tautological[121]) nor a propositional 'mirroring'[122] of the world of 'facts.' As Sextus proceeds in more overtly therapeutic terms: 'just as cathartic drugs not only flush out the bodily humours but expel themselves as well' (1996: 1:206–7) so too do 'these arguments apply to themselves along with the other arguments' (ibid.: 2:188).[123] What this transcendental disclaimer ultimately amounts to for Wittgenstein can be ascertained in the *Tractatus*'s concluding passage: 'What we cannot speak about we must pass over in silence' (1995: 7). By determining the boundaries of sense, Wittgenstein thereby demarcates what cannot be said but only *shown*; notably, the ethical and religious – or 'mystical.'[124]

Given the Pyrrhonian context in which I am situating Wittgenstein's work, and recalling what I said earlier concerning the Pyrrhonist's 'being-at-a-loss,' the *Tractatus*'s allusions to silence are pertinent. For not only is silence incorporated by Wittgenstein to safeguard the mystical from any trespassing of the natural sciences (his is a silence of respect, not one of derision[125]), it also indicates what philosophical liberation might itself involve. That is, discarding the Tractarian 'ladder' – having used it to climb out of the quagmire of philosophical confusion – not only tells us something about the therapeutic nature of the *Tractatus*'s own propositions but also provides a clue as to what 'see[ing] the world aright' (ibid.: 6.54) might encompass. Of course, this Pyrrhonian metaphor must be handled with caution, for as Wittgenstein warns elsewhere:

> I might say: if the place I want to get to could only be reached by way of a ladder, I would give up trying to get there. For the place I really have to get to is a place I must already be at now ... Anything that I might reach by climbing a ladder does not interest me.
>
> (1994a: 7)[126]

The danger with employing this spatial metaphor is that it suggests a 'somewhere else' to which one might gain access. But the place

30 *Philosophy as therapy*

Wittgenstein seeks is precisely where we now stand,[127] for it is here that 'the logic of our language is misunderstood' (1995: p. 3). What Wittgenstein is advocating is thus a radical *change of perspective* where the endless desire for 'climbing' (or the urge to try and 'look beyond' (1993: 389)) ceases to fixate and frustrate us. While it would be simplistic to equate Wittgenstein's silence with the Pyrrhonist's *ataraxia*, we should nevertheless note the practical dimension of the *Tractatus*'s 'showing' what one 'must pass over in silence.' Philosophy, we are told, 'aims at the logical clarification of thoughts,' and is defined in quasi-Pyrrhonian terms not as 'a body of doctrine' but rather as 'an activity' whose 'task' is to make 'thoughts ... clear' (1995: 4.112). There are no insoluble questions, for '[w]hen the answer cannot be put into words, neither can the question be put into words. The *riddle* does not exist. If a question can be framed at all, it is also *possible* to answer it' (ibid.: 6.5). This latter point is then applied to what Wittgenstein calls the 'problem of life,' for its 'solution' is similarly located 'in the vanishing of the problem' (ibid.: 6.521). Some years later he returns to this 'problem,' remarking:

> The way to solve the problem you see in life is to live in a way that will make what is problematic disappear ... The fact that life is problematic shows that the shape of your life does not fit into life's mould. So you must change the way you live and, once your life does fit into the mould, what is problematic will disappear ... But don't we have the feeling that someone who sees no problem in life is blind to something important, even to the most important thing of all? Don't I feel like saying that a man like that is just living aimlessly – blindly, like a mole, and that if only he could see, he would see the problem? ... Or shouldn't I say rather: a man who lives rightly won't experience the problem as *sorrow*, so for him it will not be a problem, but a joy ... a bright halo round his life, not a dubious background.
>
> (1994a: 27)

Again, there are obvious Pyrrhonian resonances here. Wittgenstein's characterization of life possessing a 'mould' into which one must 'fit' echoes the Pyrrhonist's emphasis on the need for flexibility regarding the vacillations of the natural and cultural world. Moreover, for both Sextus and Wittgenstein it is unnecessary to regard this as a lamentable restriction on oneself.[128] Rather, 'fitting' oneself into 'life's mould' will dispel all such superfluous anxieties, and this, broadly speaking, constitutes 'living rightly.' On a biographical note these passages are of additional interest insofar as they capture something of the shifting direction of Wittgenstein's own life. On completion of the *Tractatus* – a closure he thought to be an 'unassailable and definitive' (1995: p. 4) closure of philosophy – Wittgenstein changed the 'shape' of his life by withdrawing from the philosophical establishment. His sporadic attempts to abandon philosophy for the more worldly pursuits of architect, gardener, hospital porter, laboratory assistant and school teacher all proved unsuccessful, for Wittgenstein repeatedly returned to academic philosophy.[129] Nevertheless, he did continually attempt to change his life. Wittgenstein's failure to achieve this goal does not undermine the claim that his motivation remained essentially Pyrrhonian. Rather, it only suggests that Wittgenstein's philosophical standards were a little higher than those of his Pyrrhonian predecessors, that his perfectionism (or 'disease') was too resilient, or that his lack of success at non-philosophical pursuits drew him back to the one thing he knew he could do.[130] Whatever the reasons, the completion of the *Tractatus*, its internal objective of allowing one to 'transcend [its] propositions' and subsequently 'see the world aright' (ibid.: 6.54), and Wittgenstein's own attempts to abandon philosophy, are all intimately connected in a therapeutic schema that remains deeply Pyrrhonian. Having outlined some of the problems facing the *Tractatus*, I now want to return to the later writings, and specifically how the philosophical status of these 'descriptive' works is to be understood alongside their implicit normativity.

If we recall, *persuasion* is the only mode of discourse available to the Pyrrhonist – that is, of appealing to the potential convert: 'this is what my experiences cause me quite naturally to do; and this is what I have so far observed to result from these doings. See what happens in your own case' (Nussbaum 1991: 540).[131] Given her anti-dogmatic aspirations and desire for the 'life of appearances,' the Pyrrhonist must restrict herself to essentially rhetorical means. What is significant here is that a similarly rhetorical dimension emerges in Wittgenstein's later writings. Thus, in *Philosophical Investigations*, we are cautioned:

> The ideal, as we think of it, is unshakeable. You can never get outside it; you must always turn back. There is no outside; outside you cannot breathe. – Where does this idea come from? It is like a pair of glasses on our nose through which we see whatever we look at. It never occurs to us to take them off.
>
> (1958: §103)

What Wittgenstein is alluding to here is the possibility of liberation from our distorted view of language, including the picture holding us 'captive' (ibid.: §115) so vividly painted in the *Tractatus*.[132] We must remove the 'glasses through which we see whatever we look at' and expunge the Tractarian belief in an ideal language – a 'preconceived idea' to which we think the world '*must* correspond' (ibid.: §131).[133] Only abandonment of that belief opens the way to liberation. We are not, however, being asked to replace these 'glasses' but to *remove* them,[134] and this is why Wittgenstein warns his own brand of philosophizing against setting itself up as a

32 *Philosophy as therapy*

'new ... idol' (1993: 171).[135] For, as previously noted, the task facing the philosopher is not the theoretical elucidation of something 'unheard of' (ibid.: 179), but the description of what 'we have always known' (1958: §109); what lies '*right in front of* [our] *eyes!*' (1994a: 39).[136]

An essential component of Wittgenstein's new approach is his rejection of the idea that the multifarious ways language is used require philosophical justification.[137] Although I will discuss the nature and limits of justification in Chapter 2, it is nevertheless pertinent to our present concerns that in *On Certainty* Wittgenstein remarks:

> Where two principles really do meet which cannot be reconciled with one another, then each man declares the other a fool and heretic ... I said I would 'combat' the other man, – but wouldn't I give him *reasons*? Certainly; but how far do they go? At the end of reasons comes *persuasion*. (Think what happens when missionaries convert natives.)
> (1999: §§611–12)

This passage is striking, not only because it presents the question of justification and persuasion as themes of Wittgenstein's investigations, but also because it captures something of the rhetorical orientation of those very investigations. But in order to explain this it is first necessary to say something about the general style of the later writings.

It is here worth reiterating that the therapies of both Sextus and Wittgenstein ought to lead not to the theoretical solution of philosophical problems but rather to their *dissolution*.[138] I am not suggesting that the methodological maneuvers made by each philosopher are identical. After all, the standard dialectical movement philosophical texts commonly make[139] is complicated by Wittgenstein's later 'criss-cross' (1958: p. ix) style, whereas Sextus remains more obviously within the (albeit radically curtailed) dialectical model.[140] Nevertheless, even this apparent difference is not straightforward. It could be argued that Wittgenstein's work does engage in some form of dialectical movement – at least of the restricted Pyrrhonian type. For in both Wittgenstein and Sextus the first two elements of the dialectic are in operation. In Sextus' work this is represented in the opposition of theses (thereby demonstrating the *equipollence* of conflicting assertions, in turn leading to *epoche* and finally *ataraxia*), while in Wittgenstein's writings a comparable opposition appears in his strategic employment of examples showing 'intermediate' (ibid.: §122) cases. Thus, Wittgenstein speaks of the

> particular peace of mind that occurs when we can place other similar cases next to a case that we thought was unique, occurs again and again in our investigations when we show that a word doesn't have ... just one meaning (or just two), but is used in five or six different ways.
> (1993: 175)

To do justice to this quasi-dialectical feature of Wittgenstein's work would require a detailed analysis, and I will not attempt that here. Instead, I want to focus on the more obvious 'fragmentary' nature of his later writings.[141]

In the preface to *Philosophical Investigations* Wittgenstein concedes:

> I have written down all these thoughts as remarks, short paragraphs, of which there is sometimes a fairly long chain about the same subject, while I sometimes make a sudden change, jumping from one topic to another ... After several unsuccessful attempts to weld my results together into such a whole, I realized that I should never succeed. The best that I could write would never be more than philosophical remarks.
>
> (1958: p. ix)

This doomed endeavor to formalize *Philosophical Investigations* (something others have also attempted[142]) failed for more important reasons than mere ineptitude on Wittgenstein's part. Though his 'thoughts were soon crippled' by the effort of such codification, Wittgenstein explains that 'this was ... connected with the very nature of the investigation.' That is, the peculiar 'criss-cross' style of the text merely reflects the terrain of the landscape traveled 'in the course of [those] long and involved journeyings' (ibid.). Elsewhere we are told that '[w]orking in philosophy' is primarily a 'working on oneself' (1994a: 16), but this claim should similarly be handled with care. For although Wittgenstein may prioritize 'working on oneself,' he is not (as Rhees intimates[143]) thereby limiting his ambitions to his own private liberation. In this sense the tone of *Philosophical Investigations*' 'sketches of landscapes' might be described as quasi-confessional.[144] For here Wittgenstein's 'working on [him]self' nevertheless aims at the inauguration of something new;[145] a radical change in perspective or '*way of seeing*' (1990: §461) in the lives of those who similarly find themselves philosophically perplexed. (At the very least Wittgenstein wanted to 'stimulate someone to thoughts of his own' (1958: p. x).) This point is substantiated by the quasi-religious vocabulary Wittgenstein employs when characterizing philosophical perplexities as temptations or as matters pertaining to the 'will' rather than the intellect.[146] Indeed, this tendency to exploit the language of temptation, sin, responsibility and guilt makes Wittgenstein's much discussed claim '"I am not a religious man but I cannot help seeing every problem from a religious point of view"' (Drury 1981: 94) somewhat less bemusing. As I will argue in later chapters, the specificities of Wittgenstein's religiosity are obscure. But what cannot be questioned is that he found the religious life (particularly in its Tolstoyan form) enormously attractive, despite his own incapacity to enter into it fully.[147] It is therefore unsurprising that this deep religious longing should manifest itself both in Wittgenstein's often obsessive attitude toward philosophical problems and the way those problems are articulated in his writings.[148] In short, part of the sense of Wittgenstein's confessing that he could not 'help seeing every problem from a religious point of view' lies in the vocabulary he employs, and what he felt to be at stake in his being able to dissolve his own philosophical temptations and then show others how to cure themselves.[149] By means of this religious subtext Wittgenstein makes an implicit appeal to the reader to work on themselves also. As Shields puts it, in speaking of 'philosophical problems in terms of temptations' Wittgenstein effectively 'puts the moral responsibility more on the tempted individuals' insofar as 'it requires a degree of compliance on our part to make temptations into actual transgressions' (1997: 56). Mindful of this, it is interesting that in 'Lectures on Aesthetics' Wittgenstein makes the following admission:

> What I'm doing is also persuasion ... I am saying 'I don't want you to look at it like that.' ... I am in a sense making propaganda for one style of thinking as opposed to another. I am honestly disgusted with the other. Also I'm trying to state what I think. Nevertheless I'm saying: 'For God's sake don't do this.' ... How much we are doing is changing the style of thinking and how much I'm doing is changing the style of thinking and how much I'm doing is persuading people to change their style of thinking.
>
> (1994b: 27–8)[150]

Insofar as Wittgenstein here speaks candidly of 'making propaganda' and 'persuading people to change their style of thinking' this suggests that his philosophical intentions extended beyond his own personal *ataraxia*. Such passages thus undermine Rhees's suspicion that perhaps Wittgenstein was only ever speaking for himself.[151] But more needs to be said here. For there are passages where Wittgenstein's emphasis does seem to be of a more solitary nature. For example, in a note from 1947 he asks whether it is only he who 'cannot found a school ... ?' In response, Wittgenstein conjectures: 'I cannot found a school because I do not really want to be imitated. Not at any rate by those who publish articles in philosophical journals' (1994a: 61). This allusion to not wanting to be 'imitated' by others looks like corroborative evidence for Rhees's hypothesis. However, in an earlier entry Wittgenstein remarks:

> I am by no means sure that I should prefer a continuation of my work by others to a change in the way people live which would make all these questions superfluous. (For this reason I could never found a school.)
>
> (1994a: 61)

Even from these passages we can therefore conclude that Wittgenstein remained deeply ambitious (if not always optimistic[152]) that the significance of his work would be felt beyond the confines of academic philosophy, his own philosophical satisfaction and indeed lifetime. In short, while these passages do not tell us whether Wittgenstein thought himself to be alone in this pursuit, they do support the view that this quest aimed beyond a merely solitary emancipation.[153] Of course, the objective was no longer the death of philosophy *per se* (a point to which I will return shortly) but rather the possibility of deliverance for the individual philosopher so that she too may make the 'discovery' which would enable *her* to stop 'doing philosophy' (1958: §133) when *she* wants. The unfeasibility of Wittgenstein's ever 'founding a school' is thus due to the transformation he wishes to bring about not being merely theoretical, but rather, like the Pyrrhonist (and indeed genuine religiosity[154]), fundamentally practical; a 'change in the way people live' (1994a: 61).

This leads us naturally to the question of how Wittgenstein saw the future of philosophical practice? In addition to the biographical material available that elucidates his troubled relationship with academic philosophy,[155] there exist a number of allusions to this tense liaison within Wittgenstein's writings. As previously suggested, one can take Wittgenstein's remark that the 'real discovery is the one that makes me capable of stopping doing philosophy' (1958: §133) to represent his basic attitude toward philosophic practice. For what he yearned for were '[t]houghts that are at peace' (1994a: 43). This is not to say that Wittgenstein always thought philosophy's completion to be possible within his lifetime – despite the fact that upon finishing the *Tractatus* he did indeed think that the central problems of philosophy had been solved. After the *Tractatus* there is an increasing tentativeness regarding the very notion of an 'end to philosophy.' Thus, in *Zettel*, Wittgenstein cautions:

> Disquiet in philosophy might be said to arise from looking at philosophy wrongly, seeing it wrong ... But in that case we never get to the end of our work! – Of course not, for it has no end ... (We want to replace wild conjectures and explanations by quiet weighing of linguistic facts.)
>
> (1990: §447)

This admission is perfectly understandable given the proclaimed descriptive orientation of Wittgenstein's later work. That the multiplicity of language-games philosophers must now only describe 'is not something fixed, given once for all' (that 'new types of language, new language-games ... come into existence, and others become obsolete and get forgotten' (1958: §23)) would itself assure the boundlessness of the new philosophical task.[156] We might therefore say that it is precisely Wittgenstein's later recognition of linguistic-conceptual multiplicity and permutation[157] – in contrast to his earlier insensitivity to these phenomena[158] – that marks the difference in self-assurance regarding the possibility of bringing philosophy itself to a close.[159] But again, none of this detracts from Wittgenstein's underlying Pyrrhonism. At least two possible readings offer themselves here: (1) Drawing on Drury's remark that Wittgenstein had a 'persistent intention to change his whole manner of life' and 'forsake' academic philosophy (and that Wittgenstein himself identified his own 'vanity' (Drury 1981: 92) as what drew him back to philosophy[160]), and Rhees's recollection of Wittgenstein exclaiming: ' "You know I said I can stop doing philosophy when I like. That is a lie! I *can't*" ' (ibid.: 186, n. 9), the correct interpretation of such passages is that although Wittgenstein never ceased wanting to 'stop doing philosophy' his own conceit barred his way. That is, Wittgenstein's aspirations remained essentially Pyrrhonian, despite the fact that he could not manage to actualize them. (2) On a more subtle interpretation we might say that while Wittgenstein did indeed come to recognize the boundlessness of his new descriptive philosophy, this remained not only a continual source of 'wonder' (Holland 1990: 22) for him but also *itself* a potential source of liberation from the philosophic enterprise. While the task of philosophy now appeared infinite (for why should language-games ever reach a point of static equilibrium, thereby providing philosophy with a determinate field of enquiry?), that task had itself become redefined so as to allow him to embrace this essential indeterminacy without the lamentations accompanying his earlier Tractarian perfectionism.[161] Although each of these interpretations is distinct, they are nevertheless unified on one crucial point: that the practical success/failure of Wittgenstein's Pyrrhonism was 'a difficulty having to do with the will, rather than the intellect' (1994a: 17).

Reconstructing the Pyrrhonian dimension of Wittgenstein's work we can thus summarize as follows: There is a perfectionist dimension to the *Tractatus* insofar as it purports to provide a full explanation of the relationship between mind, language and world. In its strict determination of meaning, this project should thereby bring about the conclusion of philosophy. In the later writings, however, Wittgenstein's position becomes more complex insofar as meaning itself is no longer determinable in any *a priori* sense, but instead seen as the function of a variety of language practices.[162] Having thus abandoned the '*preconceived idea* of crystalline purity' (1958: §108) of the *Tractatus* there was little sense in despairing that the wheels of philosophy kept turning.[163] Wittgenstein's objective was rather to ensure that they did not continue to turn in isolation from the actual mechanisms of language usage.[164] Whereas before there had been one fixed, identifiable goal, now the philosopher was faced with many specific and constantly fluid objectives. And this is why Wittgenstein (like Sextus) makes use of the medical analogy, insisting that '[p]roblems are solved ... not a *single* problem,' and that there 'is not *a* philosophical method, though there are indeed methods, like different therapies' (ibid.: §133).

Thus far I have focused on questions pertaining to Wittgenstein's method, style and meta-philosophy. These are important themes that require considerable clarification, not least because they constitute essential preparatory material for any credible investigation of more ethical-political matters emerging from Wittgenstein's work. It is to the latter that I will now turn.

Wittgenstein and Pyrrhonian conservatism

Recalling Sextus' outline of the 'life of appearances,' I satirized the Pyrrhonist's social conformism by likening her to Heller's 'diabolical old man' (1961: 260) – a character who uncritically embraced whatever political power happened to dominate. But what was most conspicuous about Heller's character was his incessant rebuttal of his interlocutor's accusations. The old man thus reflected on the practical advantages of learning which wars to lose, and responded to the charge of 'insanity' by reminding his interrogator of both the quality and longevity of his life. Thus, at the end of this incredible dialogue, the old man proudly affirmed that 'of course' he did not have 'any principles' (ibid.: 262). The Pyrrhonian lesson here is that by inculcating the chameleon-like life one can both attain and maintain a rather unperturbed existence. But if Heller's character serves to illustrate the possible ethical-political extremes to which the Pyrrhonist may go in both acquiring and maintaining *ataraxia*, then we might ask whether such troubling implications can be found in Wittgenstein's later work? That is, in *his* yearning for '[t]houghts that are at peace' (1994a: 43) do we find an analogous ethical-political indifference at play?[165] Some commentators do detect this in Wittgenstein's mature thinking. Thus, Nyíri claims:

> [T]he specific tone of Wittgenstein's analyses, the content of many of his remarks and reflections, and the historical circumstances in which this philosophy came into being definitely invite an interpretation in the light of which there indeed emerge family resemblances between Wittgenstein on the one hand and some important representatives of conservatism on the other.
>
> (1982: 44)[166]

But this is not merely a biographical point, for Nyíri proceeds to suggest that such a reading is 'a necessary step toward a more complete picture of Wittgenstein's philosophy' (ibid.: 45).[167] On specifically methodological matters Nyíri develops this correlation by noting Kaltenbrunner's remarks concerning the conservative's general 'distaste for ... theory,' their related devotion 'to the familiar' (a 'decisive preference for the experiences of life as opposed to the constructions of the intellect'), and finally that the conservative 'always begins with that which is concrete' (ibid.: 46). On this reading of conservatism (which, for argument's sake, I will not question) the aforementioned 'hostility' towards theory finds its 'most radical expression' in a certain 'preference for silence' when faced with what is 'concrete' (ibid.: 47). In short: 'the given form of life is the ultimate givenness' (ibid.: 59).[168] Likewise, this time citing Grabowsky, the conservative's '"silent reverence for the impenetrable"' (ibid.: 56) (which encapsulates the very essence of the 'conservative attitude' (ibid.: 55)) is aligned with Wittgenstein.[169] But Nyíri is not alone in these suspicions. Bloor similarly argues that 'Wittgenstein's texts show how, time and again, he develops the characteristic themes of conservative thinkers' (1983: 161).[170] Identifying what he perceives to be the central tenets of *On Certainty*, Bloor thus provides the following synopsis:

> My life, says Wittgenstein, shows what I know and what I am certain about . . . 'My *life* consists in my being content to accept many things', he tells us elsewhere . . . A language-game, we are reminded, is not something reasonable or unreasonable: 'It is there – like our life' . . . Justification must come to an end somewhere, says Wittgenstein, but it does not end in a state of intellectual doubt or in the apprehension of self-evident truths. It ends in 'an ungrounded way of acting' . . . The difficult thing to grasp, we are told, is the groundlessness of our beliefs . . . we inherit a system of belief whose certainty derives from the fact that 'we belong to a community' . . . Doubting is parasitic: an acquired skill for directing attention at limited areas of belief . . . So there we have it. The entire categorical framework of conservative thought: authority, faith, community – all woven together to show the priority of Life over Reason, Practice over Norms, and Being over Thought.
>
> (1983: 161–2)[171]

What then are we to make of such characterizations? And more pointedly, does the Pyrrhonian dimension of Wittgenstein's thought necessarily lead to the sort of 'radical' conservatism displayed by Heller's 'diabolical old man'?

Sustaining these 'conservative' readings is not difficult. One might, for example, develop the analyses of Nyíri and Bloor by correlating these general tendencies of conservatism with the revival of Pyrrhonism during the sixteenth and seventeenth centuries, and specifically its application by Counter-Reformers to undermine the Protestant appeal to non-mediated scriptural authority.[172] This Pyrrhonian-inspired Catholic fideism is interesting because it not only brings to light Pyrrhonism's latent (though extreme) conservative implications, but also because Wittgenstein's own influence in philosophy of religion is frequently said to foster just such an anti-apologetic fideism.[173] The claims of Nyíri and Bloor might then have much in their favor. After all, Wittgenstein explicitly warns: 'Our mistake is to look for an explanation where we ought to look at what happens as a "proto-phenomenon". That is, where we ought to have said: this language-game is played' (1958: §654), and similarly: 'If I have exhausted the justifications I have reached bedrock, and my spade is turned. Then I am inclined to say: "This is simply what I do"' (ibid.: §217).[174] Although, as I will argue in Chapter 2, Wittgenstein's epistemological point here is rather deeper than that of Heller's old man, there remains a sense in which such a position *is* of potential political significance – and especially in view of his apparent[175] prohibition against philosophers 'interfering' with language-games.[176] Moreover (as previously discussed), concerning the relationship between philosophy and life[177] Wittgenstein advises that theoretical 'solutions' to the problems of life are simply *not required*, and thus neither is the philosophical quest that seeks these as its end. Life is neither made easier nor more valuable through philosophical theorizing; life *has been* and *remains* entirely livable (and not merely bearable) outside the philosophical enterprise. Thus the right way of 'solving' the problems of life (and philosophy) is to dissolve them so they are no longer experienced *as* problems. Although this therapeutic process of dissolution is rarely easy, it ultimately has a liberating effect on one's life, even becoming a source of 'joy' (1994a: 27). It would therefore seem that Wittgenstein's work, to the extent that it is Pyrrhonian, does lend itself to the conservative reading outlined above. But despite this initial plausibility, Nyíri's and Bloor's broad-brush approach ultimately distorts Wittgenstein's mature thinking.[178] For what lies at the root of these suspicions is not Wittgenstein's conservatism but rather his seemingly radical anti-foundationalism. Although the correlations Nyíri and Bloor make are interesting, their articulation of the question in such explicitly political terms tends to divert attention from the underlying philosophical issue. There *is* something ethically and politically significant about Wittgenstein's later work, but it is not adequately represented by the appeal to his alleged conservatism. Rather, it is Wittgenstein's Pyrrhonian naturalism that both opens his work to questions of ethics and politics and ultimately transcends the troubling quietism displayed by the thoroughgoing Pyrrhonist. What Nyíri and Bloor focus on is one specific – though admittedly prominent – dimension of Wittgenstein's work; namely, its apparent quasi-communitarian anti-foundationalism. But by emphasizing Wittgenstein's frequent appeals to community, tradition and training, one is prone to overlook the deeper naturalism that both underpins and also tempers such themes in his later writings.[179]

In this chapter I have already identified one aspect of Wittgenstein's naturalism; namely, his claim that philosophical perplexity is not merely the symptom of philosophical speculation but rather of both 'ordinary language' and our natural 'urge' to misunderstand its manifold functions. It is clearly significant that Wittgenstein, like Sextus, should ultimately locate both one's philosophical puzzlement and potential liberation in the natural realm. This is not, however, the most important aspect of his naturalism. Rather, as intimated above, the crucial question here is to what extent Wittgenstein's naturalism relates to ethical-political matters? In the next chapter I will pursue this by means of a detailed interrogation of *On Certainty*. Focusing on this text is necessary for three reasons because: (1) its continual emphasis on community, tradition and training would appear to corroborate the general claims made by Nyíri and Bloor, (2) here, perhaps more than anywhere else, the potential ethical-political stakes of Wittgenstein's mature thinking can be discerned most readily, and (3) despite the more obviously 'communitarian' overtones of this text Wittgenstein provides an important indicator as to the ethical implications of his naturalism in his remarks on 'learning' and 'trust' specifically.

2 Trusting in a world-picture
Knowledge, faith and ethics after *On Certainty*

> Skepticism and solutions to skepticism ... make their way in the world mostly as lessons in hypocrisy: providing solutions one does not believe to problems one has not felt.
>
> S. Cavell, *The Claim of Reason*

> Contempt for truth harms our civilization no less than fanatical insistence on the truth. In addition, an indifferent majority clears the way for fanatics, of whom there will always be plenty around ... We have the right to stand by our beliefs.
>
> L. Kolakowski, *Freedon, Fame, Lying and Betrayal*

> A good part of the problem with religion is religious people (without them, religion's record would be unblemished).
>
> J.D. Caputo, *On Religion*

Introduction

In Chapter 1 I explored the most striking correlations between Wittgenstein and Pyrrhonism.[1] But my primary interest there was the (apparently) similar ethical-political implications of each therapeutic philosophy. Thus, although the 'conservative' interpretation of Wittgenstein is not wholly unfounded, I suggested that it is nevertheless inadequate. Indeed, a detailed examination of Wittgenstein's later writings makes it increasingly difficult to determine any obvious political orientation therein. One reason for this is that the quasi-communitarian reading of Wittgenstein facilitates a number of ethical-political interpretative possibilities. It is therefore possible to identify the roots of a liberal, pluralistic,[2] and even relativistic dimension to these texts. On other occasions (particularly, as we will see, in his reflections on religious belief) Wittgenstein seems to provide an apologetic for dogmatism. Any attempt to 'politicize' Wittgenstein's work (to either identify an existent political subtext or utilize his writings to develop a particular political agenda) must therefore handle such interpretative possibilities carefully. We must, as it were, ensure that we 'put the question marks *deep* enough down' (Wittgenstein 1994a: 62).

As I will argue in Chapter 3, this necessitates an investigation into the naturalism underpinning Wittgenstein's mature work. For although this crucial dimension of his thinking is not synonymous with any specific political outlook, it is prerequisite for ethical-political theorizing *as such*. In this chapter, however, my interest lies with the apparent communitarian-relativism of *On Certainty* – a text that (allegedly) embodies the 'entire categorical framework of conservative thought' (Bloor 1983: 161–2). Although Bloor's claim warrants serious attention, there is too much at stake in *On Certainty* which leaves the role of those specific emphases Bloor identifies ('authority, faith, community' (ibid.: 162)) still undetermined.[3] Indeed, it is because of this that any defensible reading of this text must take into account Wittgenstein's other writings. I will therefore read *On Certainty* alongside Wittgenstein's reflections on religious belief, and in doing so highlight the potentially radical epistemological and ethical-political consequences of his later work. More specifically, this will enable me to: (1) address the interrelated problems of justification and relativism, (2) determine the function of rhetoric in both epistemological and ethical-political discourse (I will develop this in Chapter 3), and (3) begin to identify the crucial role 'primitive behaviors' play in this overall schema (this will be developed in Chapters 3 and 5).

Echoes of Pyrrhonism: doubt, knowledge and the groundlessness of belief

According to Edwards, *On Certainty* should not be read as a treatise on Wittgenstein's own epistemological views but as an alternative 'object of comparison' to philosophy's customary anti-skeptical foundationalism. On this view, Wittgenstein's equally convincing 'nonfoundational' picture facilitates our liberation from 'habitual ways of thinking' (Edwards 1985: 184). Edwards's portrait of Wittgenstein as argumentatively strategic and ontologically non-committal[4] thus remains distinctly Pyrrhonian.[5] Like the commentaries of Nyíri and Bloor, such interpretations are not implausible. There *is* something Pyrrhonian about *On Certainty*, but it is not to be found in its (alleged) 'nonfoundationalism.'[6] While one cannot (and perhaps should not) derive a systematic epistemological position from these notebooks, conceding this much does not commit one to such radically Pyrrhonian or anti-foundationalist conclusions. Where then does the Pyrrhonism of *On Certainty* lie? First, we should note that Wittgenstein's assault on skepticism does not prohibit a Pyrrhonian reading. The reason for this lies in those features of Pyrrhonism which distinguish it from more orthodox (broadly Cartesian) forms of skepticism. For although Wittgenstein touches on numerous philosophical issues here[7] his initial concern is to interrogate the premises upon which Moore's realist, 'common-sense' anti-skepticism operates.[8] Indeed, what makes *On Certainty* so fascinating is that it launches an attack both at traditional skepticism *and* anti-skepticism.[9] Wittgenstein's purpose here is to corroborate neither the skeptic's nor anti-skeptic's claims but, rather, to demonstrate how the entire debate spawns from grammatical confusions concerning the circumstances in which it 'make[s] sense' (1999: §2) to apply 'knowledge' and 'doubt.' This brings me to the second, more substantive point. Wittgenstein's refusal to align himself with either skeptic or anti-skeptic echoes Sextus' own treatment of the dogmatists and academics. Both philosophers avoid getting embroiled in the customary philosophical dichotomy between knowledge and doubt[10] by highlighting what skeptic and anti-skeptic have in common. Thus, as discussed in Chapter 1, the apparent distinction between dogmatist and academic in the Pyrrhonian schema is 'dissolved' insofar as each remains fixated on objective truth, or how things 'really are.' According to Sextus, only once this urge has been arrested does *ataraxia* become possible. The Pyrrhonist thus attempts to evade the assertiveness plaguing both truth-claimers (dogmatists) and truth-deniers (academics), exercising this 'third way' in terms of a therapeutically motivated agnosticism. *Ataraxia* is attained neither through dogmatic assent *nor* dissent but by relinquishing the drive toward committing oneself to anything beyond the life of subjective 'appearances.' Similarly, Wittgenstein questions Moore's defense of 'common-sense,' not because he wants to side with the skeptic but because Moore puts things 'in the wrong light' (ibid.: §481).[11] Moore's fundamental mistake lies not merely in *what* he says concerning knowledge and doubt but rather in his saying *too much*, or not knowing where to stop.[12] For Moore to offer such 'proofs' of epistemic certitude (as he does when declaring he knows that ' "here is a hand" ' (ibid.: §19)[13] and he has 'spent his whole life in close proximity to the earth' (ibid.: §93)) is to misunderstand the nature, applicability and interconnection of 'knowledge,' 'doubt' and other related concepts. Moore's assertions have no obvious application because he assumes their meaning to be guaranteed regardless of their specific context.[14] But once we remind ourselves of the 'ordinary' function of such terms,[15] the 'urge' driving Moore's assertions will be placated. In much the same way as objective truth (according to Sextus) leads one astray, so the yearning for 'metaphysical' (ibid.: §482), 'transcendent certainty' (ibid.: §47) becomes the philosophical affliction needing treatment in *On Certainty*.

This then constitutes the broadly Pyrrhonian terrain of *On Certainty*. There are, however, more specific points of contact between Wittgenstein and Sextus here. For example, a striking correlation emerges between Sextus' appeal to the realm of animality[16] and Wittgenstein's remark that the 'squirrel does not infer by induction that it is going to need stores next winter as well. And no more do we need a law of induction to justify our actions or our predictions' (ibid.: §287).[17] But given that my present interest lies with *On Certainty*'s apparent quasi-communitarianism I will leave Wittgenstein's Pyrrhonian naturalism for a moment. The more immediate correlation between Wittgenstein and Sextus is instead their mutual awareness of the (potentially) aporetic nature of judgement criteria. But before this can be properly elucidated I must first outline the main themes of *On Certainty*.

As intimated above, the most notable point of departure Wittgenstein takes from traditional philosophic practice here is the intimate grammatical relationship he perceives to be at play between 'knowledge' and 'doubt.' Contrary to a certain philosophical inheritance (itself presupposed by Moore) that presents these two concepts as wholly antithetical, Wittgenstein suggests that in their ordinary, non-philosophical application, 'knowledge' and 'doubt' are in fact two sides of the same conceptual-linguistic coin.[18] One of Moore's mistakes is to assume that 'the proposition "I know . . . "' is 'as little subject to doubt as "I am in pain"' (ibid.: §178).[19] The crucial point here is that the grammar governing 'I know' is 'restricted' (ibid.: §554) in a way quite foreign to Moore's own applications.[20] (The sort of propositions Wittgenstein has in mind are: '*here is one hand*' (ibid.: §1),[21] 'I am a human being' (ibid.: §4),[22] '[t]here are physical objects' (ibid.: §35),[23] 'the earth existed long before my birth' (ibid.: §84),[24] 'I have spent my whole life in close proximity to the earth' (ibid.: §93),[25] '[m]y body has never disappeared and reappeared again after an interval' (ibid.: §101), and 'all human beings have parents' (ibid.: §240).[26]) What Moore overlooks is the *conditionality* of the use of 'I know,' for he 'forgets the expression "I thought I knew"' (ibid.: §12).[27] To 'know' something entails that one can offer justification (evidence, reasons, and so on) for that claim,[28] and this is where Moore begins to go astray in his various attempts to articulate the absolute epistemic certitude of his propositions. In keeping with his later descriptive methodology, Wittgenstein is therefore concerned with how knowledge-claims are made 'in ordinary life' (ibid.: §406),[29] free from the 'metaphysical emphasis' (ibid.: §482) philosophers often impose.[30] This is why, for each of Moore's propositions, one 'can imagine circumstances that turn it into a move in one of our language-games, and by that it loses everything that is philosophically astonishing' (ibid.: §622).[31] In other words, it is Moore's repeated application of the phrase 'I know' outside any specific context[32] that renders it of ostensible philosophical significance. But despite this principal confusion, Moore's position remains worthy of philosophical attention. His self-assurance[33] may be of little interest in itself, but the 'propositions . . . which Moore retails as examples of such known truths are . . . interesting' because one does not 'arrive at any of them as a result of investigation' (ibid.: §§137–8).[34] That is, Moore's examples transcend the conditionality of the language-game of knowledge and doubt,[35] and thus cannot meaningfully be doubted in ordinary circumstances.[36] What Moore erroneously concludes from this is that he therefore 'knows' such propositions 'to be true' (Moore 1994a: 48).[37] Wittgenstein, however, refuses to subsume these types of proposition under the rubric of 'knowledge' because their epistemic status is more fundamental than Moore recognizes.[38] Thus, Wittgenstein remarks: 'Moore does not *know* what he asserts he knows, but it stands fast for him, as also for me; regarding it as absolutely solid is part of our *method* of doubt and enquiry' (1999: §151). One does not 'arrive at any of [these propositions] as a result of investigation' because they are a necessary part of what *constitutes* 'an investigation.'[39] Without such propositions being immune from critical interrogation 'a doubt would ... drag everything with it and plunge it into chaos' (ibid.: §613) – or at least change dramatically 'the role of "mistake" and "truth" in our lives' (ibid.: §138). In such extreme skeptical circumstances (assuming they are conceivable[40]) 'the foundation of all judging would be taken away from me' (ibid.: §614).[41] That Moore's propositions also 'stand fast' for Wittgenstein highlights that he is not rejecting the former's position, but rather attempting to determine what Moore can and cannot meaningfully say. The problem lies in Moore's casting this 'standing fast' in the conditional, hypothetical terms of the knowledge-game.[42] This misrepresents such 'absolute solidity' insofar as it radically understates it. One does not 'know' such things; rather, they *stand fast* by providing the necessary backdrop for any involvement in the knowledge-game itself.[43] Fundamental propositions are not a matter of epistemic certitude (their significance lies *deeper than epistemology*[44]), and it is due to this 'depth' that even Wittgenstein struggles to articulate their quasi-epistemic status.[45] Moore's trivializing the way such propositions 'stand fast' is thus further highlighted in Wittgenstein's repeated insistence that it is in one's relations with the entire natural and social world that the absolute, implicit, practical 'trust'[46] one has in the '*scaffolding* of our thoughts' (ibid.: §211) is manifest.[47] It is as though Moore, wanting to demonstrate his certitude, were to respond to the question: 'What would you be prepared to gamble on the earth existing for another minute?' with 'Oh, I'd bet a whole year's salary!' Such a wager would be peculiar because: (1) what is being gambled on (the continued existence of the earth) must itself be presupposed in the language-game of gambling, and (2) that a stake of 'a year's salary' is proportionally insignificant given that one's *entire life* hinges on the unshakeable stability of such a tacit commitment.[48]

I suggested above that Moore's cardinal mistake lay in his attempting to say 'too much.' There is, however, a sense in which this formulation remains insufficient. For when Wittgenstein remarks that the assertion '[t]here are physical objects' is 'a misfiring attempt to express what can't be expressed like that' (1999: §37), a telling correlation emerges with the saying/showing distinction of the *Tractatus*. For these quasi-epistemic foundations resist being spoken about directly,[49] but rather manifest themselves indirectly. That is, such 'certitude' ultimately resides in action and is thereby *shown*[50] in one's lived existence, not primarily in what one *says*.[51] These fundamental convictions are too close or familiar to us to permit adequate articulation; so 'anchored' in our life are they that we 'cannot touch [them]' (ibid.: §103).[52] Given what I said in Chapter 1 regarding

46 *Trusting in a world-picture*

Wittgenstein's account of the origins of philosophical perplexity (and specifically his warning that language has the 'power ... to make everything look the same' (1994a: 22)[53]) the problem inherent in any attempt to articulate this 'background' (ibid.: 16) certitude becomes clearer. Moore's knowledge-claims (his offering proofs, evidence, and so on) have an inevitable tendency to make foundational propositions look like empirical hypotheses.[54] But the 'essence of the language game is a practical method (a way of acting) – not speculation, not chatter' (1993: 399). Moore's assertion '"Here is one hand, and here is another"' (1994b: 82) adds nothing to the initial gesture – or to the course of daily life in which hands have a role – other than philosophical confusion. Thus, Moore's error should perhaps be located, not in his saying *too much* but rather in his 'urge' (Wittgenstein 1958: §109) to say *anything at all*; in his trying to 'express by the use of language' (*say*) what is 'embodied in ... grammar' (Moore 1993: 103) (*shown*).

If the same 'grammar' governs both doubt and knowledge then one cannot – as Descartes assumes[55] – choose to doubt *at will.* For if knowledge-claims demand the possibility of further justification and specific circumstances in which to operate, then so too must doubt-claims.[56] Thus, Wittgenstein maintains, one must have 'grounds for doubt' (1999: §122) or 'reasons for leaving a familiar track' (1993: 379). But he opposes the Cartesian method even more resolutely than this. For doubt, we are told, is essentially parasitic upon certitude;[57] if someone were to try to 'doubt everything' she would 'not get as far as doubting anything,' for the 'game of doubting itself presupposes certainty' (1999: §115):[58]

> How does someone judge which is his right and which his left hand? How do I know that my judgement will agree with someone else's? How do I know that this colour is blue? If I don't trust *myself* here, why should I trust anyone else's judgement? Is there a why? Must I not begin to trust somewhere? That is to say: somewhere I must begin with not-doubting; and that is not, so to speak, hasty but excusable: it is part of judging.
>
> (Wittgenstein 1999: §150)[59]

Answering the question: 'Why do I not satisfy myself that I have two feet when I want to get up from a chair?' one cannot provide reasons or evidence more certain than that which is in doubt.[60] And this is why Wittgenstein's own response to that question ('[t]here is no why. I simply don't. This is how I act' (ibid.: §148)) should be interpreted neither as equivocation nor – as Nyíri and Bloor would see it – as inherently 'conservative.' For if someone is continually unsure about the existence of her feet, hands, or the external world, then it would simply beg the question to suppose she should trust her reason, senses or the testimony of a third party (or any combination of these) in determining their existential status.[61]

Moore's examples are thus worthy of further attention insofar as they identify the sort of propositions only upon which learning can be 'hinged.'[62] The possibility of a child learning anything depends upon a natural orientation toward others, and specifically their first trusting or 'believing the adult.'[63] Doubt can only occur *after* belief,[64] for 'how could a child immediately doubt what it is taught? That could mean only that he was incapable of learning certain language games' (ibid.: §283). When learning about history a child must initially trust both what her teachers and 'text-books' (ibid.: §§162, 599) tell her; she must take these to be the absolute authority on such matters.[65] Of course, later she may question these sources on specific issues she formerly accepted unequivocally. But such questioning can begin only after she has learnt and accepted many other things.[66] (Indeed, even in this interrogation of her former beliefs she must at some point trust in the new evidence and research methods – which will doubtless themselves be inherited from the work and testimony of others.[67]) Reflection on one's own methods is possible; one can, up to a point, 'investigate the investigation' (ibid.: §459). But if one is to do anything (history, geography, physics, and so on) such self-reflection must terminate somewhere.[68] The central point here is that trust is a necessary condition for learning, questioning and even outright distrust.[69] Of course, at a much earlier stage of development the child's 'primitive reaction'[70] of trust is manifest with regard to its principle carer(s).[71] Here, I believe, we find *the* archetypal 'primitive reaction.' For although it may be 'impossible' to determine specifically *what* must lie 'beyond doubt' for 'there ... to be a language-game,' it is nevertheless prerequisite that *something* is trusted 'beyond doubt' (ibid.: §519).[72] It is, after all, only upon this pre-linguistic trust that the child can survive, be initiated into a community,[73] and later make judgements about further trust-relations.[74]

Focusing on the example of the young child is useful here because it highlights distinctions between trust and other related concepts. Although I will return to the example of Abraham and Isaac[75] in later chapters, this narrative is particularly instructive at this juncture (not least because Wittgenstein characterizes religious faith as a 'trusting' (1994a: 72)). In Genesis 22 we are thus told how God tested Abraham's faith by ordering him to take Isaac to Moriah and 'offer him as a sacrifice' (22:2). There are a number of things worth noting about this account. First, Abraham's two responses to God ('Here I am' (22:1, 12)) are immediate and unequivocal: 'here I am, under your eyes, at your service, your obedient servant' (Levinas 1996a: 146).[76] Moreover, having heard God's command, Abraham does not interrupt the spirit of his initial, affirmative response with appeals for justification; God is not petitioned to give 'reasons' for His sacrificial demand. The second point is that, despite Isaac's later inquisitiveness concerning Abraham's not having found a 'young beast for the sacrifice' (22:7), when it is Isaac himself who is eventually bound 'on the altar on the top of the wood' (22:9–10) this similarly does not provoke appeals to *his* father for justification.[77] In the case of both Abraham and Isaac such childlike,[78] unconditional trust can be contrasted with the conditionality of 'reliance.' When one relies on someone they are indeed 'trusted,' but only concerning a specific region of experience. Such reliance is thus conditional insofar as it remains subject to *one's own* judgement.[79] (I may even rely on someone *unconditionally* with regard to *x*. Nevertheless, in demarcating even this I have thereby demonstrated a deeper reliance on *my own* powers of judgement.) But, as Hertzberg notes, of genuine trust

> there will be no limits, given in advance, of how far or in what respects I shall trust him ... In relying on someone I as it were look down at him from above. I exercise my command of the world. I remain the judge of his actions. In trusting someone I look up from below. I learn from the other what the world is about. I let him be the judge of my actions.
>
> (1988: 314–15)[80]

Mindful of these points, it becomes clear why much more turns on Wittgenstein's reflections in *On Certainty* than the possibility of making *specific* knowledge-claims. The real stakes thus emerge when he refers not to individual propositions but to 'our frame of reference' (1999: §83),[81] one's 'world-picture' (ibid.: §§162, 167),[82] a 'whole system of propositions' (ibid.: §141),[83] and a '*totality* of judgements' (ibid.: §140).[84] What is important to note about these expressions is that, although Wittgenstein does refer to 'something universal' (ibid.: §440) ('the human language-game' (ibid.: §554) and the 'fundamental principles of human enquiry' (ibid.: §670)[85]), his dominant tendency in *On Certainty* is to speak of *our* 'frame of reference' (ibid.: §83), *this* 'point of view' (ibid.: §92), and *my* 'convictions' (ibid.: §102), without any clear indication as to the scope of the 'our,' 'this' or 'my' in such cases.[86] In short, Wittgenstein's emphasis seems potentially relativistic insofar as it lies on the *specific* community in which one is trained and through which one inherits a *specific* world-picture. Mindful of this (and Wittgenstein's more general anti-scientism), his remark that 'we should not call anybody reasonable who believed [in] something ... despite of scientific evidence' (ibid.: §324) could be taken to mean that while *we* 'belong to a community which is bound together by science and education' (ibid.: §298), other communities may not be bound in the same way. That science is *our* standard of rationality says something important about the way *our* lives are oriented, but that is all. Nevertheless, recognizing that one's own world-picture is historically and culturally situated does not mean – as relativists frequently assume – that one's attitude toward it needs be less categorical.[87] The analogy of love is particularly instructive here.[88] For example, I may hitherto have had a number of failed relationships. I may also be aware that, statistically speaking, it is probable that my new relationship will eventually go the same way as its predecessors. But none of this need undermine my unshakeable commitment to, and confidence in, my present lover. That love has failed me *in the past* (or that others do *not* (or *no longer*) love the one *I* love) is no reason to think that it will fail me *now*.[89] For part of the 'grammar' of love is that my current lover can always be taken as the exception here; that my usual doubts (indeed, the assurances of history and probability themselves) will at this point break down.[90] In short, to be self-effacing with regard to one's fundamental commitments is wholly unnecessary. Thus, according to Morawetz:

> One's own way of thinking is one's only resource for recognizing the behavior of others as 'giving grounds' or as 'making judgements,' and it is one's only measure for truth and falsity. To say that *p* is true for someone else, someone who makes judgements in a recognizably different way, is no basis at all for my saying that it is true, partly true, or something I cannot judge. The concepts one uses to describe alien ways of thinking are one's own concepts; one's attitude toward the truth and falsity of the beliefs of others is determined by one's own criteria for what is true. The question whether one's own point of view *ought* to have this role is really the nonsensical question whether what *I* call judgement and evidence are *really* judgement and evidence.
>
> (1978: 133)[91]

This passage is interesting because its anti-relativistic emphasis is an important, though easily neglected, feature of *On Certainty*.[92] It is not, however, the only emphasis, and to that extent Morawetz (for fear of the 'unsatisfactory conclusions' (ibid.: 123) alternative readings may lead to) underestimates Wittgenstein's troubled engagement with these issues.[93] Ultimately we must therefore ask whether Wittgenstein offers: (1) a credible response to the Pyrrhonist who seeks to 'ground' his quest for *ataraxia* upon 'reasoning falling into ... circularity' (Sextus 1996: 2:20),[94] and (2) a quasi-Pyrrhonian response to that challenge? I will return to these questions in a moment. First, in order to ascertain the force of Wittgenstein's allusions to a 'world-picture,' 'frame of reference' (and so on), another illustration might usefully be developed from one of Wittgenstein's own.[95] Being prone to absentmindedness I often misplace my house keys. When this happens I search my pockets, the floor, cupboards, and so on. Having checked all these possible locations I then begin to search the same places again, only this time I find the keys in my trouser pocket. I conclude from this that my original investigation was insufficiently thorough and that the keys had been there all along.[96] But what would prevent me from concluding that: (1) the keys had mysteriously 'appeared' in my pocket between the first and second investigation (and that objects do this occasionally)?, (2) a mischievous spirit likes moving my belongings around?, or (3) I had somehow 'willed' the keys into my pocket? As each hypothesis 'tallies with the facts' (Wittgenstein 1999: §199), the bare empirical situation does not compel me to any of these conclusions in particular.[97] What is ultimately at stake here is thus not merely whether (1), (2) or (3) can adequately explain this *specific* event. Rather, what is at issue is an entire 'world-picture' – that is, the extent to which conceding (1), (2) or (3) would undermine my 'whole way of looking at things' (ibid.: §292) and whether 'I could ... go on with the old language-game[s] any further' (ibid.: §617).[98]

The unconditional, primitive trusting upon which children's learning and socialization are founded must therefore be extended to encompass world-pictures more generally.[99] For the trust manifested in the life of the young child is not (unless we are referring to a 'damaged' (Hertzberg 1988: 320) life), lost or dissolved through later life, but rather, undergoes a continual process of extension and transference. One's primary trust in one's elders eventually extends to trusting: (1) *other* others, including what they tell us about the world, (2) one's *own* ability to make judgements between conflicting opinions and information, and (3) the social, political and religious *institutions* in which one is raised or later joins. Doubtless these commitments will be more or less tentative and hypothetical, but many will have a distinctly categorical character.[100] There is no linear, cumulative narrative here because the way trust dissipates will be complex and unpredictable. Neither is trusting one's family logically prior to trusting one's teachers or friends. Thus, our primitive trusting – though it provides the grounds upon which more circumscribed 'reliances' can be founded – nevertheless remains an essential part of adult life.[101] Moreover, this natural extension of trust beyond (for example) the parental relation lies at the core of the learning process. For one does not learn a series of singular propositions,[102] but rather a whole web of *mutually supportive* propositions.[103] As Wittgenstein notes, when learning what appear to be specific facts one indirectly 'acquires' (1999: §279) an entire 'frame of reference' (ibid.: §83), a 'whole system' (ibid.: §141) or 'structure' (ibid.: §102) of propositions. When learning to name different parts of the body, a child implicitly[104] learns about the stability of the physical world[105] – that one's 'hands don't disappear when [one is] not paying attention to them' (ibid.: §153),[106] or that one body-part does not suddenly mutate into another. To learn to identify *this* as 'my hand' I must also come to see 'my hand' as persisting from one day to the next (as being the *same* hand), though nobody will expressly say to me: 'This is your hand, and look! it does not suddenly disappear or change into something else.'[107] Persistent failure to identify *this* hand as both *mine* and the *same* hand today as it was yesterday would simply prevent certain language-games from being acquired[108] – as Hudson remarks, in ordinary circumstances, to 'be mistaken about that ["I have two hands"] would not be to say something erroneous about hands but to disqualify oneself from talking about them at all' (1986a: 120). Like the learning child then, without trusting in *some-*

thing and *someone* (that I have a body; that the world is not a figment of my imagination; that, as a rule, people do not try to deceive me[109]) one's orientation around the natural and social world would become hopeless.[110] And this is ultimately why it is not that Moore '*knows* something,' but rather that the propositions he offers are the 'unmoving foundation of his language-games' (Wittgenstein 1999: §403).

It is at this point that we must therefore recognize 'the groundlessness of our believing' (ibid.: §166). For if the practices of '[g]iving grounds' and 'justifying the evidence' (ibid.: §204) are but one dimension of specific language-games[111] (and all these practices require rule-governed contexts within which to 'have their life' (ibid.: §105)[112]) then such language-games cannot themselves meaningfully be said to be 'grounded' (ibid.: §205) on something else.[113] Rather, they constitute the 'given' (1958: p. 226) from which both daily practice and philosophical investigation begin.[114] 'You must bear in mind,' Wittgenstein thus cautions, 'that the language-game is so to say something unpredictable. I mean: it is not based on grounds. It is not reasonable (or unreasonable). It is there – like our life' (1999: §559). Justification and giving grounds reach their natural terminus not in the realm of theory but in human action.[115] Accordingly, the primitivity of our language-games means that they require no theoretical apologetics – not least because any such apologetic would itself necessarily rely on trust.[116] Rather, one must treat them as 'primary' (1958: §656), beyond both justification and doubt.[117] And this is why there is no compelling reason why one should question or abandon such fundamental beliefs, even in the face of apparently falsifying eventualities.[118] (I will expand on this in a moment.)

The central themes of *On Certainty* can thus be summarized as follows: (1) Echoing Sextus' treatment of the dogmatists and academics, Wittgenstein highlights the grammatical confusions plaguing both traditional skepticism and Moore's anti-skepticism. By focusing on how 'knowledge' and 'doubt' are actually used, Wittgenstein problematizes the (shared) assumption that these are wholly antithetical concepts. (2) Moore's anti-skepticism is not, however, simply erroneous. Rather, its significance lies in the sort of propositions Moore offers as 'evidence' against the skeptic. What interests Wittgenstein is how such propositions transcend the conditionality of the knowledge-game and resist explicit articulation. Indeed, it is precisely this unconditionality that Moore understates in his numerous claims to 'know' such things to be 'true.' To speak of 'knowledge' and 'doubt' here is misleading because the knowledge/doubt language-game *itself* presupposes such propositions to be beyond question. (3) What is therefore at stake here is not merely the conditions of possibility for making specific knowledge-claims but the general background required for a vast number of human activities. Learning (and social interaction more broadly) likewise requires that some things are trusted unconditionally. For if, as Wittgenstein suggests, one acquires a whole 'nest' (1999:

§225) of propositions, then, regarding the possibility of falsification, what is ultimately at stake is not this or that belief but an entire 'frame of reference' (ibid.: §83).

As I suggested earlier, one fruitful way of negotiating the central themes of *On Certainty* is through Wittgenstein's remarks on religious belief. With the previous synopsis in mind I will now indicate more precisely why this correlation is necessary for understanding the ethical-political implications of his later work.

Rock and sand: fundamental propositions and blasphemy

Although there has been relatively little commentary on the relationship between *On Certainty* and Wittgenstein's remarks on religion,[119] he in fact suggests this correlation in the following passage:

> If the shopkeeper wanted to investigate each of his apples without any reason, for the sake of being certain about everything, why doesn't he have to investigate the investigation? And can one talk of belief here (I mean belief as in 'religious belief', not surmise)?
>
> (1999: §459)

There are a number of reasons why Wittgenstein alludes to religious belief here, but most significant is the distinction he makes between belief and hypothesis.[120] Thus, in 'Lectures on Religious Belief' Wittgenstein remarks of the claim ' "These people rigorously hold the opinion (or view) that there is a Last Judgement" ' that here

> 'Opinion' sounds queer.
> It is for this reason that different words are used: 'dogma', 'faith'.
> We don't talk about hypothesis, or about high probability. Nor about knowing.
> In a religious discourse we use such expressions as: 'I believe that so and so will happen,' and use them differently to the way we use them in science.
>
> (1994b: 57)[121]

Notwithstanding some notable differences,[122] these sorts of beliefs parallel the 'hinge' propositions Wittgenstein identifies in Moore's anti-skepticism insofar as both lack the tentative conditionality associated with hypothesizing.[123] Despite a concurrence in 'surface grammar' (1958: §664), belief in the Last Judgement is not commensurate with the astronomer's belief in the pending arrival of a meteorite.[124] In the latter, evidence can be accumulated, observations and calculations made, hypotheses confirmed or refuted. For the religious believer, however, the Last Judgement stands 'on an entirely different plane' (1994b: 56)[125] to such empirical conjectures.[126] Still, as Kierkegaard cautions, the meaning of this 'category' of the 'quite differently' (1973: 253) [127] is hardly transparent. I therefore want to elucidate this important claim.

Now, the notion of 'testing' is not wholly foreign to the religious sphere. As I discussed earlier, Abraham was indeed 'tested' by God. Nevertheless, such trials of faith are notably unilateral, for here it is God who puts *us* to the test. There are, of course, apparent exceptions to this. In 1 John 4:1 the faithful are thus warned against false prophets: 'do not trust any and every spirit, my friends; test the spirits, to see whether they are from God.' Still, the sort of 'testing' advocated here is clearly not empirical or hypothetical, for no 'result' would ever sanction the conclusion that *God* had been found wanting. The most such 'testing' could demonstrate would be a failing (of faith, trust or understanding) on *our* part. This qualification aside, obvious questions arise concerning the very possibility of 'testing' religious beliefs in the aforementioned way. But this is not the point I want to pursue. Rather, what interests me is the extent to which in even *considering* such a possibility one would have already misunderstood the pivotal position such beliefs play in the religious life. Belief in the Last Judgement ought not to be interpreted as arising from quasi-inductive procedures – as though one was naturally led from experience to this belief. (As Wittgenstein remarks: 'experience does not direct us to derive anything from experience' (1999: §130).) Because such beliefs form 'the background against which [one will] distinguish between true and false' (ibid.: §94) they play a crucial part in constituting what an individual (and her community) will *count* as 'proof,' 'evidence' or a 'valid deduction.' [128] So, for example, an individual's *non*-belief need never be undermined by a 'visionary' experience. The non-believer might judge such a phenomenon to be of religious significance, and thus it might shake her world-picture at its roots. She might subsequently seek counsel from a priest. But equally might she judge the 'vision' to be of purely psychological origin, and instead seek psychiatric advice. There is nothing *in the phenomenon itself* that dictates which of these interpretations she should follow.[129] Rather, the inherited world-picture in which she has been trained and through which she acquires her judgement-criteria will, most likely, inform her response to the aforementioned 'vision.' [130] This would not be 'hasty but excusable,' rather, it is an essential part of what for her constitutes 'judging' (ibid.: §150). This is not to deny that the non-believer's world-picture *can* be undermined by such occurrences. The point is that such phenomena *need not* undermine her world-picture, for here she may simply close her eyes to doubt.[131] The non-believer's 'vision' can thus be adequately (and, given her training, more straightforwardly) explained without her entertaining a religious interpretation at all. There is, however, an instructive oversimplification in this example. For experiencing such a phenomenon as even *negotiable* (that is, subject to deliberation[132]) will likely not be considered a legitimate option from within each respective world-picture.[133] For the non-believer to even consider visiting a priest for advice would likely be judged by the non-believing community (and perhaps even herself) as demonstrating a prior 'weakening' toward the religious point of view.[134] Likewise, for those believers who consider such visions as religiously significant, to even entertain the possibility of seeking psychiatric assistance here would likely constitute a prior inclination toward the secular viewpoint (or even a sort of blasphemy). In short, at the heart of each world-picture lies a law of prohibition against seeking interpretative possibilities outside its own designated perimeters – or, for that matter, of questioning the stability of those perimeters.[135]

Foundational beliefs thus lie beyond rational justification, not because they are 'fixed in the sense that anything holds [them] fast' but because they are held in place by the practices that 'rotate' (ibid.: §152) around them; because *they* determine precisely *what* requires justification, and *when* and *how* such justification should occur.[136] Martin therefore concludes:

> [A]t the level of foundational convictions – religious or otherwise – the distinctions between reasonable and unreasonable and even between truth and falsity cannot yet be made ... the course which reason takes in sorting truth from falsity has legitimacy bestowed upon it only because a discernible matrix of axiomatic beliefs remains firmly and, as it were, *timelessly in place.*
>
> (1984: 603, my emphasis)

Martin's synopsis inadvertently highlights something crucial; namely, the role of temporality here. How then are we to understand his allusion to 'timelessness,' and why does it matter? One potentially fruitful way of approaching these questions would be to differentiate between types of fundamental proposition. Thus, Hudson suggests that Wittgenstein employs his 'river-bed' (1999: §97) metaphor to draw just such a distinction between 'some kinds of fundamental proposition' that 'may come or go, but not others' (Hudson 1986a: 124). While some fundamental propositions are like the shifting 'sand' of the riverbed, others resemble the immovable 'rock' beneath.[137] Martin's 'timeless' propositions might therefore refer to the latter type. However, as Hudson himself acknowledges, a certain shifting even 'at the deepest bedrock level of fundamental propositions' clearly 'does occur' (ibid.: 125).[138] But surely if we concede this then the distinction between 'sand' and 'rock' becomes rather superfluous.[139] Nevertheless, I think something valuable can be salvaged from this schema if we reconsider Martin's allusion to temporality in the light of Hertzberg's remarks on trust. First, we should acknowledge that any endeavor to distinguish too rigidly between types of fundamental proposition will be problematic given that there is no absolutely decisive way of distinguishing these from mere hypotheses.[140] Still, Hudson's attempt to make such a distinction reveals something important; namely, that although 'what men consider reasonable or unreasonable alters' at different 'periods' (Wittgenstein 1999: §336), for some beliefs this sort of observation will be necessarily *retrospective*.[141] While fundamental beliefs of either variety 'may come or go' (Hudson 1986a: 124), at any given time it is significantly unthinkable that *some* of these beliefs would *ever* change.[142] Here one is 'not ready to let anything count as a disproof' (Wittgenstein 1999: §245), and this is what constitutes these beliefs as 'rock.' The unconditional trust one has here parallels that of the child's primitive trusting relation to its elders, Abraham's relation to God, and Isaac's trust in Abraham.[143] It would therefore be misleading to speak of 'reliance' in this context, as this would imply that such commitments were both conditional and thereby subject to already existent judgement criteria.[144] Moreover, that such beliefs are *trusted* effectively means that 'there will be no limits, *given in advance*, of how far or in what respects' (Hertzberg 1988: 314, my emphasis) one will trust them.[145] What is deceptive about Hudson's formulation of the sand/rock distinction is that in omitting to emphasize this point about retrospection he implies that such a specification can indeed be made 'in advance.'[146] It is therefore important to note that although what was once held to be 'rock' can become displaced,[147] this could neither have been foretold nor, at that time, taken to be tentative or hypothetical. (It is conceivable that what is initially taken to be a hypothetical fundamental belief of the 'sand' variety eventually solidifies into 'rock,' and vice versa.[148]) 'Rock' convictions thus remain 'timelessly in place' (Martin 1984: 603) in the sense that any judgement concerning their shifting will be made in hindsight – that they *did* shift, not that they *might* shift.[149] With this in mind I now want to focus more specifically on Wittgenstein's account of religiosity.

In 'Lectures on Religious Belief' Wittgenstein imagines witnessing a (seemingly) 'miraculous' event.[150] Wittgenstein then confesses that, were he to encounter 'a very credulous person' who offered such a phenomenon as evidence for belief, *he* would be inclined to say: ' "Can it only be explained one way? Can't it be this or that?" ' (1994b: 60–1). In such a scenario Wittgenstein would try to persuade the 'credulous person' of other explanatory possibilities, treating the phenomenon just as one would 'treat an experiment in a laboratory' that one thought 'badly executed.' But this response Wittgenstein reserves for someone markedly gullible (someone who is perhaps prone to changing beliefs on the basis of such occurrences). By contrast, in the company of someone who 'showed an extremely passionate belief in such a phenomenon' Wittgenstein tells us that a response of the form ' "This could just as well have been brought about by so and so" ' would be inappropriate to the point of seeming like 'blasphemy on my side' (ibid.: 61).[151] Moreover, even if one were prepared to risk blaspheming here, there would be nothing to prevent the believer from retorting: ' "It is possible that these priests cheat, but nevertheless in a different sense a miraculous phenomenon takes place there ..."' or '"You are a cheat, but nevertheless the Deity uses you ... "' (ibid.). Accordingly, in *Culture and Value* we are told that '[r]eligious faith ... is a trusting' (1994a: 72), and that such belief 'means submitting to an authority.' But, Wittgenstein proceeds, '[h]aving once submitted, you can't then, without rebelling against it, first call it in question and then once again find it acceptable' (ibid.: 45).[152] In short, the 'grammar' of genuine religiosity proscribes one even entertaining the possibility of its illegitimacy in the face of (alleged or apparent) counter-evidence.[153] What therefore emerges here is not only a particular view of what constitutes blasphemy, but also a characteristic sensitivity toward what Wittgenstein deems to be *authentic* religiosity.[154] In the case of the 'very credulous person' the risk of blasphemy seems marginal insofar as here religious belief comprises more of evidential reasoning than a 'passionate commitment' (ibid.: 64)[155] or 'trusting' (ibid.: 72). What prevents Wittgenstein from combating[156] the genuine believer is the irrelevance – and thus irreverence – of providing alternative explanatory hypotheses concerning the aforementioned 'miracle.' On this view, anyone judged to be displaying the sort of quasi-empiricism attributed to the 'credulous person' is a fair combative target. Because such an individual is already – though perhaps unwittingly – involved in the hypothetical-evidential 'game' (insofar as they merely 'play with the thought' (ibid.: 33)[157] of religiosity) then responding to, and even contesting them in similar terms is quite legitimate.[158] (Indeed, it may even be appropriate, if only to demonstrate the real (hypothetical) nature of their professed faith.) One need not worry unduly about blaspheming in this case, for blasphemy would here amount to little more than offering counter-hypotheses for consideration. By contrast, to those who are deeply 'passionate' about their beliefs Wittgenstein shows considerable caution and respect. Blasphemy becomes a pressing issue here, not because counter-evidence might undermine their faith (it surely would not, or at least need not[159]), but rather because even in offering such evidence one trivializes the existential significance of their faith *per se*. Blasphemy, on this account, occurs when the rules of one discourse (here, the scientific) are unjustly used 'as a base from which to *combat*' (1999: §609) the genuinely religious. It is also worth noting that Wittgenstein often speaks of religious faith as a '*love*' (1994a: 33), '*passion*' (ibid.: 53), or that which is needed by the 'heart' and 'soul,' not the 'intelligence' or 'mind' (ibid.: 33). This is significant because comparing the believer with the lover helps counter the urge to misconstrue religious beliefs as quasi-empirical hypotheses. So, for example, blasphemy against the *genuine* believer might be compared to trying to persuade a friend that her lover is not worthy of her commitment because he lacks social etiquette or educational achievement. By contrast, in the company of someone who is prone to falling in love on a daily basis, such advice would not necessarily be either inappropriate or offensive.[160]

Fools, heretics and dogmatism: the question of religious fundamentalism

'Lectures on Religious Belief' constitutes one specific application of Wittgenstein's later descriptive method, and it is here that the normativity of his mature work (discussed in Chapter 1) becomes most conspicuous. Indeed, in my preceding discussion of blasphemy, Wittgenstein was happy to condemn the hypothetical attitude to religious belief as being not simply confused but fundamentally *irreligious*. But this inclination to denounce as 'superstitious' any believer who (for example) treated the Last Judgement as merely an anticipated empirical event – albeit of cataclysmic significance[161] – is not to deny that such beliefs might have some anticipatory, empirical element.[162] What I think Wittgenstein is rejecting is that a *genuinely* religious belief could be either reduced to, or ultimately dependent upon, this sort of expectancy. This point can be usefully developed with reference to the similarity between these sorts of commitments and Moore's 'hinge' propositions. Like the latter, such beliefs need not give way to (what others perceive to be) contradictory evidence.[163] For it is *these* beliefs that constitute the 'system of reference' for one's entire life (including one's criteria for 'contradiction'), and thereby provide the background for considerable self-sacrifice and personal risk.[164] Nevertheless, formulating an account of religiosity that can accommodate both its categorical and hypothetical dimensions soon becomes difficult, not least because the line Wittgenstein wants to draw between the genuine (categorical) and superstitious (hypothetical) believer is necessarily blurred.[165] In order to bring this difficulty into focus I want to consider one particularly salient example: contemporary Christian 'fundamentalism.'[166]

In the wake of the nineteenth-century Adventist movement in the United States, a number of now well-known – and more or less socially respectable – religious groups came into prominence. The essential feature binding such factions together (at least to the outside observer) was their often fervent millennialism; that is, the literal empirical-historical belief in the immanent 'Second Coming' or 'Day of Judgement.' Thus, on the basis of specific scriptural interpretations, the Seventh-day Adventists predicted Christ's return for 1844,[167] whereas between 1914 and 1984 Jehovah's Witnesses proffered a number of forecasts.[168] Unsurprisingly, both groups have since become more circumspect about formulating a specific timetable for Christ's return, Armageddon, or whatever the preferred terminology might be.[169] But what is pertinent about these examples is the way they complicate the Wittgensteinian picture, for they cannot easily be assigned a position in either category of 'genuine' or 'superstitious' belief. On the one hand, such groups favor the sort of literalist interpretation of scripture responsible for those predictive misadventures summarized above. For the most part they are also highly selective (and frequently mistrustful) regarding the findings of modern science, opting instead for a cosmology and natural history largely derived from Genesis.[170] Believers of this persuasion similarly tend towards a bold apocalyptic interpretation of cultural-political events, and even of natural disasters.[171] On the other hand, members of such faiths can rarely be described as anything other than defiantly categorical in their commitments, despite both their repeated predictive failures and the increasing prominence of secular world-pictures.[172] On a Wittgensteinian reading it thus remains unclear whether one could legitimately condemn such commitments as 'superstitious,' or whether their continued self-assurance in the face of predictive failure is both epistemically warranted and therein illustrative of a much deeper point concerning the limits of justification and the groundlessness of belief. After all, if it is not '*unthinkable* that [one] should stay in the saddle however much the facts bucked' (Wittgenstein 1999: §616) (if there is no necessary '*need* to give way before any contrary evidence' (ibid.: §657)) then why should this not also apply to the empirically inclined 'superstitious' believer?[173] With such examples in mind, one must inquire whether Wittgenstein merely fuels the fire of religious dogmatism, sectarianism and intolerance.[174] Likewise, when he expresses his antipathy toward religious apologetics and suggests that the 'man who stated [his belief] categorically [is] more intelligent than the man who was apologetic about it' (1994b: 62–3),[175] we might ask if there here emerges something ethically and politically menacing? Although I will develop this latter question more fully in Chapter 3, a preliminary exploration of the (apparent) affiliation between Wittgenstein's later work and religious dogmatism will here be useful.

For the aforementioned 'fundamentalists' the non-occurrence of the Last Judgement most often leads not to the abandonment of faith but rather to an 'admonishing'[176] (within the group) of those putting too much confidence in the predictions of fallible mortals.[177] Such predictive failures can easily be interpreted as a valuable – perhaps divinely orchestrated – trial to weed-out opportunists and apostates.[178] Thus, one could here simply re-emphasize the categorical nature of belief and, with Wittgenstein, respond to the question: '"What if you had to change your opinion even on these most fundamental things?"' by asserting: '"You don't *have* to change it. That is just what their being 'fundamental' is"' (1999: §512).[179] The numerous predictive failures of Jehovah's Witnesses have not in the least inhibited their global expansion. Although they have suffered temporary losses in membership at such times (notably in 1975[180]) these setbacks were remedied by some fairly minor doctrinal revisions.[181] Similar amendments were made by the Seventh-day Adventists concerning the failure of their 1844 prediction, and likewise by the Christadelphians. In short, what these revisionary maneuvers demonstrate is that '[a]ny statement can be held true come what may' if one is prepared to 'make drastic enough adjustments elsewhere in the system' (Quine

1994: 43).[182] To reiterate my earlier question, given this seemingly infinite capacity for revision – where the abandonment of faith is open to eternal deferral – what distinguishes such beliefs from *mere* dogmatism?[183] Does one ever have grounds for charging the believer with unreasonable 'stubbornness' (Kuhn 1996: 204)? On Wittgenstein's account must we exclude the possibility that someone could 'stay in the saddle' of belief when those beliefs *should* in fact be sacrificed?[184] And what are the rational grounds and status of this latter imperative?[185] One might respond to these questions by pointing out that the legitimacy of all such charges rests on the misguided assumption that what constitutes 'obstinacy,' 'unreasonableness' and 'stubbornness' is of common currency across different world-pictures. After all, '[w]hether a thing is a blunder or not – it is a blunder in a particular system. Just as something is a blunder in a particular game and not in another' (Wittgenstein 1994b: 59).[186] So, the devout Catholic might justify a change in doctrine by reference to the Will of God becoming more clearly revealed to the Papacy.[187] Likewise, the astronomer can justify their change in opinion by reference to new empirical evidence and/or better theoretical-explanatory models.[188] These adjustments are legitimate *within* their respective world-pictures, but what remains problematic on the Wittgensteinian account is the possibility of judging one by the criteria of the other.[189] The various charges of 'obstinacy' or 'stubbornness' may have a place *within* specific world-pictures, but to assume that the criteria for these various offences underpins all such world-pictures is the source of infinite philosophical confusion, if not injustice.[190]

Despite the predominantly epistemological concerns of *On Certainty*, Wittgenstein does occasionally allude to matters of a more broadly 'political' variety (something that is at least implicit in 'Remarks on Frazer's *Golden Bough*' and 'Lectures on Religious Belief'). So, for example, he remarks:

> Is it wrong for me to be guided in my actions by the propositions of physics? Am I to say I have no good ground for doing so? Isn't precisely this what we call a 'good ground'?
>
> Supposing we met people who did not regard that as a telling reason. Now, how do we imagine this? Instead of the physicist, they consult an oracle. (And for that we consider them primitive.) Is it wrong for them to consult an oracle and be guided by it? – If we call this 'wrong' aren't we using our language-game as a base from which to *combat* theirs?
>
> And are we right or wrong to combat it? Of course there are all sorts of slogans which will be used to support our proceedings.
>
> Where two principles really do meet which cannot be reconciled with one another, then each man declares the other a fool and heretic.

I said I would 'combat' the other man, – but wouldn't I give him *reasons*? Certainly; but how far do they go? At the end of reasons comes *persuasion*. (Think what happens when missionaries convert natives.)

(1999: §§608–12)

These passages might be reconstructed as follows: Because the 'principles' embodied in different world-pictures sometimes diverge radically,[191] a question arises as to whether a non-rhetorical encounter between them is possible.[192] That is, if two parties do not possess the same criteria for judging what constitutes a 'blunder' or 'false move,'[193] then the process of 'giving reasons' must terminate.[194] At this point the prospect for non-coercive, non-combative communication looks bleak, as one is forced to use increasingly rhetorical means.[195] The problem here does not merely concern how a pre-established, shared criterion is to be applied (what Lyotard calls a problem of 'litigation' (1988: p. xi)[196]), but more seriously, the *criterion itself*, concerning *what* criterion to use and how one can justify such a decision given that *that too* requires a criterion, and so on.[197] If, as *On Certainty* seems to suggest, one's criteria for judgement are a central part of one's socialization into the world-picture(s) of a specific community, then the terminus for rational argumentation between communities that train their members differently will soon be reached – assuming, of course, there is enough commonality for such argumentation to begin.[198] What is therefore in question here is whether 'making a decision' begins to lose its usual sense of being a rational, deliberative and justifiable procedure.[199] Without recourse to some shared judgement-criterion (be it one emerging from reason, human nature or divine Will) the process of decision-making between world-pictures begins to look – as the Pyrrhonists hoped to demonstrate – radically arbitrary. I would briefly like to illustrate this potential crisis of judgement with reference to Quine and, more specifically, Kuhn.

Although Quine speaks of there being 'much latitude of choice' regarding 'what statements to reevaluate in the light of ... contrary experience' (1994: 42–3) ('no statement is immune to revision,' perhaps not even 'the logical law of the excluded middle' (ibid.: 43)), he nevertheless yokes the pragmatic criteria of 'efficacy'[200] and 'simplicity' to 'our natural tendency to disturb the total system as little as possible' (ibid.: 44). Given that Quine insists that science is merely 'a continuation of common sense' (ibid.: 45) – which is itself cashed-out in terms of how human beings can most effectively work 'a manageable structure into the flux of experience' (ibid.: 44) – his movement toward ontological simplicity[201] in our belief-systems is ultimately grounded in human nature and broadly evolutionary motivations. Thus, despite the fact that Quine considers even science's ontology to be 'imported into a situation' to provide 'convenient intermediaries' which are themselves 'comparable, epistemologically, to the gods of Homer' ('the physical objects and the gods differ only in degree and not in kind. Both sorts of entities enter our conception only as cultural posits' (ibid.)), his pragmatic naturalism guarantees the superiority of the sciences over other world-pictures. A similar, though more striking, maneuver is made in Kuhn's *The Structure of Scientific Revolutions* – a text notable for echoing a number of Wittgensteinian themes.[202] Concerning the incommensurability between scientific paradigms (and pertaining specifically to the theory-ladenness of observation[203]) Kuhn makes the apparently radical claim that 'the proponents of competing paradigms practice their trades in different worlds,' and therefore 'see different things when they look from the same point in the same direction' (1996: 150). Later he comments on the 'techniques of persuasion' (ibid.: 152) subsequently employed by each competing paradigm, and how these techniques, if successful, culminate in a gestalt-like[204] 'conversion.'[205] Given his general characterization of the conceptual-revolutionary (that is, predominantly non-cumulative[206]) development of the sciences, Kuhn has been accused of relativism – an accusation he is quick to rebuff. Thus, in the postscript to *The Structure of Scientific Revolutions*, he explains further 'those parts of the book' that have erroneously led to 'charges of irrationality' (ibid.: 199). Now, the way Kuhn responds to such charges is by maintaining both a non-ontological instrumentalism[207] and a commitment to 'scientific progress' (ibid.: 206). What enables him to sustain this position is a much deeper (and homogenizing) conviction that scientific practice is essentially distinguished by its 'puzzle-solving' (ibid.: 205) capacity. With this unifying principle in place – and given that Kuhn limits his attention to the development of modern Western science – he may be justified in reassuring us that the sort of 'communication breakdown' (ibid.: 201) that concerns him is only ever 'partial' (ibid.: 198). Operating under the rubric of 'scientific practice' such competing paradigms *at the very least* find consensus in their general objectives ('puzzle-solving'), if not in their specific methods and conceptualizations. Kuhn therefore concludes that there is nothing in his work that 'implies ... that there are no good reasons for being persuaded' (ibid.: 199) of the superiority of one theory over another. More significantly for our purposes is Kuhn's further claim that this minimal unity of vision is enough to ensure not only that scientific 'progress' is possible but also that 'as argument piles on argument and as challenge after challenge is successfully met, only blind stubbornness can at the end account for continued resistance' (ibid.: 204) to the new, improved theory. Here it is possible to interrogate Kuhn on more Pyrrhonian grounds. For what he has to assume in order to avoid the perils of '*mere* relativism' (ibid.: 205) is not only that 'puzzle-solving' is essentially what science consists of (and that this minimal criterion is widely recognized and binding), but also that when such puzzles are solved in a 'better' way (with more 'accuracy of prediction ... simplicity, scope, and compatibility with other specialities' (ibid.: 206)) the new theory will only be resisted out of 'blind stubbornness' (ibid.: 204). Kuhn's rhetoric is striking, not least because he argues earlier:

> If two men disagree, for example, about the relative fruitfulness of their theories, or if they agree about that but disagree about the relative importance of fruitfulness ... neither can be convicted of a mistake. Nor is either being unscientific. There is no neutral algorithm for theory-choice, no systematic decision procedure which, properly applied, must lead each individual in the group to the same decision.
>
> (1996: 199–200)

This passage highlights something paradoxical at the heart of *The Structure of Scientific Revolutions*. On the one hand we are told that there is 'no neutral algorithm for theory-choice,' and yet Kuhn himself must presuppose that there *is* something like such a 'neutral' criterion by which to assess: (1) whether a proposed theory legitimately qualifies as a scientific theory (or even as a theory at all), and (2) the superiority of a new theory over its predecessors. Even if we accept Kuhn's definition of science as 'puzzle-solving' (and he provides no compelling reason why we should) the deeper question is how, without recourse to some quasi-transcendental criteria, we are to choose in a non-arbitrary way between competing paradigms whose respective understanding of what *constitutes* a legitimate 'anomaly' and 'solution' fundamentally differ? Likewise, when Kuhn remarks that there is nothing in his work which 'implies ... that there are no good reasons for being persuaded' (ibid.: 199) by one theory over another, Kuhn misses the point. For what is at stake here is precisely what *constitutes* a 'good reason.' Likewise, when Kuhn refers to the 'better' theory possessing more 'accuracy of prediction ... simplicity, scope' (ibid.: 206), the question remains of *what is to count* as 'accuracy,' 'simplicity' and 'scope' here?[208]

In keeping with the central themes of *On Certainty*, what Kuhn's position thus brings to the fore is: (1) the seemingly aporetic nature of judgement-criteria, (2) the limits of rational justification, and (3) the necessary unconditionality of certain beliefs if activities such as natural science[209] (or indeed any organized social activity[210]) are to be possible. Of course, for the Pyrrhonist the potential for infinite regress or vicious circularity regarding criteria is embraced as an effective rhetorical-therapeutic strategy by which to combat dogmatism and bring about *ataraxia*.[211] But given the troubling ethical-political indifference such a strategy instills I want to return to the question of justice with reference to Wittgenstein's *On Certainty* and reflections on religious belief.

Persuasion, conversion and judging others: ethical-political implications of *On Certainty*

As I have suggested, what is ultimately at stake in §§608–12 of *On Certainty* is the limit of ethical-political consensus; that is, whether in the circumstances there outlined one has only rhetorical – or even coercive[212] – strategies at one's disposal?[213] Although I will explore this further in Chapter 3 with reference to political and religious pluralism, there are a number of Wittgensteinian themes that require prior clarification. Most pressing here is the extent to which language-games can be individuated, as this is prerequisite for the problem of inter-game (and thus inter-world-picture[214]) conflict arising.

Somewhat characteristically, Wittgenstein does not present any definite judgement on this matter. Thus, the language-games catalogued in *Philosophical Investigations* present, not entire, complex social practices such as 'religious belief,' but those 'primitive' (1958: §25) language-games ('Asking, thanking ... praying' (ibid.: §23), 'Commanding, questioning' and 'recounting' (ibid.: §25)) of which such things as 'religious belief' consist.[215] But in these passages Wittgenstein also mentions the sort of practices more obviously associated with the empirical sciences ('Describing the appearance of an object, or giving its measurements ... Forming and testing a hypothesis,' 'Presenting the results of an experiment in tables and diagrams' (ibid.: §23)). What should be noted, however, is that the numerous other language-games he lists ('Giving orders, and obeying them ... Reporting an event ... Translating from one language into another' (ibid.)) cannot be allied so exclusively with either religion or science. Here then we are presented with primitive language-games which, in a non-uniform manner, touch upon the discourses of religion, science and countless other human activities. It is doubtless with this in mind, coupled with the frequent accusations of 'fideism' from critics, that philosophers with Wittgensteinian sympathies are often quick to discredit the idea that religious belief constitutes an homogeneous language-game.[216] Nevertheless, it is equally clear that Wittgenstein does perceive language-games to possess more-or-less identifiable boundaries,[217] for without the possibility of such individuation he could not speak of 'a *move* in the language-game' (ibid.: §22),[218] a language-game 'missing' (ibid.: §96), 'new language-games ... [coming] into existence' (ibid.: §23),[219] 'a different language-game' (ibid.: §195),[220] or 'using our language-game as a base from which to *combat* theirs' (1999: §609). In short, without some degree of individuation one could not speak of there being an 'inside' or 'outside'[221] of language-games, no matter how 'blurred' their 'edges' (1958: §71) might be.

What then can be said regarding communication where 'two principles really do meet which cannot be reconciled with one another' (1999: §611)? First, such an event will likely be rare as the majority of apparent incommensurabilities can be overcome by locating and building upon some common ground[222] (specifically those 'primitive' language-games that are shared[223]). But assuming there are a few troubling cases where 'two principles *really* cannot be reconciled,' discourse may here either break down entirely[224] or take a more strategic,[225] 'propagandist'[226] turn where one's objective becomes *merely* to persuade the other 'to look at the world in a different way' (ibid.: §92).[227] Given that 'reasoning' here terminates[228] (in the twofold sense that my reasons are *themselves* beyond justification, being neither 'reasonable' nor 'unreasonable' (ibid.: §559), and even the second-order reasons I can offer do not constitute what *you* recognize as 'reasons') a number of options remain.[229] I could, for example, simply 'put up with' (ibid.: §238) the differences between us – although on what grounds I *should* do this remain unclear.[230] Alternatively, I could sacrifice my own position and try to inhabit yours – though again there seems little reason why I *should* attempt this.[231] Or, assuming superiority, I might instead attempt to impose the rules and judgement-criteria of my language-game upon your 'wrong' (ibid.: §609), 'foolish,' 'heretical'[232] practices. As previously discussed, the problem with this latter response is that in judging your practices to be deficient I implicitly assume that the 'inherited background against which I distinguish between true and false' (ibid.: §94) ('good' and 'bad,' and so on) is the same as yours, and perhaps everyone else's. But again, this is precisely what is in question.[233] Asserting the superiority of my world-picture is not a matter of reason-giving[234] but of persuading you that you are mistaken (that my reasons are *good* reasons), or that you would be better off judging and living differently. Wittgenstein therefore proceeds to imagine the following scenarios:

> [W]hy should not a king be brought up in the belief that the world began with him? And if Moore and this king were to meet and discuss, could Moore really prove his belief to be the right one? I do not say that Moore could not convert the king to his view, but it would be a conversion of a special kind; the king would be brought to look at the world in a different way.
> Remember that one is sometimes convinced of the *correctness* of a view by its *simplicity* or *symmetry*, i.e., these are what induce one to go over to this point of view. One then simply says something like: '*That's how it must be.*'
> (1999: §92)

> I can imagine a man who had grown up in quite special circumstances and been taught that the earth came into being 50 years ago, and therefore believed this. We might instruct him: the earth has long ... etc. – We should be trying to give him our picture of the world.
> This would happen through a kind of *persuasion*.
> (1999: §262)

Although Wittgenstein provides no detailed account of how such rhetorical procedures operate, he does allude to religious education and conversion. These remarks are pertinent because, as I said earlier, the religious analogy is itself suggested in §612 of *On Certainty*.[235] Regarding religious education Wittgenstein thus writes:

> It strikes me that a religious belief could only be something like a passionate commitment to a system of reference. Hence, although it's *belief*, it's really a way of living, or a way of assessing life. It's passionately seizing hold of *this* interpretation. Instruction in a religious faith, therefore, would have to take the form of a portrayal, a description, of that system of reference, while at the same time being an appeal to conscience. And this combination would have to result in the pupil himself, of his own accord, passionately taking hold of the system of reference. It would be as though someone were first to let me see the hopelessness of my situation and then show me the means of rescue until, of my own accord, or not at any rate led to it by my *instructor*, I ran to it and grasped it.
>
> (1994a: 64)

Here we find a number of familiar themes – specifically those concerning a 'system of reference' constituting an entire 'way of assessing life.' But more striking is Wittgenstein's description of how one may come 'passionately' to take hold of such a 'system.' What interests me here is his emphasis upon one's *first* being made to 'see the hopelessness of [one's] situation' and only *then* shown 'the means of rescue.' Reading this schema alongside §612 of *On Certainty*, the process of persuasion might be elucidated as follows: When 'two principles really do meet which cannot be reconciled with one another' and we have reached 'the end of reasons,' I am left only with rhetorical means (assuming I do not simply recoil into silence[236]). At this point I might therefore attempt to convince you that, through your determination to 'stay in the saddle' (1999: §616) of your world-picture, you lack something which, with a little submission, you would immediately realize you could not henceforth live without. In short, what I first need to inculcate in you is a feeling of existential deficit; only then do I show you the 'means of rescue' (1994a: 64). The most effective way of generating this sense of deficiency would be through questioning, not so much the other's intelligence but their basic moral character. Condemning someone as a 'fool' or 'heretic' when 'two principles cannot be reconciled' is not to call into question their rational capacities, for if this were judged substandard then there would be little point in making such a condemnation. What such accusations amount to are denunciations of the way the other abuses or neglects (what we count as) 'rational procedures.' One accuses them of being a 'fool' or 'heretic' precisely because one perceives the other to be capable (though reluctant) of seeing things differently.[237]

The picture of religious conversion I have reconstructed from Wittgenstein's remarks parallels not only that offered by William James[238] (with which Wittgenstein was familiar) but also the work of a number of psychologists and sociologists researching the recruitment procedures of 'New Religious Movements.'[239] So, for example, it has been argued that

> 'a conversion appears to the psychologist as the disintegration on the religious level, of a mental synthesis, and its replacement by another.' Thus indicating that there were two stages in that process, a stage of disintegration and one of re-integration.
>
> (Nelson 1987: 130)

The conversion process Wittgenstein outlines most closely approximates what is best described as 'coercive,' where a 'de-structuring' takes place so 'the existing beliefs [of the individual] are broken down' (ibid.: 136), and only then does one provide the 'means of rescue' (Wittgenstein 1994a: 64) or 're-structuring – whereby a new set of beliefs is inculcated' (Nelson 1987: 136).[240] This psychological gloss is not simply saying that the 'new' world-picture replaces the 'old.'[241] Rather, it is alluding to the initially destructive measures necessary for such a substitution to take place. Moreover, given what I said above about the 'existential deficit' of the potential convert, it is notable that most New Religious Movements 'do not make a directly religious approach to potential converts,' but rather

> start by discussing the awful state of the world, with its increase in drug taking, crime, war and violence. Only if they find that the potential recruit agrees will they then proceed to hint that the only solution to these problems is to be found in the teachings of their movement.
>
> (Nelson 1987: 138)

In short, what makes such rhetorical strategies so successful is their initial appeal to human *moral* sensibilities (to features of life that *ought* to concern everyone), rather than strictly intellectual or theological matters.[242]

In *Culture and Value* Wittgenstein remarks:

> Nothing can be defended absolutely and finally. But only by reference to something else that is not questioned. I.e. no reason can be given why you should act (or should have acted) *like this*, except that by doing so you bring about such and such a situation, which again has to be an aim you *accept*.
>
> (1994a: 16)[243]

With this passage in mind, I would like to develop the illustration Wittgenstein himself provides in §§608–12 of *On Certainty*. Suppose *A*'s 'system of reference' is scientific whereas *B*'s is magical; in circumstances where *A* appeals to empirical research, *B* consults an oracle.[244] During their conversation *A* and *B* reach justificatory bedrock, for what *A* offers as 'reasons' in favor of her world-picture *B* does not recognize as such (and vice versa).[245] The quest for shared judgement-criteria has therefore failed, as each party feels 'inclined to say: "This is simply what I do."' (Wittgenstein 1958: §217). At this point *A* nevertheless feels compelled to challenge *B*, for it is an integral part of *A*'s position to consider all alternatives as mistaken.[246] She does this by providing a brief inventory of science's most impressive achievements in space travel: 'If you want to travel to other planets,' *A* proclaims, 'then Western science will get you there. Magic will not.'[247] To this *B* happily concedes: 'You are doubtless right, but *we* do not want to travel to other planets. *We* see no value in doing such things.' *A* might now accuse *B* of simply being a 'fool,' not because the latter fails to recognize the efficacy of modern science but rather because this sort of achievement *does not interest him*; it has no role in *B*'s cultural 'form of life.'[248] If *A*'s argument is to have any rhetorical force then it must simultaneously persuade *B* that activities such as space travel are themselves valuable,[249] and as such the appeal to scientific rationality here has a normative dimension.[250] Let me sharpen these points somewhat. Suppose the stakes were not the efficacy of science *vis-à-vis* space travel but rather its medical achievements. *A* thus confidently assures *B*: 'With Western medical techniques I can cure your children of river-blindness.' Surely in this scenario *B* could legitimately be condemned a 'fool' (or worse) for not accepting the challenge and/or not conceding the positive results *A*'s procedures yield. But even here the situation is not straightforward. First, there is no compelling epistemic reason why *B* should accept *A*'s challenge in the first place. What for *A* constitutes river-blindness may conceivably for *B* represent an act of divine retribution (akin to how some fundamentalists perceive AIDS) or perhaps a test of faith. Where *A* sees needless suffering, *B* might see the price paid for his ancestors' irreligiousness, and a punishment which, if interfered with (as *A* wishes to do), would constitute a sort of blasphemy.[251] But suppose that this initial obstacle was circumvented by *A*'s secretly 'curing' a child and presenting this test case to *B*. Would *B* then be compelled to admit the superiority of *A*'s world-picture – at least regarding matters of health? He would not. After all, this test case *could* be judged a fluke occurrence, having nothing to do with *A*'s medical procedures (a verdict frequently made by science against alleged 'miracle healings'[252]). Suppose then that *A* 'cures' a number of children whilst under the supervision of *B*. Throughout the process *A* 'describe[s] the actual procedure[s]' (Wittgenstein 1999: §671) of her medical intervention, explaining to *B* about infection, how the human eye functions, even perhaps showing him microscopic evidence to support her claims. (Indeed, *A* may also show *B* that she can repeatedly *cause* river-blindness and *then* cure it.) Must *B* now concede that his own world-picture is deficient and therefore needs to be either revised or abandoned? Is there any reason why he should not conclude that *A*'s apparent ability to restore sight derives from some demonic force?[253] Again, there is no *reason* why *B* must make such a concession,[254] for his resistance will never be epistemologically unfeasible. No matter how one refines this sort of scenario *B*'s determination to 'stay in the saddle' of his world-picture – however frustrating for outsiders – need never lack epistemic acumen. (Moreover, whether or not *B* accepts the *efficacy* of *A*'s world-picture, this in itself need never undermine the former's conviction that, though effective, *A*'s intervention constitutes an act of blasphemy.[255]) The two main points I here want to draw from Wittgenstein's remarks in *On Certainty* and *Culture and Value* are: (1) that there are no compelling epistemological reasons why someone *ought* to accept such things as 'scientific achievement' (or pragmatic criteria) as valuable, and (2) that 'rational,' non-coercive argument can only function upon the mutually shared bedrock of such ontological, epistemic and normative commitments – though, of course, the precise degree of such commonality may not be specifiable in advance.

As I have already suggested, Wittgenstein's remarks on the possibility of communication when two or more 'principles really cannot be reconciled with one another' are of ethical-political import. This can be readily seen in the previous scenario concerning Western medical techniques. For here *B* would indeed likely embrace *A*'s curative success, thus supplementing, amending or perhaps abandoning his own world-picture.[256] The greater rhetorical force of this example is, however, neither incidental nor necessarily an instance of 'Western imperialism.' For the question of human vulnerability presents an especially hard case for anyone skeptical about transcultural judgement-criteria and the legitimacy of judging another's world-picture. Whether or not a community happens to value inter-planetary travel is of little direct importance, and is certainly not something against which one should launch a rhetorical offensive. In these circumstances one would simply 'have to put up with' (ibid.: §238) another's world-picture differing from one's own. But whether or not a community considers it important to eliminate the suffering of children is a question that challenges the sensibilities of even the most radical pluralist or relativist. What is at issue here is not (as was the case with the space travel example) whether Western medicine can be shown to possess some 'intrinsic' value. As I remarked in Chapter 1, the value of medicine – like any therapy – is wholly dependent upon the illnesses requiring treatment. As such, rejection of the highly effective methods of Western medicine can only derive from a misunderstanding or trivialization of human suffering.[257] In circumstances where, for example, a child's expressions of pain were always treated with 'hesitation' (Wittgenstein 1993: 379), or where we witnessed a systematic failure in others to react to 'somebody's cries and gestures' (ibid.: 381), we would be inclined to condemn this as either immoral or just plain 'crazy' (ibid.: 383). That the relationship between vulnerability and trust has here degenerated to such extremes as to provoke our condemnation is significant, and not obviously indicative of arrogant self-aggrandizement. At this bedrock level of human existence such skepticism is not only epistemically puzzling, it is of the deepest moral concern insofar as it undermines the very building blocks of ethical-political life.[258] As I will argue in Chapter 3, if there is any commonality to be found between 'radically' disparate world-pictures it is to vulnerability and suffering that we must ultimately look. As Caputo rightly notes: 'Disasters . . . have an ominous sameness, which invariably involves spilled blood, limp bodies, broken minds, damaged lives' (1993: 41).[259] But in order to substantiate this claim I must first clarify a number of questions that arise in Wittgenstein's work pertaining to the issues of pluralism, tolerance, exclusivism and what might be called 'conceptual imperialism.' In other words, what requires more thorough investigation is the extent to which Wittgenstein's own methodological principle of non-interference (the prohibition against both judging one world-picture by the standards of another[260] and of interfering with 'the actual use of language' (1958: §124)[261]) has been explicitly applied to ethical-political matters.

3 Pluralism, justice and vulnerability
Politicizing Wittgenstein

> A state without plurality and a respect for plurality would be, first, a totalitarian state, and not only is this a terrible thing, but it does not work ... Finally, it would not even be a state. It would be, I do not know what, a stone, a rock, or something like that.
>
> J. Derrida, 'A Word of Welcome'

> [J]ustice always occurs only as a surprising exception, and its counterfeit, the justice that rests on mere prudence and is everywhere advertised, is related to it in quality and quantity as copper is to gold.
>
> A. Schopenhauer, *On The Basis of Morality*

> The elevation of human identity to the rank of transcendental subjectivity does not annul the effect which the penetration of metal can have, as a knife point or a revolver's bullet, into the heart of the I, which is but viscera.
>
> E. Levinas, *Of God Who Comes To Mind*

Introduction

In the previous two chapters I explored the relationship between Wittgenstein's later work and Pyrrhonian Skepticism. In Chapter 1 I pursued this by showing where the therapeutic strategies of Sextus and Wittgenstein intertwine, and specifically how each is motivated by the non-philosophical life. In Chapter 2 I extended this analysis by examining Wittgenstein's *On Certainty* – a text that Nyíri and Bloor insist betrays fundamentally 'conservative' themes. At first glance *On Certainty* does appear 'conservative' in Nyíri's and Bloor's sense. But such readings remain insufficient, for a thorough examination of Wittgenstein's later work reveals a more unifying picture that stresses the natural 'common behavior of mankind' (1958: §206). In addition to the aforementioned 'conservative' interpretation, it is often alleged that Wittgenstein was latterly concerned with radical or 'irreducible plurality' (Greisch 1999: 50). In this chapter I will argue against this view by providing a broadly Wittgensteinian critique of certain trends in contemporary pluralistic thinking. Having set up the analysis by examining Feyerabend's democratic relativism, Hick's religious pluralism, and Lyotard's politics of 'dissensus,' I will then turn to Wittgenstein's reflections on embodiment. This will enable me to demonstrate how the rhetorical force of each of the aforementioned positions hinges on a more-or-less repressed naturalism.

Politics, religion and the rhetoric of pluralism

According to Wittgenstein '[w]hat has to be accepted,' or that which is 'given,' is *'forms of life'* (1958: p. 226). Our language-practices, embedded in and underpinned by complex ways of behaving, require no justification from philosophers. Philosophy's task is rather to remind us of the multifarious ways language actually functions.[1] Between Wittgenstein's early and later writings ontology thus never entirely drops out of the picture, but rather shifts from the subterranean '*utterly simple*' (ibid.: §97) structure of the world (itself mirrored in language[2]) to the plurality of language-games in which human beings are actively engaged. The ontology of the later work may be fragmented, but it is nevertheless an ontology, and one that is necessary for Wittgenstein to place his therapeutic 'full stop' at human practices as they are 'given.' There is, of course, much else to be said on this point. But for the moment I simply want to highlight this methodological – and arguably quasi-religious[3] – commitment to the *givenness* of forms of life, and the language-games (and other behaviors) of which they comprise. Now, if we accept this picture and – as is often done – interpret 'forms of life' as something essentially cultural,[4] a number of possible ethical-political perspectives become available. Feyerabend expresses one of these when he asserts: '*Traditions are neither good nor bad, they simply are* . . . rationality is not an arbiter of traditions, it is itself a tradition or an aspect of a tradition. It is therefore neither good nor bad, it simply is.' He continues: '*A tradition assumes desirable or undesirable properties only when compared with some tradition*, i.e. only when viewed by participants who see the world in terms of its values' (1988: 243).[5] Here we find the sort of reverence for the 'given' often discernible in Wittgenstein, though employed in the service of a specific political agenda. The bedrock traditions upon which our deliberations take place (including those concerning matters of 'right' and 'wrong,' 'true' and 'false,' and so on) cannot *themselves* meaningfully be said to be 'right' or 'wrong,' 'true' or 'false' – they simply *are*. In other words, these traditions provide the conditions of possibility for all such ethical, epistemic and ontological judgements.[6] Feyerabend thus proceeds to argue that, given the fundamental diversity of 'traditions,' democratic relativism is the only legitimate political position: it is '*reasonable* because it pays attention to the pluralism of traditions and values' and '*civilized* for it does not assume that one's own village and strange customs it contains are the navel of the world' (1987: 28).[7] Combining a quasi-Wittgensteinian reverence for the 'given' multiplicity of traditions[8] with a Kuhnian incommensurability thesis, Feyerabend is an enthusiastic advocate of relativistic pluralism. No single tradition (for example, the Christian faith or Western science[9]) has a monopoly on truth, not least because 'the criteria of acceptability for beliefs change with time, situation and the nature of the beliefs' (1988: 264).[10] This claim Feyerabend justifies in broadly Quinean fashion: 'Every culture constructs entities in a way that is determined partly by accidents, partly by obstacles experienced and partly by the sequence of beliefs, needs and expectations that accompanied the way in which it dealt with the obstacles' (ibid.: 270), and concludes (though not with Quine) that the 'just' society is therefore one in which no 'particular creed' has more '*rights*,' '*power*' (ibid.: 246) or access to resources than any other. This is not to deny Western reason its place. Rather:

> [O]ne thing must be avoided at all costs: the special standards which define special subjects and special professions must not be allowed to permeate *general* education and they must not be made the defining property of a 'well-educated person'. General education should prepare a citizen to *choose between* the standards, or to find his way in a society that contains groups committed to various standards *but it must under no condition bend his mind so that it conforms to the standards of one particular group.*
>
> (Feyerabend 1988: 167)[11]

This deeply voluntaristic and normative agenda is not, of course, unproblematic.[12] Indeed, given Feyerabend's claim that '"[o]bjectively" there is nothing to choose between anti-semitism and humanitarianism' (that while 'racism will appear vicious to a humanitarian, humanitarianism will appear vapid to a racist' (1987: 8–9)) we might inquire as to the moral and epistemic status of the democratic relativism he defends, and how this imagined pluralistic society could legitimately (but *what is* and *who decides* the standard of 'legitimacy' here?[13]) resist a 'totalitarian' tradition trespassing onto *other* traditions? Appealing to the standards of democratic relativism – that it is somehow *better* to allow other traditions to flourish in peace – is already to make a substantive moral claim,[14] and thus merely begs the question. For it is precisely *that* sort of criterion the totalitarian will reject. But the stakes need not be raised as far as political totalitarianism to demonstrate the problem here. For any tradition (many religious traditions, for example) believing itself to: (1) possess the 'truth' and others to be 'in error,' and (2) have a morally binding duty to convert others, will find its activities severely restricted in Feyerabend's relativistic democracy. In short, the only traditions that could flourish in this pluralistic utopia would be traditions *already* valuing pluralistic tolerance. But this obviously conflicts with respect for traditions as they '*simply are*' (1988: 243) in their stark, incontestable 'givenness.'[15] On reflection then, the grounds upon which Feyerabend can even offer this political agenda (and how he can demand: 'one thing must be avoided at all costs ... ' (ibid.: 167)) remain unclear. After all, if traditions are multiple and only locally legitimated then this must also apply to democratic relativism. In his defense one might claim that relativism is the best ethical-political option because it seeks to maximize tolerance, thus enabling all other traditions to express themselves. This would, however, not only be contradicted by the example of religious exclusivism (to which I will return in a moment), it would again merely beg the question. For disagreement about what *constitutes* the 'best option' (and, not least, the *genuinely* 'ethical-political') will be one of the most fundamental differences between such traditions. Feyerabend's political theorizing is hopelessly simplistic. Nevertheless, the issues with which he attempts to grapple emerge in the work of other philosophers more directly associated with social-political matters – those, for example, explicitly concerned with contemporary religious pluralism.[16] Thus, in Hick's writings we find an analogous tension emerge between respect for religious traditions *as they are*, and the endorsement of (or at least 'hope' (1977: 183) for) pluralistic tolerance in a violently sectarian world.[17] It is to this more focused type of pluralism that I will now turn.

Hick is correct to insist that there is nothing *a priori* violent or homogenizing about the idea of pluralism, and that any shortcomings of the pluralistic hypothesis must not simply be assumed to be part of a broader Western 'imperialism.'[18] Indeed, in this regard it is important to acknowledge that the genealogy of pluralism, at least in its various religious manifestations,[19] is historically and culturally better established than is commonly assumed.[20] Nevertheless, Hick concedes that in recent times the West has been forced to recognize the presumptuousness of any claims it may have made regarding its own 'moral superiority' (1995: 14). As such, contemplative Christians have had to accept that the fruits of the spirit 'do *not* occur more abundantly' (ibid.: 16) within Christianity than other faiths. This awareness, coupled with the promising fact that these 'religions are now meeting one another in a new way as parts of the one world of our common humanity,' leads Hick to conclude that the 'religious imperialism' (1977: 182) hitherto endorsed by traditional Christian theology (which, at best, only pitied those of other faiths) is in desperate need of revision.[21] It is no longer legitimate to claim that 'all who are saved are saved by Jesus of Nazareth.' What the enlightened Christian can say 'gladly' is that the 'Ultimate Reality has effected human consciousness for its liberation or "salvation" in various ways' within a multiplicity of cultural-religious 'forms of life' (ibid.: 181).[22]

The main tension within Hick's position is worth exploring because it is pertinent to many of the themes discussed in Chapters 1 and 2. I am not, therefore, concerned with the finer details of how Hick proposes to revise the traditional, exclusivist theological perspective.[23] What concerns me is the essentially normative trajectory his pluralism takes, despite his attempts to secure it in 'the facts of the history of religions' (1995: 51). For while Hick rejects the idea of an homogenizing 'new global religion' (ibid.: 41), and speaks instead in quasi-Wittgensteinian terms of leaving 'the different traditions just as they are' (ibid.: 41–2),[24] he nevertheless admits that his own pluralism violates the exclusivist self-image of both traditional Christian theology and numerous other religions.[25] On this point Hick is clearly troubled by the resurgence of fundamentalism,[26] and even speculates that Christianity may soon be divided into two factions: one liberal, the other fundamentalist, with each side 'seeing the other as a religious disaster' (ibid.: 134).[27] This, he confesses, would be deeply lamentable, not least because, on the latter side of the theological-political divide, one finds 'dangerous ... extremists' responsible for much of society's 'conflicts' (ibid.). Proceeding in Feyerabendian fashion Hick thus observes how 'absolutism in religion, preaching the unique superiority of one's own tradition over against others [sic], continues to motivate young men to be willing to kill and to be killed for what they regard as a sacred cause' (ibid.: 134). Given that the 'absoluteness of the justification ... can have power to validate anything,' the only real hope for religion becoming 'a healing instead of a divisive force' is if that absolutism is 'dismantled by the realization that one's own religion is one among several valid human responses to the Divine' (ibid.: 123). If the aforementioned division at the heart of Christianity is to be avoided (assuming it is not irrevocably under way) then we must choose between 'one-tradition absolutism and a genuinely pluralistic interpretation of the global religious situation' (ibid.: 43); either we 'affirm the absolute truth of one's own tradition, or go for some form of pluralistic view' (ibid.: 48–9).[28] Indeed, the adoption of the latter is 'unavoidable' if Christianity is to be a 'credible ... faith for the twenty-first century' (ibid.: 132). In these claims it is not then merely cultural-historical awareness that holds the key to a 'better' (pluralistic) future – after all, religious exclusivists are not ignorant of the existence of other faiths. Rather, Hick is advocating a hospitable attitude in response to 'the global religious situation.'[29]

As I suggested above, the aporia here lies in Hick's position being simultaneously descriptive and normative. For while he speaks of leaving 'the different traditions just as they are,'[30] he concedes that his own agenda necessarily impinges upon exclusivism. Indeed, Hick openly condemns exclusivist tendencies within contemporary religious practice as 'treason against the peace and diversity of the human family' (ibid.: 118) – an unsurprising condemnation given that those tendencies constitute the most formidable threat to pluralism. While he recognizes that the exclusivist's position is internally 'consistent and coherent,' it is so only 'for those who can believe that God condemns the majority of the human race ... to eternal damnation' (ibid.: 19). But Hick is clear that such a position is reprehensible, even referring to the missionary activities of orthodox Christianity as 'a complete mistake' (ibid.: 117).[31] The 'ultimate ineffable

Reality,' we are thus assured, can be 'authentically experienced' in a variety of 'different sets of human concepts' (ibid.: 25). However, it is equally apparent that this does *not* apply to 'every religious movement' – not, for example, to those endorsing 'harmful practices' such as 'human sacrifice, the repression of women ... opposition to planned parenthood, discrimination against homosexuals' (ibid.: 44), and so on. Much like Wittgenstein then, Hick's criterion of what constitutes 'genuine' religiosity is neither purely descriptive nor open-ended.[32]

What this brings into focus is the lack of rhetorical force of Hick's position, for it remains unclear how he hopes to persuade the exclusivist of the value of pluralism? Thus, in order to demonstrate that the 'paradigm shift' demanded by religious pluralism is possible, Hick defines Christian belief as 'what Christians generally believe' – a web of belief that 'has varied enormously over the centuries' (ibid.: 126).[33] But if this is demonstrable proof of the possibility of a shift toward pluralism, then it can equally be offered as proof of the possibility of a shift toward fundamentalist absolutism. The claim that religious pluralism (while challenging 'some of our traditional dogmas') does 'not require that any of the basic Christian ideas be abandoned' (ibid.: 125) again begs the question, for it presupposes a consensus as to what constitutes dispensable hypothetical dogma, and what is 'basic' to Christian practice.[34] Of course, Hick is not oblivious to this tension in his thinking, and concedes that 'there's a sense in which religious pluralism does ... give a different status to the various traditions and their teachings from what they give themselves.'[35] Nevertheless, it is telling that he proceeds to describe *this* fact as a 'virtue' (ibid.: 45) of pluralism – a reassurance doubtless self-evident to other pluralists but not to the exclusivist for whom it may seem like blasphemy.[36] Hick thus faces an initial, perhaps insurmountable, problem; namely, of how to speak in a consensus-oriented fashion to the exclusivist when *their* conception of 'genuine' religiosity differs so radically from the pluralist's. This presents a particularly hard case for contemporary pluralistic thinking. Nevertheless, it is necessary to highlight it here given both Hick's specific concern with *religious* pluralism and the obvious unacceptability of his position for non-pluralists. Indeed, asking the question: 'To whom is Hick addressing himself?' is germane, for it remains unclear who his target audience is – not least because the value of pluralistic tolerance is *presumed* rather than demonstrated in his argument.[37] After all, Hick's emphasis on pluralistic tendencies in both ancient religions and contemporary interfaith dialog does nothing to undermine the exclusivist's suspicion that such phenomena merely bear witness to the dominance of impious, decadent and increasingly secular world-pictures.[38] These aporias might thus be summarized in the following Levinasian–Derridean terms (to which I will return in later chapters): Is it possible – or even desirable – to respect the other's difference if that other does not in turn respect the difference of *other* others? And if this is *not* possible – or desirable – then what remains other than the hollow tolerance of 'respecting' versions of *oneself* (one's *own* values and practices)?[39] In other words: am I only to welcome those who respond courteously to my pluralistic hospitality, or rather, is hospitality a genuine possibility only where the other poses a potential threat or 'risk' (Derrida 1995b: 68)[40] to my peaceful, pluralistic 'being-at-home'?[41]

My objective here has not been to question Hick's pluralistic motives but rather to highlight the difficulties of formulating such pluralism in the first place. By identifying the logical problems haunting Hick's argument I have thus shown how pluralism – at least in this specific form – lacks rhetorical force and ultimately only addresses those who are *already* sympathetic to its general principles and aims.[42] That our differences can be simultaneously resolved *and* respected is the central dilemma facing any such political-religious project. For identifying what differences one *can* sacrifice (or legitimately demand the other to sacrifice) for the sake of pluralistic harmony, without thereby jeopardizing the singularity of one's own (or the other's) position, is precisely what differentiates each position in the first place. Indeed, to this extent there is no better propaganda for the exclusivist and pluralist (respectively) than the practices and pronouncements *of the other*. Each could address their respective audiences by showing them the alternative world-picture and rhetorically inquiring: Is this *really* what you think God wants?

What inspires Hick's pluralism is a deep respect for 'the peace and diversity of the human family' (1995: 118). Thus, underpinning his assault on exclusivism, lies an appeal to a 'common humanity' (1977: 182) of which we are *all* a part, despite the differences between our historical, political, ethical and religious practices and status. Surin correctly identifies this unifying backdrop to Hick's narrative, but proceeds to condemn him for neglecting to notice that 'this ahistorical affirmation of "a common human history" is ... irredeemably ideological.' Indeed, in post-Enlightenment culture there is no more effective way of veiling real social-political injustices than to dress one's theorizing 'in the garbs of a universalistic "pluralism"' (Surin 1990: 120).[43] Surin's caution is not wholly unreasonable, for what lies at the heart of every pluralism is the belief that the categories of 'plurality' and 'unity' cannot be straightforwardly dissociated.[44] Nevertheless, that the conception of a 'common humanity' both *can be* and *has been*[45] used as an ideological weapon of oppression does not mean that it is an *inherently* oppressive notion.[46] It is, after all, singularly difficult to think of any principle (including Surin's respect for the 'intractable "otherness" of the Other' (ibid.: 126) and desire to 'safeguard' this unique 'strangeness' (ibid.: 125)) that could *not* be used to facilitate political violence, oppression or indifference.[47] I will return to this point later. First, however, I want to develop Surin's suggestion that the very notion of a 'human family' is simply part of a more clandestine attempt at cultural-political-conceptual homogenization (and is thus *itself* inherently exclusivist). I will do this with reference to Lyotard's more radical pluralistic vision.[48]

Totalitarianism and Lyotard's politics of dissensus

In Chapter 2 I raised a question concerning the extent to which language-games (and, by implication, world-pictures) could be individuated. This question is important here because it lies at the heart of the pluralist debate. Whether one is speaking about 'traditions' (as Feyerabend does) or 'religions' (as Hick does) the degree to which these are represented as either fundamentally *incommensurable* or *unified* will determine the sort of ethical-political conclusions one reaches. Of course, by definition all pluralisms concede a degree of plurality within the social arena. But whether this plurality is ultimately judged to be of an irreducible sort (as Surin advises it *should* be judged[49]) is another matter. Thus, Hick's acknowledgment of the 'given' multiplicity of religious traditions is tempered by what he sees as their mutual concern with human salvation and the elimination of egocentrism, and a shared 'human family' of which all 'the great world faiths' (1995: 17) are a part. These criteria enable Hick to demarcate 'genuine' religiosity from the manifold dangers of absolutism. But, as previously discussed, by this demarcation Hick marginalizes *from the start* those for whom his discourse is presumably intended; namely, religious exclusivists. According to a more radical form of pluralism, however, this tempering of singularity by positing a 'common humanity' is precisely what the question of social-political justice hinges on. For here the task is to 'define a pluralism of radical separation, a pluralism in which the plurality is not that of a total community, that of cohesion or coherence of the whole' (Derrida 1999b: 96). Thus, like Feyerabend, Lyotard employs a number of Wittgensteinian themes[50] in order to emphasize the fragmentation of contemporary social life and thereby pose the question of how we are to conceive and deploy justice when 'the position of the other remains always irreducibly other' (Barron 1992: 31). In response to this dilemma Lyotard advocates a 'pagan' attitude of 'acceptance ... that one can play several games, and that each of these games is interesting in itself insofar as the interesting thing is to play moves.' The pagan thereby tries 'to invent new games,' 'figure out new moves' previously 'unexpected and unheard of,' and even 'move from one game to another' (1985: 61).[51] What is characteristic of the *non*-pagan is their tendency to 'stick to [their] signified' and 'think that they are in the true' (ibid.: 62).[52] Such self-assured dogmatism is misplaced because, while language-games are indeed *given*, the way one proceeds to 'play' them remains essentially open.[53] On the basis of this radical individuation of language-games Lyotard thus proceeds to define 'oppression' in terms of the proclivity (of non-pagans) to 'import into a language game a question that comes from another one and to impose it' (ibid.: 53).[54] The question of justice arises because political efficacy demands that language-games employ the same conceptual vocabulary; the language of a 'common humanity' or universal 'we.'[55] The implicit injunction in traditional politics is thus 'be operational (that is, commensurable) or disappear,' and this, we are warned, inevitably 'entails a certain level of terror' (1997a: xxiv).[56] According to Lyotard, then, the most fundamental ethical-political right is the right *to be other*, to 'play' different games or the same games differently.[57] Any state that confines its members to specific, pre-established narratives is – albeit surreptitiously – essentially *totalitarian*.[58]

In *The Differend* Lyotard therefore attempts to 'do justice' to the various 'given' narratives rather than subsuming them under a general rationalization.[59] Here his primary concern is what happens, and what can be done in the name of justice when a dispute occurs between two or more incommensurable language-games[60] – or, in Lyotard's terminology, when a conflict arises that cannot be treated as a mere problem of 'litigation,' but which rather constitutes a 'differend' (1988: xi).[61] To understand this distinction one might compare a *litigation* to a dispute between two cardplayers who differ over the application of a specific rule in poker. Here a consensus-oriented compromise is possible because both players agree about the basic rules of poker (and that they are indeed both playing poker). A *differend* would occur when the divergences between each party were so radical that neither would consider the other to be even *playing* poker (or perhaps *any game whatsoever*).[62] As a 'universal rule of judgement ... is lacking in general' (ibid.) it is therefore the role of 'a certain literature, philosophy, and ... politics to bear witness to differends by finding idioms for them' (Carrol 1987: 169) which do not compromise either party. The Lyotardian objective is thus *not* one of consensus (which is necessarily violent in its diminution of the other's otherness) but rather the right of each party to have their own idiomatic voice, thereby maintaining a level of *dissensus* in the social-political realm.[63] As 'we do not have a rule for justice,' the quest for justice 'is not a matter of conforming to laws' (Lyotard 1985: 65). To embark upon such a program would be totalitarian insofar as totalitarianism is defined as the exclusion of 'the possibility of dispute' (Readings 1991: 109).[64] By claiming to have identified and fixed the meaning of the 'just,'[65] totalitarianism thereby silences dissenting voices – or at least vilifies such resistance as transgressive,[66] unnatural, demonic or 'mad' (Lyotard 1988: 8).[67]

With these points in mind, Hick's treatment of the religious exclusivist represents precisely the sort of totalitarian silencing procedure Lyotard warns against. So, by appealing to a quasi-naturalistic prevalence of 'a kind of implicit religious pluralism' (1995: 122)[68] and positing a common 'human family' (ibid.: 118) that the exclusivist disrespects, Hick effectively calls into question her *humanity*. Likewise, in his casting (a rather specific notion of) 'salvation/liberation' as central to 'each of the great world faiths' (ibid.: 17), and subsequent allusion to the self-evident repugnance of the notion of an exclusivist God,[69] Hick thereby calls into question the exclusivist's *religiosity*. Similarly, if religious pluralism is in the end 'unavoidable' (ibid.: 132) then so too must the *rationality* of the exclusivist be questioned. And finally, given that sacrificing exclusivist tendencies is an inherent 'virtue' (ibid.: 45), the *moral* bankruptcy of the persistent exclusivist should also be noted. In short, by the very parameters set by Hick's discourse, the exclusivist is judged *from the start* to be in some fundamental respects inhuman, irreligious, irrational and immoral. With these dubious credentials it is therefore unsurprising that she is deemed undeserving of a voice.

Lyotard's work presents one attempt to conceptualize an instance of 'two principles' meeting that 'cannot be reconciled with one another,' where each party simply declares 'the other a fool and heretic' (Wittgenstein 1999: §611). If, as Lyotard maintains, the imposition of the rules of one language-game upon another is 'inherent to oppression' (1985: 53), then, conversely, respect for 'difference' is the core of justice itself. What must be resisted is the temptation to consider one's own practices to be either fixed once and for all or (whether 'fixed' or not) inherently superior to the practices of others. In short, what should be avoided is the assumption 'that one's own village and strange customs it contains are the navel of the world' (Feyerabend 1987: 28). Lyotard's concern to avoid linguistic-conceptual domination[70] – and thereby 'bear witness to'[71] the absolute 'heterogeneity of language games' (1997a: xxv) – thus highlights the possible ethical-political significance of Wittgenstein's later work. I have thus far remained uncritical of Lyotard's politicization of Wittgenstein. But I would now like to consider one particularly striking example of how Lyotard's 'pagan justice' or 'politics of dissensus' has been applied by Readings – one of his chief exponents. This will enable me to focus critical attention on the Lyotardian project toward the end of the chapter.

Taking Herzog's *Where the Green Ants Dream* as his inspiration, Readings claims that what this film highlights is the incommensurability between 'Aborigines and . . . liberal capitalist democracy' (1992: 171). In its portrayal of a dispute between the Aborigines and a local mining company regarding land ownership, Herzog's film 'does not represent an other so much as bear witness to an otherness to representation, a *différend*' (ibid.: 176). Readings proceeds to summarize *Where the Green Ants Dream* in typically Lyotardian fashion:

> [T]he dispute . . . takes place at the edge of the Empire, in the Australian desert, on a site which is at the same time central to the political struggles currently animating the west: the rights of indigenous peoples in the wake of the Empire. In the course of the film a radical aporia in legal arbitration appears as a structural necessity of the modernist insistence on the representability of the human and the possibility of universal justice . . . *Where the Green Ants Dream* shows that

80 *Pluralism, justice and vulnerability*

> ethical responsibility demands a quasi-aesthetic experimentation if justice is to be done to an Aboriginal claim ... Doing justice is a matter of experimentation rather than of corresponding to models.
>
> (1992: 172–3)

And more specifically:

> During the court hearing, the Aborigines produce as 'evidence' certain sacred objects. But the sacred objects ... can only be recorded as an utter blank: 'wooden object, carved, with marking, the markings indecipherable. The significance of the markings not plain to this court' ... Governor Phillips raised his flag in 1788, around 200 years ago, more or less when the Aboriginal sacred objects were buried. But they weren't buried at the same time, since they weren't buried in the same history ... the flag is raised in western historical time and the objects are buried in a time that is not historical in any sense we might recognize ... [a] time which cannot be thought by western science.
>
> (1992: 181)[72]

The plaintiff and defendant 'do not merely speak different languages, they participate in utterly incommensurable language games' (ibid.: 180) – an incommensurability that becomes apparent in, for example, the Aboriginal understanding of temporal and spatial relations[73] and methods of enumeration.[74] But most crucial is how the Aborigines conceive their relation to the 'sacred land, where the green ants dwell,' for they 'belong to the land' in a quite specific way: 'Not belong *to* the land: there is no possibility of even a thought of separation or abstraction. They can't be transplanted, immigrate elsewhere. They have no *abstract human nature* that would survive in another place, anywhere else' (ibid.: 183). Due to the Enlightenment (and hence liberal) dream that 'all difference can be overcome' by reference to the 'universal language' or '"common law" of humanity,'[75] the Aboriginal voices are effectively silenced. It is not that the court *openly* forbids the Aborigines from speaking, but that, despite the 'sham' (ibid.: 181) of their being permitted a legal voice, in its very demand for a 'unitary "we"' (ibid.: 180) the other's language-game is inevitably suppressed. Thus, one might say, the Aborigines are rendered conceptually mute. The implicit command of the court is 'speak as *we* do!' for without this much commonality, understanding and the goal of mutual compromise become impossible.[76] For Readings, the injustice of the trial emerges from the untranslatability of the language of the Aborigines into that of 'common law,' and thus of 'common humanity.' Although an 'encounter takes place, it happens' there is 'no language available [in which] to phrase it' (ibid.: 183). What Herzog's film bears witness to 'is not an incidental act of injustice' but rather 'the necessary, structurally implicit terror that accompanies the encounter of a people that says "we" with a community that is not modern, that doesn't think itself as a people' (ibid.: 184). The 'paradox that arises is that neither side is wrong,' for ' "We" have no way of saying who is right here, the mining company or the Aborigines. No "we" can pronounce once and for all on their dispute. All we can do . . . is to try to tell another story,' namely 'one that doesn't seek to synthesize or assimilate them but to keep the dispute and the difference an open question' (ibid.: 185).[77] What Lyotard's 'paganism' thus demands is a movement away from a politics that seeks to absorb the other and deny radical difference. In much the same way as Surin criticizes Hick, for both Lyotard and Readings the 'suggestion that all cultures are fundamentally the same is the trade mark of the imperialism of modernity.' The real challenge of contemporary politics is how 'to think liberation otherwise than as an abstraction into ever more splendid (more universal) isolation'; that is, of how to rethink 'the notion of community under the horizon of dissensus rather than of consensus' (ibid.: 184).

As Readings's synopsis of *Where the Green Ants Dream* suggests, the waters of incommensurability may indeed be abyssal, but the question remains: are they *unfathomable*? In my analysis of *On Certainty* in Chapter 2 I showed how Moore misconstrues the epistemic status of his 'hinge' propositions. Keeping this in mind I now want to explore why Readings's conclusions are premature, for what requires further analysis is the possibility of there being *ethical* foundations (analogous to the trans-epistemic foundations Moore inadvertently draws attention to) upon which human interaction is 'hinged.' If such ethical foundations can indeed be identified then this would not only facilitate a more comprehensive understanding of those anxieties intermittently haunting Wittgenstein's own work (notably *On Certainty*), it would also curb Surin's worries concerning Hick's religious pluralism and, more crucially, reveal why the Lyotardian position is untenable. The best way of negotiating these issues is, indirectly, through Wittgenstein's alleged anti-foundationalism, for this reading of his later work naturally lends itself to such theoretical extravagances as Feyerabend's naive relativism and Readings's Lyotardian 'paganism.' As will become clear, however, this anti-foundationalist reading is both inaccurate and unsound.

A succinct example of the aforementioned position can be found in Greisch's recent work. For there we are told that 'Wittgenstein developed the theory of the irreducible plurality of language games anchored in "forms of life" ' where he hoped 'to resolve the difficult question of values in terms of *plurality*,' whereas (for example) 'Husserl strove towards some kind of teleological *unity*' (1999: 46).[78] According to this synopsis, then, Wittgenstein's later writings revolve around the notion of 'irreducible plurality.' Thus, having outlined Werner Marx's work on the primacy of 'sympathy' as a 'unifying principle' (ibid.: 50) in ethics, Greisch somberly concludes:

[A]nyone who is familiar with the thought of the later Wittgenstein will have difficulty sharing the optimism of [Werner Marx] who calculates that an ethics of compassion appears capable of surmounting the heterogeneity of language games and the corresponding forms of life.
(1999: 58)

What is interesting about these remarks is that they systematically overlook the primacy of 'natural reactions' in Wittgenstein's work – *including* those of 'pity' (1958: §287) and 'sympathy' (1993: 381).[79] Greisch's lamentation is therefore misplaced, for the very 'unifying principle' he discovers elsewhere lies at the very heart of Wittgenstein's own work.[80] It is this claim that I will now substantiate, first by reconstructing Wittgenstein's account of both inter-personal and inter-cultural relations, and finally by critiquing the Lyotardian position outlined above.

Body, soul, suffering and the specter of amoralism

Pain and suffering (both one's own and others') are recurrent themes in Wittgenstein's later writings. Although these phenomena are relevant to a number of epistemological questions, they are also of obvious ethical import.[81] I would like to begin to reconstruct this ethical subtext from the following passage in *Philosophical Investigations*:

> Suppose you came as an explorer into an unknown country with a language quite strange to you. In what circumstances would you say that the people there gave orders, understood them, obeyed them, rebelled against them, and so on? The common behavior of mankind is the system of reference by means of which we interpret an unknown language.
> (Wittgenstein 1958: §206)[82]

Here Wittgenstein is clear that, even when faced with cultural difference – even where language practices are seemingly *incommensurable* – one is not entirely at a loss. Despite the manifold divergences between one's own culture and that of another, the 'common behavior of mankind' is nevertheless capable of breaking through the mutual bewilderment[83] (indeed, without this underlying commonality it would be impossible to learn another's language). Encountering another culture is patently not the same as finding oneself amidst a colony of alien beings who lacked an even vaguely determinate bodily form or behavioral repertoire.[84] Aside from extreme borderline cases, one *immediately* distinguishes the human from the non-human,[85] and this reaction is deeply rooted in our 'natural history' (ibid.: §25).[86] It is of course true that, for example, after a road accident it may be difficult to distinguish the driver's body from the wreckage. Gross disfigurement – and perhaps especially of the face[87] – clearly can make such identification less than 'immediate.' But such hesitancy is

Pluralism, justice and vulnerability 83

not only relatively exceptional, it is particularly horrific precisely *because* such identification requires deliberation. This natural 'immediacy' in inter-personal relations effectively means that taking a hypothetical attitude toward others only occurs in highly 'abnormal' circumstances. And this is why Wittgenstein demarcates between having 'an attitude towards a soul' and merely being 'of the *opinion* that [someone] has a soul' (ibid.: p. 178).[88] For what it actually means to 'believe that men have souls' lies in the *practical application* of this 'picture' (ibid.: §422).[89] However, in order to appreciate both the ethical significance of these remarks and what constitutes the aforementioned 'common behavior of mankind' it is first necessary to understand something of Wittgenstein's phenomenology of the body.

That Wittgenstein should draw attention to the human face is unsurprising given that the face maintains a privileged position in our dealings with others.[90] Not only is the face capable of expressing another's more general state of being,[91] so too do we tend to place a special value on face-to-face encounters.[92] There is a natural priority[93] here, for this distinctive assemblage of features provides human beings with a vast array of expressive possibilities.[94] But the significance of Wittgenstein's treatment of the face and body lies in his attempt to undermine a more general philosophical prejudice about the nature of intersubjectivity.[95] According to Wittgenstein, the other's face (indeed, their body as a whole) does not supply a series of signs to be decoded, interpreted and then responded to. Rather, as previously suggested, the meaningful presence of the other is *immediate*.[96] When one looks into the face of another[97] one *sees* consciousness, and a 'particular *shade* of consciousness' at that.[98] When encountering the other's face one does not first 'look into' (1990: §220) oneself and then 'make inferences ... to joy, grief, boredom' (ibid.: §225) concerning them,[99] and this is why 'a tender facial expression' cannot adequately 'be described in terms of the distribution of matter in space' (1994a: 82).[100] Rather, we 'describe a face immediately as sad, radiant, bored' (1990: §225);[101] its meaning 'is there as clearly as in your own breast' (ibid.: §220).[102] The face, one might say, is the very manifestation of joy, grief, boredom and suffering, and to that extent there is nothing inherently mysterious in our relations with others.[103] Mimicking the second of Descartes' *Meditations*[104] Wittgenstein nevertheless entertains the following possibility: 'But can't I imagine that the people around me are automata, lack consciousness, even though they behave in the same way as usual?':

> If I imagine it now – alone in my room – I see people with fixed looks (as in a trance) going about their business – the idea is perhaps a little uncanny. But just try to keep hold of this idea in the midst of your ordinary intercourse with others, in the street say! Say to yourself, for example: 'The children over there are mere automata; all their liveliness is mere automatism.' And you will either find these words

> becoming quite meaningless; or you will produce in yourself some kind of uncanny feeling ...
>
> (1958: §420)

Wittgenstein's point in referring to an 'uncanny feeling' is not merely to suggest that skeptical doubt is never as radical in practice as it is in theory.[105] One might imagine what it would be for others to be like mere automata despite their apparent normality. (As philosophers know, temporary detachment from 'ordinary intercourse with others' permits one to engage in all manner of conceptual acrobatics – possibilities to which even Wittgenstein was not wholly adverse.[106]) We clearly *can* be struck by the mechanical appearance of people walking together in a crowd, chanting at a political rally, praying together, or dancing in unison. And doubtless such experiences, though necessarily short-lived, often produce 'uncanny' feelings.[107] But here we have, through an act of imagination, begun to perceive others *as if* they were machines, and it is precisely this qualification that is crucial. Imagining that the children *are* automata is quite different,[108] for now our imagining involves a crucial existential commitment (these children *are actually* machines) that cannot be divorced from our broader practical orientation toward them. Such an attitude would manifest itself, not in a mildly 'uncanny feeling' but rather in deep revulsion, horror, and so on. The accessibility of seeing the children *as if* they were automata lies in the regularity of their movement, which provides a conceptual 'peg' (Tilghman 1991: 100) upon which to hang the likeness. But to take their 'particular interplay of movements, words, expressions' (Wittgenstein 1990: §594) to be *actual* automatism has no such anchor. For their '*harmonious* behavior' (Husserl 1982: 114) is the very paradigm of the *un*mechanical 'voluntary movements of a normal human being' (Wittgenstein 1990: §594).[109] And this is why Wittgenstein phrases his initial question: 'But can't I imagine that the people around me are automata ... even though they behave *in the same way as usual?*' (1958: §420, my emphasis).

Most significant here is the role repetition plays in our encounters with others. Clearly a degree of behavioral-linguistic repetition[110] – and thereby a degree of predictability[111] – is necessary for human behavior to be meaningful, but this sort of repetition is only loosely regimented.[112] Wittgenstein illustrates a related point when he remarks: 'If a man's bodily expression of sorrow and of joy alternated, say with the ticking of a clock, here we should not have the characteristic formation of the pattern of sorrow or of the pattern of joy' (ibid.: §174). And likewise:

> Isn't it as if one were trying to imagine a facial expression not susceptible of alterations which were gradual and difficult to catch hold of, but which had, say, just five positions; when it changed it would snap

straight from one to another. Now would this fixed smile, for example, really be a smile? And why not?

(1990: §527)[113]

By conceiving such a face (or body) one is imagining someone 'dysfunctional,' acting or making a joke[114] – a 'pseudo-organism' (Husserl 1982: 114). Indeed, we might say that 'expression *consists* in incalculability,' for if one always knew 'exactly how [another] would grimace, move, there would be no facial expression, no gesture' (Wittgenstein 1994a: 73). It might, as Wittgenstein suggests, be possible in 'a certain sense' to 'keep being surprised' by a piece of music that we can anticipate note for note.[115] But the same could not, I think, be said of another's actions without something seeming awry.[116] There is clearly nothing uncanny about using the 'repeat' function on a CD player. But '[s]uppose we were to meet people who all had the same facial features: that would be enough for us not to know where we are with them' (ibid.: 75). If *this* would be enough for us to lose our footing then so too would we find ourselves perplexed by someone whose natural bodily-linguistic behaviors were completely predictable. Of course, the degree of calculability is significant here. One is continually learning how to predict when specific individuals will laugh, cry, smile and curse without that inducing an 'uncanny' feeling. Indeed, without this degree of predictability human interaction would be impossible. Predictability thus constitutes the natural substratum[117] for 'knowing someone' or having any meaningful relationship with them.[118] But the analogy Wittgenstein makes with music suggests a degree of calculability well beyond this. Here the other's behavior would be as predictable as playing a well-worn record – or one that sticks on one specific phrase. It would mean that not only would I know *when* they were going to laugh, but for *how long* that laughter would last, what *volume* and *pitch* it would reach, and so on.[119] It is doubtless impossible to identify precisely where to make the distinction between the fluid, 'iterable' sort of repetition human beings naturally display and the more stunted, catatonic variety of automata. Doubtless, too, there are borderline cases where one would be hesitant in making such a judgement. But this does not undermine the main point; that one cannot simply choose at will to view others as though they *actually were* machines dressed in 'hats and coats' (Descartes 1976: 73).[120]

Given Wittgenstein's preoccupation with embodiment, his numerous references to the 'soul'[121] may seem rather surprising. But again, what interests Wittgenstein is how the grammar of this term actually functions.[122] After analysis it thus becomes clear that 'soul' does not operate as a designator for some mysterious inner substance. Extending the applicability of the word 'soul' to non-human animals, Wittgenstein therefore remarks:

> We do not say that possibly a dog talks to itself. Is that because we are so minutely acquainted with its soul? Well, one might say this: If one sees the behavior of a living thing, one sees its soul.
>
> (1958: §357)[123]

The meaning of saying that someone (or some 'thing') 'has a soul' is again manifested, not in one's hypothetical beliefs but rather through one's general orientation toward them.[124] In other words, to 'believe that men have souls' lies in the application of this 'picture' (ibid.: §422), and this is why '[m]y attitude towards him is an attitude towards a soul. I am not of the *opinion* that he has a soul' (ibid.: p. 178).[125] Given this deeply non-hypothetical characterization of 'attitude,' it is clear why such a 'picture' is central to our sense of ethical concern for others who are 'mortal ... [and] vulnerable to misfortune' (Gaita 2000: 239).[126] Contrary to Surin, Lyotard and Readings there is something primordially significant about the human form – so much so that it determines the limits of what or who the concepts 'pain,' 'consciousness' and 'soul' can be meaningfully attributed to.[127] That people campaign for the rights of non-human animals and the unborn fetus is not unintelligible, even to those who passionately disagree.[128] It is not as though such individuals were campaigning for the rights of carpets or iron filings – which clearly would raise questions concerning what such 'rights' could possibly amount to.[129] Indeed, it is in this sense that caution is needed when speaking of the 'intractable "otherness" of the Other' (Surin 1990: 126).[130] For any criterion that proscribes such markedly peculiar claims about the 'rights' of carpets and iron filings would be enough to incur limitations on the very notion of the *radically* 'other.'[131]

Our responsiveness to others should not, however, be construed as deliberative,[132] or resulting from a reasoning 'by analogy' (Wittgenstein 1990: §537).[133] Rather, we must 'remember that it is a primitive reaction to tend, to treat, the part that hurts when someone else is in pain; and not merely when oneself is':

> But what is the word 'primitive' meant to say here? Presumably that this sort of behavior is *pre-linguistic*: that a language-game is based *on it*, that it is the prototype of a way of thinking and not the result of thought.
>
> 'Putting the cart before the horse' may be said of an explanation like the following: we tend someone else because by analogy with our own case we believe that he is experiencing pain too ...
>
> (Wittgenstein 1990: §§540–2)

In other words:

> Being sure that someone is in pain, doubting whether he is, and so on, are so many natural, instinctive, kinds of behavior towards other

Pluralism, justice and vulnerability 87

> human beings, and our language is merely an auxiliary to, and further extension of, this relation. Our language-game is an extension of primitive behavior.
>
> (Wittgenstein 1990: §545)[134]

None of this is to deny that there are times when the meaning and sincerity of another's behavior is in question,[135] but rather to suggest that in principle: '"I can only *believe* that someone else is in pain, but I *know* it if I am"' is only to say that 'one can make the decision to say "I believe he is in pain" instead of "He is in pain". But that is all ... Just try – in a real case – to doubt someone else's fear or pain' (1958: §303).[136] To reiterate a familiar Wittgensteinian theme from Chapter 2, in such circumstances one needs 'reasons for leaving a familiar track,' for '[d]oubt is a moment of hesitation and is, *essentially*, an exception to the rule' (1993: 379).[137] That is:

> The game doesn't begin with doubting whether someone has a toothache, because that doesn't – as it were – fit the game's biological function in our life. In its most primitive form it is a reaction to somebody's cries and gestures, a reaction of sympathy or something of the sort. We comfort him, try to help him.
>
> (Wittgenstein 1993: 381)[138]

The point I want to emphasize here is that if, as Wittgenstein maintains, language is 'auxiliary to,' an 'extension' (1990: §545), 'refinement' (1994a: 31) or 'replacement'[139] of primitive reactions, then moral deliberation concerning *when, how* and *to whom* we should attend (be it the musings of a child as to whether a trapped insect is suffering, or the heights of abstract ethical theorizing[140]) is grounded upon pre-linguistic natural or 'primitive' reactions toward others.[141] This is not to contest the obvious anthropological fact that the manner in which different cultures organize and implement their moral values may vary. Nor is it necessarily to deny that, as Caputo puts it, 'flesh and pain have a history' – that, for example, there might be a 'difference between the experience of pain before and after the discovery of anesthetics, inside and outside medical-technological civilizations, inside and outside of one religion or another' (1993: 208).[142] What it does suggest, however, is that the depth of such cultural diversity is *not* (as Readings suggests) unfathomable, but necessarily circumscribed both by pre-linguistic behaviors and fundamental physiological-biological facts concerning the inherent vulnerability of mortal, embodied beings.[143] In other words, the various trajectories taken in the course of historical-cultural practice and rational ethical-political deliberation are only possible on the grounds of a much more natural concern for others.[144] What Wittgenstein therefore draws to our attention is the necessary backdrop or 'tacit presupposition[s]' (1958: p.179) our lives hinge upon:[145]

> The concept of pain is characterized by its particular function in our life.
>
> Pain has *this* position in our life; has *these* connexions; (That is to say: we only call 'pain' what has *this* position, *these* connexions).
>
> Only surrounded by certain normal manifestations of life, is there such a thing as an expression of pain. Only surrounded by an even more far-reaching particular manifestation of life, such a thing as the expression of sorrow or affection. And so on.
>
> (1990: §§532–4)

This, then, is why the amoralist's demand for cogent 'reasons' why they should care about anything or anyone is so troubling. For, as Williams puts it: 'it is very unclear that we can in fact give the man who asks it a reason – that, starting from so far down, we could *argue* him into caring about something.' What such a person requires is 'help, or hope, not reasonings' (1973: 17).[146] If the amoralist is (in a quasi-Pyrrhonian sense[147]) 'at a loss' as to why the needless suffering of children is a tragedy, then initially one must ask whether some tragedy has befallen *them*; whether *their* life has been damaged in such a way that they cannot feel 'the force of pity' (Nuyen 2000: 421).[148] Reactions of moral indifference often bear witness to temporary moral exhaustion. While there are obvious correlations between the symptoms of exhaustion and amoralism, and while the former provides a fairly secure route to the latter, to find oneself buckling under the weight of others' suffering should not be confused with the persistent indifference displayed by the genuine amoralist. Here *we* need to distinguish, and in turn respond to, what is effectively an *appeal for assistance*. If, as Wittgenstein suggests, belief in predestination is 'less a theory than a sigh, or a cry' (often born from 'the most dreadful suffering' (1994a: 30)), then much the same might be said of extreme moral skepticism.[149] In this sense then even the genuine amoralist does not challenge the *authority* of morality.[150] Amoralism does not provide grounds for a radical critique of our normal moral reactions and sensibilities. Nor does it establish grounds for *our* becoming skeptical. On the contrary, the provocation of amoralism lies in its capacity to call *our own* potential for moral responsiveness into question.[151] That is, what the amoralist challenges is the 'good conscience' we may harbor regarding our own competence at helping the helpless or giving hope to the hopeless. Morality is far from being undermined here, for we are, implicitly, being petitioned to be *more* moral – probably more than we can bear. In this respect the genuine amoralist is the most helpless and hopeless individual one is ever likely to encounter.

Mindful of these points it becomes clear why the idea of a 'moral community' is fundamentally dissimilar to, for example, that of a 'scientific community' or 'artistic community.' As Winch rightly notes: 'there could not be a human society which was not also, in some sense, a moral community.' Moral concern cannot adequately be described as either a 'form of activity' or – as Lyotard suggests – a 'form of life' (or 'language-game') which one may choose to either partake in or ignore.[152] Rather, moral problems 'force themselves on you' insofar as they emerge from the 'common life between men and do not presuppose any particular forms of activity in which men engage together' (Winch 1960: 239–40).[153] What constitutes suffering is not primarily an epistemic or hypothetical matter; it is central to the natural life of human beings. The other's suffering *commands* us to help, his misery 'calls for action: his wounds must be tended' (Tilghman 1991: 113), for it is part of the 'grammar' of others' suffering that one is thereby placed under obligation. As Schopenhauer remarks of 'natural compassion': 'It calls out to me "Stop!"; it stands before the other man like a bulwark, protecting him from the injury that my egoism or malice would otherwise urge me to do' (1995: 149).[154] Though one may or may not respond to this 'call,' to not *hear* it is to not recognize suffering *qua* suffering; it would, for example, be to perceive only indentations in another's flesh, as though these were mere marks on a paving stone.[155] In the company of the genuine amoralist rational argumentation would indeed be to no avail, for the efficacy of such argumentation requires some commonality to already be in place. Without this shared natural 'background' (Wittgenstein 1990: §567) against which to debate – or against which to simply *show* her an instance of suffering and await an appropriate response – there is nothing more to say. This is why '[t]here can be no more dramatic way of falling away from the ethical than seriously to doubt its reality' (Gaita 2000: 179). Giving reasons cannot start 'from so far down' (Williams 1973: 17)[156] because here reasoning 'comes to an end' (Wittgenstein 1999: §192)[157] – indeed, with the genuine amoralist, reasoning does not even get a chance to begin. In such cases one must try to ascertain how deep her indifference runs. But with regard to the persistent amoralist ultimately all we have recourse to is '*persuasion*' (ibid.: §262, 612), whatever that might entail.[158]

As mentioned earlier, Wittgenstein is sometimes characterized as *the* philosopher of linguistic-conceptual plurality; a pluralism that (allegedly) becomes most conspicuous in his vocabulary of 'language-games,' 'forms of life' and 'world-pictures.' But what this reading neglects is that beneath all the 'differences'[159] Wittgenstein shows us lies a more unifying naturalism. Indeed, it is precisely this that enables him to escape the snares of Lyotard's portrayal of *radical* social fragmentation. When exploring Wittgenstein's naturalism, however, 'Remarks on Frazer's *Golden Bough*' demands particular attention.[160] Rather than attempt a survey of the disproportionately large secondary literature this text has provoked, I will instead reconstruct its central themes in order to address the specific ethical-political implications of Wittgenstein's suggestion that 'man is a ceremonial animal' (1996a: 67).

The primitive and the modern: Wittgenstein on Frazer's *Golden Bough*

Despite its fragmentary nature, 'Remarks on Frazer's *Golden Bough*' can be roughly divided into three parts: those remarks pertaining to (1) methodological issues, (2) 'opinion,' 'reason' and 'ritual,' and (3) the relation between the 'primitive' and 'modern' subject. I will return to (2) and (3) later. First, I want to focus on the methodological distinctions Wittgenstein draws between his own project and Frazer's anthropology.

Although Wittgenstein concedes in *Philosophical Investigations* that his 'interest certainly includes the correspondence between concepts and very general facts of nature,' he does not want to 'fall back upon these possible causes of the formation of concepts' because in the end he is 'not doing natural science; nor yet natural history – since we can also invent fictitious natural history for our purposes.'[161] He proceeds:

> [I]f anyone believes that certain concepts are absolutely the correct ones, and that having different ones would mean not realizing something that we realize – then let him imagine certain very general facts of nature to be different from what we are used to, and the formation of concepts different from the usual ones will become intelligible to him.
>
> (1958: p. 230)[162]

In short, the concepts and practices we have are not *a priori* necessary or determined. This implies two things: (1) given the facts of our actual natural history, a considerable degree of conceptual variety is nevertheless possible, and (2) were this natural history different then so too would our present concepts and practices. In effect what we are presented with here is simultaneously a recognition of cultural diversity *and* a commitment to the basic commonality of human life as it is 'given.'[163] It is in large part the philosophical-anthropological necessity of maintaining this dual emphasis that 'Remarks on Frazer's *Golden Bough*' addresses.

For Wittgenstein the central problem with Frazer's anthropology is its implicit scientism, and specifically Frazer's tendency toward interpretation and explanation. According to Wittgenstein the 'very idea of wanting to explain a [religious] practice ... seems wrong' (1996a: 61), for one should 'only describe and say: this is what human life is like' (ibid.: 63). Echoing numerous other passages in his later writings,[164] Wittgenstein here highlights both his ontological commitments regarding the 'givenness' of language practices and how this ought to determine the philosophical enterprise insofar as we cannot explain *why* a certain form of life exists, '[a]ll we can do is to describe it – and *behold* it!' (Malcolm 1993: 76).[165] Having 'put the question mark deep enough down' (having gone 'right down to the foundations' (Wittgenstein 1994a: 62)) explanatory and justificatory discourse 'comes to an end' (1999: §204). At this point 'all one can say is: where that practice and these views occur together, the practice does not spring from the view, but they are both just there' (1996a: 62). That 'the practice does not spring from the view' is an important and recurrent theme in 'Remarks on Frazer's *Golden Bough*,' not least because Frazer misrepresents 'the magical and religious views of mankind' as pseudo-scientific '*errors*' or 'pieces of stupidity.'[166] But, Wittgenstein insists, religious and magical rituals can only be 'erroneous' to the extent that they 'set forth a theory' (ibid.: 61) and thereby constitute hypothetical speculation.[167] For Wittgenstein, however, '[n]o opinion serves as the foundation for a religious symbol' (ibid.: 64), and 'the characteristic feature of primitive man is that he does not act from opinions (contrary to Frazer)' (ibid.: 71).[168]

A question of primacy naturally arises here of whether reason grounds action or vice versa? But the problem with framing things in these terms is that one thereby makes an implicit distinction between language and behavior. This is why Wittgenstein is reluctant[169] to talk of 'primacy,' and instead stresses the simultaneity of these phenomena.[170] Nevertheless, there is a genuine ambiguity here. For elsewhere, as has already become clear, Wittgenstein emphasizes the *derivative* nature of language-behavior from 'primitive reactions.'[171] Thus, language *and* reasoning are said to have their roots in natural, pre-linguistic behavior. The primary function of language is not to report or describe such primitive reactions – though this is something one eventually acquires the skill to do. Rather, language is both taught and learnt in an *auxiliary* role; as an *extension* of such natural behaviors.[172] One might therefore talk of the 'primacy' of action (primitive behaviors) over reason (deliberation), so long as that is not taken to mean that 'the natural' determines the *specificities* of 'the cultural' – and, by implication, that the latter could simply be reduced to or deduced from the former. What the former does provide, however, are the boundary conditions only within which the latter can develop in its various forms.

As we have begun to see, what troubles Wittgenstein about Frazer's anthropology is its speculative character and the way it misrepresents the 'primitive' religious rituals under analysis. For by characterizing such practices in pseudo-scientific garb Frazer trivializes them as mere 'pieces of stupidity' (ibid.: 61). The Wittgensteinian corrective can immediately be seen in the following passage:

> [O]ne could begin a book on anthropology by saying: When one examines the life and behavior of mankind throughout the world, one sees that, except for what might be called animal activities, such as ingestion, etc., etc., etc., men also perform actions which bear a characteristic peculiar to themselves, and these could be called ritualistic actions.
>
> (1996a: 67)

92 *Pluralism, justice and vulnerability*

Wittgenstein thus effectively closes the divide (a potentially Lyotardian '*differend*') between the 'primitive' and 'modern' subject – a lacuna Frazer not only assumes to be in place but takes to be primarily epistemic. For

> the principle according to which these practices are arranged ... is a much more general one than in Frazer's explanation and it is present in our own minds, so that we ourselves could think up all the possibilities ... Indeed, if Frazer's explanations did not in the final analysis appeal to a tendency in ourselves, they would not really be explanations.
>
> (1996a: 65–6)

The possibility for Frazer to even formulate his explanatory hypotheses is itself grounded upon those cultural practices he describes *not* being wholly alien to his (or our) own. We can make *some* sense of these rituals (and indeed, of Frazer's own analyses) precisely because the differences between the 'primitive' and 'modern' are *not* 'radical' in the Lyotardian sense.[173] This is not to say that what essentially unites these epochs is a shared epistemology; it is not that we can make sense of such rituals because they represent childish versions of our modern scientific world-picture. (Though were they 'to write it down, their knowledge of nature would not differ *fundamentally* from ours' (ibid.: 74).) Rather, the important connection lies in the 'more general' fact that we share *a common humanity* comprising of shared instinctive, natural behaviors. Indeed, only once 'a phenomenon is brought into connection with an instinct which I myself possess' (ibid.: 72) is the difficulty of understanding those cultural practices resolved:

> Frazer: ' ... That these observances are dictated by fear of the ghost of the slain seems certain ... ' But why then does Frazer use the word 'ghost'? He thus understands this superstition very well, since he explains it to us with a superstitious word he is familiar with. Or rather, this might have enabled him to see that there is also something in us which speaks in favor of those savages' behavior. – If I, a person who does not believe that there are human-superhuman beings somewhere which one can call gods – if I say: 'I fear the wrath of the gods,' that shows that I can mean something by this, or can give expression to a feeling which is not necessarily connected with that belief.
>
> (1996a: 68)[174]

What Frazer thus fails to appreciate is the nature of the 'kinship' between 'those savages' behavior' (ibid.: 70) and 'any genuine religious action of today' (ibid.: 64). In other words: 'All these different practices show that it is not a question of the derivation of one from the other, but of a common spirit' (ibid.: 80) or a 'general inclination' (ibid.: 78)[175] – that is, *natural* propensities that relate to Wittgenstein's various remarks on 'primitive behaviors' and 'instinct reactions' previously discussed. One might therefore say that the initiation and longevity of religious rituals are dependent upon their ability to bear witness to the most basic tendencies and concerns of human beings,[176] and thus are not, as Frazer construes them, rooted in confused quasi-scientific conjectures. Frazer's mistake is to take instrumental, means–ends oriented actions to be the archetype of all meaningful human activities. Assessing ritual activities in this way clearly does render them epistemically impoverished, but it is Frazer's own model of comparison that generates this apparent deficiency.[177] After all, as Wittgenstein notes:

> When I am furious about something, I sometimes beat the ground or a tree with my walking stick. But I certainly do not believe that the ground is to blame or that my beating can help anything. 'I am venting my anger'. And all rites are of this kind. Such actions may be called Instinct-actions. – And an historical explanation, say, that I or my ancestors previously believed that beating the ground does help is shadow-boxing, for it is a superfluous assumption that explains nothing. The similarity of the action to an act of punishment is important, but nothing more than this similarity can be asserted.
> (1996a: 72)

> Burning an effigy. Kissing the picture of one's beloved. That is obviously not based on the belief that it will have some specific effect on the object which the picture represents. It aims at satisfaction and achieves it. Or rather: it aims at nothing at all; we just behave this way and then we feel satisfied. One could also kiss the name of one's beloved, and here it would be clear that the name was being used as a substitute.
> (1996a: 64)[178]

The point to be emphasized here is that we all, *qua* human beings, engage in ritualistic activities. And it is in this sense that 'man' might be said to *be* 'a ceremonial animal' (ibid.: 67). These activities should not be sneered at as remnants of an unenlightened, superstitious age,[179] or as a 'false physics.' To judge them, as Frazer does, according to scientific criteria is not only erroneous[180] and 'foolish' (ibid.), it is also fundamentally unjust.[181] Keeping these central themes of 'Remarks on Frazer's *Golden Bough*' in mind I finally want to cast a critical eye back over Lyotard's radical pluralism.[182]

Reconsidering Lyotard's pagan justice

In 'Pagans, Perverts or Primitives?' Readings concludes that it is the 'assumption of our common humanity' that 'lights the way to terror' (1992: 186). Indeed, according to him, 'it is unjust to the cultural diversity of the Aborigines to presume that they are human' (ibid.: 185). But Readings's skepticism is misplaced, for his own argument (like Frazer's) must in some important respects presuppose the *falsity* of this extreme position. First, we can reasonably assume that even Readings would only affix the term 'culture' (and thus also 'cultural diversity') to *human beings*[183] – or at least to that which 'resembles' (Wittgenstein 1958: §281)[184] the human. His argument is thus paradoxical, for if the other – here the Aborigines – were truly 'other' (that is, the very epitome of unintelligibility, incommensurability, untranslatability and conceptual difference) then how could Readings himself: (1) identify them *as such*, and (2) bear witness to their predicament – or for that matter bear witness to the need for politics *itself* to 'bear witness' to their predicament? If the other is indeed *radically* 'other' then how could one *ever* know that there had been an encounter, for *as such* the other 'would not even show up' (Derrida 1992a: 68)?[185] Second, Readings (like Surin[186]) is right to be circumspect concerning the predication of 'human nature' insofar as any such predication can facilitate political exclusion, marginalization and violence.[187] But all this really warns us against is a certain *type* of predication. If one characterizes 'human nature' too narrowly then of course the possibility of 'racism, sexism and homophobia' (Readings 1992: 174) becomes dangerously grounded.[188] But then Readings's own respect for radical 'cultural diversity' could *itself* simply reinforce the undesirable ethical-political traits of fear, misunderstanding, distrust or patronizing exoticism. There is a corresponding danger here that in over-emphasizing the 'otherness of the other' one might unwittingly encourage the tendency toward alienation that is so integral to precisely those injustices Readings identifies.[189] And third, while Readings may also be right that positing a 'common humanity' necessarily entails the possibility of excluding individuals from that category, even this is not *inherently* unjust. As previously discussed regarding the amoralist, in extreme cases where reasons and justification have been *thoroughly* 'exhausted' (Wittgenstein 1958: §217)[190] it is not merely excusable but the only appropriate response to claim that someone has 'lost their humanity' – albeit temporarily.[191] The neo-fascist who tours Auschwitz to laugh at the photographs of mass graves, or to entertain a friend by climbing into the incineration ovens[192] (in short, the man who persistently indulges in an utterly 'malicious joy at the misfortune of others' (Schopenhauer 1995: 135)), can indeed be said to have 'lost his humanity' in this sense. His failing is not epistemic; he has neither merely nor primarily made an error of judgement.[193] Rather, his moral reactions and priorities have become so skewed that he no longer understands what it means to make such a judgement in the first place. (This is also why the counter-exclamation: 'How could anyone do such a thing?' is not appealing for explanatory answers.[194] This exclamation is, again, more 'a sigh, or a cry' (Wittgenstein 1994a: 30); an appeal for hope, comfort, or a concession of shared bewilderment from another.[195]) That this individual might be said to 'not live in our world' (Cavell 1979: 90) or to be 'inhuman' (though *not*, I will argue in later chapters, 'an animal') is no mere rhetorical extravagance. It is absolutely fitting.[196]

What is striking about Readings's account of the predicament of the Aborigines is that it necessarily presupposes that *these* beings possess the capacity to suffer an injustice in the first place. In his essay Readings expresses no doubt concerning this potentiality. Indeed, if there were any doubt about *that* then his entire argument would be superfluous, and we could only consider it a matter of contingency that his meditations focus on the plight of the Aborigines and not on the numerous 'injustices' suffered by carpets or iron filings. This highlights another important point concerning the Lyotardian project more generally. The notion of a *differend* relies, we will recall, on the possibility of *radical* conflict.[197] But, one might ask, how would such a conflict manifest itself? In order for there to be a conflict *as such* there must be some commonality between conflicting parties – there must at least be 'conflicting parties.' Thus, a conflict between judgement-criteria can only meaningfully be said to occur between those who employ judgement-criteria, and this is partly why one cannot be said to be 'in conflict' with stones, carpets, trees, and so on. Likewise, conflict between (allegedly) incommensurable language-games or world-pictures presupposes that *both* parties 'play' language-games or 'partake in' world-pictures.[198] In short, what is again necessarily presupposed here is that both the Aborigines and their opponents share the (human) form of life only within which language-games and world-pictures have a function. As I said earlier of the notion of 'radical otherness,' a genuinely *radical* conflict would not even disclose itself *as* a 'conflict.' (Paradoxically, a *radical* conflict might be exactly like love, peace or friendship.) Readings's polemic thus possesses considerable rhetorical force precisely because the Aborigines *are human beings* and as such are capable of suffering injustice or being 'damaged'[199] in analogous ways to ourselves.[200] While it may not be possible to derive a substantive ethical code from Wittgenstein's minimal naturalism, it does demonstrate that the proclamation (explicit or otherwise) of a 'we' is not merely 'hasty but excusable' (1999, §150); it is absolutely necessary for ethical-political theorizing to even get off the ground.[201]

4 Interlude
On preferring peace to war

> That a people, as a people, 'should accept those who come and settle among them – even though they are foreigners,' would be the proof [*gage*] of a popular and public commitment [*engagement*], a political res publica that cannot be reduced to a sort of 'tolerance,' unless this tolerance requires the affirmation of a 'love' without measure.
>
> J. Derrida, 'A Word of Welcome'

> 'There is neither God nor the Good, but there is goodness' – which is also my thesis. That is all that is left to mankind ... There are acts of stupid, senseless goodness.
>
> E. Levinas, *Is It Righteous To Be?*

> Conversation requires renunciation, the renunciation of the power to persuade someone by illegitimate means.
>
> R. Gaita, *A Common Humanity*

In the preceding chapters I have argued that Wittgenstein's naturalism is not only an essential – albeit frequently understated – component of his later work but that it is also of considerable ethical-political significance. Before moving on, it will be helpful to summarize the main themes of the discussion so far.

In Chapter 1 I showed how both Sextus and Wittgenstein share a certain therapeutic teleology, where the possibility for emancipation from abstract theoretical anxieties constitutes the objective of good philosophical practice. I also noted how this liberation was rendered possible only through embracing the 'natural.' For the Pyrrhonist this involved two main elements: (1) eradicating belief and thereby submitting oneself to the life of immediate phenomenological experience, and (2) simultaneously assimilating oneself into surrounding social-cultural practices. Only in this way, the Pyrrhonist argues, can one achieve and maintain *ataraxia*. For Wittgenstein, attaining the non-philosophical life is intimately connected with the 'grammatical' nature of philosophical problems. Language *itself* leads us astray here – an estrangement that is exacerbated by philosophers. The new descriptive procedures Wittgenstein advocates thus aim at recontextualizing language within 'ordinary,' non-philosophical life. By providing these grammatical reminders of how language actually functions, philosophical perplexities are thereby dissolved. In short, Wittgenstein attempts to free us from certain misleading assumptions about language by situating it within practical human activities. Most significant in this regard is his insistence that language functions in an auxiliary role to natural, instinctive behaviors. Now, Wittgenstein's deeply anti-philosophical project of linguistic-conceptual recontextualization has led some commentators to draw quasi-Pyrrhonian conclusions about the ethical-political implications of his later work. Here Wittgenstein is characterized as a fundamentally 'conservative' thinker whose overriding preoccupation lies with training, rule-following and conforming to the mores of one's community. In Chapter 2 I explored these allegations by considering the central motifs of *On Certainty* – Wittgenstein's last, and purportedly most 'conservative' writings. Given his numerous reflections on the limits of justification, the legitimacy of holding fast to one's inherited worldpicture, and the role of persuasion in rational argument, this text does indeed appear to advocate a certain epistemic-cultural dogmatism (something that also emerges in the anti-apologeticism of 'Lectures on Religious Belief'). Nevertheless, I argued that a more tormented subtext haunts *On Certainty*. This problematizes the aforementioned 'conservative' reading insofar as Wittgenstein is frequently torn between: (1) an epistemological relativism (what some have interpreted as his later 'pluralism'), and (2) a deeper, unifying naturalism. In response to this ambiguity, I suggested in Chapter 3 that one must situate *On Certainty* alongside other of Wittgenstein's writings, not least because this reveals how his naturalism tempers the potentially radical epistemological relativism of the later descriptive-therapeutic philosophy. Thus, what emerges in 'Remarks on Frazer's *Golden Bough*' (a text to which I will return in Chapter 5), is a much deeper commitment to the underlying commonality of humankind. While Wittgenstein far from trivializes cultural-conceptual 'difference,' he nevertheless insists that in the aforementioned 'primitive' human behaviors (and, I would add, particularly those associated with suffering) emerges something capable of bridging the seemingly radical divide that separates: (1) presently existent human communities, (2) modern (or for that matter 'postmodern') forms of cultural life and those of antiquity, and (3) the human and non-human animal.

Recalling the comparative analysis of Wittgenstein and Sextus in Chapter 1, these main points can be summarized as follows: While both philosophers practice therapeutic techniques aimed at alleviating conceptual anxieties, and identify such liberation with immersion into a more 'natural' way of life, they differ fundamentally as to the *ethical* implications of this naturalism. While the Pyrrhonist sees this return to the natural as *also* a liberation from ethical concerns (advocating a troubling social-cultural parasitism), for Wittgenstein the realm of the natural contains the very instinctive-behavioral building blocks upon which ethical life is founded. That is, while the Pyrrhonist hopes to extricate moral burdens by abandoning belief, she fails to recognize that the realm of the natural is *already* 'contaminated' by the ethical. Thus, Wittgenstein's *philosophical* 'ideal' may be 'a certain coolness' (1994a: 2) or '[t]houghts that are at peace' (ibid.: 43), but this is not – as it is for the Pyrrhonist – an *ethical* ideal. These, then, are the central themes of the previous three chapters. But in order to set the stage for the proceeding discussion, I would briefly like to comment on two passages; the first from Wittgenstein's *Zettel*, the second from Levinas's 'Meaning and Sense.'

In accordance with much of what Wittgenstein says in *On Certainty* about 'stay[ing] in the saddle' (1999: §616) of belief and our learning 'not *one* proposition but a nest of propositions' (ibid.: §225), in *Zettel* he remarks:

> If someone does not believe in fairies, he does not need to teach his children 'There are no fairies': he can omit to teach them the word 'fairy'. On what occasion are they to say: 'There are . . . ' or 'There are no . . . '? Only when they meet people of the contrary belief.
> (1990: §413)

The logical point here is straightforward enough. When educating a child one need not account for all those things which the imparted world-picture *excludes* – just as one does not teach her all the ungrammatical ways of structuring sentences in her natural language.[1] Invariably the child of the atheist (for example) will at some point ask her parents about God, heaven, immortality (and so on), but such an inquiry does not arise because her parents have overlooked something in her education. Rather, she will here come to experience a lacuna in her own conceptual vocabulary when faced with others whose world-pictures include such concepts.[2] What the passage above thus brings to our attention is the disruptive potential of encountering others who have 'contrary' beliefs. This is worth noting because, as was seen in Chapter 2, the general thrust of *On Certainty* appears to emphasize the unnecessary hospitality of engaging with an 'alternative' world-picture in this way. Although 'staying in the saddle' of one's world-picture is epistemically justifiable, such a position becomes problematic (if not potentially tyrannical) on explicitly ethical grounds. More specifically, the passage above suggests that such self-assurance becomes destabilized when one is faced by another who contests it, and who (as will be seen in Chapter 5) has the capacity to 'contest' even in her simply *being-there*.[3] I will come back to this in a moment. First, I want to turn to Levinas.

Regarding the possibility of learning another's language, in 'Meaning and Sense' Levinas writes:

[W]hat has not been taken into consideration in this case is that an *orientation* is needed to have the Frenchman take up learning Chinese instead of declaring it to be barbarian (that is, bereft of the real virtues of language) and to prefer speech to war. One reasons as though the equivalence of cultures, the discovery of their profusion and the recognition of their riches were not themselves the effects of an orientation and of an unequivocal sense in which humanity stands ... One reasons as though peaceful coexistence did not presuppose that in [human] being there is delineated an orientation which gives it a unique sense.

(1996a: 46)

Keeping §413 of *Zettel* in mind, what Levinas says here concerning the acquisition of natural languages might equally be applied to Wittgenstein's 'world-pictures.' That is, the question Levinas provokes is: How are we to understand one's peaceful 'orientation' toward another's world-picture? How are we to make sense of the fact that, very often, encountering a world-picture that differs from one's own does *not* lead to our 'declaring it to be barbarian,' but rather to our 'preferring speech to war'?[4] As Levinas points out elsewhere:

[T]he great problem placed in the path of those who expect the end of violence starting from a dialogue that would only need to perfect knowledge is the difficulty ... of bringing to this dialogue opposed beings inclined to do violence to each other. It would be necessary to find a dialogue to make these beings enter into dialogue.

(1998a: 142)[5]

The point I want to make here is that, again, on purely epistemic grounds (assuming there could be such a thing) one would simply disregard, reject, or denounce another's world-picture. In short, there are no compelling *reasons* why one should 'prefer speech to war' – or for that matter the Pyrrhonist's shrug of indifference.[6] That typically one does *not* castigate the other in this way (Wittgenstein's own engagement with the religious is one notable example) indicates that intersubjectivity is not wholly saturated with – and thus confined by – epistemological categories, but that somehow ethical sensibilities play an ineliminable and epistemically disruptive role. That generosity, hospitality and the gift, even to the point of self-sacrifice,[7] are possible – that sometimes you *do* 'give up the mastery of your space, your home, your nation' (Derrida 1999a: 70) – should neither be forgotten nor trivialized.[8] While ethics is generally recognized to involve epistemic concerns (a point I do not want to dispute), it is not so well acknowledged that ethics also necessarily permeates the epistemological; that there is a 'mutual contamination'[9] here.

I said above that 'somehow' ethics plays an irreducible role in our relations with others. I remained tentative here because the nature of this ethical relation has yet to be adequately delineated. More specifically, it has yet to become clear how 'concern for the other man' might transcend 'the complacency in ideas agreeing with the particularism of a group and its interests' (Levinas 1998a: 9). Although Wittgenstein's naturalism provides important clues as to where to begin looking for this 'orientation' toward others, my contention is that it is through Levinas's work – and Derrida's cautious development of it – that we gain a deeper sense of how this preference for 'peace over war' might emerge. In the remaining chapters it is this claim that I will substantiate.

5 Wretchedness without recompense
Wittgenstein on religion, ethics and guilt

[T]here is no small probability that with the irresistible decline of faith in the Christian God there is now also a considerable decline in mankind's feeling of guilt; indeed, the prospect cannot be dismissed that the complete and definitive victory of atheism might free mankind of this whole feeling of guilty indebtedness toward its origin, its *causa prima*. Atheism and a kind of *second innocence* belong together.
F. Nietzsche, *On the Genealogy of Morality*

[T]he experience of the impossible ... [is] the sole true provocation to be reflected upon. Thinking takes place not on what we can do, but beginning with what we cannot do.
J. Derrida, *Negotiations*

I do not think the craving for placidity is religious; I think a religious person regards placidity or peace as a gift from Heaven, not as something one ought to hunt after.
L. Wittgenstein, quoted in R. Rhees, *Ludwig Wittgenstein*

Introduction

In Chapter 3 I explored both the natural limits that frame intersubjectivity and how even the 'radical' pluralism of Surin, Lyotard and Readings necessarily presupposes such boundaries. While Wittgenstein's later work seems to emphasize the 'irreducible plurality of language-games' (Greisch 1999: 50), this appearance is deceptive. For while the diversity of cultural practices should not be underestimated, the basis for any recognition and understanding of such practices (even *as* 'cultural practices') lies in those 'fundamental notions' that 'determine the "ethical space," within which the possibilities of good and evil in human life can be exercised' (Winch 1964: 322). When faced with contemporary theorizing of 'otherness' and 'radical difference' we should therefore remember that in any justifiable designation 'other culture' one has *already* identified 'the other' in some minimally intelligible way.[1] For radical pluralists like Surin, Lyotard and Readings such identification constitutes a violation of the other's alterity insofar as it (allegedly) renders her *essentially* a reflection of oneself. On this account the other's 'absolute singularity' is degraded in the positing of a more-or-less homogeneous 'we.' But, as Derrida notes, we should be careful when condemning this as 'violence,' for it is 'at the same time nonviolence, since it opens the relation to the other' (1997c: 128–9).[2] That is, this 'preethical violence' (ibid.: 128)[3] marks the very beginning of ethics, politics and justice.[4] The purpose of the following two chapters is to determine: (1) how the ethical and political are constituted through such an ineliminable 'violence,' and (2) what this 'violence' amounts to. In the present chapter I will begin by considering the function of guilt in Wittgenstein's treatment of a number of religious and ethical themes. The extent to which his naturalism figures in these engagements is crucial, and specifically how the practical setting to which Wittgenstein returns religious beliefs is delineated as an 'ethical space.' Nevertheless, due to the piecemeal way Wittgenstein deals with these issues, in Chapter 6 they will be developed with explicit reference to Heidegger and Levinas. This is not to suggest that Wittgenstein's thinking represents a mere preamble. On the contrary, what will emerge toward the end of Chapter 6 is how both Heidegger's and Levinas's radical conceptions of guilt (and despite their suspicions regarding 'ordinary' experience and language) are actually substantiated by what might be called the 'grammar' of moral guilt. This then is the broader context into which the following twofold analysis of guilt is situated. But to frame my analysis properly it is first necessary to attend to Wittgenstein's sympathetic – albeit frequently troubled – engagement with a number of ethical-religious concepts.

The consequences of belief: understanding Wittgenstein's hesitancy

In 'Lectures on Religious Belief' Wittgenstein is candid about his bewilderment regarding belief in immortality. This bewilderment should not, however, be confused with the dissent of the atheist. For in response to the petition: 'What do you believe, Wittgenstein? Are you a skeptic? Do you know whether you will survive death?' all he could say with any confidence is 'I don't know' (1994b: 70) or similarly 'I can't say' (ibid.: 55). But neither should we conclude that this constitutes mere equivocation. On the contrary, the specter of silence (be it the reverent silence concluding the *Tractatus*, or the hesitancy punctuating 'Lectures on Religious Belief') is of philosophical significance throughout Wittgenstein's writings. Nevertheless, in their later manifestation the function of these silences becomes more obscure, and for this reason demands textual clarification. Wittgenstein's reluctance to either embrace or renounce belief in immortality is due to his experiencing a particular *kind* of incomprehension and hesitancy resulting from his initial inability to apply the 'picture' (ibid.: 54) presented by the statement 'I don't cease to exist' after the demise of my body.[5] Here Wittgenstein does not yet have any 'clear idea' what is being said or what 'consequences' (ibid.: 70) are to be drawn. It is, in part, for this reason that his deeply respectful (often desirous[6]) attitude toward the believer is both distinctive and more deeply rooted than a mere 'inability to decide' – or, for that matter, the Pyrrhonist's radical hesitancy discussed in Chapter 1.[7] Indeed, although it is tempting to describe Wittgenstein as 'agnostic' this would be misconceived,[8] not least because he would judge the rationally prolonged hesitancy of the agnostic to be inherently irreligious rather than theologically neutral. (I will return to this later). Wanting to avoid the traditionally polarized stances of belief and nonbelief (including agnosticism), Wittgenstein thus casts his own bewilderment otherwise. Any straightforward dissent is problematic here since *denying* the validity of this picture would presuppose comprehension of what one was in fact denying, and thus of what the picture involved.[9] But, he proceeds:

> If you ask me whether or not I believe ... in the sense in which religious people have belief in it, I wouldn't say: 'No. I don't believe there will be such a thing.' It would seem to me utterly crazy to say this. And then I give an explanation: 'I don't believe in ... ', but then the religious person never believes what I describe.
>
> (1994b: 55)

In other words, when explaining to the believer what it is *I deny*, this is rarely felt to have adequately represented what it is *she believes*. Obviously there may be occasions when the believer judges such a paraphrase to be sufficiently representative, but such assurances become less likely the higher the existential stakes rise – that is, the more one proceeds from discussing specific theoretical or doctrinal matters to the deeper normative role those play in the believer's life. The point is nicely illustrated in Tolstoy's *A Confession*. This text is pertinent, not only because Wittgenstein's attitude to religion owes much to Tolstoy's vision, but also because the following passages highlight a common 'fideistic' misinterpretation of Wittgenstein's work on religious belief. Despite his 'recognition of the existence of God,' Tolstoy thus describes his anguish at not being in 'relationship' with Him as follows: 'I fell into despair and felt that there was nothing else I could do except kill myself. And worst of all was that I did not even feel I could do that' (1987: 64). Tolstoy proceeds, however, to speak of 'joyous waves of life' breaking through this desolation, where everything around him 'came to life and took on meaning.' But such rapture was short-lived, for Tolstoy kept returning to abstract theological matters. It was not a 'concept of God' that he sought, but rather, that 'without which there cannot be life.' Momentarily tempted (again) by thoughts of suicide, Tolstoy recalls that he had 'only lived during those times when [he] believed in God,' for '[t]hen, as now, I said to myself: I have only to believe in God in order to live. I have only to disbelieve in Him, or to forget Him, in order to die.' This momentous self-revelation, experienced 'more powerfully than ever before' (ibid: 65), cast everything in a new light which was henceforth never extinguished. Without suggesting that what Tolstoy describes here is typical of all believers, these passages illustrate not only the depth at which religious faith can be experienced but, moreover, the immense existential stakes that can rest on such commitments.[10] That Tolstoy's *entire life* could only find meaning through a relationship with God[11] could surely only be articulated by someone who has shared a similar experience. (I will return to this potentially problematic claim in a moment.) As a non-believer one might be able to paraphrase another's belief concerning matters of Christology. It is, however, significantly less assured that one could adequately represent the existential significance of Christ's sacrifice for their daily life. This is why a thorough grounding in theology or metaphysics guarantees nothing with regard to acquiring (or maintaining) genuine religious faith. Analogously, any attempt to elucidate the reasons for one's non-belief would, to both believer and non-believer, seem necessarily obtuse,[12] for the presentation of such 'reasons' would be akin to paraphrasing an unacceptable hypothesis.[13] In specifying what it is *I* do not believe, the believer may well agree that neither does *she* believe *that*. That she would feel fundamentally misrepresented by such a hypothetical gloss is often enough to indicate that one has inadvertently distorted her beliefs. Indeed, one might suggest that such a representation – if it remains wholly insensitive to the believer's protestations – constitutes what Wittgenstein refers to as a philosophical 'dogmatism' (1994a: 26), 'prejudice' (1958: §340) or 'injustice.'[14] And this is in part why he 'would be reluctant to say':

> 'These people rigorously hold the opinion (or view) that there is a Last Judgement'. 'Opinion' sounds queer.
> It is for this reason that different words are used: 'dogma', 'faith'.
> We don't talk about hypothesis, or about high probability. Nor about knowing.
> In a religious discourse we use such expressions as: 'I believe that so and so will happen,' and use them differently to the way in which we use them in science.
>
> (1994b: 57)[15]

Wittgenstein thus warns that between the respective claims of believer and non-believer lies a vast conceptual-linguistic chasm. There is in fact no 'contradiction' (ibid.: 53) here because such people 'think entirely differently'; they have 'different pictures' (ibid.: 55) or an 'entirely different kind of reasoning' (ibid.: 58).[16] He proceeds:

If some[one] said: 'Wittgenstein, do you believe in this?' I'd say: 'No.'
'Do you contradict the man?' I'd say: 'No.'
If you say this, the contradiction already lies in this.
Would you say: 'I believe the opposite', or 'There is no reason to suppose such a thing'? I'd say *neither*.
Suppose someone were a believer and said: 'I believe in a Last Judgement,' and I said: 'Well, I'm not sure. Possibly.' You would say that there is an enormous gulf between us. If he said 'There is a German aeroplane overhead,' and I said 'Possibly. I'm not so sure,' you'd say we were fairly near.
It isn't a question of my being anywhere near him, but on an entirely different plane which you could express by saying: 'You mean something altogether different, Wittgenstein.'

(1994b: 53)[17]

With this in mind the aforementioned suggestion that 'the religious person never believes what I describe' (ibid.: 55) can be elucidated further. Such a discrepancy occurs due to a certain negligence of the practical setting within which religious beliefs have their life. That my representation seems artificial to the believer (that she is compelled to reject my gloss as insufficient, mistaken, or perhaps blasphemous) should lead to a different style of philosophical analysis.[18] Rather than assuming religious claims to be quasi-empirical hypotheses, philosophers must 'only describe' (1958: §124) such language use.[19] This descriptive analysis must do more than merely catalog religious utterances. Indeed, that a concern with 'words alone' (1990: §144) would lead to the sort of representational problems already mentioned, is why Wittgenstein urges us to attend to language rooted in its various practical settings.[20] (This is also what turns on his distinction between 'surface' and 'depth grammar' (1958: §664).) What requires descriptive analysis is not only what is said but also the way what is said integrates with one's practical orientation toward life. But neither is Wittgenstein concerned with drawing up an inventory of 'words' on the one hand, and corresponding 'actions' on the other, for this would still presuppose exactly what his later work repudiates – namely, that linguistic and non-linguistic behavior are discrete phenomena (hence Wittgenstein's vocabulary of 'language-games'). What calls for description is rather the complex web of relationships only *within which* linguistic and non-linguistic behavior has meaning. In this way, then, 'Lectures on Religious Belief' maps onto a much broader philosophical strategy.[21] In the previous chapter I discussed Wittgenstein's naturalism with specific reference to 'Remarks on Frazer's *Golden Bough*.' What remains to be examined is the relationship between this naturalism and his reflections on religious belief. This is important, not only because it holds the key to a proper understanding of Wittgenstein's views on religion and their place in his broader therapeutic philosophy but also because without appreciating the role of his naturalism we will likely misconstrue the ethical implications of his work.

As previously noted, Wittgenstein suggests that there is no 'contradiction' between the believer and non-believer because their respective discourses operate on 'entirely different plane[s]' (1994b: 53). Such passages seem to reveal precisely the sort of relativistic fideism that I have hitherto been arguing against. For here it is tempting to read Wittgenstein as describing a Lyotardian 'differend' between believer and non-believer that renders their positions *radically* incommensurable. Likewise, when I suggested that Tolstoy's confession could only be understood by someone who had experienced 'something similar,' this might be taken to mean that only religious 'insiders' could begin to comprehend his anxieties. Doubtless some interpretative work is needed here, but, mindful of the broader philosophical-naturalistic perspective Wittgenstein presents, this potential fideism can be circumvented – though not, as Drury implies,[22] by appealing to Wittgenstein's 'pluralism.' The point I want to stress here is analogous to that highlighted in Chapter 3 concerning the 'primitive' and 'modern'; namely, that (in the present example) although the conceptual-linguistic-practical space between theist and atheist may often be vast, it is not unfathomable. For despite such differences, both believer and non-believer remain united by certain primitive, natural human activities.[23] As such, the 'entirely different planes' Wittgenstein refers to cannot be 'radical.'[24] Thus, returning to the believer and non-believer, some '*connecting links*' (1996a: 69) might be located between: (1) certain religious and non-religious acts of 'piety' (ibid.: 66),[25] (2) a confession of sins and a confession of love or guilt,[26] (3) the adoration of a religious image and the devotion exhibited toward a picture or name of a loved one,[27] (4) talk of ghostly 'visitations' by the dead (and crediting such spirits with the 'power of stealing the souls of the living' (Frazer 1993: 185)) and one's being 'haunted' by conscience or the memory of another,[28] (5) the absolute trusting demanded by religious faith and that which governs the maternal relation,[29] (6) prayer and expressions of basic human vulnerabilities and needs (thus paralleling the child's appeals for help, comfort and love[30]), (7) notions of fate and predestination, and natural feelings of helplessness in the face of the world's vacillations,[31] and (8) following Wittgenstein's own suggestion that '[c]alling something "the cause" is like pointing and saying: "*He's* to blame!"' (1993: 373), certain eschatological beliefs might similarly correspond to a natural desire or hope for justice.[32] In more general terms, then, the 'connecting links' Wittgenstein refers to are often – though, as the previous inventory suggests, not exclusively – found in those basic human activities associated with mortality, the parental relation, and suffering.[33] As Clack notes, what is most interesting in Wittgenstein's reflections on religion is his suggestion that 'the origins and nature of religion must be attributed to human nature, that its roots lie in humanity's natural responsiveness to the world' (Clack 1999: 120).[34] But, we might ask, if such analogies can be justified then what are we to make of his *general* approach to religious belief? To what extent does Wittgenstein's naturalism undermine the *religiosity* of religious beliefs by linking them to natural human behaviors? Wittgenstein is not being intentionally reductive,[35] but surely it would be strange for someone to come to accept this account and yet remain as firmly in the 'saddle' of his or her religious world-picture as before. Likewise, it is most unlikely that anyone could be 'converted to Christianity having understood it in Wittgenstein's terms' (ibid.: 125). Framing the question in this way inevitably leads toward atheistic conclusions concerning Wittgenstein's work.[36] On this view Wittgenstein's remark that it is 'always a tragic thing when a language dies. But it doesn't follow that one can do anything to stop it doing so. It is a tragic thing when the love between a man and wife is dying; but there is nothing one can do. So it is with a dying language' (Drury 1981: 152)[37] could be similarly applied to his views on religious belief. That is, Wittgenstein's position is 'atheistic' to the extent that he recognizes (and even laments) the death of a certain way of life. As Clack summarizes, this is a 'despairing, apocalyptic atheism ... the frustrated and bitter recognition that the passionate beauty of the religious life is no longer open to us' (1999: 129). While Clack's reading has some biographical plausibility, it is, philosophically speaking, neither the most fruitful nor interesting. Wittgenstein's naturalization of religious belief is better understood not as a sort of naturalistic-anthropological apologetic or lamentation but rather as something distinctly *cathartic*; a re-description of religious practice that 'aims at' the 'satisfaction' (Wittgenstein 1996a: 64) of his aforementioned 'bewilderment.' Thus, in 'Remarks on Frazer's *Golden Bough*,' we are cautioned that a 'hypothetical explanation will be of little help to someone, say, who is upset because of love,' for 'it will not calm him' (ibid.: 63). Being troubled by love (by the end of an affair, or by the longing for love) will not be eased by theoretical formulations. Indeed, often all one can say in such circumstances is 'this is what human life is like' (ibid.: 63). Analogously, being troubled by religious belief (by a crisis of faith, or by the desire for faith[38]) will not be abated by theorizing, even of an 'evolutionary' sort. What Wittgenstein's naturalism offers is a way to 'sharpen [one's] eye' for '*connecting links*' (ibid.: 69) between seemingly incommensurable human activities. Such a 'perspicuous representation' thus enables Wittgenstein to account for his own sympathetic attitude toward religious practice (*his* 'religious point of view' (Drury 1981: 94) and tendency to speak of religion 'with a sort of *religio*-sity' so as 'not to introduce anything alien' (Derrida 1998b: 23)), despite being unable to immerse himself fully in any particular religious world-picture.[39] In short, we should interpret Wittgenstein's reflections on religion as one way of reconciling these apparently conflicting inclinations by tracing those recurrent patterns of behavior that manifest themselves in 'the life of mankind' (1994a: 70). We should also remember that what Wittgenstein finds objectionable about

Frazer's anthropology – and the 'narrow spiritual life' (1996a: 65) to which it bears witness – is Frazer's apparent incapacity to suspend his own reductive scientism.[40] All Frazer discerns in the practices he seeks to 'explain' are epistemic blunders and inferior methods of handling the natural environment. What he overlooks is, as Wittgenstein puts it, that one 'can fight, hope and even believe without believing *scientifically*' (1994a: 60).[41] On Frazer's account, between 'primitive' and 'modern' society lies an epistemic gulf in virtue of which we 'civilized' Westerners can legitimately judge the former to be *essentially* impoverished. Wittgenstein's point is that not only are our respective epistemologies not '*fundamentally*' (1996a: 74) different[42] but, more crucially, neither is the religious-ritualistic life of the 'primitive' so far removed from our own 'civilized' existence. *Their* practices may seem at odds with those of modern Western society, but scratch the surface of the latter and one soon finds the same non-instrumental, ritual activities that are (to the Western eye) more immediately conspicuous in the former.[43]

What I referred to above as Wittgenstein's project of 'reconciliation' is not therefore merely of biographical import concerning his own self-understanding (though it may indeed begin there[44]). Other religious believers and non-believers alike (not to mention radical pluralists like Surin, Lyotard and Readings) would benefit from reminding themselves that, despite the linguistic-conceptual gulf that sometimes divides human beings, there nevertheless remain *natural* grounds upon which mutual understanding can be built – though, of course, 'peaceable' intercourse can never be guaranteed.[45] This is not, as it is for Frazer, simply to render 'foreign' practices palatable to people who think as *we* do.[46] Rather, such 'connecting links' between the life of religious belief and non-belief (or between different faiths, cultures, and so on) demonstrate the 'common spirit' (ibid.: 80) we share *as human beings*. But neither is this to suggest that religious practices can simply be reduced to primitive human activities.[47] Such a position would not only render Wittgenstein's account fundamentally atheistic, it would also underestimate the inherent complexities of such practices as they have hitherto developed and continue to change.[48] Maintaining that ritual is not an activity peculiar to the explicitly 'religious' sphere – but rather finds a place in many regions of human life[49] – is not to trivialize religious rituals in their particularity but simply to deny their *radical* singularity. For without rooting such activities in 'primitive' human tendencies they would become irredeemably alien phenomena, and as such unidentifiable *as* 'religious rituals' – or indeed as 'rituals' of any sort.

This, then, is how Wittgenstein's naturalism feeds into his account of religious belief. It also suggests how Wittgenstein's later work need not be silent regarding questions of social justice. But, as previously suggested, this naturalism leads him to a distinctly ethical interpretation of specific religious concepts. It is to these that I will now turn.

Immortality and ethical responsibility

Regarding the notion of immortality, Wittgenstein elucidates further his reason for hesitancy between assent and dissent:

> 'If you don't cease to exist, you will suffer after death', there I begin to attach ideas, perhaps ethical ideas of responsibility. The point is, that although these are well-known words, and although I can go from one sentence to another sentence, or to pictures [I don't know what consequences *you* draw from this statement].
>
> (1994b: 70, my emphasis)[50]

Again, what is expressed here is puzzlement regarding religious notions, despite the familiarity of their 'surface' grammar. Yet, in what becomes a characteristic move in Wittgenstein's work, he thereby also presents the key to understanding such beliefs by asking what 'consequences' subsequently procure?[51] – 'consequences' that are, of course, not merely logical but also practical. Of particular interest here are how these 'consequences' are taken to likely involve 'ethical ideas of responsibility.' Wittgenstein continues:

> A great writer said that, when he was a boy, his father set him a task, and he suddenly felt that nothing, not even death, could take away the responsibility [in doing this task]; this was his duty to do, and that even death couldn't stop it being his duty. He said that this was, in a way, a proof of the immortality of the soul – because if this lives on [the responsibility won't die.]
>
> (1994b: 70)[52]

This was not an isolated remark, for Malcolm similarly recalls Wittgenstein suggest that 'a way in which the notion of immortality can acquire a meaning is through one's feeling that one has duties from which one cannot be released, even by death' (1958: 71):

> Wittgenstein did once say that he could understand the conception of God, in so far as it is involved in one's awareness of one's own sin and guilt. He added that he could *not* understand the conception of a *Creator*. I think that the ideas of Divine judgement, forgiveness, and redemption had some intelligibility for him, as being related in his mind to feelings of disgust with himself, an intense desire for purity, and a sense of the helplessness of human beings to make themselves better. But the notion of a being *making the world* had no intelligibility for him at all.
>
> (Malcolm 1958: 70–1)

Such passages testify to Wittgenstein's general orientation toward bringing the ethical and religious spheres together. As I have been arguing, reclaiming religious utterances 'from their metaphysical to their everyday use' (1958: §116) need not undermine them.[53] Rather, no real sense can be made of religious beliefs (even those which appear wholly ontological) which are *not* rooted in the practical-ethical lives of those professing them.[54] Thus, recalling Tolstoy's *A Confession*, one might 'believe *that* God exists' and yet from this nothing else follows.[55] After all, belief in the *being* of God could take the form of a quasi-cosmological judgement about which one remains existentially unaffected. There is a stark contrast, however, between this and 'belief *in* God.' Although the latter must in some sense require a latent commitment to the being of God, the point is that no meaningful access can be gained to the ontological conception except through the ethical.[56] Belief *in* God is (as we saw in Chapter 2) more akin to what Wittgenstein calls an absolute 'trusting' (1994a: 72) or 'passionate commitment' (ibid.: 64) by means of which the 'shape'[57] of one's life is both changed and continually molded.[58] In short, one's application of 'the word "God" does not show *whom* you mean – but, rather, what you mean' (ibid.: 50). For the genuine believer the question pertaining to God's *existence* becomes a question regarding the orientation of their *life as a whole*, a question to which they can only adequately respond by 'showing' that orientation. Thus, in a markedly Tolstoyan passage, Wittgenstein concludes:

> Suppose somebody made this guidance for this life: believing in the Last Judgement. Whenever he does anything, this is before his mind. In a way, how are we to know whether to say he believes this will happen or not?
>
> Asking him is not enough. He will probably say he has proof. But he has what you might call an unshakeable belief. It will show, not by reasoning or by appeal to ordinary grounds for belief, but rather by regulating for all in his life.
>
> ... Suppose you had two people, and one of them, when he had to decide which course to take, thought of retribution, and the other did not. One person might, for instance, be inclined to take everything that happened to him as a reward or punishment, and the other person doesn't think of this at all.
>
> (1994a: 53–4)[59]

As Malcolm intimates, this emphasis on the practical setting only within which 'words [get] their sense' (Wittgenstein 1994a: 85) results in drawing ethical and religious concepts together. Wittgenstein's bemusement regarding an essentially ontological conception of God leads him not to a dogmatic atheism but rather to a sympathetic appreciation of religious concepts in terms of sin, guilt and ethical responsibility. And as I said above, this is not merely a biographical point, for what Wittgenstein here bears witness to is the broader possibility of making sense of religious concepts in terms of those behaviors we share *as human beings*.[60]

In keeping with this, Wittgenstein writes:

> If someone who believes in God looks around and asks 'Where does everything I see come from?', 'Where does all this come from?', he is *not* craving for a (causal) explanation; and his question gets its point from being the expression of a certain craving. He is, namely, expressing an attitude to all explanations. – But how is this manifested in his life?
>
> (1994a: 85)[61]

There are obvious resonances between this and Wittgenstein's 1929 'A Lecture on Ethics'[62] where, struggling to find an adequate expression, he remarks:

> I believe the best way of describing [this feeling] is to say that when I have it *I wonder at the existence of the world*. And I am then inclined to use such phrases as 'how extraordinary that anything should exist' or 'how extraordinary that the world should exist.'
>
> (1993: 41)

Unsurprisingly, Wittgenstein's subsequent emphasis lies on the way a 'characteristic misuse of our language runs through *all* ethical and religious expressions' (ibid.: 42).[63] But still, some nine years earlier than 'Lectures on Religious Belief,' he concludes in characteristically sympathetic fashion that this 'running against the walls of our cage is perfectly, absolutely hopeless ... But it is a document of a tendency in the human mind which I personally cannot help respecting deeply and I would not for my life ridicule it' (ibid.: 44).[64] That this primitive 'impulse' (1978: 80) to speak of ethics and religion is simultaneously futile *and* worthy of profound respect is important to remember when considering the appropriation of Wittgenstein's early work by the Logical Positivists.[65] For while both might be said to have placed the term 'God' under erasure, for Wittgenstein such a 'boundary line' (1958: §499) was not a mark of disavowal but rather 'a way ... to save the name of God, to shield it from all onto-theological idolatry' (Derrida 1995c: 62).[66] Nevertheless, these sentiments of ontological wonderment become more intelligible against the practical backdrop of the later writings' contextualization of language-usage, and, not least, in the light of Wittgenstein's suggestion that the ontological question 'gets its point from being the expression of a certain craving' (that one is here 'expressing an attitude to all explanations' that is 'manifested in [one's] life').[67] Genuinely religious utterances do not describe a transcendent reality. Rather, they express a fundamental orientation toward one's terrestrial life.[68] If such utterances 'describe' anything, it is not to the supernatural realm that we should direct our attention but to the human.[69] Hence, 'Christianity is not a doctrine' – that is, 'not ... a theory about what has happened and will happen to the human soul' – but rather 'a description of something that actually takes place in human life.' In other words: '"consciousness of sin" is a real event and so are despair and salvation through faith,' and '[t]hose who speak of such things ... are simply describing what has happened to them, whatever gloss anyone may want to put on it' (1994a: 28). In such passages we again get a sense of Wittgenstein's normativity, for it is clear that for *some* the notion of immortality does denote the continuation of the self beyond the demise of the body. But it would be wrong to consider this belief to be inherently 'religious.' For one may profess such convictions 'either religiously or nonreligiously' (Malcolm 1972: 215); that is, either with or without a practical-ethical attitude. There is nothing to prevent someone from believing that they will 'survive death' as though this was merely an incidental, quasi-empirical fact. It is not *necessary* that anything need follow from such a conviction.[70] Of course, this is not to suggest that such classificatory 'wrong turnings' (Wittgenstein 1994a: 18) are easily avoided.[71] On the contrary, what often leads us astray is the 'power language has to make everything look the same' (ibid.: 22) when abstracted from its manifold practical settings.[72] The notion of immortality – like Moore's fundamental propositions discussed in Chapter 2 – begins to look like a quasi-empirical hypothesis due to the very language in which it is couched.[73] As Wittgenstein notes, we naturally become confused 'by certain analogies between the forms of expression in different regions of language' (1958: §90), not least because 'our language has remained the same and keeps seducing us into asking the same questions' (1994a: 15).[74] Thus:

> Philosophers who say: 'after death a timeless state will begin', or: 'at death a timeless state begins' ... do not notice that they have used the words 'after' and 'at' and 'begins' in a temporal sense, and that temporality is embedded in their grammar.
>
> (1994a: 22)[75]

Talk of immortality thereby lends itself to certain misunderstandings.[76] Due both to the temporality rooted in language, and the 'urge' (1958: §109) to assume that language functions in one way,[77] we are prone to misconstrue the notion of immortality quantitatively as more-of-the-same; *more* life after this life, *more* time after death. But what separates the believer and non-believer here is not a difference in their respective *post-mortem* anticipations. Rather, the difference is exhibited in their respective existential attitudes towards *this* life.[78] By bringing words back 'to their everyday use' (ibid.: §116) and rejecting explanation in favor of 'description alone' (ibid.: §109), Wittgenstein thus attempts to show that talk of immortality is essentially of practical-ethical significance.

Of course, these conditions apply when talking about numerous other religious concepts and practices. But in 'The Groundlessness of Belief' Malcolm brings to light something else of particular significance for the present analysis. There, Malcolm remarks that while he (like Tolstoy) finds 'great difficulty with the notion of belief in *the existence* of God,' the idea of 'belief *in* God' is quite 'intelligible.' For if

> a man did not ever pray for help or forgiveness, or have any inclination toward it; nor ever felt that it is 'a good and joyful thing' to thank God for the blessings of his life; nor was ever concerned about his failure to comply with divine commandments – then ... he could not be said to believe in God ... [B]elief in God in any degree does require, as I understand the words, some religious action, some commitment, or if not, at least a bad conscience.
>
> (1972: 211)[79]

All of this is in keeping with Wittgenstein's own views. But it is Malcolm's closing remark that is striking; that a 'bad conscience' is the minimal manifestation required of the authentically religious life. Wittgenstein emphasizes the same thing when he remarks: 'People are religious to the extent that they believe themselves to be not so much *imperfect*, as *ill*. Any man who is half-way decent will think himself extremely imperfect, but a religious man thinks himself *wretched*' (1994a: 45).[80] It is to this dramatic characterization of the 'religious man' that I will now turn.

Sin, wretchedness and bad conscience

As we have begun to see, Wittgenstein's religiosity is far from transparent. Indeed, this ambiguity is compounded insofar as it becomes central to his philosophical treatment *of* religious belief. It is thus sometimes difficult not to become impatient with Wittgenstein's aforementioned 'hesitancy' on such matters. One source of dissatisfaction here can be located in his demarcation between decency and religiosity when characterizing the genuinely 'religious man' as thinking himself to be not merely 'imperfect' but positively '*wretched*.' For here we are presented with a portrait that immediately calls to mind Wittgenstein himself.[81] But again, this is not merely of biographical interest. Thus Drury recalls Wittgenstein once remarking: 'If you and I are to live religious lives, it mustn't be that we talk a lot about religion, but that our manner of life is different. It is my belief that only if you try to be helpful to other people will you in the end find your way to God.'[82] Drury then proceeds: 'Just as I was leaving [Wittgenstein] suddenly said, "There is a sense in which you and I are both Christians"' (1981: 129–30). Whatever contingent circumstances might have prompted Wittgenstein's remark, it raises a more general question regarding his approach to religious belief; namely, is it possible (and if so, what might it mean) to 'live a Christian life' *without* actually 'being a Christian'? For if to be a Christian is essentially to 'live a Christian life,' then the latter must surely amount to more than practicing a Christian ethic (assuming there is such a thing[83]), or of merely trying 'to be helpful to other people.' This question is germane because it is not clear that Wittgenstein's work provides any obvious response.[84] One reason for this is the deeply Tolstoyan picture of Christianity he tends toward.[85] For in both thinkers we find a certain idealization of what Tolstoy describes as the 'true' faith of the 'illiterate peasant' (1987: 71) or 'simple working people' (ibid.: 63).[86] Alongside this portrait emerges a deep suspicion of the theology of 'learned believers' (ibid.: 72) (which destroys 'the thing it should be advancing' (ibid.: 74))[87] and institutionalized ritual practice.[88] This concurrence is worth noting because it is precisely the Tolstoyan dimension of Wittgenstein's work that becomes potentially disabling at a philosophical level.[89] For if one undermines the significance of doctrinal and theological tradition in distinguishing believers from non-believers – in short, if one is denied recourse to the sort of organizational 'trappings' of religion that Wittgenstein appears to have thought to be 'pretentious' (1994a: 30)[90] – then one is in danger of rendering that very distinction superfluous.[91] In what substantive 'sense' might one understand Wittgenstein's claim that both himself and Drury were Christians? A plausible response to this question can be formulated, but only by returning to the deeper naturalism orienting Wittgenstein's treatment of religiosity. Although he may not do justice to the 'trappings' of religious practice – and despite the fact that such phenomena as 'hierarchy, honours and official positions' (ibid.) or the importance of one's 'saying alot of prayers' (Drury 1981: 109) are extremely marginal in the Wittgensteinian account – this marginality is due not to their being *inherently* 'pretentious'[92] but because for someone at his 'level' (Wittgenstein 1994a: 32) of belief they could hardly appear otherwise.[93] Wittgenstein focuses on those beliefs that have a more obvious ethical dimension because it is only by means of these deeply *human* phenomena that he can even begin to make sense of the particularities of Christianity.[94] Thus, although we are warned that '[e]verything ritualistic (everything that, as it were, smacks of the high priest) must be strictly avoided, because it immediately turns rotten,' Wittgenstein nevertheless proceeds: 'Of course a kiss is a ritual too and it isn't rotten, but ritual is permissible only to the extent that it is as genuine as a kiss' (ibid.: 8).[95] Wittgenstein's attitude is not therefore condemnatory toward institutionalized practices *per se*. Rather, he is recommending vigilance with regard to their inherent seductions. And it is on the basis of this sensitivity toward both the fundamentally ethical orientation of religious faith and the importance therein of *genuine* ritual that Wittgenstein can, without excessive hyperbole, describe himself as being in 'a sense' a Christian.

Reading Wittgenstein against the backdrop of the Christian conception of original sin, Shields suggests that Wittgenstein's work represents a sort of exorcism of philosophical 'temptations' (Shields 1997: 61).[96] By emphasizing Wittgenstein's continued preoccupation with 'the thought of absolute dependence on arbitrary power'[97] Shields reasonably claims that 'one point is clear ... Wittgenstein shows that this is not a warm personal God but a fearful Power whose main attribute is his otherness' (ibid.: 33).[98] Wittgenstein stresses this, we are told, by reference to the sheer 'givenness' of 'the world,' 'logical form,' 'form[s] of life' and 'grammar' (ibid.: 34) that are 'not of our own making' but rather 'thrust upon us' (ibid.: 36).[99] Indeed, '[m]eaning is given like a gift, or a covenant of God made toward the undeserving' (ibid.: 46).[100] Now, although Shields's account is compelling, some restraint is nevertheless needed when applying the notion of 'original sin' here. As I previously suggested with reference to Tolstoy (and as Shields himself notes), Wittgenstein's work does often display a certain 'nostalgia' (ibid.: 88) for the honest, simple faith of the 'peasant.' Still, the sort of 'wretchedness' Wittgenstein perceives to lie at the heart of the genuinely religious life problematizes the reparative teleology of the Christian concept of original sin. (In this sense we might ask whether Wittgenstein's conception of religiosity is more Judaic than Christian?) In view of Wittgenstein's focus on the categorical nature of religious belief,[101] I would therefore like to pursue other interpretative possibilities. Most striking in this regard is his warning in *Culture and Value*:

> 'God has commanded it, therefore it must be possible to do it.' That means nothing. There is no '*therefore*' about it ... in this context 'He has commanded it' means roughly: He will punish anybody who doesn't do it. And nothing follows from that about what anybody can or cannot do.
>
> (1994a: 77)

While this passage bears witness to Wittgenstein's tendency to characterize God as 'a fearful Power' (Shields 1997: 33), what should also be noted is the way God's having 'commanded' something dislocates the conceptual-practical boundaries which ordinarily circumscribe human responsibility. For when *God* commands me this does not necessarily entail the possibility of my being able to *fulfill* that injunction.[102] God's commandments come from a moral 'height' outside the customary rules governing ethical discourse.[103] And it is this severing of the realm of responsibility (the ethical *ought*) from that of possibility (the ontological *can*) that enables us to relocate the feeling of 'wretchedness' Wittgenstein describes outside the teleology of original sin. As previously noted, Wittgenstein makes a connection between 'the immortality of the soul' and an experience of responsibility 'that even death couldn't stop' (1994b: 70).[104] In this coupling it is evident that the usual criteria of moral responsibility are similarly disrupted, for here not even death relieves the moral burden.[105] In these passages responsibility is therefore presented as *unconditional*; what

116 *Wretchedness without recompense*

God demands never logically entails the possibility of one's satisfying that demand, and, likewise, the notion of the immortal soul may itself gain its sense from the 'feeling' that even my (or the other's) death cannot always annul my duty to another.[106] Now, it might appear that these remarks provide striking examples of language going '*on holiday*' (1958: §38), becoming 'like an engine idling' (ibid.: §132) and thus of lacking 'practical consequences' (1999: §§450, 668). That is, it may seem as though divorcing the ethical 'ought' from the ontological 'can' effectively severs the normal connection between linguistic and non-linguistic behavior. If I am 'commanded' to do something that I cannot *possibly* do, or if even death does not cancel my responsibilities to another, then surely any subsequent talk of obligations, duties, guilt (and so on) can lead only to conceptual confusion. That such notions *can* have important practical-ethical consequences will be central to my examination of Levinas in Chapters 6 and 7. But in order to prepare the way for those analyses, I would first like to show how, even in Wittgenstein's earlier writings (where ethics is described as 'supernatural' (1993: 40)), this correlation between guilt and responsibility plays an important role.

Guilt, being judged and Dostoyevsky's imperative: religion without recompense

Although 'A Lecture on Ethics' post-dates the *Tractatus* by eight years or so, this text possesses a distinctly Tractarian atmosphere.[107] Thus, echoing a number of his earlier ideas, Wittgenstein there remarks:

> Suppose one of you were an omniscient person and therefore knew all the movements of all the bodies in the world dead or alive and that he also knew all the states of mind of all human beings that ever lived, and suppose this man wrote all he knew in a big book, then this book would contain the whole description of the world; and what I want to say is, that this book would contain nothing that we would call an *ethical* judgement or anything that would logically imply such a judgement.
>
> (1993: 39)

Developing Kant's distinction between hypothetical and categorical imperatives,[108] Wittgenstein maintains that whereas the former (judgements of 'relative' value) can be translated into the language of ontology, the latter (judgements of 'absolute' value) cannot.[109] (I will return to this distinction later.) The contents of this imagined 'world-book' would thus consist only of facts all 'stand[ing] on the same level' (ibid.), from which no judgements of absolute value could be derived.[110] Indeed, Wittgenstein proceeds to suggest that 'if a man could write a book on Ethics which really was a book on Ethics, this book would, with an explosion, destroy all the other books in the world ... Ethics, if it is anything, is supernatural and our words will only express facts' (ibid.: 40). Meaningful language, on this early account, is tethered to mirroring the structure of the world. But, as previously noted, Wittgenstein repeatedly emphasizes that although attempting to speak of the ethical may be 'hopeless' it nevertheless remained a human 'tendency' (ibid.: 44) he respected.[111] It is therefore significant that in a letter to von Ficker he should remark of the *Tractatus* itself:

> [T]he point of the book is ethical. I once wanted to give a few words in the foreword which now actually are not in it, which, however, I'll write to you now because they might be a key for you: I wanted to write that my work consists of two parts: of the one which is here, and of everything which I have *not* written. And precisely this second part is the important one.
>
> (1996b: 94)[112]

On this account the *Tractatus* performs a sort of negative theology that, indirectly, '*points to something*' (1978: 81).[113] By remaining (almost) silent about the ethical, Wittgenstein nevertheless maintains that it is this (almost) unspoken part of his book that is 'the important one.' By determining what could – and thus could not – be meaningfully said within the language of ontology, the *Tractatus* positions the realm of the ethical 'outside the world' (1995: 6.41), thereby exiling it from meaningful, fact-stating speech.[114] In order to 'write a book on Ethics which really was a book on Ethics' would therefore be to write the book Wittgenstein did not himself write – and presumably did not think could be written; the silent, co-present underside of the *Tractatus* itself.[115] Of course, the metaphysical vision underpinning the *Tractatus* (and specifically the account of language expounded therein) is at odds with Wittgenstein's later thought, and it is this that primarily concerns me. Nevertheless, by returning to 'A Lecture on Ethics' it will become clear how, even here where ethics is described as 'sublime' and 'supernatural' (1993: 40), human guilt plays a central role.

When distinguishing between relative and absolute value judgements, Wittgenstein employs the following illustration:

> [I]f I say that it is *important* for me not to catch cold I mean that catching a cold produces certain describable disturbances in my life and if I say that this is the *right* road I mean that it's the right road relative to a certain goal. Used in this way these expressions don't present any difficult or deep problems. But this is not how Ethics uses them.
>
> (1993: 38)

He then proceeds:

> Supposing that I could play tennis and one of you saw me playing and said 'Well, you play pretty badly' and suppose I answered 'I know, I'm

playing badly but I don't want to play any better,' all the other man could say would be 'Ah then that's all right.' But suppose I had told one of you a preposterous lie and he came up to me and said 'You're behaving like a beast' and then I were to say 'I know I behave badly, but then I don't want to behave any better,' could he then say 'Ah, then that's all right'? Certainly not; he would say 'Well, you *ought* to want to behave better.' Here you have an absolute judgement of value, whereas the first instance was one of a relative judgement.

(1993: 38–9)

My not wanting to play tennis 'any better' presents no direct ethical problem. Any suggestion that one *ought* to want to play 'better' would only be commensurate to certain other relatively valuable states of affairs (such as 'you will get fitter'), the importance of which I could still reasonably contest.[116] But my not wanting to 'behave any better' is not dependent on such additional commitments. This is why, in the above scenario, such an exclamation would likely be treated as facetious or met with bewilderment. For there is no 'right time' (no specific or determinable occasions) in which to seek the *moral* good.[117] You might find it odd that I do not want to play tennis 'any better,' but you would not perceive this listlessness to be a deep moral character flaw.[118] The differences that separate these two cases will thus likely be shown in: (1) the extent to which you would employ your powers of persuasion to convince me that I am mistaken, and/or (2) what you would ultimately risk on account of it. In short, having exhausted your reasons and rhetoric, there will be little option but for you to re-evaluate the basis, depth and prospects of our relationship. Wittgenstein then concludes:

> The right road is the road which leads to an arbitrarily predetermined end and it is quite clear to us all that there is no sense in talking about the right road apart from such a predetermined goal. Now let us see what we could possibly mean by the expression, '*the* absolutely right road.' I think it would be the road which *everybody* on seeing it would, *with logical necessity*, have to go, or be ashamed for not going. And similarly, the *absolute good*, if it is a describable state of affairs, would be one which everybody, independent of his tastes and inclinations, would *necessarily* bring about or feel guilty for not bringing about. And I want to say that such a state of affairs is a chimera. No state of affairs has, in itself, what I would like to call the coercive power of an absolute judge.

(1993: 40)

What is noticeable here is the vocabulary Wittgenstein employs in discussing this 'chimera.' For he does not simply say that failure to follow 'the absolutely right road' or pursue 'the absolute good' would be wrong or bad. Rather, Wittgenstein explicitly cashes out the latter in terms of guilt, shame and the wrath of an 'absolute judge.'

To the extent that Wittgenstein's emphasis on guilt (notably in those passages from 'Lectures on Religious Belief' and *Culture and Value*) disrupts orthodox ethical precepts by divorcing the 'ought' from the 'can,' it may seem merely paradoxical, no matter how biographically revealing.[119] But despite the piecemeal nature of Wittgenstein's reflections on guilt, they do suggest another, more strictly philosophical rendering. First, one can begin to piece together a rather different conception of 'genuine' religiosity that emphasizes its *fundamentally* categorical structure. Just as inquiring: '*Why* should I be good?' or 'What's in ethics *for me*?' would be to erroneously conceive of the categorical in hypothetical terms, so too would it be mistaken to ask of religion: '*Why* should I believe that?' or again, 'What's in it *for me*?'[120] Doubtless non-believers frequently ask such questions of believers. Doubtless too, the apologetic responses of the latter to such petitions can often be cashed out in similarly prudential terms ('*If* you want salvation *then* . . . '; '*If* you do not want to suffer God's wrath *then* . . . '). But these sorts of responses are themselves profoundly *irreligious*. The person who loves another essentially because *they love him* can never be said to have truly *loved* the other, for 'love exists without worrying about being loved' (Levinas 2001: 143).[121] Likewise, giving gifts only to those who one knows will compensate with a gift in return is a similarly hollow practice. Analogously, she who decides in favor of 'being moral' because we convince her that (*qua* the Pyrrhonist) it is *prudent* to do so, can hardly be said to be genuinely moral.[122] And he who decides in favor of Christian belief because it promises salvation is not merely superficially religious, he is not religious *at all*.[123] This, then, is the deeper meaning to draw from Wittgenstein's claim (referred to in Chapter 2) that he who states his belief 'categorically' is 'more intelligent than the man who [is] apologetic about it' (1994b: 63). Such remarks do not bear witness to a dogmatic fideism – though they might lend themselves to that reading. Rather, they say something important about the grammar of *genuine* religiosity. With this in mind, it here seems natural to raise questions concerning the possibility of a purely categorical religion that says only '*Do this!*' (Wittgenstein 1994a: 29) without promising *anything at all* – or, more radically perhaps, that promises only *losses*.[124] As Levinas asks:

> Are we entering a moment in history in which the good must be loved without promises? Perhaps it is the end of all preaching. May we not be on the eve of a new form of faith, a faith without triumph, as if the only irrefutable value were saintliness, a time when the only right to a reward would be not to expect one?
>
> (1999: 109)

Is it therefore conceivable that one might 'believe' *beyond* the economics of eschatological-salvationist hope; *beyond* the 'promise ... of the Happy End' (Levinas 1988a: 175)? Could religious faith consist in an *absolute expenditure* without the assurance, faith or hope that one will be 'well paid' (Nietzsche 1968: §188)?[125] To these questions I will return in later chapters, but Wittgenstein's remarks on immortality already gesture in this general direction. For, we will recall, it is the feeling that 'even death couldn't stop' a sense of 'duty' to another that is said to provide a 'proof of the immortality of the soul – because if [the soul] lives on' then so too would the 'responsibility' not 'die' (1994b: 70). Here the reality of the immortal soul does not offer potential recompense for (or an annulment of) one's mortal ethical responsibilities. Rather, the 'proof' that the soul is immortal lies in the sense that one's obligations to another hold even *beyond death.* In short, the immortal soul does not achieve Pyrrhonian *ataraxia* but instead retains its state of 'wretchedness' eternally. The second point to note here is how many of Wittgenstein's reflections provoke a rethinking of ethical responsibility itself, and specifically how much traditional ethical theory constitutes the theoretical circumscription of a primordially boundless responsibility – itself prompted by a certain experience of guilt.[126] As Levinas suspects, and as I will discuss in Chapter 6, perhaps the realm of the 'human' in general (and 'scruples' in particular) 'are always already remorse' (1999: 179).

It is widely acknowledged that Dostoyevsky's work fascinated Wittgenstein at least as much as Tolstoy's.[127] Indeed, Malcolm recalls that when Wittgenstein was incarcerated at Monte Cassino 'he and a fellow prisoner read Dostoyevsky together ... it was this writer's "deeply religious attitude" that commended him to Wittgenstein' (1993: 8). Redpath similarly notes that Wittgenstein read *Crime and Punishment* 'at least ten times, and both in that novel and in *The Brothers Karamazov* he thought Dostoyevsky expressed "a whole religion"' (1990: 53).[128] And likewise, Monk reports that Wittgenstein had read the latter text 'so often he knew whole passages of it by heart' – indeed, *The Brothers Karamazov* was one of the very 'few personal possessions' (1991: 136) he had taken to the Eastern Front in 1916. We can only speculate as to what portions of Dostoyevsky's work Wittgenstein had deemed worthy of committing to memory, but there is one passage in *The Brothers Karamazov* (a passage that preoccupies Levinas) that encapsulates perhaps the most significant aspect of Dostoyevsky's work; namely, its treatment of guilt as 'having a positive function' (Johnston 1991: 123). There he writes:

> 'every one of us is responsible for everyone else in every way, and I most of all.' Mother could not help smiling at that. She wept and smiled at the same time. 'How are you,' she said, 'most of all responsible for everyone? There are murderers and robbers in the world, and what terrible sin have you committed that you should accuse yourself

before everyone else?' 'Mother ... my dearest heart, my joy, you must realize that everyone is really responsible for everyone and everything. I don't know how to explain it to you, but I feel it so strongly that it hurts ... '

(Dostoyevsky 1967: 339)[129]

This excerpt highlights many of the themes in Wittgenstein's work discussed in this chapter[130] – notably those remarks pertaining to the relationship between responsibility and a certain 'experience ... of feeling guilty' (1993: 42), and his characterization of the 'religious man' as '*wretched*' (1994a: 45).[131] What might be said to be prerequisite for genuine religiosity is not merely the '"belief that only if you try to be helpful to other people will you in the end find your way to God"' (Drury 1981: 129), but the conviction that the greatest immorality and blasphemy is to be found in the experience of *good* conscience;[132] in believing that one's duty has been done and one's responsibilities placated before God or one's neighbor.[133]

Given that Wittgenstein's treatment of these themes is not systematic, it is necessary to look elsewhere for a way to clarify the relationship between guilt and responsibility. This, I believe, can best be approached through Levinas's work. Shifting between not only specific philosophers but also (alleged[134]) philosophical traditions, is beneficial for both sides of the so-called 'Analytic/Continental divide.' For while Levinas provides a crucial supplement to Wittgenstein's reflections on both the face (discussed in Chapter 3) and the relationship between guilt and ethics, the internal complexities of Levinas's own thought can be unraveled by bringing to our reading many of the themes already considered. Indeed, the first obstacle facing the uninitiated reader of Levinas is that his work seldom progresses in an orthodox linear fashion. Of course, much the same might be said of Wittgenstein, but in Levinas's writings the matter seems more complex. For there we find a number of apparently synonymous ideas – and a steady accumulation of metaphors – revolve in such a way as to intimate a nucleus.[135] Some tentativeness is unavoidable here because it is not made clear by Levinas (or his commentators) that there is such a pivotal point around which his thinking moves. And while those that *are* suggested (for example, Levinas's conviction that philosophy has systematically annulled the 'alterity of the other') are not inaccurate, they tend to compound the internal difficulties of his work. I will instead argue that this challenging body of work is best understood as an extended meditation on what we might – along with Wittgenstein – refer to as a certain 'experience of feeling guilty.'[136]

6 Trespassing
Guilt and sacrifice in Heidegger, Levinas and ordinary life

> [N]o profit can be made except at another's expense ... let anyone search his heart and he will find that our inward wishes are for the most part born and nourished at the expense of others.
>
> M. Montaigne, *Essays*

> 'You shall not steal! You shall not kill!' – such words were once called holy; in their presence people bowed their knees and their heads and removed their shoes. But I ask you: Where have there ever been better thieves and killers in the world than such holy words have been? Is there not in all life itself – stealing and killing?
>
> F. Nietzsche, *Thus Spoke Zarathustra*

> Where is the main stress ... in *being-there*: on *being*, or on *there*? In *there* – which it would be better to call *here* – shall I first look for my being?
>
> G. Bachelard, 'Trust and Antitrust' *The Poetics of Space*

Introduction

If the question emerging from both Wittgenstein's *Tractatus* and 'A Lecture on Ethics' ultimately concerns the possibility of writing on ethics in a conceptual vocabulary too ontologically laden (indeed, this 'running-up against the limits of language is *Ethics*' (Wittgenstein 1978: 80)), then Levinas's work represents one attempt to do precisely this.[1] That is, Levinas endeavors 'to run against the boundaries' (Wittgenstein 1993: 44) of a language that seems to prohibit any genuine expression of the ethical, and this leads him toward writing philosophy 'as a *poetic composition*' (Wittgenstein 1994a: 24).[2] It would be an exaggeration to suggest that Levinas succeeds in writing the explosive 'book on Ethics' Wittgenstein refers to – indeed, it will become clear later why the very notion of 'success' is problematic here.[3] Nevertheless, the general aspirations of Levinas's work can initially be framed in this way. An important question thus arises: If both Levinas *and* the later Wittgenstein can be read as responding to the challenges outlined in the *Tractatus* and 'A Lecture on Ethics,' to what (if any) extent do their respective responses intertwine? One recent commentator approaches this question by recommending that Levinas's work be read as a non-foundationalist[4] account of *the* 'transcendental language game' (Greisch 1991: 70).[5] Provocative though this suggestion is, I will resist its 'non-foundationalist' trajectory, not least because it is inconsonant with the deeper spirit of both philosophers' work.[6] What is more philosophically interesting is the extent to which Wittgenstein and Levinas each bear witness to a certain experience of *guilt*.

Toward the end of Chapter 5 I cited a passage from *The Brothers Karamazov* that usefully brought together a number of Wittgenstein's concerns. But that excerpt was selected for another, equally important, reason. For Levinas is also much taken with Dostoyevsky (along with those other Russian literary figures who were to influence his early thinking[7]), and expressly the idea that 'every one of us is responsible for everyone else in every way, and I most of all' (Dostoyevsky 1967: 339).[8] What fascinates Levinas about this passage is, as I will argue later, the way in which both: (1) *my* responsibility is presented as exceeding the reciprocal economics of what he deems to be 'traditional' ethical thinking (including Buber's *I and Thou*[9]), and (2) subjectivity itself can be characterized in terms of 'an originary ... responsibility or guilt' (Robbins 1999: 147).[10] However, in order to illuminate how guilt functions in Levinas's work it is first necessary to situate it in relation to Heidegger's exposition of Conscience and Guilt[11] in *Being and Time* – a text Levinas considered 'one of the finest books in the history of philosophy' (1992: 37) (despite the fact that its author has 'never been exculpated ... from his participation in National-Socialism' (ibid.: 41)).[12] The extent to which Levinas transforms Heidegger's ontological analyses into something distinctively ethical should not be underestimated. But the root of Levinas's thinking here is not exclusively Heideggerian. Close attention must also be paid to the profound influence the Holocaust has on both the rhetoric and substance of his work.[13] Only through a combined appreciation of these two sources will we be in a position to discern the pivotal position Guilt plays in his philosophy.

Conscience and guilt in Heidegger's *Being and Time*

In keeping with the enterprise of 'fundamental ontology,' Heidegger claims that his analysis of Conscience and Guilt diverges from the 'manifold ways' (1999: 313) such phenomena have hitherto been dealt with by anthropology, psychology and theology.[14] This is not to say that such traditional investigations, or our 'everyday' (ibid.: 314) understanding, are entirely worthless. Rather, Heidegger's project aspires to operate on a more fundamental philosophical level, providing the ontological grounds for all such interpretations.[15] But what is most distinctive about Heidegger's approach can best be seen by reviewing his more 'positive' (ibid.: 341) reflections on these themes.

Dasein, we will recall, is defined as that being that has as its Being a

124 *Trespassing, guilt and sacrifice*

'potentiality-for-Being' (ibid.: 315).[16] In other words, Dasein is distinct from other beings because 'in its very Being, that Being is an *issue* for it' (ibid.: 32). Dasein is thus to be determined not by reference to 'a "what" of the kind that pertains to a subject matter' but rather as that being which 'always understands itself in terms of its existence – in terms of a possibility of itself: to be itself or not' (ibid.: 32–3). In this way then Dasein is *in its very Being* concerned with its own potentialities.[17] Moreover, the sort of Being Dasein 'has' is originally social. For even when Dasein is 'alone,' this solitude is possible only because its primary mode of Being is Being-with-others.[18] Indeed, this essential *Being-with* structure is already present in Dasein's self-concerned involvement with the inanimate world.[19] Thus, in its practical dealings with worldly objects, Dasein is presented with implicit reference-relations to *other* Daseins[20] – to those who have perhaps constructed these objects, or who may later encounter and use them for themselves.[21] Taking clothing as his example, Heidegger thus writes: 'In the work [the thing produced] there is also reference or assignment to "materials": the work is dependent on leather, thread, needles, and the like. Leather ... is produced from hides. These are taken from animals ... someone else has raised.' He proceeds:

> The work produced refers not only to the 'towards-which' of its usability and the 'whereof' of which it consists: under simple craft conditions it also has an assignment to the person who is to use it or wear it. The work is cut to his figure; he 'is' there along with it as the work emerges ... Thus along with the work, we encounter not only entities ready-to-hand but also entities with Dasein's kind of Being – entities for which, in their concern, the product becomes ready-to-hand; and together with these we encounter the world in which weavers and users live, which is at the same time ours. Any work with which one concerns oneself is ready-to-hand not only in the domestic world of the workshop but also in the *public world*.
>
> (1999: 100)[22]

I will return to this idea in later chapters, for such characterizations of *Being-with* are only part of the Heideggerian narrative. Like Sextus and Wittgenstein, Heidegger does not escape a certain normativity here[23] insofar as he repeatedly warns Dasein of its tendency to lose itself in 'inauthenticity' (ibid.: 312),[24] or of letting itself be '*dispersed*' (ibid.: 167) into the anonymous collectivity of *das Man* (the 'nobody' (ibid.: 312) or the 'they'[25]). When one programmatically does (or omits to do) something simply because this is how the majority act,[26] or when one appeals to social convention and justifies oneself that 'this is what is expected of me,' one thereby relinquishes responsibility for choosing what *oneself* is to be.[27] This is a radically non-Pyrrhonian vision, for, as Kellner puts it, to 'be authentic one must resolutely choose to liberate oneself from domination by social conventions and inauthentic ways of being and liberate oneself for one's own projects and self-determination' (1992: 202). In *Being and Time* we are thus presented with 'a model of the individual struggling against society' where only the inauthentic person 'blindly follows social convention, evades decisive choice by losing itself in distraction, or ineffectually surmising what it should do.' An *in*authentic person 'surrenders to the way things have been publicly interpreted and falls into the ways of being that are socially prescribed and recommended' (ibid.).[28] Due to what Heidegger describes as Dasein's being 'thrown *into existence*' (1999: 321)[29] it is thereby 'factically submitted' (ibid.: 344) to the world. That is, through being 'brought into its "there" ... *not* of its own accord' (ibid.: 329) Dasein's potentiality-for-Being is inevitably restricted.[30] But even taking into account that such 'thrownness' often renders choice difficult, Dasein is always able to make *some* choices.[31] Absorbed in the everyday anonymity of the 'they' Dasein is prevented 'from taking hold of [its] possibilities' (ibid.: 312) and subsequently 'kept away' from authentic Being.[32] Dasein cannot simply escape responsibility by losing itself in the 'they,' for this 'losing oneself' (or choosing not to choose[33]) still constitutes a choice for which Dasein is responsible.[34] In other words, although Dasein cannot escape choosing, *what* it chooses is always (relatively) open.[35]

It is at this juncture that Heidegger introduces the notion of 'Conscience.' As traditionally delineated the 'call of conscience' provides an inner voice of moral guidance. More specifically, this 'ordinary' experience of conscience is thought to occur '*after* the deed has been done or left undone' (ibid.: 335–6) and thus 'follows the transgression and points back to that event which has befallen and by which Dasein has loaded itself with guilt' (ibid.: 336–7). In its Being-toward-death, however, 'Dasein "is" ahead of itself,' for although the voice of Conscience 'does call back ... it calls beyond the deed which has happened ... to the Being-guilty into which one has been thrown, which is "earlier" than any indebtedness' (ibid.: 337) (I will return to this later). Heidegger's concept of Conscience therefore differs from the traditional rendering insofar as the former is *constitutive* of Dasein's Being, and as such is 'manifestly not present-at-hand' (ibid.: 343). Conscience calls with a commanding voice, 'wrenching' Dasein 'away from *das Man*' (Macann 1992: 230). Furthermore, in contrast to the 'ontical common sense' (Heidegger 1999: 314) interpretation, Conscience lacks explicit content[36] and thereby demands a special sort of 'hearing' (ibid.: 314). The call of Conscience, Heidegger claims, 'asserts nothing, gives no information about world-events, has nothing to tell.' Nevertheless, this '*keeping silent*' (ibid.: 318) – though informationally barren – possesses 'the momentum of a push – of an abrupt arousal' (ibid.: 316) in its invoking 'the Self to its potentiality-for-Being-its-Self' (ibid.: 319). That is, the 'call of conscience has the character of an *appeal* to Dasein by calling it to its ownmost potentiality-for-Being-its-Self,' and 'this is done by way of *summoning* it to its ownmost Being-guilty' (ibid.: 314).[37]

126 *Trespassing, guilt and sacrifice*

Given that Conscience is said to both 'appeal' to Dasein and constitute Dasein's Being, the relationship between that which *calls* and that which is *called* requires elucidation. According to Heidegger then, this 'alien' (ibid.: 321) call does not come from anywhere other than Dasein's own Being.[38] From its 'lostness' (ibid.: 319) or 'hiding-place' in the 'they,' Dasein 'gets brought to itself by the call' (ibid.: 317). But this is not simply a moment of soliloquy, for in its disclosure[39] the call possesses the capacity to *surprise* Dasein; to come 'against [its] expectations and even against [its] will' (ibid.: 320). In being called by Conscience Dasein is thus forcefully summoned 'to its ownmost Being-guilty' (ibid.: 319). 'Where ... shall we get our criterion for the primordial existential meaning of the "Guilty!"?' Heidegger rhetorically inquires:

> From the fact that this 'Guilty!' turns up as a predicate for the 'I am'. Is it possible that what is understood as 'guilt' in our inauthentic interpretation lies in Dasein's Being as such, and that it does so in such a way that so far as any Dasein factically exists, it *is* also guilty?
>
> (1999: 326)

The crucial point here is that Dasein – in its very status as an 'I am'[40] – '*is guilty*' (ibid.: 331), and it is this 'primordial' (ibid.: 332) Guilt that arouses the call of Conscience.[41] Moreover, the charge of 'Guilty!' picks out Dasein as a *particular* 'I.'[42] On this view, then, the notion of a 'public conscience' is little more than 'the voice of the "they."' As Heidegger caustically remarks: 'A "world-conscience" is a dubious fabrication, and Dasein can come to this only *because* conscience, in its basis and its essence, is *in each case mine*' (ibid.: 323). Insofar as Dasein's Guilt has thus been divorced from any common, social morality, one might ask *what* it is that Dasein is supposed to be Guilty *of?* But for Heidegger, posing the question this way would be simultaneously problematic and philosophically revealing insofar as it perpetuates certain errors inherent in the 'common sense,'[43] 'ordinary' (ibid.: 327),[44] 'everyday' (ibid.: 336) understanding of being-guilty. Asking '*What* Dasein is Guilty *of?*' implies a specific object *of* Guilt, and thereby lends itself to the economic interpretation of guilt as '"owing", of "having something due on account"' or 'as "*having debts*"' (ibid.: 327) commonly proffered by the 'they.'[45] For the latter guilt is like a 'business procedure that can be regulated' (ibid.: 340), but the ontological understanding both grounds and undercuts this economic model: '*Being-guilty does not first result from an indebtedness ... but that, on the contrary, indebtedness becomes possible only "on the basis" of a primordial Being-guilty*' (ibid.: 329).[46] According to Heidegger then, the 'they' understand Being-guilty as a being-in-arrears; as a situation 'in' which one *sometimes* finds oneself.[47] This interpretation suggests the possibility of neutralizing the burden of debt by 'reckoning things up' or 'balancing them off.'[48] (At the very least it suggests that the occasions of one's being-guilty might be 'balanced off' against periods of innocence.) But for Heidegger Dasein's Being-guilty prohibits such compensatory moves, and this is why here 'there is no counter-discourse in which ... one talks about what the conscience has said, and pleads one's case. In hearing the call understandingly, one denies oneself any counter-discourse' (ibid.: 342).[49] In short, the primordiality of Heideggerian Guilt renders all apologetics – ontologically speaking – both impotent and inauthentic.

Now, although Heidegger problematizes any talk of 'what' Dasein's Being-guilty amounts to, he does suggest one way of approaching this question:

> Dasein is its basis existently – that is, in such a manner that it understands itself in terms of possibilities, and, as so understanding itself, is that entity which has been thrown. But this implies that in having a potentiality-for-Being it always stands in one possibility or another: it constantly is *not* other possibilities, and it has waived these in its existentiell projection ... what we have here is ... something existentially constitutive ... The nullity we have in mind belongs to Dasein's Being-free for its existentiell possibilities. Freedom, however, *is* only in the choice of one possibility – that is, in tolerating one's not having chosen the others and one's not being able to choose them.
>
> (1999: 331)

This is, I believe, the key passage to understanding Heidegger's notion of Conscience and Guilt if one is to understand Levinas – and arguably Derrida too. Heidegger's general point is straightforward enough. Dasein's Being is a 'potentiality-for-Being' (ibid.: 315),[50] for in its having been 'thrown *into existence*' (ibid.: 321) Dasein 'understands itself in terms of possibilities' (ibid.: 331). However, in its pursuit of every such possibility Dasein must simultaneously exclude all *other* possibilities. In its essential finitude Dasein can only ever pursue 'one possibility or another' (ibid.), and as such its Being is inherently *sacrificial*.[51] Naturally, the dimensions of the negative side of such choices (the sacrificial 'not') are vast.[52] Dasein's Being-guilty can therefore be described in terms of the trace of all those possibilities it cannot pursue in every pursuit of *this* or *that* possibility. Hence 'a "not" ... is constitutive for [the] *Being* of Dasein' (ibid.: 330).[53] The call of Conscience can therefore be 'heard'[54] to haunt Dasein with the latter's necessarily manifold omissions.[55] And the emphasis here must (again) be placed on the *necessity* of these sacrificial omissions; that is, on their constitutive and ontological nature. For it is not as though such negativities represented mere 'privations' which could in turn be replenished without thereby excluding *other* possibilities. And this accounts for Heidegger's further suspicions regarding the common economic interpretation of both good and bad conscience.[56] For what Dasein is summoned to by the call of Conscience is to face its primordial, inescapable Being-guilty

128 *Trespassing, guilt and sacrifice*

'resolutely,'[57] and thus to resist the good conscience of the 'they' and their tendency to neutralize '"guilt and innocence"' by 'balancing them off' (ibid.: 338).

This then is how Guilt and Conscience are explained in *Being and Time*. With Heidegger's analysis in mind I now want to turn to Levinas, for here one finds many of Heidegger's basic insights at work – though negotiated rather differently. Now the emphasis lies on an ethics that, in Levinas's view, severely problematizes Heidegger's prioritization of ontology, and specifically Dasein's essential self-concern.[58]

Levinas's ghosts: trespassing and the violence of being

I referred above to Dasein's being 'haunted' by those possibilities-for-Being it necessarily excludes in every word (or silence) and deed (or inaction). This spectral metaphor becomes increasingly relevant when reading Levinas insofar as he provides an account of subjectivity that *ethicalizes* the Heideggerian 'not' discussed above. But there is another sense in which Levinas's work undergoes a certain 'haunting.'[59] As will become clear, Levinas's 'ghosts' emerge from the Nazi death camps of the 1940s.[60] But what makes this haunting so philosophically important is the specific way it transcends anything one might locate historically as 'the Holocaust' or 'Shoah.'[61] Indeed, this is why Levinas's work runs counter to any project attempting to attain '[t]houghts that are at peace' (Wittgenstein 1994a: 43).

Approaching Levinas by way of the Holocaust is not, however, to take interpretative liberties. For Levinas himself acknowledges that the 'explicitly Jewish moment' in his thought is indeed 'the reference to Auschwitz, where God let the Nazis do what they wanted.' He proceeds:

> Consequently, what remains? Either this means that there is no reason for morality and hence it can be concluded that everyone should act like the Nazis, or the moral law maintains its authority. Here is freedom; this choice is the moment of freedom ... before the twentieth century, all religion begins with the promise. It begins with the 'Happy End'. It is the promise of heaven. Well then, doesn't a phenomenon like Auschwitz invite you, on the contrary, to think the moral law independently of the Happy End? That is the question ... The essential problem is: can we speak of an absolute commandment after Auschwitz? Can we speak of morality after the failure of morality?
>
> (1988a: 175)[62]

Levinas's personal history would be significant here were my objective to provide a biographical reconstruction of his thinking.[63] But what I want to highlight are those recurrent themes within Levinas's philosophy that demand to be read alongside what we can begin to know and imagine of the horror of the Nazi death camps. Of specific interest here is Levinas's

Trespassing, guilt and sacrifice 129

repeated emphasis on the 'trespassing'[64] nature of being-in-the-world; that *in my very being* I thereby take the place of (or sacrifice) *another*. One can begin to trace this theme in the following confessional remarks:

> No one has forgotten the Holocaust, it's impossible to forget things which belong to the most immediate and most personal memory of every one of us, and pertaining to those closest to us, who sometimes make us feel guilty for surviving.
> (Levinas 1996b: 291)

Most striking here is Levinas's reference to feeling 'guilty for surviving'[65] – a sentiment repeated elsewhere and which Derrida has also recently noted.[66] While the experience of 'survivor's guilt' is (psychologically speaking) of common heritage, this remark is illuminating when reading Levinas's philosophy.[67] For it is a distinct rhetoric he employs when describing being-in-the-world as an 'exclusion' or 'exiling' (1996b: 82) of another human being.[68] Thus, Levinas asserts: 'This is in fact the question one must ultimately pose. Should I be dedicated to being? By being, by persisting in being, do I not kill?' (1992: 120). He proceeds elsewhere:

> Language is born in responsibility. One has to speak, to say I, to be in the first person, precisely to be me . . . But from that point, in affirming this me being, one has to respond to one's right to be . . . My being-in-the-world or my 'place in the sun', my being at home, have these not also been the usurpation of spaces belonging to the other man whom I have already oppressed or starved, or driven out into a third world; are they not acts of repulsing, excluding, exiling, stripping, killing? . . . A fear for all the violence and murder my existing might generate . . . It is the fear of occupying someone else's place . . .
> (1996b: 82)[69]

That Levinas here has *Being and Time* in mind becomes clear when he re-casts this general point as follows:

> The self is the very crisis of the being of beings in the human . . . because I myself already ask myself if my being is justified, if the *Da* of my *Dasein* is not already the usurpation of someone's place. A bad conscience which comes to me from the face of the other who, in his mortality, uproots me from the solid ground where, as a simple individual, I stand and persevere naively – naturally – in my stance. A bad conscience which puts me in question.
> (1998b: 148)[70]

This 'bad conscience' resulting from my being 'accused' for my 'very presence' (1999: 21) is not therefore to be understood in wholly Heideggerian

130 *Trespassing, guilt and sacrifice*

terms. For my being-in-the-world is *already* my 'being-in-question' (ibid.).[71] Thus, when Pascal suggests that 'the primitive model for the usurpation of the whole earth' lies in the naive and natural exclamation 'this is my place in the sun' (1961: §231),[72] Levinas adds that it is to this extreme point that 'Pascal's "the *I* is hateful" must be thought through' (1999: 22).[73] Indeed, it is in this way that 'the subjective' is irrevocably 'knotted in ethics' (1992: 95), for, as Caputo rightly notes, Levinas has 'installed bad conscience as a kind of structural feature of ethical life' (2000: 116).[74]

This is only a preliminary sample of such murderous reflections in Levinas's work, but it provides enough of a backdrop against which to read more confessional Holocaust writers. Thus, in *The Drowned and the Saved*, Levi similarly laments:

> [A]lmost everybody feels guilty of having omitted to offer help. The presence at your side of a companion who is weaker ... or too young, hounding you with his demands for help or with his simply being there, which is itself an entreaty, is a constant in the life of the Lager. The demand for ... a human word, advice, even only a listening ear, was permanent and universal but rarely satisfied.
>
> (1998: 59)[75]

He then proceeds to interrogate himself:

> Are you ashamed because you are alive in place of another? And in particular, of a man more generous, more sensitive, wiser, more useful, more worthy of living than you? You cannot exclude this: you examine yourself, you review your memories, hoping to find ... that none of them are masked or disguised; no, you find no obvious transgressions, you did not usurp anyone's place, you did not beat anyone ... you did not steal anyone's bread; nevertheless, you cannot exclude it. It is no more than a suspicion, indeed the shadow of a suspicion; that everyone is his brother's Cain, that everyone of us ... has usurped his neighbour's place and lived in his stead. It is a suspicion, but it gnaws at us ... [that] I might be alive in the place of another, at the expense of another; I might have usurped, that is, in fact killed.
>
> (1998: 62)[76]

The concurrence between Levi's rhetoric[77] and Levinas's own becomes even more striking when the latter speaks of being held 'hostage' (1996a: 91) and 'persecuted' (ibid.: 89)[78] by the other, of my 'occupying someone else's place,' my 'usurpation of spaces belonging to the other man,' my 'repulsing ... stripping, killing' (1996b: 82) and 'despoiling' (1999: 23) another, and not least in his numerous references to the neighbor as 'exposed' (1993: 94), 'defenseless' (ibid.: 158), 'destitute' (1996c: 75), 'impoverished' (1992: 86), 'frail' (1988a: 170), 'vulnerable' (1996a: 102) and 'naked' (1993: 102).[79] This deliberately shocking vocabulary is not, however, *mere* rhetoric.[80] Rather, it is employed to remind us that even the most peaceable life is possible *as such* only to the extent that it is *also* sacrificial and murderous. In this terrifying thought – in this 'shadow of a suspicion' as Levi puts it – it would be negligent not to hear resonances of the daily realities of Auschwitz, Treblinka and the life of the Lager as Levi and others describe it.[81]

Before leaving Levi's work, I want to draw attention to a specific passage from *If This is a Man*. There we are told of those new prisoners who 'through basic incapacity, or by misfortune, or through some banal incident ... are overcome before they can adapt themselves' to the harsh realities of the Lager, that '[t]heir life is short, but their number is endless; they ... the drowned, form the backbone of the camp, an anonymous mass ... of non-men who march and labor in silence.' Levi then confesses: 'They crowd my memory with their faceless presences, and if I could enclose all the evil of our time in one image, I would choose this image' (1996: 96).[82] Such 'imagery' played an important part in my discussion of Wittgenstein in Chapter 3, and specifically of how the body and face can be described as 'a moral space' or 'the locus of ... the basis of moral life' (Tilghman 1991: 115). The face *imposes* ethical questions on us,[83] and Wittgenstein's work goes some way toward bearing witness to this primitive fact. However, it is in the unique way that the face haunts Levinas's thinking that we discover more explicit connections between the face, Guilt and responsibility. Although Levinas's reflections on the face are complex – and will therefore take up part of the next chapter – in order to see how his analyses supplement Wittgenstein's, it is to this 'image' that I will now turn.

Guilt and the grammar of the face

While it would not be wholly inaccurate to describe Levinas's reflections on the face[84] as phenomenological (not least because he always saw himself indebted to that tradition[85]), his relationship with phenomenology is tense. For one of his main objectives is to highlight the inadequacies of how Western thought, culminating in the work of Husserl and Heidegger, has construed intersubjectivity.[86] Levinas is uncomfortable speaking of a phenomenology of the face since 'phenomenology describes what appears' (1992: 85) and 'the face is special' insofar as it transcends 'an exact phenomenological description.' At the very most such an analysis would be 'negative' (1988a: 168). In other words, Levinas suspects that the face cannot be understood as 'a phenomenon,' for appearance is not its primary 'mode of being' (ibid.: 171).[87] A straightforward phenomenology is problematic here in much the same way as a spatial-geometrical account of the face was inadequate for Wittgenstein.[88] As I discussed in Chapter 3, the ethical significance of the face is due to its being saturated with

132   *Trespassing, guilt and sacrifice*

meaning from the start.[89] With this Levinas would agree – indeed, Wittgenstein's insistence that here one does not 'make inferences' (1990: §225) parallels Levinas's own claim that what the face expresses 'is not just a thought which animates the other; it is also the other present in that thought,' for the 'expression does not speak about someone, is not information about a coexistence, does not invoke an attitude in addition to knowledge ... Expression is ... the archetype of direct relationship' (1987: 21).[90] For both philosophers then, the face is not primarily an object of comprehension toward which consciousness is coolly directed.[91] Rather, as Levinas puts it: 'access to the face is straightaway ethical' (1992: 85).[92] The face does not wait to be deciphered as a collection of distinguishing features, for it is not 'the mere assemblage of a nose, a forehead, eyes, etc.; it is all that, of course, but takes on the meaning of a face through the new dimension it opens up in the perception of a being' (1997a: 8),[93] and this is why 'the word *face* must not be understood in a narrow way' (1998b: 231). Levinas summarizes: 'The best way of encountering the Other is not even to notice the color of his eyes! When one observes the color of the eyes one is not in social relationship with the Other' (1992: 85).[94] Levinas's treatment of the face thus not only parallels Wittgenstein's own, it also deepens the former's more general attempt to question the traditional philosophical prioritization of knowledge over responsibility (or ontology over ethics).[95] Still, in order to situate Levinas's account of the face within this broader critical enterprise I would like to draw on some phenomenological observations Wittgenstein makes in *Zettel*. Although these passages refer to the face (specifically the eyes), my initial interest here is methodological – that is, with Levinas's broader suspicion of visual metaphors and his subsequent tendency to describe the face in auditory terms.

In *Zettel* Wittgenstein writes:

> We do not see the human eye as a receiver, it appears not to let anything in, but to send something out. The ear receives; the eye looks. (It casts glances, it flashes, radiates, gleams.) One can terrify with one's eyes, not with one's ear or nose. When you see the eye you see something going out from it. You see the look in the eye.
>
> (1990: §222)

> (I have never yet read a comment on the fact that when one shuts one eye and 'only sees with one eye' one does not simultaneously see darkness (blackness) with the one that is shut.)
>
> (1990: §615)

When one encounters the other's face, her eyes are not entirely passive; one experiences 'the look in the [other's] eye.'[96] (As will become clear later, a central part of Levinas's own work is to elucidate the ethical meaning of this 'look.') But what these passages highlight is the wider function of the ocular in Levinas's work.[97] For while Levinas must – despite his protestations[98] – rely upon visual metaphors simply in virtue of his emphasis on the *face* (a face that is both 'what is *seen* ... and also that which sees' (Derrida 1997c: 98)) it becomes apparent that this same metaphor motivates his criticism of philosophy's *misrepresentation* of the other. According to Wittgenstein, the eye might be said to be ravenous for the world in a way that the ear (or nose) is not,[99] and this is why 'one does not simultaneously see darkness' when one eye is closed. This broadly phenomenological point corresponds to Levinas's general characterization of philosophy from 'Aristotle to Heidegger' (1996c: 189) as a similarly insatiable enterprise committed to a knowledge that seeks the systematic 'assimilation' (1992: 60) of the world to understanding.[100] As Derrida summarizes, for Levinas philosophy's quest for 'inhuman universality' (1997c: 97) represents an attempt to 'bring the other back into the midst of the same' (ibid.: 96) and is thus 'in its meaning and at bottom' (ibid.: 91) an 'imperialism' (ibid.: 84)[101] or 'totalitarianism' (ibid.: 91) – indeed, traditional philosophies are 'summoned' by Levinas to 'transpose themselves into [his] language by confessing their violent aims' (ibid.: 97). To this extent Levinas engages in a deliberate act of synesthesia as his work moves toward an increasingly auditory characterization of a face that *speaks*, *accuses* and *commands*.[102] Levinas emphasizes this because the visual metaphor harbors precisely those dangers he thinks should be guarded against; namely, the assimilation of what is 'other' to ontological-epistemological categories.[103] In short, while sight is perhaps the most voracious of senses,[104] hearing is markedly more passive[105] and vulnerable – themes central to Levinas's thinking.[106]

These points may seem to be only of general methodological interest. However, if we keep this synesthetic movement in mind the significance of Levinas's characterization of the other's face (and specifically the 'language of the eyes' (1996c: 66)) as the 'meaning prior' (1998a: 13) to language that embodies the commandment '"Thou shalt not kill ... "' (1992: 89) becomes clearer. In Levinas we find numerous remarks pertaining to the face as 'an order issued to me not to abandon the other' (1993: 44), as 'the categorical imperative' (ibid.: 158), and likewise as not being 'offered to serene perception' but rather as 'summoning' or 'recalling' me 'to a responsibility I incurred in no previous experience' (ibid.: 93–4).[107] And it is precisely this 'active' dimension of the face that lies at the heart of Levinas's rejection of a purely empirical exegesis thereof (thus deepening the ethical significance of Wittgenstein's aforementioned observations on the 'look' (1990: §222)). The central point here is that, while the face 'presents' itself to me, insofar as I am thereby also *faced* by the face,[108] its meaning transcends what would otherwise be a pure plasticity.[109] As Harvey notes: '*le visage* is not translatable into English as simply "the face" without a violent ... reduction of its meaning.' Rather, '[*l*]*e visage* is "a facing" more precisely; it is an opening of the face and is therefore

134 *Trespassing, guilt and sacrifice*

expression as well as face as such' (1986: 171). Although inanimate objects might be said to 'face' me, the manner in which the other's *face* 'faces' me is unique. But Levinas develops this in a rather specific way: 'The face is exposed, menaced, as if inviting us to an act of violence. At the same time, the face is what forbids us to kill' (1992: 86):

> The first word of the face is the 'Thou shalt not kill.' It is an order. There is a commandment in the appearance of the face, as if a master spoke to me. However, at the same time, the face of the Other is destitute; it is the poor for whom I can do all and to whom I owe all.
> (Levinas 1992: 89)[110]

This seems to complicate matters insofar as the face is here presented as both masterful *and* impoverished; both forbidding *and* inviting violence.[111] Indeed, Levinas acknowledges 'these two strange things in the face: its extreme frailty – the fact of being without means and, on the other hand, there is authority' (1988a: 169).[112] This characterization thus suggests strength[113] and weakness simultaneously;[114] the authority of a commanding position of 'height' (1996a: 12)[115] which is also a pleading.[116] For 'in its expression, in its morality, the face before me summons me, calls for me, begs for me ... and in doing so recalls my responsibility, and calls me into question' (1996b: 83).[117] But this dual emphasis is not as paradoxical as it might first appear. The wailing of a young child (for example) might be described as simultaneously an appeal *and* a demand.[118] (Likewise, the exclamation 'Do not kill me!' can be simultaneously an entreaty *and* commandment for mercy – if not also a counter-threat.[119]) According to Levinas then, the face of the other 'calls me into question' through the 'extreme exposure'[120] of her inherent 'defenselessness, vulnerability' (1998b: 145),[121] 'dereliction,' 'timidity' (1996a: 69), 'destitution,'[122] 'poverty' (1992: 86), 'nakedness' (1993: 102),[123] 'loneliness' (ibid.: 158), 'decomposition,'[124] 'frailty,'[125] 'original frankness' (1996d: 95), and shivering 'nudity' (1996a: 54). That is, the authority of the face and its capacity for 'awakening and sobering [me] up' (1998b: 114)[126] lies precisely in its *fragility*.[127]

From these reflections Levinas argues that the other's face challenges the particular 'I'[128] as it has variously been construed by Western thought, including Heidegger's Dasein.[129] On Levinas's view all such characterizations participate in a fundamental spirit of egocentrism – what might be called a domestication of the 'foreigner.' Philosophy's treatment of the other human[130] thus represents simultaneously the most important and lamentable instance of its broader 'assimilating'[131] trajectory toward 'a reduction of all experience ... to a totality wherein consciousness embraces the world, leaves nothing other outside of itself' (1992: 75).[132] According to Levinas, the 'I' has been construed primarily in terms of self-presence or self-coincidence (what he refers to as the 'haughty priority of the A *is* A' (1998a: 174)), where any relation to others is seen to form a

Trespassing, guilt and sacrifice 135

secondary, derivative layer to this prior 'egotism of the *I*' (1998b: 189).[133] From this perspective others are essentially another species of object (albeit a particularly interesting sort) to be known, and are thereby approachable only insofar as they reflect oneself, one's interests, potentialities-for-being, and so on.[134] In other words, philosophy has treated the social relation as being either structurally symmetrical and reciprocal,[135] or dissymmetrically weighted on the side of the ego.

Much of what I said above concerning the 'authority' of the face is relevant here. For what Levinas emphasizes is the disruption[136] of the philosophical-egological account of the subject.[137] If this latter model can be characterized by its appeal to self-sufficiency and self-coincidence (a certain 'being at home with oneself' (1994a: 178)[138]) then Levinas's conception of subjectivity can, by contrast, be characterized as one of essential displacement, uneasiness and 'bad conscience' (1998a: 174).[139] What the other's face interrupts is consciousness returning safely to itself in self-consciousness, 'into an *I think*' existing primarily 'for [it]self' (1996a: 143):[140]

> [A] face imposes itself upon me without my being able to be deaf to its call or to forget it, that is, without my being able to suspend my responsibility for its distress. Consciousness loses its first place ... Consciousness is called into question by the face ... Visitation consists in overwhelming the very egoism of the I ... A face confounds the intentionality that aims at it ... The I loses its sovereign self-coincidence, its identification, in which consciousness returns triumphantly to itself to rest on itself. Before the exigency of the Other ... the I is expelled from this rest ...
>
> (Levinas 1996a: 54)[141]

Levinas proceeds elsewhere:

> As soon as I acknowledge that it is 'I' who am responsible, I accept that my freedom is anteceded by an obligation to the other. Ethics redefines subjectivity as this heteronymous responsibility in contrast to autonomous freedom. Even if I deny my primordial responsibility to the other by affirming my own freedom as primary, I can never escape the fact that the other has demanded a response from me *before* I affirm my freedom not to respond to his demand.
>
> (1984: 63)[142]

Although *my* exclusion of the *other* is here couched in a violent terminology (and could indeed be understood as the originary condition of all violence) it would be mistaken to read such passages as representing the *ethical* relation as something essentially savage[143] or tragic.[144] It would, for example, be mistaken to here join Baudelaire and lament 'the tyranny of the human face' (1996: 53). Such a Sartrean[145] gloss would miss Levinas's point that there is no pre-existent 'I' *to which* this disruption 'happens.' Only if this were the case would the vocabulary of violence (or tragedy) be appropriate, for only then would an existential nostalgia be possible:[146]

> [T]he responsibility for the other ... is the contracting of an ego, going to the hither side of identity – identity gnawing away at itself – in a remorse. Responsibility for another is not an accident that happens to a subject, but precedes essence in it, has not awaited freedom, in which a commitment to another would have been made. I have not done anything and I have always been under accusation – persecuted.
> (Levinas 1994a: 114)[147]

That the face 'calls me into question' is thus not the clearest way for Levinas to express himself, as this does seem to imply a prior 'me' *to which* being 'called into question' *happens*.[148] Levinas provides a better formulation when he remarks: 'One comes not into the world but into question' (1996b: 81),[149] and similarly: 'Responsibility ... is not a simple attribute of subjectivity, as if the latter already existed in itself, before the ethical relationship. Subjectivity is not for itself; it is ... initially for another' (1992: 96).[150] The 'I' is thus actually 'defined' in its exposure to another human being, for the 'ethical I is a being who asks if he has a right to be!, who excuses himself to the other for his own existence' (1984: 62–3).[151]

Earlier I discussed Wittgenstein's remark to Drury that there was 'a sense in which' they were 'both Christians' (Drury 1981: 130). Although I will return to this in Chapter 7, it is here worth noting that Derrida similarly recalls Levinas once describe himself as being (in some sense) 'Catholic'; a remark that would 'call for long and serious reflection' (Derrida 1996c: 9). It is reasonable to suppose that this meditation would involve Derrida considering the place of Guilt (and perhaps confession) in Levinas's work.[152] But I allude to Levinas's 'Catholicism' because his treatment of Guilt, though rarely named as such, requires careful negotiation.[153] As previously suggested, Levinas does not seek atonement or liberation from his 'ghosts,' and thus his preoccupation with Guilt is, contrary to the intimation above, emphatically *not* that of Catholic orthodoxy, or of Christian theology more generally.[154] Although both Catholic and Levinasian Guilt recast the self as ethically burdened, for Levinas this burden is not merely of ancient origin, but *immemorial*. That is, the Guilt around which Levinas's thought revolves remains Heideggerian insofar as it does not first emerge through *specific* acts or omissions perpetrated. Neither can it be subsumed under the rubric of 'original sin' or any other archaic inheritance.[155] For although the mark of original sin in its various Christian formulations may cut deep into human nature, insofar as this notion maintains an origin – and thereby the potential for nostalgia – it simultaneously remains tethered to the possibility of reparation, salvation and eventual good conscience.[156] But it is precisely this 'promise ... of the "Happy End"' (1988a: 175) or of 'divine pardon' (1998b: 18) that the face of the other calls into question. In 'the augmentation of guilt,' Levinas thus remarks, 'there is no rest for the self' (1996a: 144):

> Conscience welcomes the Other. It is the revelation of a resistance to my powers that does not counter them as a greater force, but calls in question the naïve right of my powers, my glorious spontaneity as a living being. Morality begins when freedom, instead of being justified by itself, feels itself to be arbitrary and violent.
>
> (1996c: 84)[157]

On this account, to be 'in the first person' (1996b: 82) is *already* to be a trespasser. It is not that I am first – or potentially (even by the grace of God) – an innocent subject *upon* whom guilt and responsibility are inscribed. Rather, we must think of subjectivity as being *in its meaning* accountable to the other.[158] I am a trespasser because, simply through my being-in-the-world, I am Guilty of *taking another's place*. And it is on account of this that one must attempt to think beyond the economics of Catholic guilt to 'a debt in the *I*, older than any loan' (1998b: 227).[159] ('What is an individual if not a usurper?' Levinas further inquires, 'What is signified by the advent of conscience, and even the first spark of spirit, if not the discovery of corpses beside me and my horror of existing by assassination?' (1997a: 100).[160]) In short, I occupy a site that can only be conceived as 'rightfully mine' by indulging in what Derrida calls the 'scandal ... [of] good conscience' (1999: 67).[161] Thus, contrary to the Heideggerian account, my primordial Guilt is not to be understood in terms of the necessary exclusion of my *own* latent possibilities, but in terms of my exclusion of an *other*. For Levinas my responsibility is therefore due to a certain play of absences of those others denied such a place by *my-being-here*. My existence might therefore be described as 'differentially constituted'[162] insofar as it carries along with it a 'trace' of the other whose 'place' (1996b: 82) I continually occupy.[163] And it is with this 'irremissible guilt with regard to the neighbor' (1994a: 109) in mind that the 'I' can be said to be 'constituted by a certain work of mourning' (Derrida 1997a: 14).[164]

Even with these points in mind, it is easy to misconstrue Levinas's position. For there are times when he appears to advocate little more than a distributive justice; as when, for example, he remarks of the face's command 'Thou shalt not kill':

> This does not mean simply that you are not to go around firing a gun all the time. It refers, rather, to the fact that, in the course of your life, in different ways, you kill someone. For example, when we sit down at the table in the morning and drink coffee, we kill an Ethiopian who

138 *Trespassing, guilt and sacrifice*

doesn't have any coffee. It is in this sense that the commandment must be understood.

(1988a: 173)[165]

Here we might hear an echo of Rousseau's *Discourse on the Origin of Inequality*.[166] Reading Levinas in this way would, however, lead to misunderstandings. For while the development of a Levinasian politics (assuming such a thing is conceivable[167]) may naturally take this trajectory, Levinas's position is neither reducible to a 'scarcity argument' nor a straightforward rebuttal of the 'acts and omissions' distinction. For one should again recall: *my* responsibility for *you* does not spring from, and is not simply proportionate to, our relative material assets or 'proprietorship' (Rousseau 1930: 220). Rather, my asymmetrical responsibility *precedes* the responsibilities arising from such material inequalities.[168] I am responsible, not in virtue of what I *have* or can *do*, but in virtue of the fact *that I am*.[169] In the concluding part of this chapter I want to bring these points together by: (1) demarcating where the Heideggerian and Levinasian projects both intertwine and part company, and (2) explaining why Wittgenstein remains of crucial importance here.

Confessions: the singularity of guilt and ordinary experience

Like Wittgenstein's portrayal of one's being 'addressed' (1990: §717) by God, the 'calls' of both Heideggerian Conscience and the Levinasian other have authority due to their capacity to summon and accuse the 'I' in its particularity.[170] Both 'calls' resist thematization into a simple informational content and manifest themselves as an interruption of the subject in its various states of good conscience, tearing it out of its domestic and cultural retreats.[171] On this the Heideggerian and Levinasian projects are in broad agreement. However, they differ on the specific nature and source of this 'call.' While for Heidegger the call constitutes an appeal that summons Dasein *to itself*, for Levinas it is the *other* who calls me – even, as Levi puts it, by 'his simply being there' (1998: 59). Likewise, on Heidegger's account, the call's interruption of good conscience is primarily the interruption of Dasein's lostness in the anonymous inauthenticity of the 'they.' But, according to Levinas, Dasein's aspiration for resolute self-sufficiency does not escape the other's accusation. It is not the good conscience of the 'they' that primarily concerns Levinas but rather the subject's attempted withdrawal into the '"nobility," [and] proud virility' (1998b: 226) of its own authentic relation to Being[172] (a relation that, Levinas reminds us, is not primarily concerned either with its 'owing anything to anyone' (ibid.) or 'giving, feeding the hungry and clothing the naked' (ibid.: 116)). Although Heidegger characterizes Dasein as fundamentally '"not-at-home"' (1999: 321)[173] in its thrownness,[174] what distinguishes the Levinasian subject from Dasein is that, in the latter, this primordial 'anxiety'[175] concerns 'its ownmost potentiality-for-Being' (ibid.). In its finitude Dasein is never able to achieve full authenticity,[176] but its primary concern nevertheless remains (or ought to remain) with the project of authenticity. Because Heidegger's analyses are therefore essentially egological,[177] Levinas seeks to uncover the 'bad conscience that is not the finiteness of existing signified in [Heideggerian] anguish' (1999: 28).[178]

On the question of Guilt similar points of convergence and divergence emerge between Heidegger and Levinas. Both resist a more judicial-economic understanding, and instead stress the primordiality and singularity of a Guilt that both precedes any particular act or omission and also identifies *me alone* as responsible. Primordial Guilt is not something that befalls a pre-existent 'I' by virtue of specific crimes or misdemeanors. Rather, it is constitutive of one's very being-in-the-world; to be an 'I' is *already* to be Guilty. But it is the nature of this 'being-in-the-world' that again indicates the difference between Heidegger and Levinas. For the former, Being-in-the-world is essentially a Being-before-Dasein's-own-potentialities. I am (as Dasein) primordially Guilty face-to-face with *myself,* and specifically with my 'ownmost potentiality-for-Being' (1999: 321). For Levinas, however, the 'I' is Guilty face-to-face with the *other* who reminds it of the murderousness of its very being.[179] Finally, Heidegger's emphasis on the 'nullity' or 'not' (ibid.: 331) constitutive of Dasein's Being is taken up by Levinas (and Derrida) and given a distinctly ethical twist. Although I will turn more explicitly to Derrida in Chapter 8, it is here worth citing one particularly striking reformulation of Heidegger's 'not.' In *The Gift of Death* Derrida writes:

> The absoluteness of duty and of responsibility ... calls for a betrayal of everything that manifests itself within the order of universal generality ... In a word, ethics must be sacrificed in the name of duty ... What the knights of good conscience don't realize, is that 'the sacrifice of Isaac' illustrates ... the most common and everyday experiences of responsibility. The story is no doubt monstrous, outrageous, barely conceivable ... But isn't this also the most common thing?
> (1995b: 66–7)

In other words: 'what binds me thus in my singularity to the absolute singularity of the other, immediately propels me into the space or risk of absolute sacrifice' because there are 'innumerable' *other* others 'to whom I should be bound by the same responsibility' (ibid.: 68). What Derrida is highlighting here is that in any response to the 'call' of *this* other (here, facing me) I necessarily sacrifice countless *other* others. That is, 'I always betray someone to be just; I always betray one for the other, I perjure myself like I breathe' (2001b: 49):[180]

By preferring my work, simply by giving it my time and attention, by preferring my activity as a citizen or as a ... philosopher, writing and speaking here in a public language ... I am perhaps fulfilling my duty. But I am sacrificing and betraying at every moment all my other obligations: my obligations to the other others whom I know or don't know, the billions of ... my fellows who are dying of starvation or sickness ... to those who don't speak my language ... to those I love in private, my own, my family, my son, each of whom is the only son I sacrifice to the other, every one being sacrificed to every one else in this land of Moriah that is our habitat every second of every day.

(1995b: 69)[181]

The trace of Heidegger here is relatively transparent (certainly it is more difficult to locate anything in Levinas's work that echoes Heidegger so conspicuously). Nevertheless, the essential point is that for both Derrida and Levinas it is not the necessary exclusion of my *own* possibilities that is of primary importance but rather the necessary exclusion of the *other* other (in even the most generous, hospitable and 'responsible' of acts) that marks my being-in-the-world as primordially Guilty.[182] It is, one might say, the very condition of possibility of my having possibilities-for-Being that I take the place of another. Although Heidegger maintains that Being-guilty is 'the existential condition for the possibility of the "morally" good and for the "morally" evil – that is, for morality in general' he quickly adds that this 'primordial "Being-guilty" cannot be defined by morality, since morality already presupposes it for itself' (1999: 332).[183] According to Heidegger then, insofar as Dasein is first Guilty *before itself*, morality is a subsidiary issue.[184] For Levinas, however, given that I am first Guilty *before the other*, ethics has philosophical primacy: 'In the responsibility for the other person, my being calls for justification' because the '*Da* of *Dasein* is already an ethical problem' (1993: 48).[185] If Heidegger's Dasein can be said to be haunted by the trace of its *own* excluded possibilities-for-Being, then for Levinas (and Derrida) it is the trace of the excluded *other* who haunts the subject's Being-in-the-world.[186]

In his refusal to offer an 'optimistic philosophy for the end of history' (ibid.: 114), Levinas's is indeed an 'austere doctrine' (1997a: 20) – if not in some sense 'masochistic' (2001: 46). There is no Pyrrhonian *ataraxia* in this conception of ethics, and no safe haven (not even the domestic home, as we will see in Chapter 8) in which to shield oneself from the other. And yet Levinas's work does not appear excessively dark or brooding. His overt rejection of the religious-eschatological assurance of the 'Happy End'[187] is not then *mere* renunciation or protest. From a life scarred by the Nazi horror, and a philosophy continually haunted by the countenance of the other,[188] Levinas finds something affirmative to say: I am primarily *for*-the-other. Indeed, were this otherwise then there would be no goodness in

Trespassing, guilt and sacrifice 141

the world, not even the everyday 'after you.'[189] All this is doubtless 'not pleasant' or 'enjoyable, but it is "good"' (2001: 135).

Earlier I highlighted those passages in Wittgenstein's writings that gesture toward a notion of responsibility beyond the traditional moral principle that 'ought implies can.'[190] Wittgenstein never systematically works through these ideas – although certain biographical facts[191] are relevant here. Due to this insufficiency in Wittgenstein's work I turned to the Heideggerian and Levinasian analyses of Guilt, indicating where these respective projects both intersect and diverge. What I would finally like to suggest is how a more Wittgensteinian approach might be developed to integrate with both the analysis of Guilt provided in Heidegger's 'fundamental ontology,' and the sense of 'bad conscience' motivating Levinas's ethics. This is important because, while Levinas does occasionally allude to 'everyday' phenomena in an affirmative manner[192] (the aforementioned 'after you' being perhaps the most notable example), his more general attitude echoes Heidegger's own suspicion of 'ordinary' language and 'everyday' concepts.

In *Robinson Crusoe* (a text to which Levinas refers on a number of occasions[193]) Defoe tells us of the protagonist's thoughts of suicide upon finding himself to be the sole survivor of a shipwreck. Tortured by feelings of both relief (for himself) and remorse (for his companions) Crusoe reproves his 'pensive' state as follows:

> Well, you are in a desolate condition, 'tis true, but pray remember, where are the rest of you? Did not you come eleven of you into the boat? where are the ten? Why were they not saved and you lost? Why were you singled out? Is it better to be here or there? and then I pointed to the sea. All evils are to be considered with the good that is in them.
>
> (Defoe 1985: 80)

In this way Crusoe keeps a tight rein on his 'melancholy' (ibid.: 81). Mindful of Crusoe's predicament, Levinas's reading of Genesis 4:9 becomes pertinent:

> [W]hen someone says to [Cain]: 'Where is your brother?' He answers: 'Am I my brother's keeper?' ... We must not take Cain's answer as if he were mocking God or as if he were answering as a little boy: 'It isn't me, it's the other one.' Cain's answer is sincere. Ethics is the only thing lacking in his answer; there is only ontology: I am I, and he is he.
>
> (1998b: 110)[194]

Insofar as the others' deaths haunt Crusoe's own survival, his pragmatism is (ontologically speaking) perfectly *reasonable*[195] – after all, what third party would contest his motives? Analogously, Cain's response to God is hardly exceptional: Abel is not an infant requiring constant supervision. Still, the responses of Crusoe and Cain are by no means inevitable; that 'there is only ontology' here is not, as it were, predetermined. Such pragmatism is, for example, lacking in Rousseau's *The Confessions*. There we are told how, upon his father's homecoming from Constantinople, Rousseau himself became 'the unhappy fruit of his return.' An 'unhappy fruit,' not merely due to his being a 'poor and sickly child' who was 'almost born dead,' but specifically because this birth 'cost [Rousseau's] mother her life':

> I never knew how my father stood up to his loss, but I know that he never got over it. He seemed to see her again in me, but could never forget that I had robbed him of her; he never kissed me that I did not know by his sighs and his convulsive embrace that there was a bitter grief mingled with his affection ... When he said to me, 'Jean-Jacques, let us talk of your mother,' I would reply: 'Very well, father, but we are sure to cry.' 'Ah,' he would say with a groan; 'Give her back to me, console me for her, fill the void she has left in my heart! Should I love you so if you were not more to me than a son?'
>
> (1953: 19)[196]

Rousseau thus proceeds to describe his birth as 'the first of my misfortunes,' later pardoning his principal carers for 'causing me to live' (ibid.). Doubtless one could speculate on the relationship between this and Rousseau's soon-discovered masochism[197] (if not also between this masochism and his desire to make his 'soul transparent' (ibid.: 169)[198] and lay himself entirely 'open to human malice' (ibid.: 65) in *The Confessions* itself). But what these passages also highlight is, again, an experience of guilt that disrupts the customary precepts of moral culpability. What then is one to make of Rousseau's ghosts? Are they only of biographical (or pathological) significance?

With these examples in mind it is notable that, in his commentary on Heidegger, Kellner should berate moral philosophy for being 'merely prescriptive or emotive, confessional (or trivial, apologetic, and conformist, as in the case of much "ordinary language" ethics)' (1992: 207). What Kellner is presumably attacking here is the reparative nature of ethical theory, and specifically its preoccupation with an essentially economic understanding of guilt.[199] But does this appraisal do justice, not so much to moral philosophy but more particularly to the 'ordinary language' Heidegger[200] (and Levinas[201]) treats so disparagingly? Or might there be a certain 'grammar' of guilt that would account for Rousseau's experience and also bear witness to precisely those characteristics of Guilt emphasized by Heidegger and Levinas? What is at stake here is the assumption that the 'ordinary' understanding of guilt is inherently deficient, and that a proper conception would demand an entirely 'new vocabulary' (ibid.: 209). Such skepticism is, I believe, both misplaced and liable to blind philosophers sympathetic to Heidegger and/or Levinas to features of 'everyday' discourse that actually substantiate their own objectives. I will now explain how.

Gaita recalls a specific episode of the documentary series *The World at War* where a Dutchwoman was interviewed about the Nazi death camps:

> She had given shelter to three Jews fleeing the Nazis, but after some days she asked them to leave because she was involved in a plot to assassinate Hitler and judged that it would be at risk if she were caught sheltering Jews. The three were caught within days of leaving her house and murdered in a concentration camp. She said Hitler had made a murderess of her.
>
> (1991: 43)

Although the woman clearly 'was not a murderer: no court would judge her to be that ... no one could seriously say to her, nor even of her, that she was, morally speaking, a murderess' (ibid.), it is nevertheless meaningful for her to feel remorse for her actions.[202] Gaita thus rightly concludes that it is the 'tendency to connect moral responsibility too tightly to culpability' that 'leads to a moralistic distortion in much contemporary discussion of moral responsibility' (ibid.: 44).[203] A similar example of this occurs toward the end of Spielberg's *Schindler's List*. There, the morally ambiguous figure of Schindler realizes that, despite his contribution to the safekeeping of 'his' Jews, he could nevertheless have done *so much more*. The 'Schindler Jews' attempt to curb what seems to them a perversely harsh self-condemnation (earlier, Schindler is assured that what he was doing was an 'absolute good'). But for Schindler this provides little solace as he continues to interrogate himself regarding how many *more* lives could have been saved had his lifestyle during the war been less opulent – despite the fact that it was precisely this opulence that had enabled him to safeguard 'his' Jews in the first place. Both the Dutchwoman and Schindler thus bear witness to a remorseful guilt that no third party could ever seriously endorse. In short, theirs is a guilt marked by its 'radical singularity.'[204] As Gaita puts it, whatever reassurances are offered by others, it 'should be no consolation if what we did was also done by the best of people' (ibid.: 49), for 'there can be only corrupt consolation in the knowledge that others are guilty as we are' (ibid.: 47). A final example from Wittgenstein's own life illustrates the point well. In the 1930s Wittgenstein delivered a 'confession of sins' to a number of friends.[205] One of those recipients, Fania Pascal, has since confessed her own 'feeling of guilt' (1996: 45) for her 'coldness and for being at a loss what to say' (ibid.: 49) in response. After contemplating the possible reasons for Wittgenstein's confession she proceeds: 'These are idle speculations. Yet the question seems relevant:

144 *Trespassing, guilt and sacrifice*

should he not have realized that many people live with a constant feeling of guilt?' (ibid.: 49–50). What is interesting about Pascal's question is how, having suggested that *Wittgenstein's* confession was unnecessary because 'many people live with a constant feeling of guilt,' she does not excuse *her own* confession and guilt in the same way. Why? Because while it may be perfectly natural and justifiable to say to the *other* 'Take comfort; *you* do not need to confess. After all, we are *all* similarly guilty,' to console *oneself* with such sentiments could only reveal an indecent and questionable presumptuousness.[206] Recalling Dostoyevsky's remarks in *The Brothers Karamazov*, while I might concede that 'every one of us is responsible for everyone else in every way,' this is not to say that such responsibility divides equally amongst us: *I* may still be guilty 'most of all' (1967: 339). In Heidegger's terms, what is being resisted by the Dutchwoman, Schindler and Pascal is the possibility of falling into the good conscience of the 'we'; of saying '"I am good"' (1999: 338) because 'they' assure me so.[207] Here too, then, guilt functions outside the rules that, according to Heidegger and Levinas, govern the 'everyday,' reparative model. But although their characterization may fit a certain legal-judicial model of guilt, it is unlikely *that* model adequately represents how *moral* guilt functions 'ordinarily' (ibid.: 314). In other words, it is unclear that this 'radical singularity' or 'mineness'[208] is not already inscribed into the grammar of moral guilt. If this is correct then Guilt does not need a 'new vocabulary' (Kellner 1992: 209). Rather, what is required is more attentiveness regarding our 'ordinary' language – a language that is often quite 'extraordinary' (Derrida 2000a: 415).[209]

Although the previous examples dramatize my main point, their lesson is by no means exceptional. Indeed, such phenomena are so commonplace we often fail to notice them.[210] It is not unusual to feel guilty for having done or said something (or omitted to do so) to someone who is now long since dead.[211] This guilt might persist beyond any possible reparation, haunting us for the rest of our lives[212] – even though, as others remind us, the offended party did not die with any sort of grudge. Indeed, the offence in question might itself be spectral, having been explicitly forgiven long before the other's demise. One might, for example, feel an unshakeable guilt for having omitted to tell a partner 'I love you' on the morning of their death – a morning that lacked any special reason for intimacies of this sort. With a variety of such facts others may try and console us. But *this* was the morning of their death, and no recourse to circumstantial details need ever relieve our bad conscience. Of course, this sense of guilt is prone to 'egocentric corruptions' (Gaita 1991: 52), where one adorns oneself in the garbs of guilt to wallow in self-pity or play the role of martyr.[213] In this respect the mere recognition of *bad* conscience can itself simply disguise a deeper *good* conscience.[214] Piety, or any ritualized activity that is not 'as genuine as a kiss' (Wittgenstein 1994a: 8), is something to be wary of here too,[215] as is the descent into narcissistic self-destruction. Thus, recalling Crusoe, it may sometimes be a proper rebuke against moral haughtiness and *hubris* to remind someone who judges their failings of character too harshly that they are only human, meaning, that they should gain a perspective on their failings by remembering they are not alone in such failings.

(Gaita 1991: 49)

Nevertheless, it is often quite 'different with guilt':

It should be no consolation if what we did was also done by the best of people. That is not pride because remorse does not focus on what kind of person we are: its focus is on what we have become ... It is therefore not inaccurate or fanciful to say that the guilty, in recognition of what they have become, have a sense of being placed elsewhere: *placed*, because of their concentrated radical singularity under judgement; *elsewhere*, because their suffering can find no relief in a humbling acknowledgement of their humanity.

(Gaita 1991: 49–50)

Rephrasing this in the vocabulary of *On Certainty* (discussed in Chapter 2) we can summarize as follows: When faced with another suffering such a 'radically singular' guilt it would be natural to try and ease their burden by stressing our common humanity and finitude, or by appealing to the pragmatic necessity of them not *over*burdening themselves to the point of incapacity. All such rhetorical strategies – and countless others – could be employed here. However, one could *not* (in the sort of examples I have been considering) simply pronounce the other to have made a 'blunder' (Wittgenstein 1994b: 59) in their reasoning. For how does one reason from a common ground or shared criterion when what is in question (one's *own* guilt) operates precisely where appeals to universality break down? Here, it would seem, one finds a paradigm case of what Wittgenstein refers to as a 'fundamental' (1999: §512), 'groundless' (ibid.: §166) and 'unshakeable' (ibid.: §86)[216] conviction. At this juncture one might attempt to provide reasons against another's guilt, but 'how far do they go? At the end of reasons comes *persuasion*' (ibid.: §612).[217]

It is in this sense that the possibility of a 'radically singular' guilt disrupts the notion of a 'we' or 'common humanity.' But this admission does not demand that we abandon such categories altogether, for this 'radicality' is not a quasi-Lyotardian space of fathomless incommensurability. As previously argued, those passages from *On Certainty* cited above should not be taken on face value, but rather read alongside Wittgenstein's naturalism. Only by tempering the apparently resignatory (or 'conservative') spirit of such remarks in this way can one properly understand his later work. More pointedly, this unifying naturalism is itself necessary for understanding the 'singularity' of guilt expounded by Heidegger and Levinas. For while it is doubtless true that a profound disturbance occurs here in the (potential) good conscience of the appeal to an underlying 'common humanity,' this nevertheless remains a *disturbance* and not a total dissolution of this category. Recognizing one's natural commonality with others does not mean that *my* guilt cannot be disproportionately excessive. Moreover, though no 'relief' from guilt may be found 'in a humbling acknowledgement of [one's] humanity,'[218] this does not mean that *my* guilt is wholly idiosyncratic or incommunicable. The claim that the guilty can find themselves 'placed elsewhere' by the 'radical singularity' of their guilt[219] must not therefore be taken in the extreme Lyotardian sense criticized in Chapter 3. Indeed, Rousseau's *The Confessions* is instructive on precisely this point. For although its author is at pains to stress the singularity of his revelatory exercises,[220] in his attempt to make his 'soul transparent to the reader's eye' by presenting the minutiae of his life 'from all points of view, to show it in all lights, and to contrive that none of its movements shall escape his notice' (1953: 169) (that is, in his frequent appeal to the reader[221]), Rousseau thereby bears witness to the *natural limits* of this singularity. The signature Rousseau wants to inscribe in his confession is not – and cannot be *qua* signature – wholly singular.[222] For despite the remarkable frankness of *The Confessions*, this does not render it unintelligible.[223] The very possibility for the reader to 'follow' Rousseau 'in all the extravagances of [his] heart and into every least corner of [his] life' (and, not least, for Rousseau to thus lay himself 'sufficiently open to human malice by telling [his] story' (ibid.: 65)) necessarily depends upon there being *some* degree of commonality between author and reader. There are doubtless times in *The Confessions* where one wonders precisely why Rousseau is divulging certain events, yet even here it would be a gross exaggeration to suggest that these peculiar expositions are *radically* singular in the Lyotardian sense.

This cautionary point is, however, of additional significance when approaching Levinas's work. For it is a remarkable philosophical move he makes when claiming that 'What I say here of course only commits me!' (1992: 114).[224] This quasi-confessional moment – though of obvious interest given the specific relationship we have traced between Levinas's work and the Holocaust – would seem to abandon all the standard criteria of philosophical argumentation. At this juncture we might reasonably ask: If all this only commits *Levinas* then why should *we* bother to read him – or at least bother to read him *philosophically*? This is an important question. But again, I do not think that one is forced to make such a dismissive gesture. It is true that Levinas seems largely preoccupied with the 'encounter with the face' that lies '[b]eneath solidarity, beneath companionship, before *Mitsein*' (Derrida 1997c: 90) – an emphasis that tends to marginalize questions pertaining to the gritty realm of political contingency.[225] (Indeed, it is the former preoccupation that prevents him from expounding any definitive moral code.[226]) Nevertheless, what Levinas says regarding the asymmetrical nature of responsibility does not – as it presumably would were this singularity *radically* 'radical' – commit him to a solitary, quietistic mysticism.[227] The rhetorical force of Levinas's vocabulary of trespassing and Guilt[228] lies rather in its ability to touch upon very basic (though rarely thematized) human tendencies. While he may not be able to *compel* us to acknowledge our own primordial Guilt before the face of the other – which would, after all, only amount to a 'forced confession' – Levinas must at least hope for a change of perspective in his readership. This point is, however, important for a more pressing reason. I said above that Levinas's work tends to pass over the political contingencies of the historical-cultural world. Given his repeated emphasis on both the face-to-face relation and the asymmetrical singularity of my responsibility for the other, the orientation of Levinas's work may thus appear to be fundamentally *a*-political – if not in fact *anti*-political. On such a reading, what he invokes is at best a quasi-Rousseauistic state in which one is, like Crusoe, faced by *an* other. What Levinas (allegedly) underestimates, however, is the brute fact that in my being-in-the-world I am always also faced by *many* others; *many* different and incompatible claims on my responsibility. While the primordial Guilt Levinas alludes to is not *radically* singular (it is not simply *Levinas's own*), it is not yet clear precisely how such Guilt functions in the ethical-political realm. It is to this important question that I will now turn.

7 The unreasonableness of ethics
Levinas and the limits of responsibility

> For the first time I began to perceive that true sympathy cannot be switched on and off like an electric current, that anyone who identifies himself with the fate of another is robbed to some extent of his own freedom.
>
> S. Zweig, *Beware of Pity*

> If you offer a sacrifice and are pleased with yourself about it, both you and your sacrifice will be cursed.
>
> L. Wittgenstein, *Culture and Value*

> So long as ethics cannot point to a foundation ... it may carry on its disputations and make a show in the lecture halls, but real life will make it an object of ridicule. I must, therefore, give the teachers of ethics the paradoxical advice of first looking around a little at the lives of men.
>
> A. Schopenhauer, *On The Basis of Morality*

Introduction

In Chapter 3 I argued that characterizing the human body as a 'moral space' facilitates a deeper understanding of the ethical terrain of Wittgenstein's later work.[1] What he calls into question is the assumption that ethics constitutes a subsidiary layer of experience that is essentially parasitic on more fundamental philosophical issues.[2] This is not to deny reason its place, but rather to highlight the 'common behavior of mankind' (1958: §206) *upon* which reason – including ethical-political deliberation – is hinged. Levinas also questions philosophy's prioritization of knowledge and reason over ethical responsibility, and similarly denies that the latter is 'superimposed ... as a second layer' (1998a: 11).[3] On this point the Wittgensteinian and Levinasian projects are in broad agreement. However, this accord comes unstuck at the level of the 'natural.' Despite their mutual preoccupation with the face and vulnerability, a crucial disparity occurs at the precise moment Wittgenstein's unifying naturalism is revealed. My objective in this chapter is to: (1) elucidate this tension between the Levinasian and Wittgensteinian projects, and (2) provide a Wittgensteinian corrective to Levinas's anti-naturalism. But in order to do this a number of additional Levinasian themes need to be explored. Thus, developing my previous analysis of the face, I will first assess the significance of Levinas's 'religious' conceptual vocabulary (specifically with reference to his account of the 'third-party'), and then critique his 'inhospitality' toward the non-human animal.

Thanking God for the third party: the haunting of the political/Levinas's prayer

Although Levinas distinguishes between his philosophical writings and those of a more religious and confessional bent,[4] this demarcation is far from clear-cut. As Derrida rightly notes, in Levinas's work there lies a certain 'complicity of theology and metaphysics' (1997c: 109).[5] So, for example, Levinas describes the face as 'the *indispensable circumstance* of the meaning' of the word 'God,' and likewise as the 'first prayer' and 'first liturgy' (1993: 94) coming 'from most high outside the world' (ibid.: 103).[6] What then should we make of such passages, and what (if any) substantive philosophical work are they doing? The first thing to note here is that, despite Levinas's insistence that the face and the 'transcendent' are intimately associated, it is not clear that his remarks compel us toward an explicitly 'religious' interpretation of the latter. Such passages might be read in a more straightforwardly phenomenological way, where the 'transcendence' of the other represents only the ineptitude of consciousness to 'grasp' them fully (thereby retaining *their* 'otherness' and demanding of *us* a little 'faith' (Ward 1998: 188)). In other words, Levinas's religious vocabulary might allude only to the difference between one's experience of objects[7] (which are always open to verification and therein 'appresented' in their partial manifestation[8]) and one's experience of other people.[9] Thus interpreted, Levinas's terminology becomes something of a rhetorical extravagance,[10] and his work an unnecessarily spiritualized development of the fifth of Husserl's *Cartesian Meditations*.[11] This is one possible reading, but not one Levinas would endorse. For him, the 'transcendent,' 'God,' the 'Infinite'[12] and 'most high'[13] are not translatable into even *quasi*-epistemological terms.[14] The otherness of the other, Levinas insists, is not simply a 'not-knowing' or 'privation of knowledge.' It is not merely that the other is incalculable or 'unforeseeable,' just as it is 'not as a miscarried knowledge that love is love' (1992: 66–7).[15] One must therefore take Levinas's (philosophical) religiosity seriously. For when he claims that 'the relation to God is ... a relation to another person' he denies that this is 'a metaphor'; on the contrary 'it is literally true. I'm not saying that the other is God, but that in his or her face I hear the Word of God' (1998b: 110).[16] According to Levinas then, the face is inextricably linked to the religious, and the latter is not shorthand for the limits of epistemology. A lot turns on this point, for as Derrida notes, Levinas will actually describe 'this being-together as separation ... [as] *religion*' (1997c: 95)

150 *The unreasonableness of ethics*

or the 'religious relation ... the religiosity of the religious' (ibid.: 96).[17] Ultimately I will argue against this account in favor of something more naturalistic (in the Wittgensteinian sense). Nevertheless, it is first necessary to tease more from Levinas's religious imagery, and thereby identify some important ambiguities within his broader project.

Levinas's religiosity is far from orthodox, for here God is emphatically not conceived as ontological – not even as 'the *being* ... par excellence' (1996a: 129–30).[18] In keeping with Wittgenstein's (and Malcolm's) bewilderment concerning the notion of God as 'creator,' Levinas warns that God's reality 'cannot be proved.' Rather, the existence of God 'is sacred history itself, the sacredness of man's relation to man through which God may pass' (1984: 54).[19] Thus, regarding Picard's suggestion that '*the face of man is the proof of the existence of God*,' Levinas remarks:

> Clearly the concern here is not with deductive proof, but with the very dimension of the divine ... disclosing itself in that *odd configuration of lines that make up the human face*. It is in the human face that ... *the trace of God is manifested, and the light of revelation inundates the universe*.
> (1996d: 95)

In the other's face one does not 'see' the face of God.[20] Neither does one infer from it that God exists.[21] Rather, the other's face testifies to the divine in a way that cannot be assimilated to epistemic categories.[22] Obviously the face can be treated as merely one object among many[23] (as can the other more generally[24]), and this possibility is why Levinas cautions that the 'best way of encountering the Other is not even to notice the color of his eyes!' (1992: 85). Estheticizing the other in this way bypasses the social relation and results in an essentially pornographic encounter. But while Levinas avoids speaking of the face in purely surface terms, so too does he want to avoid any suggestion that the face is a material obstacle to the divine.[25] It is not that the phenomenal appearance of the face (including the other's capacity to use it as a 'mask') is irrelevant to the social relation – how could it be? What Levinas is resisting is the reduction of its meaning to these material features.[26] But a familiar problem re-emerges here, for opposing the tendencies of reductionism does not necessarily liberate us from the categories of knowledge – assuming we seek such liberation. Even if we concede that the face should not be 'understood' solely in terms of its surface qualities,[27] it remains unclear whether Levinas's point is not fundamentally epistemological. Again, how is it possible to think the transcendent without a more-or-less implicit appeal to knowledge – albeit the *impotence* of knowledge and ontological language here?[28] Thus, one might say, Levinas's negative theology of the face is – like all negative theologies perhaps – not *sufficiently* negative.[29]

Still, Levinas's denial that the face provides a 'proof of the existence of God' but rather represents 'the *indispensable circumstance* of the meaning of that word' (1993: 94)[30] opens another possible avenue for exploring his intermingling of philosophy and religion. The intimate relation between the face and language is clearly insinuated in Levinas's remarks on 'prayer' and 'liturgy' cited above. But why should he mention these specific discourses? As previously suggested, one potentially fruitful way of approaching this question would be through Wittgenstein's remarks on religious belief. That the face testifies to the Infinite (that it is 'the locus of the ["Thou shalt not kill"] of God' (Levinas 1999: 104)) could then be understood in terms of its 'imperative' (1993: 158), commanding authority.[31] That is, the face of the other in Levinas's work functions in much the same way as God's command does in Wittgenstein's observation that one can only 'hear God speak' if one is 'being addressed' (1990: §717) – a point Levinas himself makes.[32] Indeed, the authority Levinas claims on behalf of the face mirrors Wittgenstein's more general remarks on the categorical nature of genuinely religious utterances.[33] A further correlation between Levinas and Wittgenstein emerges here insofar as the face of the other alludes to killing in the twofold sense that I am both 'straightaway' (Levinas 1992: 85)[34] commanded not to kill *and* simultaneously accused of having killed (and indeed of continuing to be an 'accomplice' (1998b: 186) to murder) through my very being-in-the-world.[35] The face's command 'thou shalt not kill' (ibid.: 168) is, like Wittgenstein's example in *Culture and Value*,[36] an *impossible* command; a mandate I have necessarily already violated and continue to violate with every breath, word and deed. The face both warns *and* accuses me of crimes already committed, and this is why 'in approaching the neighbor' I am 'always late for the appointed time' (Levinas 1996a: 106).[37] In short, there is an important and telling concurrence between the 'depth grammar' of religion and the face.[38] With these points in mind, we are now better placed to understand Levinas's remarks that:

> The infinite does not announce itself in the testimony as a theme. In the sign given to the other ... in my 'here I am' – immediately present in the accusative – I testify to the Infinite ... The sentence in which God comes forth, for the first time, and mingles with words, cannot be expressed: 'I believe in God.' Testifying to God does not consist in stating this extraordinary word or phrase ... 'here I am' signifies me in the name of God, in the service of men ...
>
> (1996a: 105–6)

And similarly:

> I am a testimony ... The Infinite is not 'in front of' me; I express it, but precisely by giving a sign of the giving of signs, of the 'for-the-other' in which I am dis-interested: here I am (*me voici*)! The accusative here is remarkable: here I am, under your eyes, at your

service, your obedient servant ... The religious discourse that precedes all religious discourse is not dialogue. It is the 'here I am' ...

(1996a: 146)[39]

The meaning of the 'here I am' is therefore similarly twofold: (1) 'here I am' offering myself to you, 'at your service,'[40] and (2) 'here I am' accused and guilty. Situated before the other's face the 'I' is at once both *submissive* to her demands and *confessional* regarding the violence of its own being-in-the-world. In this second sense the 'here I am' constitutes a 'testimony' to one's primordial Guilt; it is nothing short of a confession of mass murder.[41] Indeed, given Levinas's occasional denial of the universality of his claims, and his emphasis on both primordial Guilt and the apologetics of language, I would suggest that the increasing difficulty of his writings is due to their fusion of philosophical and confessional genres. While Levinas begins as a fairly orthodox phenomenologist, that career eventually culminates in a number of semi-phenomenological confessional performances – most notably *Otherwise than Being*. In attempting to *say* the ethical whilst avoiding the lures of philosophical 'totalization,' Levinas engages in a confessional discourse that elucidates the meaning of responsibility by *saying* 'Here *I* am, accused and guilty.'[42]

Recalling Levinas's claim that 'the face before me summons me, calls for me, begs for me' (1996b: 83), this testimonial-confessional dimension facilitates a better understanding of the relation between the face and language. Levinas's terminology here is far from incidental,[43] but when he states that the 'face speaks' (1992: 87)[44] the point is not merely physiological (that one 'could not speak without a face' (1988a: 174)); rather, it is the face that provides the *ethical* conditions of possibility for discourse.[45] For it is *from* the (vulnerable) authority of the other's face that the silent[46] demand that I justify myself first comes, and *toward* the (authoritative) vulnerability of the face that my response is ultimately addressed.[47] That is:

> [T]he beginning of language is in the face ... Language does not begin with the signs that one gives, with words. Language is above all the fact of being addressed ... One speaks to someone ... And to speak to someone is not simply to speak in front of the plastic form that the other is ... I am called upon to respond ... the first language is the response.
>
> (Levinas 1988a: 169–74)[48]

That the face inaugurates language is a common theme in Levinas's writings.[49] As Derrida notes: 'the face is given simultaneously as expression and as speech. Not only as glance, but as the original unity of glance and speech, eyes and mouth, that speaks, but also pronounces its hunger.' That is, the face 'does not incarnate, envelop, or signal anything other than self, soul, subjectivity ... The other, therefore, is given "in person" and without allegory only in the face' (1997c: 100–1). Though characteristically attentive, Derrida's synopsis is also instructively misleading in suggesting that the face 'does not signal anything other than self.' For, according to Levinas, the other's face is *not* in the end saturated with meaning of such an intimate sort; *other* others are also therein 'presented,' and thus we find ourselves in the realm of politics. It is to this that I now want to turn.

As previously noted, Levinas's claim that the face inaugurates discourse is not merely a physiological point. But this becomes even clearer when Levinas extends the meaning of 'face' to encompass the 'whole sensible being, even in the hand one shakes' (1993: 102). Indeed, it is in this sense that 'the whole human body is ... more or less face' (1992: 97).[50] As discussed in Chapter 3, Wittgenstein makes a similar claim,[51] but Levinas's subsequent remark that the 'human face is the face of the world itself, and the individual of the human race' (1996a: 73) suggests that there is something more radical at stake here. What ultimately turns on this point is elucidated in the following passage:

> Everything that takes place here 'between us' concerns everyone ... Language as the presence of the face does not invite complicity with the preferred being, the self-sufficient 'I-Thou' forgetful of the universe; in its frankness it refuses the clandestinity of love ... The third party looks at me in the eyes of the Other – language is justice ... the epiphany of the face qua face opens humanity. The face in its nakedness as a face presents to me the destitution of the poor one and the stranger ... the whole of humanity, in the eyes that look at me.
> (Levinas 1996c: 212–13)[52]

How, then, are we to understand this extension of the meaning of 'face' to the 'whole of humanity'? Again, in a more strictly phenomenological manner, one might suggest that the *other* others are 'co-presented' in the face of this *particular* other insofar as the

> existence-sense [*Seinssinn*] of the world and of Nature in particular, as Objective Nature, includes ... thereness-for-everyone. This is always cointended wherever we speak of Objective actuality ... These Objects, in respect of their origin and sense, refer us to subjects, usually other subjects, and their actively constituting intentionality. Thus it is in the case of all cultural Objects.
> (Husserl 1982: 92)[53]

In other words, even if one were to take the face in its 'plasticity'[54] as merely another 'cultural Object,' its sense *as such* refers us to *other* others in its being part of a 'common surrounding world' (Husserl 1989: 201).[55] However, constituting the *other* others in such a way would, for Levinas, still be too ontological[56] in its safely housing the 'I' in a community of observers.[57] This broadly phenomenological point Levinas thus ethicalizes as follows:

> [I]n the relationship with another I am always in relation with the third party. But he is also my neighbor. From this moment on, proximity becomes problematic: one must compare, weigh, think; one must do justice, which is the source of theory. The entire recovery of Institutions ... is done ... starting from the third party ... we must have comparison and equality: equality between those that cannot be compared. And consequently, the word 'justice' applies much more to the relationship with the third party than to the relationship with the other. But in reality, the relationship with another is never uniquely the relationship with the other: from this moment on, the third is represented in the other; that is, in the very appearance of the other the third already regards me.
> (1998a: 82)

The problem that now emerges is how 'to reconcile ... the infinite ethical requirement of the face that meets me ... and the appearance of the other as an individual and as an object' (1998b: 205).[58] According to the passage above the relation to both the singular other and the third party must be understood in terms of the demand for worldly justice.[59] Although, as discussed in Chapter 5, Levinas tends to focus on the relationship with the singular other, here he insists that such a relationship is (though in a rather specific sense) a fiction; 'in reality, the relationship with another is never uniquely the relationship with the other.'[60] Levinas's preoccupation with the 'uniqueness of the *other* man' is not therefore 'a repudiation of politics' (ibid.: 195).[61] For if

> there was only the other facing me, I would say to the very end: I owe him everything. I am for him ... I am forever subject to him. My resistance begins when the harm he does me is done to a third party who is also my neighbor. It is the third party who is the source of justice, and thereby of justified repression; it is the violence suffered by the third party that justifies stopping the violence of the other with violence.
> (1998a: 83)

In short, the 'Other's hunger – be it of the flesh, or of bread – is sacred; only the hunger of the third party limits its rights' (1997a: xiv). Levinas's reservations concerning the 'society of love' (1998b: 20) (namely, the society that perceives love to be the social relation *par excellence*) are pertinent here. For what remains problematic about the relation between lovers is precisely their tendency toward I-Thou exclusivity, and thus their forgetting of the third party. In the face of the lover one tends to see *only* the lover – the lover's face is saturated with its own intimate significance and thereby 'does not ... signal anything other than [it]self' (Derrida 1997c: 100).[62] But at the heart of the love relation lies an easily neglected sacrificial injustice insofar as one always loves the beloved 'to the detriment of another' (Levinas 1998b: 21).[63] *If* there were only two (you and I), our relation could indeed be understood in terms of the intimacy of 'love.' But we are not alone; there is a third party who also demands love, and who is therefore 'wounded' by *our* 'amorous dialogue' (ibid.). Thus, Levinas concludes, insofar as 'the lover and the loved one' exist *as though* they 'were alone in the world ... love is not the beginning of society, but its negation' (ibid.: 20). To summarize: If there were only two of us I would be infinitely indebted to you – even being obliged to suffer at your hand. Between only the two of us there would be no possible question of (or appeal to) justice, and to *that* extent 'there wouldn't be any problem' (ibid.: 106).[64] However, given that we are not alone in this way, any violence you (as other) perpetrate against a third (*another* other) demands justice[65] – indeed, this is the very birth of justice, political-economic institutions and the world-pictures of which they are a part. Here I must make a 'judgement' (ibid.: 202) between parties and thus 'calculate with the incalculable' (Derrida 1990: 947)[66] in order to ascertain 'which of the two takes precedence' (Levinas 1998b: 104).[67] In this way a 'measure superimposes itself on the "extravagant" generosity of the "for the other," on its infinity' (ibid.: 195). If necessary, I will now appeal to the political establishment and official powers.[68] And if these appeals fail, or if the mechanisms of legal arbitration are too cumbersome or ponderous, *I* might have to repress, silence and confront you with violence.[69] Not, however, for my *own* well being, but *for the sake of the other*; your 'neighbor' (1994a: 157) or 'brother' (ibid.: 158) whom you wrong. This movement from the infinite responsibility for the singular other to the more measured realm of politics is crucial to understanding Levinas's work. Indeed, it is here that the quasi-genealogical dimension of his philosophy comes to the fore. On the one hand, the face-to-face relation with the singular other is essentially mythical, for there *never was* such an ethically 'pure' encounter between just two.[70] Yet, on the other hand, in *every* encounter with another there remains a trace of just such a 'pure' relation. As Levinas remarks: 'what seems to me very important, is that there are not only two of us in the world. But I think that everything begins *as if* we were only two' (1988a: 170, my emphasis). Thus, in every *actual* relation with another (which is also a relation with the third party) it is *as if* I were 'reminded' of the one-to-one relation of infinite ethical expenditure.[71] And this quasi-remembrance is of ethical-political import insofar as it raises a question of priority. For the pragmatic demands of worldly justice inaugurated with the third party must always be 'held in check' (2001: 132) by the 'initial charity' (1998b: 104) of the face-to-face relation.[72] In short, the political realm is *haunted* by the ethical.

I referred above to the 'quasi-genealogical' dimension of Levinas's

156   *The unreasonableness of ethics*

work. I would now like to substantiate this characterization by briefly comparing Levinas's position here with Rousseau's lamentations in *A Discourse on the Origin of Inequality* (a text to which I referred in Chapter 6).[73] This will enable me to highlight a number of important – though again, easily misconstrued – points about the Levinasian project.

In *A Discourse on the Origin of Inequality* Rousseau presents a quasi-Pyrrhonian characterization of 'natural man' whose 'first care [was] that of self-preservation' and whose life was, like the animal, 'limited ... to mere sensations' (1930: 207).[74] For Rousseau this primitive self-concern is not to be scorned. On the contrary, it is *sociality* and the awareness of others[75] that ultimately corrupts the blithe animality of 'infant man.'[76] It would therefore be mistaken to assume 'that man is naturally cruel, and requires civil institutions to make him more mild,' for there is nothing 'more gentle than man in his primitive state ... restrained by natural compassion' (ibid.: 213)[77] where he 'lived [a] free, healthy, honest and happy' (ibid.: 214) life. According to Rousseau then, 'from the moment one man began to stand in need of the help of another ... equality disappeared, property was introduced ... [and] slavery and misery were soon seen to germinate' (ibid.: 214–15).[78] Along with society 'each became in some degree a slave even in becoming the master of other men':

> [T]here arose rivalry and competition on the one hand, and conflicting interests on the other ... All these evils were the first effects of property ... Usurpations by the rich, robbery by the poor, and the unbridled passions of both, suppressed the cries of natural compassion.
> (Rousseau 1930: 218–19)

According to this genealogy, 'natural compassion' was eventually smothered by the need to compete with our neighbors – this competitive drive finding its impetus in the emergence of a sense of property inaugurated by the 'first man who, having enclosed a piece of ground, bethought himself of saying *This is mine*' (ibid.: 207). There are two things worth noting about Rousseau's speculations here: (1) his emphasis on the 'usurpation'[79] that lies at the heart of socio-political reality, and (2) his nostalgia concerning both the goodness of 'natural man' and the relative simplicity of that pre-social stage of human existence. It is clear that Rousseau's reflections on the inherent violence of property[80] strike a chord with certain Levinasian themes.[81] But Rousseau's second point (that pre-social existence was an essentially *simple* affair) also seems to find a parallel in Levinas's work. For, as previously discussed, it is only with the advent of the third party ('from this moment on' (Levinas 1998a: 82)) that my responsibility to the other becomes increasingly compromised and 'problematic' (ibid.).[82] With the third party the sacrificial component of ethical responsibility is no longer merely a matter of my own *self*-sacrifice (my being-for-the-other without reserve), but also my sacrificing the demands and needs of the *other* other

The unreasonableness of ethics 157

for the sake of *this* other. The call for justice thus augments bad conscience ever further: Between only the two of us I simply owe everything, although I can never rest assured that I have done *enough* (hence bad conscience). But along with the third party, not only is *this* level of guilt maintained, it is infinitely supplemented by the fact that, in my choosing *you* over him or her or them (and, I would suggest along with Derrida, even the 'it' of the animal[83]), I am additionally guilty. Indeed, the *more* I do for *you*, the *less* I have done for the *other* other.[84] In short, if it were not for the third party my relation to the other would be *straightforwardly* asymmetrical.[85] Of course, the respective emphases of Rousseau and Levinas differ in one very important sense: Rousseau's interest lies with the life experienced by 'infant man' (1930: 207) in glorious isolation from others (or at least in a primitive, pre-linguistic, pre-rational form of sociality[86]), whereas Levinas would question Rousseau's valorization of this state of natural 'self-preservation' (ibid.). (I will return to the latter.) These differences aside, it is nevertheless striking that both philosophers stress the inherently problematic nature of being-with-(*other*)-others. To what (if any) extent then does Levinas share Rousseau's nostalgia? As Derrida has recently inquired,[87] might Levinas's claim that 'there wouldn't be any problem' (1998b: 106) if there were only two of us constitute a *lamentation* regarding the way the third party becomes a 'complication' (1997b: 82) to the face-to-face relation? These important questions can, I think, be answered with reference to the following passages from *Otherwise than Being*:

> In the proximity of the other, all the others than the other obsess me, and already this obsession cries out for justice, demands measure and knowing ... The other is from the first the brother of all the other men. The neighbor that obsesses me is already a face, both comparable and incomparable, a unique face and in relationship with faces, which are visible in the concern for justice ... The relationship with the third party is an incessant correction of the asymmetry of proximity in which the face is looked at. There is weighing, thought, objectification, and thus a decree in which my anarchic relationship with illeity is betrayed ...
>
> (Levinas 1994a: 158)

Thus far Levinas could be read as indulging in precisely the sort of Rousseauist lamentation previously mentioned; a mourning, 'complaint' or 'cry' (Derrida 1999a: 68) concerning the way responsibility for the singular other is 'betrayed' by the third party.[88] But Levinas proceeds to dispel this suspicion:

> There is betrayal of my anarchic relation with illeity, but also a new relationship with it: it is only thanks to God that, as a subject incomparable with the other, I am approached as an other by the others, that

158 *The unreasonableness of ethics*

is, 'for myself.' 'Thanks to God' I am another for the others ... The passing of God, of whom I can speak only by reference to this aid or his grace, is precisely the reverting of the incomparable subject into a member of society ... It is thus that the neighbor becomes visible, and, looked at, presents himself, and there is also justice for me.
(1994a: 158–9)

This 'Thanks to God' (or similarly ' "with the help of God" ' (ibid.: 160)) could be variously interpreted. So, for example, Critchley suggests that this phrase refers to something 'classical[ly] Christian'; namely, that 'the universality of fraternity is ensured through the mediation of the divine' (1999b: 273). But Levinas does not offer any clear indication how this 'Thanks to God' ought to be understood in relation to the question of the third party. I would therefore like to offer the following interpretation. Given that Levinas claims not to be offering a hypothesis concerning God's existence, the 'Thanks to God' might be understood as 'less a theory than a sigh, or a cry' (Wittgenstein 1994a: 30). Where Derrida discerns a 'cry' of 'complaint' (1999a: 68) in Levinas's remarks on the third party, one should instead hear rejoicing. Although it is only through this 'new relationship' that *I* 'become an other like the others' (Levinas 1994a: 161) and thereby have care owed to myself, this need not be taken as the *primary* source of Levinas's 'Thanks to God.' The fact that the *other* other demands justice may mean that I can legitimately care (and demand justice) for myself, but what motivates this is not primarily my *own* needs (for myself), but rather the needs of the other.[89] That is, '[m]y lot is [also] important' (ibid.) insofar as it provides the requisite protection and provisions *to aid the other*, and it is in this sense that worldly justice rightly permits *me* a degree of self-preservation. On this reading Levinas's 'Thanks to God' does not constitute an expression of self-satisfaction ('Thanks to God I am now unburdened of infinite responsibility!'). One might indeed discover a certain relief here, but this is again relief *for the other* whose suffering can now be eased from *other* resources (to which *I* do not have access) in addition to my own limitless efforts in this regard. The point I want to make here is that, contrary to both Rousseau's genealogy and Derrida's suspicions, the co-presence of the third party is a cause for adulation rather than bemoaning. Thus, if the 'Here I am!' before the face of the singular other constitutes the 'first liturgy' (1993: 94) (even 'the origin of language' (2000: 192)) I would suggest that the third party and her demand for worldly justice constitutes the 'Amen' at the close of Levinas's own philosophical confession.

For Levinas and Wittgenstein (as for Derrida too[90]) the meaning of religion is thus *fundamentally* ethical rather than onto-theological. As discussed earlier, Wittgenstein not only naturalizes religious belief, he also stresses the ethical dimension such beliefs have – or at least ought to have if they are to qualify as 'genuinely' religious. I now want to consider further Levinas's own conception of religion. By this I am not referring primarily to his Judaism, as this would go against his own intentions to elucidate 'a human fact, of the human order, and entirely universal' (1988a: 177).[91] Rather, I am concerned with what Derrida refers to as the 'religiosity of the religious' (1997c: 96) or the 'morality of morality' (1995c: 16), specifically in relation to Levinas's anti-naturalism.

The unreasonableness of ethics: Levinas's anti-naturalism

Levinas is emphatic that he is 'not afraid of the word God, which appears quite often in my essays.' As discussed earlier, the reason for this boldness is that 'the Infinite comes in the signifyingness of the face. The face *signifies* the Infinite' (1992: 105). Levinas need not be 'afraid' of this word because the only thing to be apprehensive of here is falling into idle onto-theological speculation, and he would be the first to condemn such a maneuver.[92] This is, no doubt, how Levinas would perceive the situation. But then what remains of the significance of this most provocative of terms? And what becomes of religion once its theological voice is so dramatically curtailed? The recurrent emphasis in Levinas's work is that religion and one's relation to others are *inextricably* connected:

> 'Going towards God' is not to be understood here in the classical ontological sense of a return to, or reunification with, God as the Beginning or End of temporal existence. 'Going towards God' is meaningless unless seen in terms of my primary going towards the other person. I can only go towards God by being ethically concerned by and for the other person.
>
> (1984: 59)

That is, '[f]aith is not a question of the existence or non-existence of God. It is believing that love without reward is valuable' (1988a: 176).[93] That both 'going towards God' and 'faith' should here be explicated in ethical rather than theological terms makes Levinas's orientation clear, and there are numerous other passages which demonstrate this transcription of the religious into the ethical.[94] That 'the Infinite enters into language,' that 'the subject who says "Here I am!" testifies to the Infinite' (1992: 106), and that 'responsibility ... is a way of testifying to the glory of the Infinite' (ibid.: 113) are familiar themes by now. But they pose one of the most difficult questions regarding the Levinasian project; namely, whether – despite his protestations[95] – Levinas's conception of God is in any substantive way distinguishable from the other *human*?[96] If the only 'access' to the divine is through the inter-human encounter, and one is denied a traditionally onto-theological voice, then why preserve this distinctly religious terminology? That Levinas's thinking is in danger (assuming it is a danger) of collapsing into 'mere' humanism – where 'God' and the 'Infinite' become *thoroughly* saturated with the human – is implicit here.[97] I therefore want to follow Levinas's own advice and negotiate this question through his belief in the possibility of 'love without reward.'[98] To do this I will use the previously outlined relationship between the face and language as an interpretative template.

As discussed in Chapter 5, the face is simultaneously a *facing*. While the face cannot be thought without recourse to its material embodiment, neither can its meaning be reduced to this 'plasticity.' Now, Levinas makes a parallel claim about language, again emphasizing the inseparability yet non-reducibility of its twin dimensions. Thus, regarding Western philosophy, he wonders whether

> in that whole tradition, language as *Said* has not been privileged, to the exclusion or minimizing of its dimension as *Saying*. There is, it is true, no Saying that is not the saying of a *Said*. But does the *Saying* signify nothing but the *Said*? Should we not bring out, setting out from the *Saying*, an intrigue of meaning that is not reducible to the thematization and exposition of a *Said* . . . ?
>
> (1993: 141)

According to Levinas, philosophy has concerned itself only with the *content* of language (its Said) and thereby its capacity to facilitate the exchange of 'information' (1996a: 80).[99] What has passed relatively unnoticed is the significance of the *Saying* of the Said – that is, the elementary 'movement toward the other' (1994b: 48), ' "hello" ' (1999: 98) or 'gift' (Derrida 1997c: 148) necessary for all such informational (or indeed performative[100]) exchanges to be possible.[101] In short, what interests Levinas is language as 'contact' (1996a: 80) with another human being.[102] In a striking passage he illustrates this with reference to Defoe's *Robinson Crusoe* (a text discussed in Chapter 6), and specifically Crusoe's first encounter with Man Friday. Defoe describes this initial meeting as follows:

> I smiled at him, and looked pleasantly, and beckoned to him to come still nearer; at length he came close to me . . . I took him up, and made much of him, and encouraged him all I could . . . he spoke some words to me, and though I could not understand them, yet I thought they were pleasant to hear, for they were the first sound of a man's voice that I had heard, my own excepted, for about twenty five years . . .
>
> (1985: 207)

But Levinas reads much more into this encounter. Having described the 'sounds and noises of nature' as 'words that disappoint us' (and again warned philosophy of its neglect of the 'direct social relations between persons speaking'[103]), he thus remarks:

The unreasonableness of ethics 161

But this is a disdain that cannot gainsay a situation whose privileged nature is revealed to Robinson Crusoe when, in the tropical splendor of nature, though he has maintained his ties with civilization through his use of utensils, his morality, and his calendar, he experiences in meeting Man Friday the greatest event of his insular life – in which a man who speaks replaces the ineffable sadness of echoes.

(1993: 148)

Here Levinas seems relatively unconcerned with Friday's pending 'subjection, servitude, and submission' (Defoe 1985: 209) at the hands of Crusoe. Indeed, this apparent nonchalance toward the colonialism at the heart of Defoe's narrative is manifest in Levinas's silence concerning Friday's subsequent 'education' – and, not least, that the second word Crusoe would teach him was 'Master' (ibid.).[104] Rather, what preoccupies Levinas is the way Friday's utterances *despite their unintelligibility* figure as the most momentous 'event' in Crusoe's 'silent life' (ibid.: 81).[105] Putting this in more theoretical terms, what concerns Levinas is that:

Beyond the thematization of the Said and of the content stated in the proposition ... The proposition is proposed to the other person ... It is communication not reducible to the phenomenon of the *truth-that-unites*: it is a non-indifference to the other person, capable of ethical significance.

(1993: 142)[106]

In short, the Said is always simultaneously a Saying *of* the Said, and while there is no 'access' to (ethical) Saying aside from its inevitable crystallization into a (ontological) Said, the meaning of the Saying is not therein exhausted.[107] Now, this characteristic Levinasian move whereby a mundane phenomenon is imbued with significance beyond its 'ordinary' function – yet while at the same time retaining this 'ordinariness' as the necessary vehicle *through* which this excess of meaning flows – is echoed in what might be called Levinas's 'religious humanism.' For while the religious cannot be *reduced* to a secular humanism, neither can it be approached in entirely non-humanistic terms. What (allegedly) distinguishes Levinas's humanism from more traditional humanisms is the sheer 'gratuitousness'[108] of the former – indeed, its very 'unreasonableness' in this regard.[109] What Levinas wants to emphasize here (on one occasion he describes it as the 'principal thesis' that embodies his 'entire philosophy') is the way 'the human breaks with pure being' (1988a: 172). (I will return to this claim later.) That is, a 'being is something that is attached to being, to its own being ... However, with the appearance of the human ... there is something more important than my life, and that is the life of the other.'[110] This possibility of putting the other first is striking because it is 'unreasonable.' 'Man,' it

162 *The unreasonableness of ethics*

would seem, insofar as 'he' is ethical, is 'an unreasonable animal' (ibid.).[111]

> Most of the time my life is dearer to me, most of the time one looks after oneself. But we cannot not admire saintliness ... that is, the person who in his being is more attached to the being of the other than to his own. I believe that it is in saintliness that the human begins; not in the accomplishment of saintliness, but in the value. It is the first value, an undeniable value ... I maintain that [the] ideal of saintliness is presupposed in all our value judgements.
> (Levinas 1988a: 172–7)[112]

The universality of this 'ideal' is reiterated where Levinas claims that the 'only absolute value is the human possibility of giving the other priority over oneself. I don't think that there is a human group that can take exception to that ideal, even if it is declared an ideal of holiness' (1998b: 109),[113] and likewise:

> [W]hat emerges is the valorization of holiness as the most profound upheaval of being and thought, through the advent of man ... the human (love of the other, responsibility for one's fellowman, an eventual dying-for-the-other, sacrifice even as far as the mad thought in which dying for the other can concern me well before, and more than, my own death) – the human signifies the beginning of a new rationality beyond being. A rationality of the Good higher than all essence.
> (1998b: 228)

On this account, traditional secular humanism establishes itself upon a being-*with* or -*alongside* others, and thereby begins in the assumed equality and similitude of individual 'I's' – a sort of egological economics.[114] Secular humanism is thus presumptuous because it starts with the third party without understanding the nature of the relation with the singular other.[115] But for Levinas 'it is ethics which is the foundation of justice' not the inverse. Indeed, even *within* the realm of politics 'justice is not the last word,' for therein a certain excessiveness is still at work insofar as 'we seek a better justice.'[116] And this, accordingly, bears witness to the inherent superiority of liberal democracy: 'The truly democratic state,' Levinas claims, 'finds that it is never democratic enough' (1988a: 175). It is Levinas's emphasis on the excessiveness (and, by implication, ineliminable bad conscience[117]) governing one's relation with the other that distinguishes his humanism from more traditional forms. Whatever reciprocity the mechanisms of state, politics, law and justice might demand, the ethical conditions of possibility[118] for these lie in my *non-*reciprocal, *a-*symmetrical responsibility.[119] It is in this sense that Levinasian humanism can be described as simultaneously an *anti-*humanism; not merely because it deviates from humanism's more measured, orthodox forms but because it demands that we transcend the animality of human being to become, as it were, *more* human. In short, humanism 'has to be denounced ... because it is not sufficiently human' (1994a: 128).[120]

It is clear that much of Levinas's anxiety concerns Heidegger's prioritization of ontology. But at this point one might also ask whether Levinas's apprehensions are simultaneously focused (like Wittgenstein's) on what he perceives to be the dangers of scientism. Thus, Levinas warns (rather implausibly) of the acquiescence between physics and 'the interiority of pure being before or without ethics' that is 'already a metaphor for the cruelty of the cruel in the struggle for life and the egotism of wars' (1998b: 201–2).[121] More notable, however, is where Levinas proposes a certain complicity between Heideggerian ontology and Darwinism insofar as both (allegedly) allude to a being that 'is something that is attached to being, to its own being ... a struggle for life.' He proceeds: '*Dasein* is a being who in his being is concerned for this being itself. That's Darwin's idea: the living being struggles for life. The aim of being is being itself' (1988a: 172).[122] What distinguishes the truly *human* from such a characterization is that here it first becomes possible to speak of there being 'something more important' than myself; namely, 'the life of the other' (ibid.).[123] Ethics is '*against nature* because it forbids the murderousness of my natural will to put my own existence first' (1984: 60).[124] With the 'awakening to the human' thus comes an 'ideal of holiness contrary to the laws of being' (1998b: 114). Indeed, this is why the human – insofar as it 'interrupts the pure obstinacy of being and its wars' (ibid.: 231) – is nothing less than 'a scandal in being' (ibid.: 115).[125] The orientation of such passages is clear enough. But although Levinas is candid regarding *what* this break with 'pure being' (1988a: 172) inaugurates (namely, the possibility of saintly self-sacrifice), it remains unclear precisely *how* this rupture is supposed to occur.[126] While Levinas is 'not saying men are saints, or moving toward saintliness,' but rather that 'the vocation of saintliness is recognized by all human beings as a value, and that this recognition defines the human' (1999: 171), there here lies an ambiguity concerning the extent to which his point is essentially descriptive or prescriptive (or both). Do all human beings *actually* recognize 'the vocation of saintliness ... as a value,' or is this the criterion for 'genuine' humanity? Is Levinas alluding to a fact about human beings *qua* human beings, and if so is he identifying a more-or-less latent capacity on the part of human beings for 'saintliness'? On this latter reading Levinas's point may be both descriptive (human beings do possess the *capacity* to transcend their animal nature) *and* prescriptive (human beings *should* pursue such 'saintliness'), but the constitution of this 'capacity' still remains obscure. It presumably cannot be a *rational* capacity as this would make being-for-the-other essentially a matter of deliberation, and thus relative to the subject's own cognitive powers.[127] If it is a *natural* capacity then can one be so assured that it is peculiar to

164 *The unreasonableness of ethics*

human beings? If it is neither rational nor natural then how does it arise? – presumably not from God mysteriously endowing the human with a spark of the divine. Given that Levinas is 'not saying men are saints, or moving toward saintliness' (1999: 171), it would seem that he does not want to suggest that human beings are essentially constituted by 'saintliness' – as though saintliness were somehow unavoidable. But even here things are not straightforward. For Levinas does suggest that something 'saintly' precedes (or is at least co-extensive with) *every* encounter with the other – even encounters of an explicitly violent sort. (To put this differently, the *Saying* remains 'saintly' regardless of what transpires in its being *Said*.) Levinas provides no clear answer to these questions, but his general motivation is patently exclusivistic: that *only we* (that is, *not the non-human animal*) possess the capacity to even aspire to such saintliness.[128] Much like Heidegger's descriptive-prescriptive account of authenticity, insofar as we are constituted by an ineliminable Guilt, 'pure' saintliness is necessarily impossible. Nevertheless, in our practical dealings with others we can approach the saintly more-or-less adequately. The 'human' in Levinas's work thus appears to be more an ethical than biological category. In other words, the 'break' with the natural realm is not something that has, in any determinate sense, 'occurred,' but is rather something that we need continually to attempt. For Levinas, being (biologically) human is therefore the necessary condition for (ethical) saintliness. It is not, however, a sufficient condition.

According to Levinas then, it is the potential for self-sacrifice that constitutes the 'meaning of the human adventure' (ibid.: 227):

> Goodness, a childish virtue; but already charity and mercy and responsibility for the other, and already the possibility of sacrifice in which the humanity of man bursts forth, disrupting the general economy of the real and standing in sharp contrast with the perseverance of entities persisting in their being.
>
> (1998b: 157)[129]

In the realm of pure animality one's interests move circularly from self to world and back again. Like a love, gift or confession that ultimately seeks its own satisfaction, Being is marked by its continual recuperation, replenishment and nostalgic homeward-ness.[130] Such a model is thus marked by what Levinas describes as the interestedness of 'need' (1996a: 51).[131] But the other disrupts this economy of satisfaction, interjecting the exuberance of 'desire' (ibid.)[132] into an otherwise egological narrative.[133] Henceforth the inter-human relation can be 'considered from another perspective':

> [As] concern for the other as other, as a theme of love and desire which carries us beyond the finite Being of the world ... God, as the

God of alterity and transcendence, can only be understood in terms of that interhuman dimension which, to be sure, emerges in the phenomenological-ontological perspective of the intelligible world, but which cuts through and perforates the totality of presence and points towards the absolutely Other.

(1984: 56–7)

Levinas proceeds elsewhere:

> Need opens up a world that is *for me*: it returns to itself. Even a sublime need, such as the need for salvation, is still a nostalgia, a longing to go back. A need is return to self, the anxiety of the I for itself, egoism ... In Desire the I is borne toward the Other (*Autrui*) in such a way as to compromise the sovereign self-identification of the I, for which need is only nostalgia ... The movement toward the Other (*Autrui*), instead of completing me or contenting me, implicates me ... The Desirable does not gratify my Desire but hollows it out, and somehow nourishes me with new hungers ... The Desire for the Other (*Autrui*), which we live in the most ordinary social experience, is the fundamental movement, a pure transport, an absolute orientation, sense.
>
> (1996a: 51–2)

Like Derrida's analyses of the gift, this emphasis on 'desire' enables Levinas to speak of an orientation toward the other that never seeks a return; an absolute or 'pure' gratuitousness that disrupts the economy of Being.[134] Desire, in order to be worthy of that name, must be distinguished from need insofar as the former maintains its own insatiability[135] – it is, in Derrida's words, 'without horizon of expectation' (2002d: 106).[136] Levinas thus relates desire to a specific type of sensibility; the touch of the caress 'where the subject who is in contact with another goes beyond this contact ... what is caressed is not touched, properly speaking':

> It is not the softness or warmth of the hand given in contact that the caress seeks. The seeking of the caress constitutes its essence by the fact that the caress does not know what it seeks. This 'not knowing', this fundamental disorder, is the essential. It is like a game with something slipping away, a game absolutely without project or plan, not with what can become ours or us, but with something other, always other, always inaccessible, and always still to come ...
>
> (1997b: 89)[137]

In short, the desire for the other subverts ontological being-in-the-world by denying the subject its 'needful' intentionality and nostalgia.[138] And it is

166 *The unreasonableness of ethics*

precisely this emphasis on the gratuitousness of desire that enables Levinas to position himself politically[139] and also respond to the charge that his work is fundamentally a-political.[140]

Versions of the natural: Levinas, Nietzsche and Wittgenstein

Levinas's work may not therefore be a-political, but it remains deeply anti-naturalistic, and this restricts its ethical scope. It has already become clear that his characterization of the natural realm is, contra Rousseau,[141] profoundly bleak.[142] Indeed, Levinas's harsh vision of 'natural man' echoes some of the Enlightenment's darker philosophical figures.[143] According to Helvétius, for example, human nature is fundamentally 'bloodthirsty' (1969: 46) and 'deaf to the cry of pity' (ibid.: 45) if not 'civilized' by moral education. De Sade agrees, yet goes further in actively recommending this 'primal sentiment' (1991a: Dialogue 3) of cruelty.[144] But in Nietzsche's work a more subtle and challenging vision of the relationship between nature, humanity and morality emerges. Nietzsche's naturalism is particularly interesting here because it inverts almost all of Levinas's central themes.[145] For this reason it will be instructive briefly to reconstruct the Nietzschean account.

Focusing his critical naturalistic gaze on morality, Nietzsche remarks: 'When it is trodden on a worm will curl up. That is prudent. It thereby reduces the chance of being trodden on again. In the language of morals: *humility*' (1972: p. 26),[146] and likewise: 'The beginning of justice, as of prudence, moderation, bravery – in short, of all we designate as the *Socratic virtues*, are *animal*: a consequence of that drive which teaches us to seek food and elude enemies.' One might therefore 'describe the entire phenomenon of morality as animal' (1977: §67), for all the so-called virtues are in fact just 'physiological *conditions* . . . refined *passions* and enhanced states.' So, for example, '[p]ity and love of mankind' are really the 'development of the sexual drive.' Justice is the 'drive to revenge,' while virtue is the 'pleasure in resistance, [the] will to power,' and honor is the mere 'recognition of the similar and equal-in-power' (1968: §255). One gets a flavor of Nietzsche's more substantive views on nature and ethics when he castigates traditional morality as 'a piece of tyranny against "nature"' insofar as the 'essential and invaluable element in every morality is that it is a protracted constraint' (1987: §188). What the latter amounts to is elucidated a few pages later:

> One altogether misunderstands the beast of prey and man of prey . . . one misunderstands 'nature', so long as one looks for something 'sick' at the bottom of these healthiest of all tropical monsters and growths . . . as virtually all moralists have done hitherto. It seems . . . that there exists in moralists a hatred for the jungle and the tropics . . .
> (Nietzsche 1987: §197)

The unreasonableness of ethics 167

On this account the concepts of selfishness *and* self-sacrifice are therefore 'psychologically nonsense,' for morality has systematically 'falsified all *psychologica* to its very foundations – has *moralized* them – to the point of the frightful absurdity that love is supposed to be something "unegoistic"' (1992a: p. 45).[147] For Nietzsche, traditional morality spawns from a certain weakness, and constitutes the preferred 'form of revenge of the spiritually limited on those who are less so' – or a way (for the former) to recompense themselves for 'having been neglected by nature' (1987: §219). Accordingly, a distinction must be drawn between 'healthy' (natural) and 'unhealthy' (anti-natural) morality. Healthy morality is driven by 'an instinct of life,' whereas its unhealthy, anti-natural counterpart (morality's most dominant form) stands '*against* the instincts of life,' offering only '*condemnation* of these instincts' (1972a: p. 45).[148] Insofar as morality represents 'the judgement of the judged' (ibid.: p. 46), 'Man is finished when he becomes altruistic' (ibid.: p. 87). Given that morality thus constitutes the revenge of the weak upon the strong,[149] Nietzsche's avowed intention is 'to re-translate the apparently emancipated and denatured moral values back into their nature – i.e., into their natural "*immorality*"' (1968: §299).[150]

Unsurprisingly, Christianity gets singled out in this 'cult of altruism' (ibid.: §297)[151] as nourishing the aforementioned 'sickness' through its systematic (and seemingly insatiable) attempts to burden humanity with bad conscience.[152] In effect, Christianity has rendered our natural inclinations 'inseparable from [our] "bad conscience"' (1992b: Essay 2, §24). These mongers of guilt thus utilize religion in order 'to drive [man's] self-torture to its most gruesome pitch of severity and rigor.' Here God becomes the 'ultimate antithesis' of humanity's 'ineluctable animal instincts' whereby 'man'

> ejects from himself all his denial of himself, of his nature, naturalness, and actuality, in the form of an affirmation ... as God, as the holiness of God, as God the Judge ... as torment without end, as hell, as the immeasurability of punishment and guilt.
> (Nietzsche 1992b: §22)

Here we thus find a certain 'madness of the will' to judge ourselves 'guilty and reprehensible to a degree that can never be atoned for'; to be 'punished without any possibility of the punishment becoming equal to the guilt' (ibid.).[153] Such Judaic-Christian virtues as neighborly love are, Nietzsche insists, 'always something secondary ... when compared with *fear of one's neighbor*' (1987: §201).[154] That is, 'the emancipated are ... the underprivileged whose deepest instinct is revenge' (1992a: p. 46).[155] While more '*noble* cultures' judge neighborly love, pity and selflessness to be 'something contemptible' (1972a: p. 91), *we* have taken cruelty and transformed it into 'tragic pity, so that it is denied the name of cruelty' (1968: §312).

168 *The unreasonableness of ethics*

And it is for these reasons that Nietzsche questions the teleology of Darwinism:

> As regards the celebrated 'struggle for *life*,' it seems to me for the present to have been rather asserted than proved. It does occur, but as the exception; the general aspect of life is *not* hunger and distress, but rather wealth, luxury, even absurd prodigality – where there is a struggle it is a struggle for *power* ... Supposing, however, that this struggle exists – and it does indeed occur – its outcome is the reverse of that desired by the school of Darwin, of that which one *ought* perhaps to desire with them: namely, the defeat of the stronger, the more privileged, the fortunate exceptions. Species do *not* grow more perfect: the weaker dominate the strong again and again ...
> (1972a: pp. 75–6)

Continuing his assault on the naive belief (or apparent *need* to believe[156]) that '*we have really grown more moral*' (ibid.: p. 89), Nietzsche proceeds to condemn our 'modern' era as 'a *weak* age.' Indeed, these virtues are '*demanded* by our weakness' (ibid.: p. 91). Thus, our 'belated constitution, a weaker, more delicate, more vulnerable one, out of which is necessarily engendered a morality *which is full of consideration*' does not betoken any moral advancement. On the contrary, it 'represents ... our general decay of *vitality*,' for here, where 'everyone helps everyone else ... everyone is ... an invalid and everyone a nurse.' Among those 'who knew a different kind of life, a fuller, more prodigal, more overflowing life,' this alleged virtue 'would be called something else: "cowardice", perhaps, "pitiableness", "old woman's morality".' In short: 'Our softening of customs ... is a consequence of decline' (ibid.: p. 90).

Mindful of these passages, one can imagine what a Nietzschean critique of Levinas would look like, for each account represents the pathological shadow of the other. Indeed, given Levinas's emphasis on Guilt and asymmetrical responsibility (in Nietzschean terms, given Levinas's profound '*condemnation* of [the] instincts' (1972a: p. 45) or 'tyranny against "nature"' (1987: §188)) Nietzsche's critique of Christianity would become even more caustic. In this respect it is notable that Nietzsche refers to the 'madness' of 'man' having judged 'himself guilty ... to a degree that can never be atoned for' (1992b: Dialogue 2, §22). (Indeed, Levinas not only refers to one's being accused by the other as 'a seed of madness ... a psychosis' (2000: 188),[157] he suggests that his conception of ethics is in some sense 'masochistic' (2001: 46).) Both Nietzsche and Levinas could agree that morality is fundamentally against the (allegedly) most primitive of human drives toward self-assertion, and thereby '[*a*]*nti-natural*' (Nietzsche 1972a: p. 45). Likewise, there is a sense in which Nietzsche's claim that morality 'is the judgement of the judged' (ibid.: p. 46) might also ring true for Levinas.[158] Indeed, Levinas could even accept that 'Man is finished when he becomes altruistic' (ibid.: p. 87), if by this one means *natural* 'man' immersed in the egotistic 'instinct of life' (ibid.: p. 45). Both philosophers therefore demand that we become *more* human, but while for Levinas this requires a radical break from the natural instinct of self-preservation, according to Nietzsche we need rather to rediscover our naturalness and thereby be liberated from our 'unnaturalness,' our degenerate, otherworldly 'spirituality' (ibid.: p. 23). What Nietzsche's untimely vision thus bears witness to is precisely what Levinas most fears of the natural realm – namely, the subject's primitive drive toward self-assertion over the 'suffering and unfortunate' (Nietzsche 1968: §217).[159] The questions I want to draw from Nietzsche are as follows: Is Levinas's anxiety regarding human nature justified? Is the realm of the natural really incommensurable with that of the ethical? In order to answer these questions I want to briefly return to Wittgenstein, for it is specifically through his later work that Levinas's (and by implication, Nietzsche's) savage characterization of 'the natural' can be shown to be fundamentally misleading.

Although 'the human' has a certain priority in Wittgenstein's work,[160] this should not be exaggerated. For Levinas 'the human is a new phenomenon,' and subsequently any responsibilities toward other beings are merely an extension from the human realm. While one *may* procure certain responsibilities to other living beings, 'the prototype of this is human ethics' (1988a: 172), for the 'human face is completely different and only afterwards do we discover the face of the animal' (ibid.: 171–2).[161] This anthropocentrism (which he inherits from Heidegger[162]) constitutes a troubling ethical blind spot in Levinas's work, given its alleged 'radicality.' However, Wittgenstein's prioritization of 'the human' is not of this sort. Indeed, it provides an important corrective to Levinas's anthropocentrism and anti-naturalism. For Wittgenstein the human face and body may enable a far greater degree of expressivity than other beings,[163] but this is indeed a matter of degree, not of kind.[164] Although the archetype of *human* animality in part circumscribes that to which one can meaningfully attribute suffering,[165] the boundaries of this are notably broad. Thus, for example, Wittgenstein writes:

> Look at a stone and imagine it having sensations. – One says to oneself: How could one so much as get the idea of ascribing a *sensation* to a *thing*? One might as well ascribe it to a number! – And now look at a wriggling fly and at once these difficulties vanish and pain seems able to get a foothold here.
>
> (1958: §284)

This passage is interesting for a number of reasons. First, it problematizes Wittgenstein's often quoted remark: 'If a lion could talk, we could not understand him' (ibid.: p. 223). This passage is, I believe, poorly expressed and thus frequently misconstrued as signifying a *radical* incommensurability (that is, the sort of 'break' Levinas envisages) between the human and animal realms. This remark is incongruous because: (1) elsewhere Wittgenstein describes language as 'an extension of primitive behavior' (1990: §545),[166] and (2) according to §284 of *Philosophical Investigations* (quoted above) there is enough commonality between the 'wriggling fly' and manifestations of human suffering for the notion of pain 'to get a foothold here.' Given these two points it seems reasonable to suppose that were a lion to 'speak' its language *would* have important points of contact with our own. On matters pertaining to birth, sex, death[167] and suffering the lion's 'form of life' is not *radically* different from the human. Indeed, we already (*without* the lion's 'speaking') perceive such connections, so why assume that its acquisition of language would not extend these further? (What Wittgenstein perhaps ought to have said is: 'If a *stone* could talk, we could not understand it.') With this in mind Wittgenstein's occasional remarks on other *humans* being 'a complete enigma' (1958, p. 223) – and similarly: '"These men ... have nothing human about them"' (1990: §390) – should be treated with caution. But a further point can be drawn from §284 of *Philosophical Investigations* regarding Levinas's emphasis on the 'otherness' of the other. For Levinas must presuppose some sort of recognition of (or, more naturalistically, reaction to) the human *qua* human in order to assert that 'the prototype ... is human ethics' (1988a: 172) and '[t]he human face is completely different and only afterwards do we discover the face of the animal' (ibid.: 171–2).[168] In other words, Levinas must *already* presuppose that the 'human' is significantly distinguishable from the realm of either inert nature or 'mere' animality.[169] As such, his emphasis upon the *radical* otherness of the other (who, we are repeatedly told, transcends all traditional philosophical categories) turns out to be not so 'radical' after all. As I suggested in Chapter 3 and earlier in this chapter (and as Derrida himself intimates[170]), for another to be *absolutely* 'other' would mean that that other remained wholly unrecognizable even *as* an other to whom one was ethically bound.[171] Indeed, without this identification we would be forever 'at a loss' as to whether such an encounter was taking place, or had *ever* taken place.[172] In short, this would plunge Levinas into the most extreme form of ethical skepticism or Pyrrhonian quietism.[173] Thus, his recurrent claim that the 'human community ... does not constitute the unity of genus' (1996c: 213–14),[174] or that the other is 'irreducible ... to the individual of the human race' (1998a: 10) must be treated with the same degree of circumspection as Surin's, Lyotard's and Readings's (not to mention Levinas's own[175]) suspicion of positing a human 'we.' It is, of course, correct to insist that the singular other (here, face to face with me) is not experienced merely as a *specific* incarnation of the 'human race as a biological genus' (Levinas 1996c: 213),[176] or a *specific* 'instance of humanity' (Winch 1987: 174), for such a picture of intersubjectivity would be absurdly deliberative. It is also correct to highlight the ethical significance of our 'involvement with ... particular human beings' (ibid.: 172), each with 'his own nature and history' (ibid.: 174).[177] Yet while the other should not be construed as merely one replaceable (and to that extent more-or-less anonymous) sample of 'the human,' neither is her specificity radically separable from 'the human.' This is why the minimal naturalism I have been drawing from Wittgenstein is important, for without it sensitivity toward the singular other would be rendered a *fundamentally* mysterious phenomenon.[178]

If we recall, Levinas is concerned with language as a medium through which the ethical passes.[179] The face, after all, addresses me in its 'mute and accusatory eloquence' (Derrida 1992b: 117).[180] Here Levinas decomposes language into its dual function as: (1) informational-communicative content (Said), and (2) quasi-performative offering or gift (Saying),[181] thus extending the ethical significance of language beyond a mere '*truth-that-unites*' (1993: 142).[182] Consequently the linguistic realm is demarcated from the 'sounds and noises of nature' that merely represent 'words that disappoint us' (ibid.: 148). In order to explore this demarcation I want to turn to Levinas's brief discussion of 'Bobby,' a stray dog who (albeit temporarily) reconfirmed Levinas's humanity during his wartime incarceration.

The bark of a dog: the other (as) animal

Although Levinas refers to Bobby as 'the last Kantian in Nazi Germany,' it is apparent that Bobby's 'jumping up and down and barking in delight' – his 'friendly growling, his animal faith' (1997a: 153) – is here celebrated only as a hollow counterfeit of the fully 'human.'[183] Despite his exuberant affection, in his 'brutish dumbness' (1995: 110) Bobby functioned only as a momentary relief from 'the children and women who passed by and sometimes raised their eyes – [stripping] us of our human skin' (1997a: 152–3).[184] Bobby thus granted Levinas and his fellow prisoners a precious distraction in the midst of human misery. But, as one commentator notes, there is good reason to believe that Levinas 'would consider it crucial for his account whether Bobby merely barks or whether in doing so he can say *Bonjour*' (Llewelyn 1991: 56). Although Levinas is hesitant when pressed on the question if 'the animal has a face' (ibid.: 57) – remarking cautiously that a 'more specific analysis is needed' – his general position is that the ethical significance of the animal derives from the human.[185] Levinas thus observes: 'Children are often loved for their animality. The child is not suspicious of anything. He jumps, he walks, he runs, he bites. It's delightful' (1988a: 172). Bobby's playful enthusiasm may be similarly 'delightful,' but it remains highly doubtful that for Levinas this delight harbors anything of direct ethical import.[186] As discussed earlier with reference to *Robinson Crusoe*, what is striking about Levinas's commentary is his prioritization of human language over the 'sad echoes' or 'failed words' (1993: 148) of the natural world.[187] But such a position does little more than reiterate traditional philosophical prejudices concerning the alleged 'dignity of man.' Indeed, that the realm of the human does *not* constitute a radical 'break' (1988a: 172) with nature is one important – albeit frequently overlooked – dimension of Wittgenstein's later work. Thus, as previously noted, Wittgenstein variously characterizes language as 'auxiliary to,' an 'extension' (1990: §545), 'refinement' (1994a: 31) or 'replacement'[188] of 'primitive behavior' (1990: §545).[189] This is not to question the complexity and subtlety of human linguistic communication, for doubtless 'the *language* of sensation provides finer descriptions of sensation than would be possible with purely non-linguistic behavior' (Malcolm 1986: 304). Neither is it to suggest that other species possess a communicative system analogous to human language.[190] The point is rather to ask why is such increased complexity *ethically* significant? More precisely, if language acquisition is an extension or replacement of primitive behaviors (for example, of non-linguistic pain behavior – including reacting to *other's* pain) then there is no reason to attribute any more ethical weight to language-use (or language-users) than to those primitive behaviors upon which language-use is grounded.[191] Levinas's mistake lies in his needing to know whether Bobby's bark was really a 'Bonjour,' for this question presupposes a sharp boundary between 'mere' behavior and 'genuine' language.[192] Whether Bobby's behavior can be translated into something linguistic is beside the point, for if Bobby howls when abused can we meaningfully doubt he is suffering?[193] When *Bobby's* 'content of suffering merges with the impossibility of [his] detaching [himself] from suffering' (Levinas 1997b: 69) (when *he* experiences the 'blindness of pain ... interiority of agony ... solitude of misery ... the worldlessness of suffering' (Caputo 1993: 205)[194]), is this any less certain or deplorable than our human neighbor's simply because the former *does not speak*?[195] With Levinas in mind, it is notable that Picard claims that 'the perfection in animals' lies in the fact that 'there is no discrepancy in them, as there is in man, between being and appearance, inward and outward nature' – indeed, it is this 'perfect correspondence' that 'constitutes the innocence of animals' (1948: 109). Picard's assertion is partly correct; human infants and most non-human animals can be neither dishonest nor insincere. However, he misrepresents the nature of pain. For, even in *human* suffering (including *another's* suffering) this inner/outer dualism remains questionable. As Wittgenstein suggests:

> [W]ords are connected with the primitive, the natural, expressions of the sensation and used in their place. A child has hurt himself and he cries; and then adults talk to him and teach him exclamations and, later, sentences. They teach the child new pain behavior ... the verbal expression of pain replaces crying and does not describe it.
>
> (1958: §244)

Whereas for Levinas ethics is fundamentally *anti*-naturalistic, Wittgenstein's suggests that ethics is only possible on the grounds of certain 'natural, instinctive, kinds of behavior' (1990: §545) toward others; our language-games are 'based *on it* . . . it is the prototype of a way of thinking and not the result of thought' (ibid.: §§540–1).[196] This point runs contrary to (for example) Trigg's recent claim that, for Wittgenstein 'the world is merely the world revealed in language . . . In a real sense, according to Wittgenstein, society determines what it is to be human, since it is in society that language is learnt' (1999: 176–7). Unsurprisingly, Trigg proceeds to emphasize the 'relativistic' (ibid.: 178) interpretation of Wittgenstein I have argued against, and to conclude that 'the possibility of understanding alien societies' in the wake of Wittgenstein's later work becomes 'very problematic' (ibid.: 179). But Trigg's error is to read Wittgenstein as 'stressing the distinct nature of the human social world and its separation from the animal world' (ibid.: 180). Though it is true that Wittgenstein suggests that 'an education quite different from ours might also be the foundation for quite different concepts' (1990: §387), it would be mistaken to interpret this as meaning that our concepts are *entirely* unbounded, or as denying that certain primitive 'concepts' (pain, for example) will always play some role in human affairs. At this juncture it is worth recalling Levinas's claim that ethics is 'unreasonable' and 'Man is an unreasonable animal' (1988a: 172) insofar as being-for-others ruptures both the natural drive for self-preservation and the pragmatic-economic calculations necessary for political life. That ethics is, at its root, not 'reasonable' Wittgenstein would agree. However, conceding this much is not to say that ethics is *un*reasonable; to speak of 'reason' (even of 'unreason') here overlooks the natural basis upon which being-for-others is hinged. To ask whether our primitive ethical responses are 'reasonable' would be as misconceived as inquiring whether other parts of 'our natural history' (such as 'walking, eating, drinking, playing' (Wittgenstein 1958: §25)) are also 'reasonable'? Ethics is indeed 'not based on grounds,' if one takes that to mean rational-deliberative grounds. (In this restricted sense Wittgenstein's work is indeed anti-foundationalist.) It is, however, 'grounded' insofar as it represents an extension of primitive, natural reactions that are 'not reasonable (or unreasonable)' but simply 'there – like our life' (1999: §559). The problem that Levinas simply reiterates – if not compounds further in his spiritualized humanism – is succinctly expressed by Wittgenstein in the following passage:

> Reason . . . presents itself to us as the gauge *par excellence* against which everything that we do, all our language games, measure and judge themselves. – We may say: we are so exclusively preoccupied by contemplating a yardstick that we can't allow our gaze to *rest* on certain phenomena or patterns. We are used, as it were, to 'dismissing' these as irrational, as corresponding to a low state of intelligence, etc. The

174 *The unreasonableness of ethics*

yardstick rivets our attention and keeps distracting us from these phenomena, as it were making us look beyond . . .

(1993: 389)

While both Wittgenstein and Levinas agree that ethics does not ultimately have a rational ground, Levinas's error is to conflate what is *reasonable* with what is *natural*.[197] For Levinas ethics cannot be grounded in the natural because he assumes that the realm of the natural is saturated with the egological 'instinct of life' (Nietzsche 1972a: p. 45). It thus only becomes possible to speak of ethics when this natural drive toward being-for-oneself is disrupted by concern for another.[198] And this, we should recall, is precisely what Levinas claimed was missing from Cain's response to God ('Am I my brother's keeper?') for here '[e]thics is the only thing lacking in his answer; there is only ontology: I am I, and he is he' (1998b: 110). In other words, for Levinas, Cain's response is entirely rooted in his *animal nature*.[199] It does not seem significant to Levinas that it is *also* 'a primitive reaction to tend, to treat, the part that hurts when *someone else* is in pain; and not merely when oneself is' (Wittgenstein 1990: §540, my emphasis).[200]

Earlier I discussed how, on Levinas's account, the other's face embodies the commandment 'thou shalt not kill' (1992: 87–8), and thereby constitutes 'the categorical imperative' (1993: 158) or 'order issued to me not to abandon the other' (ibid.: 44). All this lies in the face that faces me. But, as I also noted, Levinas contrasts these more active determinations by suggesting that the face is simultaneously 'exposed, menaced, as if inviting us to an act of violence. At the same time, the face is what forbids us to kill' (1992: 86). The face is thus the very junction at which authority and vulnerability meet – indeed, its authority *is* its fragility. For Levinas all these characterizations pertain explicitly to the human face.[201] But here I want to suggest that the vulnerability he attributes to the face of the other lies not in their humanity but in their *animality* – that is, in their elementary needs for sustenance, shelter and care.[202] Thus, where Levinas discerns a spark of the 'divine' in the eyes of the other, we should instead rediscover the *animal* in the other's eyes.[203] With this in mind, it is interesting that Derrida should draw attention to a passage in Baudelaire, where a beggar's gaze of '"mute eloquence"' is explicitly associated with '"the tear-filled eyes of a dog being beaten".' Why should Baudelaire make this comparison? Perhaps, as Derrida suggests, because the 'poor man is a dog of society, [and] the dog is the fraternal allegory of social poverty, of the excluded, the marginal, the "homeless"' (1992b: 143). But Derrida goes further than Baudelaire, declaring that '[n]othing is less stupid, less beast-like than "dogs being beaten" and whose "tear-filled eyes" speak the infinite demand' (ibid.: 167).[204] Must one take these latter remarks metaphorically and thereby conclude that such sentiments are (as Levinas maintains) only possible because the 'prototype . . . is human ethics' and concern for non-human animals 'arises from the transference to [them] of the idea of suffering' (1988a: 172)? In short, what is to be gained by endorsing Levinas's claim that '[i]n my relation to the other, I hear the Word of God. It is not a metaphor ... it is literally true' (1998b: 110), rather than evacuating the unnecessary metaphysics?[205]

In Chapter 2 I explored Wittgenstein's remarks on 'trust' in *On Certainty*, and specifically how distrust belongs to 'a fairly advanced stage of human relations' (Hertzberg 1988: 318). The child thus displays a 'primitive' trusting toward its principal carers, only upon which subsequent (and increasingly deliberative) trust-relations can be founded. Regarding this sort of unconditional trust – as opposed to 'reliance' – Hertzberg thus claimed:

> [I]n so far as I trust someone, there will be no limits, given in advance, of how far or in what respects I shall trust him ... In relying on someone I as it were look down at him from above. I exercise my command of the world. I remain the judge of his actions. In trusting someone I look up from below. I learn from the other what the world is about. I let him be the judge of my actions.
>
> (1988: 314–15)

Now, Levinas accepts that the child 'is a pure exposure of expression' or a 'pure vulnerability,' not least because she 'has not yet learned ... to deceive, to be insincere' (1984: 64).[206] It is, one might say, through the inherent vulnerability of the child that her unconditional trust is manifest, and that this primitive (pre-linguistic, pre-rational) trusting demands the responsibility of others.[207] But if this is true regarding the human infant, then it also pertains to non-human animals. Moreover, Hertzberg's remarks enable us to say something, not only about the natural vulnerability of the *other* but also about the subject who responds to the vulnerable other. In short, the minimal naturalism I have been defending cuts both ways in the ethical relation. Thus, at a primitive level, the dog (for example) is the very epitome of Levinasian responsibility; that is, of an unconditional 'love without reward' (or 'gratuitous gift of ... friendship' (Gaita 2003: 10)), even in the face of violence. Pure animality is pure trust, faith and obedience to the demands of another who is absolute authority. The dog responds without concern for reciprocity, for, as Levinas remarks of Bobby, he lacks 'the brain needed to universalize maxims' (1997a: 153). Of course, this rational incapacity excludes the non-human animal from playing an active[208] role in the realm of justice – where, for the sake of the third party, reciprocity, equality and calculation become necessary. But this should not blind us to the fact that the complex, often agonizing decisions justice requires can only arise *as such* against a backdrop of primitive, natural behaviors – many of which we share with non-human animals.[209] Thus, when Levinas claims that the

176   *The unreasonableness of ethics*

'Here I am!' constitutes the 'religious discourse that precedes all religious discourse' (1996a: 146),[210] this casts things in the wrong light. It would, I believe, be better to say that the 'Here I am!' is in fact the natural 'discourse' that precedes all discourse, including the 'religious.' In this regard it is notable that Levinas (again, like Rousseau[211]) should allude to 'the original language, a language without words or propositions ... a communication without phrases or words' (1987: 119–20). For, as previously noted, he is adamant that the 'sounds and noises of nature' merely represent 'words that disappoint us' (1993: 148). To reiterate my earlier question: Why should Bobby's bark need to be translated into a 'Bonjour' to gain ethical significance? In keeping with Levinas's views on the superficial 'noises of nature,' Picard writes:

> It is true that the raven croaks, the dog barks, and the lion roars. But animal voices are only chinks in the silence. It is as though the animal were trying to tear open the silence with the force of its body.
>
> 'A dog barks today exactly as it barked at the beginning of Creation', said Jacob Grimm. That is why the barking of dogs is so desperate, for it is the vain effort, since the beginning of creation until the present day, to split the silence open, and this attempt to break the silence of creation is always a moving thing to man.
>
> (1948: 111)[212]

Thus, according to Picard, what is so 'desperate' about the bark of a dog is its *sameness*. From its inaugural performance in the Garden of Eden to the present day, the dog's bark has remained the same, and it is this relentless futility that 'moves' us. But Picard overlooks something crucial here. For not only does he fail to distinguish between the bark of a 'friendly' (Levinas 1997a: 153) and maltreated dog,[213] he omits to note that the cry of *human pain* is similarly marked by its sameness across the ages. Doubtless new forms of suffering have become possible in different historical periods, but the anguished cries of broken human bodies span the millennia in the same way as the bark of the maltreated dog. Indeed, as already suggested, it is precisely in those phenomena associated with finitude and vulnerability that the natural commonality between the human and non-human animal is manifest. If one is to take seriously what Levinas says concerning the Said and Saying, I want to suggest that the latter is best thought of in terms of the non-propositional 'sounds and noises' of the human infant and the non-human animal. In short, if Levinas wants to attempt the impossible and think the 'Saying without [the] Said' (1996a: 103),[214] then he could do no better than recall and reflect more deeply on the bark of Bobby, 'the last Kantian in Nazi Germany' (1997a: 153).

Something animal

In his striking 'inhospitality' toward the animal Levinas reiterates some of the founding assumptions of the traditional humanism he aims to transcend. For despite his attempt to rethink language and ethics, Levinas fails to rid himself of certain philosophical presuppositions concerning (most notably) the relationship between linguistic and non-linguistic behavior. As has become clear, in Levinas's schema the human is that unique being through whom a trace of God passes, thus breaking the relentless domination animality would otherwise have over the mortal realm. From a Levinasian perspective one might therefore supplement Wittgenstein's remark that 'When you see the eye you see something going out from it' (1990: §222) by suggesting that what one 'sees' is a spark of the divine in the eyes of the other human. What can be said of the eyes of the non-human animal? For Levinas, these signify only a dumb, brutish concern for self-preservation; a moral lacuna. ('If a lion could talk,' Levinas would say, 'it would speak only the language of ontology.') Indeed, even in the eyes of an animal like Bobby – who appears to demonstrate otherwise – one could not describe his 'goodness' without considerable anthropomorphic distortion. But against this picture I have argued that, from the ideal of saintly holiness to the one who says simply 'after you,' we discern a 'spark' of the *animal* in the other's face. Not, that is, the egoistic brute Levinas sees, but those propensities and reactions upon which ethical life is founded (most notably a natural vulnerability and orientation toward others).[215] In the final part of this chapter I want to highlight this latter point by turning to Derrida's recent remarks on Levinas. Although I have hitherto alluded to Derrida only in passing, his distinct contribution to Levinasian scholarship deserves attention, and in Chapter 8 I will elaborate on his cautious reformulation of certain Levinasian themes. Of more immediate concern is how Derrida misrepresents Levinas on a crucial point when he claims that the latter possesses 'no concept of nature' (1999b: 90). Clearly, given my previous analysis, this assertion is problematic. Nevertheless, Derrida's additional remarks on Levinas correlate with the broadly naturalistic position I have been defending.

Despite Derrida's criticisms of both Levinas's and Heidegger's anthropocentric bias[216] (Derrida even claims that his account of iterability 'should be valid beyond the marks and society called "human"' (1997d: 134)[217]) it nevertheless remains unclear whether his own understanding of the ethical[218] hinges upon Levinas's presupposition that the human 'bursts forth' (1998b: 157) from the natural, thereby representing a 'scandal in being' (ibid.: 115).[219] This ambiguity emerges in those passages (cited above) where Derrida refers to the 'beaten dog' as the 'fraternal allegory of social poverty, of the excluded, the marginal, the "homeless"' (1992b: 143), and his subsequent remarks on the 'infinite demand' (ibid.: 167) spoken by the eyes of such a creature. For here it is precisely the *non*-human animal that is characterized, not as Levinas's dumb brute[220] but as the very epitome of the vulnerable other. A particularly interesting complication emerges, however, when Derrida begins to trace 'the logic of an extremely complex relation' between Levinas and 'the Kantian tradition' (1999b: 48–9). The crux of the matter here is that Kant thinks 'hospitality ... must be [politically] instituted in order to interrupt a bellicose state of nature' (a 'natural hostility,' for 'nature ... knows only actual or virtual war'), whereas, according to Derrida, for Levinas there lies 'a backdrop of peace' and 'hospitality that does not belong to the order of the political' (1999b: 49).[221] Although this claim is not wholly improvident (Levinas does indeed speak of a 'prior non-indifference to the other man' (1998a: 141), the 'religious discourse that precedes all ... discourse' (1996a: 146), and so on[222]), Derrida's reading nevertheless underestimates Levinas's anti-naturalism. Indeed, later in his commentary Derrida compounds this oversight by suggesting that 'there is no concept of nature or reference to a state of nature in Levinas ... and this is of the utmost importance.' He then proceeds to reiterate the significance of this (alleged) omission in the Levinasian project:

> [E]verything [for Levinas] seems 'to begin,' in ... the welcoming of the face of the other in hospitality, which is also to say, by its immediate and quasi-immanent interruption in the illeity of the third ... [Levinas] suggests that war, hostility, even murder, *still* presuppose and thus *always* manifest this originary welcoming that is openness to the face ...
>
> (Derrida 1999b: 90)[223]

As I said, this reading is not without some legitimacy, for Levinas does place ethics before (or 'above') ontology. Nevertheless, given what Levinas says about the radical 'break' humanity makes with natural animality – not to mention the anomaly between genuine language and the disappointing 'sounds and noises of nature' (1993: 148)[224] – Derrida's claim that the former lacks a 'concept of nature' is mistaken. While we might accept that there is no *analysis* of 'the natural' in Levinas's work, this is precisely the problem insofar as his treatment of the natural hinges on a number of misguided assumptions. Derrida's oversight is thus perhaps due more to an ambiguity within Levinas's work. But what primarily interests me is how this oversight again raises the question whether goodness (generosity, hospitality, and so on) can be said to have its roots in the natural realm? Earlier in his exposition Derrida makes a very pertinent remark in this regard. There, referring to Levinas's account of intersubjectivity, he speculates: 'It is as if the welcome, just as much as the face, just as much as the vocabulary that is co-extensive and thus profoundly synonymous with it, were a first language, a set made up of quasi-primitive ... words' (1999b: 25).[225] I have already alluded to the notion of a 'first

The unreasonableness of ethics 179

language' in Levinas's work, and specifically how this might be thought of in more naturalistic terms. Nevertheless, Derrida's allusion to the 'quasi-primitive' offers something of much broader significance for my argument. Of course, one is here faced with a slight equivocation: it is *as if* the welcome, generosity and hospitality consisted of something 'primitive' before or beneath culture, society and politics. Although the 'as if' (and the 'if there is') has a crucial and unequivocal function in Derrida's work,[226] on this point such a qualification seems to me unnecessary. To put it bluntly, why not simply drop the 'quasi' and say with Wittgenstein that 'it is a primitive reaction to tend, to treat, the part that hurts when someone else is in pain; and not merely when oneself is' (1990: §540), and likewise that 'this sort of behavior is *pre-linguistic*: that a language-game is based *on it*, that it is the prototype of a way of thinking and not the result of thought' (ibid.: §541).[227] Why posit a mysterious pre-natural dimension of hospitality[228] when the natural *itself* proves adequate to the ethical task?[229] Interestingly, in another recent text (concerned with issues of 'forgiveness'), Derrida addresses 'the question of the animal' as follows: 'it would be very imprudent to deny all animality access to forms of sociality in which guilt, and therefore procedures of reparation, even of mercy – begged or granted – are implicated in a very differentiated way.' Derrida then suggests that, just as there is an animal 'act of war,' there is 'no doubt' an animal 'thank you,' 'shame, discomfort, regret, anxiety' and 'remorse' – indeed, in the realm of the animal one can also witness 'rites of reconciliation, of the interruption of hostility, of peace, even of mercy' (2001b: 47).[230] In short, without wanting to deny the significance of 'verbal language' for these complex phenomena, the 'possibility, even [the] necessity of extra-verbal forgiveness' (ibid.: 48) must be acknowledged. *If there is* such a thing as a 'pure' gift, hospitality and generosity, and *if there is* such a thing as giving without calculation or the expectation of return (and I take Derrida's point to be that one can only have faith that such things occur[231]), then I want to say that they happen *blindly* every day as a '"goodness without thought"' (Levinas 1999: 108).[232] In other words, these occurrences are – like the violence of being itself – *so* ordinary, *so* banal that one does not even designate them as such. The 'impossible' that Levinas invests so much faith in has 'already occurred' (Derrida 1997c: 80) as an entirely *natural* phenomenon – that is, as 'something animal' (Wittgenstein 1999: §359).

8 Contaminations
Levinas, Wittgenstein and Derrida

> A man is capable of infinite torment . . . and so too he can stand in need of infinite help.
> L. Wittgenstein, *Culture and Value*

> Hearts open very easily to the working class, wallets with more difficulty. What opens with the most difficulty of all are the doors of our own homes.
> E. Levinas, *Nine Talmudic Readings*

> [T]he problem of hospitality [is] coextensive with the ethical problem. It is always about answering for a dwelling place, for one's identity, one's space, one's limits, for the *ethos* as abode, habitation, house, hearth, family, home.
> J. Derrida, in Derrida and Dufourmantelle, *Of Hospitality*

Introduction

In the preceding chapters we have been concerned with 'hauntings' of various sorts; of knowledge by doubt, reason by rhetoric, politics by ethics, justice by violence, good conscience by Guilt, and the human by 'the animal.'[1] Throughout these analyses I have referred to Derrida's work on numerous occasions. In this final chapter I want to bring the aforementioned themes together by releasing Derrida from his (as yet) somewhat spectral presence. In particular I want to explore: (1) the extent to which Derrida's work has become increasingly possessed by Levinasian themes, and (2) how Wittgenstein might in turn be invited to 'haunt' Derrida.[2] In a number of recent texts the influence of Levinas on Derrida's thinking is prominent – most notably where Derrida focuses on the aporetic demands of 'hospitality.'[3] As we will see, these 'quasi-prophetic' (Caputo 1993: 91) interventions demonstrate that there is perhaps nobody more attuned to the question of what Levinas's thinking might mean for contemporary ethical-political theorizing.[4] Of course, the precise degree of proximity between Levinas and Derrida remains contentious.[5] Nevertheless, the continual reformulation of Levinasian motifs in Derrida's writings is, I believe, undeniable.[6] In the following discussion I will summarize how Derrida has developed and politicized Levinas's work. More specifically, what interests me here are: (1) what Derrida's explicit reflections on hospitality owe to Levinas's phenomenology of 'home' (outlined in *Totality and Infinity*[7]), (2) how the question of hospitality figures as a backdrop to Derrida's work on 'iterability,' and (3) how his remarks on testimony, trust and faith might be read along broadly Wittgensteinian lines. As we will see, these three topics are intimately connected.

Haunted houses: Levinas's phenomenology of home

Near the beginning of his phenomenology of 'home,' Levinas identifies the existential stakes involved in this 'privileged' theme when he claims that the 'recollection necessary for nature to be able to be represented and worked over, for it to first take form as a world, is accomplished as the home' (1996c: 152). That is:

> Man abides in the world as having come to it from a private domain, from being at home with himself, to which at each moment he can retire ... Concretely speaking, the dwelling is not situated in the objective world, but the objective world is situated by relation to the dwelling.
>
> (1996c: 152–3)[8]

To truly 'have a world' presupposes that one first 'have a home' – no matter how temporary or fragile the latter might be. 'Home' here signifies a site *from* which the subject's worldly excursions are oriented, and *to* which they return, thereby maintaining a 'circular ... law of economy' (Derrida 1992b: 7–8) between self and world.[9] And it is in this sense that the home (including the 'mobile home'[10]) is 'not a possession in the same sense as the movable goods it can collect and keep' (Levinas 1996c: 157). Of course, insofar as the home provides a 'refuge' (ibid.: 154)[11] or site of 'withdrawal from the elements' (ibid.: 153), it thereby constitutes a break with 'natural existence' (ibid.: 156).[12] Levinas's point is that this taking refuge is, existentially speaking, more significant than a mere sheltering from natural forces.[13] In the subject's 'recollecting' itself in the 'dwelling,' both 'labor and property [become] possible.' (Indeed, recalling what I said in Chapter 6 of Levinas's misgivings concerning the visual metaphor, it is notable that he here describes the 'window' as that which 'makes possible a look that dominates' – that, when viewed from the home, the 'elements remain at the disposal of the I – to take or to leave' (ibid.: 156).) The 'raw material' (ibid.: 159) of the natural world is thus 'fixed between the four walls of the home' and to that extent becomes 'calmed in possession' (ibid.: 158). The home would therefore appear to be 'in fact egoist' insofar as it is first 'hospitable for its proprietor' (ibid.: 157).[14] Thus far the subject has been described as if it existed in glorious isolation – like

Crusoe's 'insular life' (1993: 148) before meeting Friday. That is to say, the home understood as essentially a 'project of acquisition' (1996c: 162) cannot as yet, it seems, be described as a 'violence' because, Levinas suggests, here acquisition and possession concern 'what is faceless' (ibid.: 160).[15] But, like the lover's relation with her beloved (discussed in Chapter 7), this economy of 'intimacy' (ibid.: 153) – and the domestic good conscience it spawns – is little more than an egoistic fantasy. For 'possession itself refers to more profound metaphysical relations'; namely, 'the other possessors – those whom one cannot possess – [who] contest and therefore can sanction possession itself.' That is, in the 'face of another being' (ibid.: 162) the subject's home (and all 'possession' manifest therein) is called 'in question' (ibid.: 163),[16] and this is why the '*somewhere* of dwelling' constitutes 'a primordial event' (ibid.: 168).

It is at this point that the question of hospitality arises – or, more accurately, shows itself to have already arisen. For now the issue is not primarily about the home as 'hospitable for its proprietor' (ibid.: 157) but rather about the 'welcome [that] the Home establishes' (ibid.: 170–1), or my knowing how to '*give* what I possess' and thereby 'welcome the Other who presents himself in my home by opening my home to him' (ibid.: 171). Levinas thus concludes:

> [N]o face can be approached with empty hands and closed home. Recollection in a home open to the Other – hospitality – is the concrete and initial fact of human recollection and separation; it coincides with the Desire for the Other absolutely transcendent. The chosen home is the very opposite of a root ... The possibility of the home to open to the Other is as essential to the essence of the home as closed doors and windows. Separation would not be radical if the possibility of shutting oneself up at home with oneself could not be produced without internal contradiction as an event in itself, as atheism.
> (1996c: 172–3)[17]

These points might be summarized as follows: In order for a thing (a found natural object, for example) to become a possession *for me* it must also be possible for *another* to possess it.[18] In an analogous way the home's being made 'hospitable for its proprietor' (ibid.: 157) (that *I* can occupy *this* site as home) refers to *other* possible proprietors.[19] Indeed, it is this necessary possibility to which the face of the other gestures when it accuses me of taking the place of another and thereby partaking in the violence of being. My-dwelling-here is therefore necessarily 'haunted' (Derrida 1999b: 112)[20] by the ghosts of others 'whose presence is discreetly an absence' (Levinas 1996c: 155).[21] As such, Levinas insists, 'my' home can never be described as thoroughly 'intimate'[22] or 'calm,'[23] never a total 'secrecy' (ibid.: 156) or 'refuge' (ibid.: 154) – indeed, not even as wholly 'mine.'[24]

With these general points in mind, Derrida's allusion to the etymological link between '*host* and *hostage*' (1999b: 57) (and specifically why the 'host ... is a hostage insofar as he is a subject put into question' (ibid.: 56)[25]) becomes extremely pertinent. It is to this that I will now turn.

The perils of hospitality

While Derrida maintains that the 'separation' between self and other 'is the condition of the social bond' (1999a: 71)[26] (even of 'love' and 'friendship' (1997e: 14)[27]), he seems more willing than Levinas[28] to cast this in quasi-epistemological terms. So, for example, Derrida remarks that this 'nonknowledge is the element of friendship or hospitality for the transcendence of the stranger, the infinite distance of the other' (1996c: 6).[29] This reference to 'hospitality' is significant, not only because I previously identified a certain Levinasian 'inhospitality' toward the animal but more particularly because it is around this Levinasian theme that Derrida develops a number of ethical, political and quasi-religious concepts.[30] Employing Derrida's conceptual vocabulary, intersubjectivity can be cashed out as follows: The other *qua* other (that is, if she is not merely a reflection of myself[31]) can always *surprise* me.[32] That is, for 'the other to happen, to come to me' (1997a: 5) means that I find myself in the domain of the 'unforeseeable' (2002a: 361) or 'perhaps' (1997a: 5).[33] (Levinas similarly remarks that the 'perhaps' is 'the modality of an enigma, irreducible to the modalities of being and certainty' (1996a: 75).[34]) As discussed in Chapter 3, Wittgenstein makes a number of related points when contrasting 'fixed' behaviors with a natural 'liveliness' (1958: §420),[35] 'incalculability' (1994a: 73) and 'unpredictability of human behavior' (1990: §603).[36] But Derrida's emphasis on the other's unforeseeableness takes on more explicitly political overtones when he proceeds to distinguish between the 'invitation' and 'visitation' (or hospitality).[37] In the *invitation* – by which Derrida is primarily referring to the closed invitation ('Come at 4 o'clock'), not the open invitation ('Come whenever you want'[38]) – the coming of the other is brought under regulatory control; you are invited and I am therefore 'expecting you and am prepared to meet you' (1999a: 70).[39] Though even here there remains a necessary possibility (otherwise this would be mere coercion[40]) that the other *will* surprise me by coming sooner or later than requested – or even not at all[41] – the function of the invitation is to inhibit such possible interruptions of my being-at-home.[42] The grammar of the invitation thus shows it to be infused with conditionality insofar as it neither stands indefinitely nor precludes its later amendment or withdrawal.[43] More specifically, this conditionality is ultimately founded upon notions of property rights; my being 'at home' (Derrida 2000b: 51).[44] What the invitation effectively says is: You are permitted to come and I will thereby grant you some of 'my' space and time, for I *rightfully belong here, I* am not (and *here* cannot be) a trespasser.[45] These

184 *Contaminations*

presuppositions are clearly problematic on Levinasian grounds, for, as previously discussed, 'the Other ... calls me into question' and 'paralyzes possession, which he contests by his ... face' (Levinas 1996c: 171).[46] Given this fundamentally 'accusative' (Levinas 1998b: 111) structure of intersubjectivity, one is never simply or unproblematically 'at home.' Rather, as Derrida puts it, one is always the 'stranger at home' (1993b: 10), for 'my home' undergoes a continual haunting by the other: '[h]ospitality is the deconstruction of the at-home' (2002a: 364).[47] In contrast to the economics of the invitation (though, as we will see, this demarcation is necessary blurred), hospitality (subject to the *visitation*) knows no such prudence.[48] Like Derrida's account of the 'pure' gift,[49] hospitality is without 'ruse' (1995c: 74) and 'supposes a break with reciprocity, exchange, economy and circular movement' (1999a: 69).[50] Genuine hospitality depends rather upon one's being open to the possibility of 'an absolute surprise,'[51] for the other, 'like the Messiah, must arrive whenever he or she wants' (ibid.: 70) not when I decide they are least inconvenient.[52] This '*messianicity*' (1998b: 17) or not-knowing *when, how* or even *if* the Messiah will arrive[53] is 'the unconditional law of hospitality ... [which] gives us the order or injunction to welcome *anyone*' even 'without checking at the border who he or she is, what his or her nationality is.' The law of hospitality is therefore 'a way of being open whoever comes. Whoever comes should feel at home here' (1997a: 8).[54] If 'I am unconditionally hospitable,' Derrida concludes, 'I should welcome the visitation,' not merely the 'invited guest' (1999a: 70).[55]

According to Derrida then, I must be vigilant in my nonvigilance, '*ready to not be ready*' (2002a: 361) or 'prepared to be unprepared' (1999a: 70).[56] Unsurprisingly, this curious practice of interminable openness to the other (this 'madness ... linked to the essence of hospitality' (1998c: 89, n. 9)[57]) brings in its wake considerable risks.[58] As previously noted, the 'invitation' represents one way of circumscribing such perils. But, as also became clear, it is precisely the desired *in*vulnerability (or quasi-Pyrrhonian *ataraxia*) motivating such practices that renders them ethically problematic. Regarding the 'visitation,' however, such risks play a constitutive role. That the visitor *might* come bearing tribulations and catch me 'without protection ... incapable of even sheltering [myself]' (1993b: 12) (that she *might* oppose my being-at-home to the point of 'ruin[ing] the house' (2000a: 353), or even by bringing death) is a necessary condition of hospitality *qua* hospitality.[59] It is also, we should note, a necessary condition for the home to be a home, and not some self-regulated quarantine, that I am vulnerable in this way.[60] (I will return to the notion of quarantine later.) If there is such a thing as 'pure' hospitality one cannot therefore 'exclude the possibility that the one who is coming ... is a figure of evil' (1997a: 9) – even of '*radical evil*' (1998b: 17),[61] and the force of this prohibition is not merely empirical, but structural, or part of the grammar of hospitality. In other words, evil is always a risk, but this risk is not *itself* evil. Rather, such risk constitutes the very chance of hospitality. Of course, in 'ordinary circumstances' the visitor is most often courteous toward the hospitality she receives; trespassing, burglary and eviction are more-or-less exceptional occurrences. But in keeping with his preoccupation with the 'production of the extraordinary *within* the ordinary' (2000a: 415), Derrida insists that this customary goodwill can neither be demanded nor pre-programmed.[62] Locking away one's valuables to avoid their possible theft by the visitor, or physically restraining her upon entering one's home for fear of possible violence; these sorts of practices (no matter how *reasonable* in specific circumstances) would be incommensurable with pure hospitality, just as a necessary condition for the gift to be a gift (and not merely an item of exchange) is the possibility of it being unwanted, inappropriate or offensive.[63] In much the same way as an authentic prayer must not be merely repeated 'mechanically' (1992a: 269), so a 'gesture "of friendship" or "politeness" would be neither friendly nor polite if it were purely and simply to obey a ritual rule' (1995c: 7).[64] In short, '[f]or an event to happen, the possibility of the worst, of radical evil, must remain a possibility ... Otherwise the good event, the good Messiah, could not happen either' (1997a: 9).[65] That is, 'what threatens is also what makes possible' (2002c: 135).

In some wonderfully evocative passages, Bachelard writes that 'the door is an entire cosmos of the Half-open' (1994: 222), for 'a mere door ... can give images of hesitation, temptation, desire, security, welcome and respect.' He then inquires: 'onto what, toward what, do doors open? Do they open for the world of men, or for the world of solitude?' (ibid.: 224). The pertinence of this question for our analysis is clear enough. Indeed, earlier Bachelard asks the following (and notably Levinasian) question: 'Where is the main stress ... in *being-there*: on *being*, or on *there*? In *there* – which it would be better to call *here* – shall I first look for my being?' (ibid.: 213). He then provides a rather convenient synopsis of what, I have argued, preoccupies both Levinas and Derrida:

> Outside and inside are both intimate – they are always ready to be reversed, to exchange their hostility. If there exists a border-line surface between such an inside and outside, this surface is painful on both sides ... The center of 'being-there' wavers and trembles.
> (Bachelard 1994: 218)[66]

The 'at home' can 'project an image ... of closedness, of selfish and impoverishing and even lethal isolation,' but this very same 'at home' is 'also the condition of openness, of hospitality, and of the door' (Derrida 2002d: 81). That is to say, the '*at-home* has always been tormented by the other, by the guest, by the threat of expropriation. It is constituted only in this threat' (ibid.: 79). Although '[w]alls and closed doors have always been experienced as invitation to trespass' (Harries 1998: 168), this is not

186 *Contaminations*

an empirical failing or lamentable vulnerability of the home. Rather, these 'threats' represent the home's positive condition of possibility. For 'in order to constitute the space of a habitable house and a home, you also need an opening, a door and windows ... a passage to the outside world. There is no house or interior without a door or windows' (Derrida 2000b: 61).[67]

Now, such aporias of giving are hardly new concerns for Derrida.[68] For the risk inscribed in hospitality (what sometimes appears as a hazardous moment of theodicy in his work[69]) relates directly to his reflections on 'writing' and 'iterability.'[70] Thus, the necessary threat of death can be seen to haunt language *in general* insofar as: (1) the human (linguistic) subject is vulnerable and mortal, and (2) language, in its structure, transcends the empirical conditions of this mortality.[71] It is to the relationship between language and finitude that I now want to turn.

From the law of iterability to the confessional

Whatever particular theory of language we might favor, one thing remains incontestable: some day I will utter my last words (or, more precisely, I *will have uttered* my last words for 'those who remain' (Heidegger 1999: 282)[72]). Moreover, barring an impossibly rigorous quarantine – where not only my environment but every physio-biological process were subject to the strictest surveillance and prediction (something only God could oversee[73]) – never can I be sure whether *these* words *at this very moment* will not turn out to be my unwitting valediction.[74] No matter how expected my death might be, it can always come sooner than anticipated and, like the visitor or Messiah who 'comes like a thief in the night' (1 Thessalonians 5:2),[75] catch me unawares.[76] Sooner than I have time to compose myself (my location, posture, or preferred 'last words'), death can always arrive as a surprise[77] – indeed, as the ultimate surprise, for I will have nothing to say about it; I will barely even experience its arrival.[78] Insofar as *these* might be my last words,[79] 'last words' are, structurally speaking, remarkably unremarkable.[80] But this structural 'ordinariness' has further implications. It is not merely that *any* word could, as a matter of fact, prove to be my last, but rather, that *every* word functions *as if it were* my last.[81] That is, it remains essential to the functioning of language *qua* language that a sign (written or otherwise) be detachable from its 'source,' and that this source be capable of being absent to the point of death. It seems obvious that 'my' words are in a relation of authorial dependence upon 'me.' But this picture is misleading insofar as any word I offer must, by definition, be capable of surviving me – whether this 'survival' pertains to a breach with my intentions, my spatio-temporal location, or my actual death.[82] As such, even the most direct and mundane acts of communication between determinate subjects already gesture toward their indeterminate dissemination.[83]

There are doubtless affinities between these points and Wittgenstein's remarks on 'private language'[84] and following a rule 'only *once*' (1958: §199).[85] But Derrida's account of iterability can also be approached through Wittgenstein's suggestion that it is often illuminating to 'invent [a] fictitious natural history' where 'very general facts of nature' (ibid.: p. 230) are different from those with which we are familiar. One might, for example, imagine a world where the subject and her written word were inextricably bound, and even determined by her mortality.[86] Here, the death of the subject naturally results in the disappearance of her written word from the world. (One might further imagine that her death obliterates the memories of others concerning anything she may have written during her lifetime.[87]) The point of this thought experiment is to illustrate not only how strange the world would be were language confined by human finitude but, more radically, whether the concepts of 'language,' 'writing' and 'communication' (and, not least, the very distinction between 'author' and 'text') could even get a foothold.[88] That the *mortality* of the (linguistic) subject needs to be contrasted with the *immortality* of the language she 'uses' is, to borrow Wittgenstein's words, something about 'the natural history of human beings' (ibid.: §415) which does 'not strike us because of [its] generality' (ibid.: p. 230).[89] It is doubtless this 'generality' that has contributed to the ill reception of Derrida in certain philosophical circles (and specifically to his being charged with making 'trivial' (1995a: 420) propositions). Of course, were Derrida's point left in the stark formulation 'language *is* . . . "immortal"' (2000a: 402) then it would indeed appear to be of little philosophical interest.[90] What *is* significant is the way such general 'observations which no one has doubted' (Wittgenstein 1958: §415) – once their implications are pursued – necessarily effect other, more specific areas of philosophical, political and ethical concern. Recalling my earlier remarks on Levinas's preoccupation with Guilt, and the seemingly 'trivial' assertion (made above) that I will *some day* utter my 'last words,' we can now bring these two themes together: With each word *I testify to my mortality*,[91] and, by implication, to my having escaped death *thus far*. As Derrida puts it, I write, speak, act (and so on) in the name of my 'survival' (1995a: 346),[92] and as such my activities (linguistic or otherwise) constitute a 'living death liturgy' (1993a: 137).[93] But as I argued in Chapter 6, my 'survival' is problematic insofar as *to be* is 'already an ethical problem' (Levinas 1993: 48).[94] Granted, I am now surviving; this is the condition of possibility of being an 'I.' But, as Levinas inquires, at 'whose cost' (1999: 179) is this survival?[95] To the extent that my activities (or 'writing' in the broader sense Derrida assigns that term) testify to my survival, they simultaneously testify to my Guilt *for* surviving,[96] and in doing so betray their inherently confessional, apologetic nature.[97] Levinas thus speculates:

> I wonder whether there has ever been a discourse in the world that was not apologetic, whether . . . our first awareness of our existence is

an awareness of rights, whether it is not from the beginning an awareness of responsibilities, whether, rather than comfortably entering into the world as if into our home, without excusing ourselves, we are not, from the beginning, accused.

(1994b: 82)

To *be* is already to be *in the confessional mode* – or, in Derrida's words, '[o]ne always writes in order to confess ... in order to ask forgiveness' (2001b: 49); one 'confesses, even when [one] does not confess or denies confessing' (2002a: 383).[98] Indeed, he explicitly links this request for forgiveness to the fact that 'one is always failing, lacking hospitality ... one never gives enough' (ibid.: 380),[99] and, more significantly, to the 'guilt ... for living, for surviving ... for the simple fact of being there' (ibid.: 383).

Skepticism, trust and violence

Derrida's work continues to provoke both venomous hostility and uncritical imitation. The latter does not interest me unduly. The former, however, is pertinent to my analysis insofar as the pervasive suspicion here is that Derrida's thinking betrays a radical skepticism. Now, one only has to consider Derrida's frequent use of the qualifier 'if there is such a thing' (1993b: 79)[100] (notably in his ethical-political work) to see how a cursory reading can generate such anxieties. The surface grammar of such remarks does indeed lend them to skeptical interpretation, but, like Wittgenstein's hesitancy between religious belief and denial, Derrida's caution here is not fundamentally skeptical.[101] The comparison with Wittgenstein is germane, for – as we will see – just as he speaks of religion out of a certain religiosity,[102] so too does Derrida speak in the name of a minimal (and ineliminable) trust or faith.[103] Derrida thus insists that the apparently circumspect 'if there is' is actually *constitutive* of responsibility, the decision, hospitality, and so on. These are not merely themselves empirically impossible, but rather the 'very figure of the impossible' (1992b: 7).[104] It is not that specific instances of a 'pure' hospitality (gift, decision, and so on) *never actually* happen, but that such things *never could* be said to have 'happened,'[105] and this is an essential feature of what they are. Their impossibility is thus not to be lamented as an insufficiency or failing – which would indeed render Derrida's account skeptical in the traditional sense. On the contrary, they owe their very life to such impossibility. In a similar manner, Derrida's account of iterability[106] may appear skeptical insofar as any meaningful sign (linguistic or otherwise[107]) is inscribed with the necessary possibility of 'failure' (1971: 325).[108] Contrary to Austin's analysis of performatives,[109] Derrida insists that the 'risk' of performative failure Austin highlights does not 'surround language like a kind of *ditch*, a place of external perdition into which [it] might never venture' (ibid.: 325). Rather, this 'risk' is an 'essential predicate or *law*' (ibid.: 323)[110] that actually constitutes language's 'power' (1992a: 42)[111] and 'internal and positive condition of possibility' (1971: 325).[112] For a sign to function 'normally'[113] (to reach its intended destination, to be understood, and so on) one cannot, as Austin attempts to do, exclude the possibility of its 'going astray.'[114] Indeed, even when a sign does function 'successfully' its failure remains inscribed as a necessary *possibility*.[115] Again then, iterability does not call for philosophical bemoaning because this is a law not a 'lure' (ibid.: 327). In keeping with Wittgenstein's reminders in *On Certainty* concerning the intimate grammatical relationship between 'knowledge' and 'doubt,'[116] Derrida reminds us that the possibility for sincerity, authenticity, success, truthfulness (and, not least, hospitality, friendship and goodness) necessarily depends upon the ineliminable potential for insincerity, inauthenticity, failure, lying (hostility, enmity and evil). In short, there is a necessary 'reciprocal contamination' (1984: 122) between the grammar of these concepts.[117] (As Wittgenstein suggests in *Philosophical Investigations*, this is why one cannot, without a certain distortion, describe the 'unweaned infant' (1958: §249) – or many non-human animals[118] – as 'sincere,' 'honest' or 'truthful.'[119]) Of course, circumstances may indicate that danger is at hand, be it in the form of physical violence or mere insincerity. But even here 'transcendent certainty' (Wittgenstein 1999: §47)[120] is neither available nor required, and thus cannot be an object of philosophical nostalgia. There is no way of determining a 'total context,'[121] not least because one 'cannot precisely describe' what constitutes 'normal circumstances' (ibid.: §27).[122] After all, what possible contextualization could provide quarantine against *any* utterance being used ironically or in quotation?[123] Indeed, to this extent Derrida's misgivings concerning the simple demarcation between 'ordinary' and 'extraordinary' language (because what he is 'trying to find ... [is] the production of the extraordinary within the ordinary, and the way the ordinary is ... "vulnerable" to or not "immune" to what we understand as extraordinary' (2000a: 415)[124]) are in line with much of Wittgenstein's later work. Thus, recalling Wittgenstein's remarks on 'trust' and 'foundational propositions' in *On Certainty*, we can re-cast a number of Derrida's points on iterability as follows: I have to trust what the other says to me – or at least trust my own judgement that she is not to be trusted.[125] Likewise, I trust that what I say will be believed and understood as it was intended.[126] More radically perhaps, I must even trust that I will survive to the end of this sentence,[127] and that you will survive too, no matter how undetermined the 'you' is here.[128] (In other words, I trust that the Apocalypse will not arrive in the meantime.[129]) Such 'primitive' (Wittgenstein 1999: §475),[130] 'elementary faith' (Derrida 1998b: 45) is not therefore 'hasty but excusable' (Wittgenstein 1999: §150), for without it one would simply be 'incapable of learning,' and subsequently engaging in 'language games' (ibid.: §283).[131] In this crucial sense then, trust is not one language-game among others.[132] Rather, it constitutes that which *all* language-games[133] are hinged upon.[134] As Derrida remarks, there could be 'no society ... without trust in the other ... [without] this minimal act of faith' (1997e: 23), or, in Winch's words, the 'notion of a society in which there is a language but in which truth-telling is not regarded as the norm is a self-contradictory one,' and therefore it would 'be nonsense to call the norm of truth-telling a "social convention", if by that were meant that there might be a human society in which it were not generally adhered to' (1960: 242–3).[135] That is, 'some concern with the virtue of truthfulness is a necessary background condition in any society in which it is possible for anyone to make true statements' (ibid.: 244).[136] At its root such trust is neither reasonable *nor* unreasonable,[137] not least because 'it may never have been expressed' or even 'thought' (Wittgenstein 1999: §159).[138] On this point, I want to suggest, the Wittgensteinian naturalism I have hitherto been defending is itself minimal enough to be read into Derrida's remarks on 'testimony' and 'trust.'[139] Thus Derrida variously remarks: 'Testimony, which implies faith or promise, governs the entire social space ... theoretical knowledge is circumscribed within this testimonial space' (1999a: 82):

> [O]ne can *testify* only to the unbelievable. To what can, at any rate, only be believed; to what appeals only to belief and hence to the given word, since it lies beyond the limits of proof, indication, certified acknowledgement ... and knowledge ... when we ask others to take our word for it, we are already in the order of what is merely believable. It is always a matter of what is offered to faith and of appealing to faith ... Such is the truth to which I am appealing, and which must be believed, even, and especially, when I am lying or betraying my oath.
>
> (1998c: 20–1)

> Take, for example, trusting someone, believing someone. This is part of the most ordinary experience of language. When I speak to someone and say 'Believe me', that is part of everyday language. And yet in this 'Believe me' there is a call for the most extraordinary. To trust someone, to believe, is an act of faith which is totally heterogeneous to proof, totally heterogeneous to perception.
>
> (2000a: 418)[140]

As I discussed in Chapter 2, if one's survival (be it one's communicative-social or physio-biological survival[141]) is to be possible, one cannot *begin* with doubt in this regard.[142] For this 'elementary trust ... is involved ... in every address of the other. From the first instant it is co-extensive with this other and thus conditions every "social bond", every questioning, all knowledge, performativity' (Derrida 1998b: 63),[143] and this is why 'there is no culture that is not also a culture of hospitality' (2002a: 361).[144] Trusting the other is logically prior to any suspicion one might later harbor because suspicion is itself necessarily grounded upon what is not open to suspicion.[145] But as soon as one is surviving (one of 'the survivors' (Derrida 1988e: 593)) doubt becomes inscribed as a necessary – though, I would add, local[146] – possibility. Insincerity, distrust, doubt and lying may be logically 'parasitic' upon sincerity, trust, certainty and truthfulness, but this can do nothing to quarantine the social-moral arena – and again, this is a structural point rather than a lamentable failing.[147] Likewise, that a certain pre-performative truthfulness (an implicit 'believe me' (Derrida 1998b: 63)[148] and '"unconditional" affirmation' or 'yes' 'independent of every determinate context' (Derrida 1997d: 152)[149]) remains co-extensive with every utterance, does not inhibit the possibility for deceit. Rather, it is what makes deceit both possible and especially easy with regard to children and many non-human animals. In an analogous way to Wittgenstein's suggestion that Moore misrepresents 'foundational propositions' by claiming to '*know* what he asserts' (1999: §151), so Derrida argues that Austin's account of performatives misrepresents deceit by characterizing it as something 'accidental' (Derrida 1971: 323), 'unhappy' (Austin 1976: 15) or 'infelicitous.'[150] Although the implicit normativity in Austin's serious/non-serious distinction provokes Derrida to wonder about the political significance of the term 'parasite' in speech-act theory,[151] I want to return to ethical-political matters of a different kind.

Earlier I discussed how the possibility for hospitality is haunted by evil insofar as it is structurally necessary that the guest can always manifest herself as radically inhospitable. There are no absolute safeguards against this possibility, and if there were then hospitality *as such* would be a hollow concept. The possibility for my being hospitable thus depends upon a certain intractable vulnerability, both of the relation of hospitality in general (the contexts of its occurrence) and of its specific 'participants' therein.[152] Clearly measures can be taken to render hospitality less susceptible to breaches of trust. But if, as Derrida sometimes suggests, a *measured* hospitality is no hospitality at all,[153] then how can such cautious maneuvers be justified?[154] To answer this question we must here recall the structural importance of the 'third party' in Levinas's work. To recap: If there were only two of us inhospitality would indeed be unjustifiable. But given that the third party also addresses me in the face of the singular other, my responsibility toward this *other* other must be given due consideration. Only in this way does inhospitality become inscribed into the demands of hospitality itself.[155] 'One must be *responsible* for what one gives and what one receives,' Derrida notes, because even the 'excess of generosity of the gift – in which the pure and good gift would consist' can turn into 'the bad ... even the worst' (1992b: 63–4).[156] With the third party (who, let us recall, has *always already* 'arrived' in the face of the singular other), not only do we find the birth of theory, justice and institutions, it is 'now' that the call for legitimate violence can be heard. Thus, if I am protecting *x* from the violence of *y*, then my *inhospitality* to *y* becomes an essential component of my *hospitality* toward *x*, my *inhospitality* toward *y* constitutes the conditions of possibility of my being *hospitable* toward *x*.[157] As Schopenhauer pithily remarks, while on the one hand 'friendship is only limitation and partiality' insofar as 'it is the restriction to one individual of what is due of all mankind,' on the other hand 'the man who is everyone's friend is no one's friend' (1918: 123).[158] The paradox that arises here is that a 'pure' hospitality would be indistinguishable from the Pyrrhonist's radical indifference, where one *nonchalantly* said

> yes *to who or what turns up*, before any determination ... before any *identification*, whether or not it has to do with a foreigner, an immigrant, an invited guest, or an unexpected visitor, whether or not the new arrival is the citizen of another country, a human, animal, or divine creature, a living or dead thing, male or female.
> (Derrida 2000b: 77)

It is in this way that there (again) remains a necessary mutual 'contamination' (1992a: 68)[159] between pure hospitality and inhospitality, between '*the* unconditional law of hospitality' and 'conditional ... laws of hospitality' (2000b: 79),[160] between love and violence, friendship and enmity.[161] Here the categories of 'exclusion and inclusion are inseparable' (ibid.: 81), and as such '[h]ospitality is a self-contradictory concept' (2000c: 5).[162] For Derrida then, violence (and thus an ineliminable bad conscience) is inscribed into the gratuitousness of Levinasian ethics insofar as: (1) the other first needs to be identified *as such* – that is, as *an other*, (2) I can never rest assured that I have done enough or made 'the just choice' (2001e: 56) for *this* other, (3) any ethical relation I have with *this* other (or *these* others) is always at the expense of *another* other (or *those* others), and (4) my responsibility to *this* other (or *these* others) may thereby demand my violence toward *another* other (or *those* others).[163] In short, there is a necessary 'infidelity at the heart of fidelity' (2002a: 388), and this is why Derrida insists that 'bad conscience ... is the main motivation of my ethics and my politics' (2001b: 69).[164] Ultimately it may not be possible to 'derive a politics' from Derrida's (Levinasian) notion of hospitality, but (again, like Levinas) Derrida insists: 'a politics that does not retain a reference to this principle of unconditional hospitality is a politics that loses its reference to justice' (2002d: 17).[165]

Thus far I have been concerned with certain contaminations between hospitality and violence, truthfulness and insincerity, and so on. What Derrida thus brings to our attention is how a Levinasian ethics of 'pure' generosity is *necessarily* impossible.[166] It is this intermingling of the possible and impossible that I now want to focus on.

(Deciding) On the impossible

In 'A Lecture on Ethics' Wittgenstein maintains that a 'characteristic misuse of our language runs through *all* ethical and religious expressions' (1993: 42). Yet the futility of this 'tendency in the human mind' to 'run against the boundaries of language' does not prevent him from 'respecting [it] deeply' (ibid.: 44). Likewise, God's commanding something beyond the realms of possibility[167] does not prompt Wittgenstein to dismiss such grammatical peculiarities as instances of language 'idling' (1958: §132) or having gone '*on holiday*' (ibid.: §38).[168] Rather, he wants to preserve these aporias as essential to the genuinely religious life.[169] In Derrida's work similar tendencies emerge insofar as justice, responsibility, hospitality, the gift (and so on) demand that we 'endure'[170] the 'experience of the impossible' (1995a: 359)[171] – or the 'experience of the desire for the impossible' (1999c: 72).[172] To take one particularly striking example, Derrida remarks that 'the so-called responsible decision' must not merely be the 'technical application of a concept' or 'the consequence of some preestablished order' (1993b: 16–17)[173] (as though one were following 'a doctor's prescription' (Wittgenstein 1994a: 53)[174]). Rather, 'the decision must arise against a background of the undecidable ... As a condition of the decision as well as that of responsibility, the undecidable inscribes threat in chance, and terror in the ipseity of the host' (Derrida 1998c: 62).[175] Providing an ethical twist to the Pyrrhonian narrative discussed in Chapter 1, Derrida insists that this backdrop of undecidability neither constitutes nor sanctions 'paralysis' (1999a: 66)[176] or 'resignation' (2001e: 56) in the face of mutually incompatible choices. For 'there would be no decision ... in ethics, in politics, no decision, and thus no responsibility, without the experience of some undecidability' (1999a: 66).[177] This is not, however, to say that undecidability is mere indeterminacy. Rather: 'I am in front of a problem and I know that the two determined solutions are as justifiable as one another. From that point, I have to take responsibility' (ibid.).[178] (That is, in a given situation I know that my options are x and y. As far as possible I know how to implement x and y and the likely outcome of each. The problem is that between these two determinate choices I do not know how to justify deciding on x rather than y (or vice versa), as the reasons and justifications for either x or y seem equally distinct, compelling and legitimate. This then is the moment of undecidability Derrida is referring to, not the sort of quandary resulting from x and/or y *themselves* being ambiguous or indeterminate.[179]) Although Derrida acknowledges the aporetic nature of judgement criteria[180] – an aporia that occasionally prompts him to speak of the necessity for a quasi-Kierkegaardian 'leap' (ibid.: 73)[181] – he nevertheless resists the Pyrrhonian teleology of *ataraxia*. There is no liberation from responsibility or the 'madness' (1995c: 59)[182] that constitutes the decision, for here there could only be the corrupt assurance of 'good conscience'

194 *Contaminations*

(1999a: 67);[183] of having applied the rule absolutely correctly or of only having 'obeyed orders.'[184] After all, how does one justify applying *this* criterion and not another, or account for the necessary exclusion of *other* programs by the adoption and implementation of *this* one?[185] And how does one justify applying a rule *in this way* rather than *that*? As I argued in Chapters 2 and 3, appealing to one's inherited world-picture may have epistemic acumen but it will never be ethically sufficient to justify good conscience. For any world-picture must *as such* be inhabitable by *other* others; there can no more be a private world-picture than there can be a private language. My world-picture is no less haunted than are those 'internal' features (my decisions,[186] my home,[187] my friendships and loves[188]) previously discussed. If the other 'haunts' (Levinas 1984: 63)[189] my being-in-the-world *as such*, then the specificities of my world-picture will provide neither an adequate means of exorcism nor quarantine in which to withdraw:

> [S]ince there is ... no hospitality without finitude, sovereignty can only be exercised by filtering, choosing, and thus by excluding and doing violence. Injustice, a certain injustice, and even a certain perjury, begins right away, from the very threshold of the right to hospitality.
>
> (Derrida 2000b: 55)

That I choose you over her, friends over strangers, my family or community (or even species) over 'foreigners' – all this I routinely justify. But that in this very process of justification I apply *this* set of criteria over another, I cannot justify.[190] In short: 'I will never know that I have made a good decision' (Derrida 2001b: 62). We must of course 'calculate'[191] between possible choices; Derrida is not advocating random[192] or arbitrary action, neither of which would constitute a 'decision.'[193] Likewise, we have a responsibility to accumulate as much knowledge as possible in order to make judgements.[194] We must not be willfully *anti*-rational (after all, how could this be justified without appealing to another rationality?[195]). But the decision to calculate is not *itself* 'of the order of the calculable' (Derrida 1990: 963).[196] More specifically, the 'decision between just and unjust is never insured by a rule' (ibid.: 947) because the justice of the *rule* – and there might always be a *better* justice and a *better* rule[197] – would thereby have to be assumed. Recalling the paradox of Pyrrhonian quietism discussed in Chapter 1, we are always already *within* the decision: '[t]he decision takes place' (2002f: 312). Even when I am *indecisive* (even when I say 'No!' to the incessant demands of decision) I have already said 'Yes' to indecision.[198] This being-in-the-decision is not itself deliberative or quasi-contractual, but due to the very structure of human finitude.[199] In this way, then, Derrida is not advocating a voluntaristic decisionism but rather attempting to articulate (which is difficult, if not impossible, insofar as every discourse or meta-discourse presupposes the pre-performative 'Yes' for itself[200]) the affirmative backdrop against which all particular deliberations occur.[201]

Despite this 'always already' of one's being-in-the-decision – and some avowedly 'hazardous' reflections regarding Heidegger's 'inexcusable silence' on 'Auschwitz and many other topics' (1988a: 147)[202] – Derrida does not (as Heidegger seems to[203]) cast suspicion upon apologetic-confessional practice *per se*. Rather, what he emphasizes is the necessary, though again impossible, vigilance demanded by such practices;[204] a vigilance that would both maintain bad conscience and yet also ensure that such bad conscience never simply masked a deeper good conscience.[205] (Though even in this risky formulation Derrida would question the ethicality of a bad conscience that could be 'ensured.') There may seem to be something 'terrible' (1997b: 20)[206] about all this, but, let us recall, these aporias do not delineate a 'trap.' Rather, they are the very 'condition of a decision' (1999a: 69) and thus of responsibility itself. What characterizes the experience of the impossible is a 'perpetual uneasiness' (1984: 120) in acknowledging that my worldly activities – insofar as they are necessarily sacrificial[207] – are never wholly just(ifiable).[208] As such, 'remorse' becomes 'an essential predicate of the relation we have to any decision' (1998a: 37), for 'in our relations with others ... we should never be sure of having done the right thing' (1997b: 23):[209]

> [T]he mortal ... is someone whose very responsibility requires that he concern himself not only with an objective Good but with the gift of infinite love, a goodness that is forgetful of itself. There is thus a structural disproportion or dissymmetry between the finite and responsible mortal on the one hand and the goodness of the infinite gift on the other hand. One can conceive of this disproportion without assigning to it a revealed cause or without tracing it back to the event of original sin, but it inevitably transforms the experience of responsibility into one of guilt ... What gives me my singularity ... is what makes me unequal to the infinite goodness of the gift that is also the first appeal to responsibility. Guilt is inherent in responsibility because responsibility is always unequal to itself: one is never responsible enough.
> (1995b: 51)[210]

In other words, my Guilt is not predicated on any specific act or omission – not even upon the inheritance of original sin. (Derrida instead refers to this as 'original sin prior to any original sin' (2002a: 388), and my being '*a priori* guilty' (ibid.: 384).) Rather, Guilt is a constitutive part of my 'finite and ... mortal' being-in-the-world; my being-*here* (which is a usurpation of *another*), my attending to *this* other rather than *that* other, and the illegitimacy of ever assuring myself that I have been 'responsible enough' to *any* other.

Derrida recalls Levinas once disclosed that his real interest was 'not ethics alone, but the holy, the holiness of the holy' (Derrida 1996c: 4).[211] In the political realm Levinas thus refers to 'a religious breath or a prophetic spirit' (1998b: 203) insofar as 'within justice, we seek a better justice' (1988a: 175)[212] – that is, because 'the ceaseless deep remorse' (1998b: 229) or 'bad conscience' (ibid.: 230) of justice keeps *good* conscience at bay.[213] Similarly, Derrida remarks that 'justice is not the law' because '[j]ustice is what gives us the impulse, the drive, or the movement to improve the law' (1997e: 16). Justice 'is always unequal to itself ... the call for justice is ... never fully answered,' and this is why it is impossible to 'say "I am just"' (ibid.: 17) without corruption.[214] To this extent, Levinas insists, there 'is no moral life without utopianism' (1988a: 178) – though, of course, this utopianism is profoundly a-teleological.[215] Indeed, it is the possibility for 'gratuitous' (1998a: 147)[216] self-sacrifice or 'saintliness'[217] that Levinas describes as the 'essence of human conscience' (1998b: 107) or '*religion*' (ibid.: 7). With this in mind, I want to close with a few remarks on Derrida's distinction between 'religion' and 'faith.'

Enduring faith

As noted previously, Wittgenstein maintains that the 'tendency' of those who attempt 'to run against the boundaries of language' when talking about ethics and religion 'is perfectly, absolutely hopeless' (1993: 44). Though worthy of respect, such endeavors nevertheless attempt the impossible. But, as discussed in Chapter 5, Wittgenstein does not leave us stranded in the silent landscape of the *Tractatus*. Despite his claim that 'Ethics, if it is anything, is supernatural' (ibid.: 40), Wittgenstein provides some clues as to the terrestrial dimension of ethical life in his subsequent references to 'shame' and feeling 'guilty' (ibid.: 40). Although for both Levinas and Derrida the 'desire for the impossible' is more directly linked to the question of good conscience and Guilt, to what extent Derrida shares Levinas's religiosity is difficult to determine. Thus, in keeping with both Levinas and the later Wittgenstein, Derrida cautions: 'We should stop thinking about God as someone, over there, way up there, transcendent,' and instead 'think of God and of the name of God without such idolatrous stereotyping or representation' (1995b: 108). But, we might ask, what then *can* be said about God? What viable function can this term now have? Interestingly, in 'Circumfession' Derrida claims that 'nobody understands anything' about his 'religion' (1993a: 154) – not even his mother 'who asked other people a while ago, not daring to talk to me about it, if I still believed in God.' He proceeds: 'but she must have known that the concept of God in my life is called by other names, so that I quite rightly pass for an atheist' (ibid.: 155). As Caputo notes, to 'pass for an atheist' seems a rather cryptic formulation[218] – one might – like the culturally assimilated Pyrrhonist – 'pass for' many things without that determination getting to the heart of the matter. Here we might recall Wittgenstein's own remarks concerning the 'sense in which' (Drury 1981: 130) he could be called 'a Christian.' Conversely, there is a 'sense in which' Derrida 'quite rightly' passes for an atheist because 'God' goes relatively unnamed (or at least 'by other names') in his life and work. The situation is complicated, not least because Derrida wonders whether it is even 'possible to think of responsibility, decision, remorse, and so on ... outside of a Christian tradition' (1997b: 21).[219] But it is not difficult to see what 'other names' might pertain to the divine in Derrida's writings. His preoccupation with confession, negative theology, the messianic and even prayer[220] are pertinent here, as are his numerous reflections on sacrifice, mourning and conscience. Of course, one should not base too much on a man's 'circumfession,' but it might still be asked whether Derrida shares Wittgenstein's preoccupation with trying to make sense of the religious in non- or quasi-religious terms. As intimated above, I am not suggesting that these Derridean themes can be straightforwardly interpreted as 'religious' (after all, it is not clear that even Levinas's work demands an explicitly 'religious' interpretation). Indeed, Derrida denies that such motifs 'mean that I am simply a religious person or that I am simply a believer':

> For me, there is no such thing as 'religion' ... Within what one calls religions ... there are again tensions, heterogeneity, disruptive volcanoes, sometimes texts, especially those of the prophets, which cannot be reduced to an institution, to a corpus, to a system.
>
> (1997e: 21)

Derrida is wary of the term 'religion' because it implies homogeneity within the realm of 'the religious.' As discussed in Chapter 3, such caution is judicious, but his emphasis on the 'heterogeneity' of 'what one calls religions' should not be exaggerated to the point of a *radical* (Lyotardian or quasi-Wittgensteinian fideistic) incommensurability thesis. For having expressed a certain admiration for Kierkegaard's 'paradoxical' (ibid.) faith, Derrida proceeds to draw the following distinction between 'religion and faith':

> [W]hat I call faith in this case is like something that I [say] about justice and the gift, something that is presupposed by the most radical deconstructive gesture. You cannot address the other, speak to the other, without an act of faith, without testimony ... This 'trust me, I am speaking to you' is of the order of faith, a faith that cannot be reduced to a theoretical statement ... So this faith is not religious, strictly speaking; at least it cannot be totally determined by a given religion. That is why faith is absolutely universal.
>
> (1997e: 22)

No critique of *religion*, or of *each determinate* religion, however necessary or radical that critique may be, should or can, in my view, impugn *faith* in general ... the experience of belief, of credit, of faith in the pledged word (beyond all knowledge and any 'constative' possibility) is part of the structure of the social bond or the relation to the other in general, of the injunction, the promise, and the performativity that all knowledge and all political action, and in particular all revolutions, imply. The critique of religion itself, as a scientific or political undertaking, makes appeal to this 'faith'. It therefore seems to me impossible to eliminate all reference to faith.

(1999d: 255–6)[221]

Like Wittgenstein, Derrida does not commit himself to any specific religious world-picture, and to this extent his position might be described as atheistic. However, insofar as *all* world-pictures – indeed, *every* human (and perhaps animal) activity, including deconstruction – are governed by a 'minimal' (ibid.: 23) faith, this hesitancy regarding the religious is not straightforwardly atheistic.[222] Indeed, that *religious* faith is itself dependent upon a more 'elementary faith' (1998b: 45) is consistent with my own suggestion that the absolute 'trusting' (Wittgenstein 1994a: 72) demanded by religion finds a natural counterpart in the 'primitive' trusting manifest in (for example) the parent–child relation.[223] In short, the 'testimonial space' Derrida maintains 'governs the entire social space' (1999a: 82) is a *natural* horizon which, as Wittgenstein might put it, is 'given' (1958: p. 226), or 'there – like our life' (1999: §559).[224]

Synopsis

From ancient Pyrrhonian skepticism to Derrida's most recent ethical-political thinking, in the preceding chapters we have covered a very broad philosophical terrain. Although Chapter 8 brought the main preoccupations of these analyses together, I would here like to offer a brief synopsis of the five central themes of the book.

1. Wittgenstein's later philosophy shares a number of striking similarities with the therapeutic practices of ancient Pyrrhonian skepticism. However, unlike the Pyrrhonists, his search for 'peaceful thoughts' does not represent an ethical-political ideal. In this crucial sense the claims of some commentators that Wittgenstein is a 'conservative' thinker are fundamentally mistaken. Likewise, that Wittgenstein is frequently taken to be primarily concerned with the 'radical plurality' of language-games, forms of life and world-pictures overlooks his underlying naturalism, for this presents a distinctly unifying picture of human life. More specifically, the minimal naturalism underpinning (for example) Wittgenstein's remarks on 'trust' in *On Certainty* identifies the necessary preconditions for ethical-political theorizing and practice.

2. Contrary to the suspicions of a number of philosophers, the deep anti-apologeticism of Wittgenstein's remarks on religious belief does not necessarily lead to a troubling relativistic fideism. What Wittgenstein cautions against is rather a conception of religiosity too closely tethered to both hypothetical speculation and what is practically 'reasonable.' Genuine religious belief is, according to him, a categorical commitment or 'trusting' insofar as what is demanded of the believer may be neither possible nor profitable. In short, Wittgenstein raises the possibility of thinking of religiosity beyond the inherent economics of eschatological-salvationist hope. This can be seen most clearly in his remarks on guilt, the 'wretchedness' of belief, and a sense of ethical responsibility that transcends even death.

3. Mindful of these latter themes, Levinas's work can best be understood as an extended meditation on existential guilt, or the 'guilt of the

survivor.' This notion has broadly Heideggerian roots, but its primary source must be located in the impact of the Holocaust on Levinas's thinking. Because *in my very being* 'I take the place of another' Levinas's fundamental question is not 'Why is there something rather than nothing?' but rather 'Do I have a right to be?' My ethical standing before the face of the other is therefore essentially apologetic and confessional. However, due to the 'primordiality' of such guilt no apologetic discourse can ever be complete. In short, 'bad conscience' is an ineliminable feature of the human condition.

4   While Wittgenstein's naturalism has tended to be underestimated by commentators, it is Levinas's *anti-*naturalism that has been neglected. Only if we take this latter omission into account will we properly understand both the philosophical motivations behind his explicitly 'religious' conceptual vocabulary, and his persistent anthropocentrism. Levinas's conception of 'religion' ultimately hinges on his conviction that 'love without reward' is both possible and of the utmost value. However, given Wittgenstein's insistence that language is a natural extension of pre-linguistic 'primitive behaviors' (of, for example, 'pain behavior'), his minimal naturalism provides not only an important corrective to Levinas's 'inhospitality' toward the non-human animal but also a more naturalistic perspective from which to account for the aforementioned possibility of 'love without reward.'

5   Derrida's recent work on 'hospitality' (and related themes) takes its lead from Levinas's brief sketch of a phenomenology of 'home' in *Totality and Infinity*. Nevertheless, Derrida teases out the internal aporias of the Levinasian account, arguing that the distinction between hostility and hospitality is necessarily blurred insofar as each 'contaminates' the other. Both the 'trust' demanded by hospitality and its inherent risks are not, however, contingent or empirical facts warranting philosophical lamentation. Rather, such mutual contamination constitutes the positive condition of hospitality *per se*. It is in this important sense that the *conditions of possibility* of hospitality are simultaneously its *conditions of impossibility*. Hence, Derrida's overriding (and avowed) ethical-political concern lies with the 'scandal of good conscience' and one's being '*a priori* guilty.'

Notes

Introduction

1 See Kerr 1997: Chs 1–6.
2 See Chapter 2.
3 See also Wittgenstein 1993: 40–4; 1996b: 94–5. As I explain in later chapters, a 'desire for the impossible' preoccupies both Levinas and Derrida.
4 Although Derrida's earlier work is intimately related to these recent preoccupations, I only indicate some of their more striking correlations (see also Bernstein 1991: 172–98). The tendency of some commentators (notably Baker 1995: 97–116; Patrick 1997: 71–90) has been to examine the 'ethics' of deconstructive practice. Interesting though these analyses are, their broad methodological focus often obscures the ethical terrain of Derrida's thinking.
5 See Caputo 1993; Bernasconi 1997; Critchley 1999a, 1999b; De Vries 1999; Bennington 2000b: Ch. 3; Llewelyn 2002.
6 See Staten 1986; Garver and Lee 1994; Glendinning 1998; Wheeler 2000.
7 Greisch (1991: 69–74) and Werhane (1995: 61–3) suggest some possible correlations between Wittgenstein and Levinas.
8 Clack (1999) is a notable exception.
9 For his later work Wittgenstein chose '"I'll teach you the differences"' as his preferred 'motto' (Drury 1981: 171).
10 Although I allude to a number of biographical details (on both Wittgenstein and Levinas), nothing philosophical ultimately turns on them.
11 Though this multiplicity is 'not ... fixed, given once for all' (Wittgenstein 1958: §23).
12 In Chapter 8 I develop this point in relation to Derrida's remarks on 'testimony' and 'faith.'
13 See also Schutz 1964: 234.
14 See Nielsen 1967; Clack 1999: 78–89. That is, the view that the 'internal' rule-bound religious practices of specific communities are quarantined from the critical assessment of those 'outside.'
15 See Nielsen 1967: 193, n. 1.
16 See Trigg 1999: 178.
17 See Nielsen 1967: 191.
18 Unlike Wittgenstein, Frazer's use of this term is pejorative.
19 See also Wittgenstein 1996a: 64–6, 68, 70, 72–4.
20 As will become clear in later chapters, I would here add 'vulnerability' and 'suffering.'
21 As I argue in Chapter 3, this is why Wittgenstein has interested 'radical' pluralists like Lyotard.
22 I develop this in Chapters 2 and 3.

202 Notes

23 Similar ideas emerge in Wittgenstein's suggestion that God's having 'commanded' something does not entail that it is even 'possible' (1994a: 77) to meet that demand. I explore this in Chapter 5.
24 As Derrida remarks of his own work: 'What I am trying to do is to find ... the production of the extraordinary *within* the ordinary' (2000a: 415).
25 This has partly been due to Levinas (and Derrida) frequently being described as 'postmodernists' – an unhelpfully vague term that tends to be used as a synonym for 'skepticism' and 'relativism' (Gellner 1993: 22–4; Gaita 2000: 15–16, 184–5, 258; Graham 2001: 21, 47, 203–4).
26 See Gellner 1993: 23; Davis 1996: 3.
27 See, for example, the essays collected in Campbell and Shapiro 1999. I refer to a number of these in later chapters.
28 See Chapter 3.
29 One might argue that the *genuinely* 'radically other' is not to be found in the familiar realm of sentient beings, but in the realm of *inanimate objects* (where the 'radically other' has never even been acknowledged *as such*). I return to this in Chapter 3.
30 See also Bernstein 1991: 74.
31 For a recent (though problematic) 'naturalistic' reading of Levinas, see Nuyen 2000.
32 See Derrida 1995a: 219.

1 Peaceful thoughts

1 For a condensed version of the present chapter see Plant 2004b.
2 See Drury 1981: 161.
3 See Derrida's criticism of Wittgenstein (1993a: 62–3), and the former's more recent 'confession' of his 'failure' (2000a: 351) to address Wittgenstein's work properly.
4 See Wittgenstein 1993: 462. For some notable exceptions see Drury 1981: 102–8.
5 I here take my lead from Fogelin's remarks on Wittgenstein and Pyrrhonism (1986, 1987: Ch. XV; see also Hardwick 1971: 24; Hookway 1990: 16). Fogelin suggests that this correlation has been overlooked due to the seeming perversity of reading Wittgenstein alongside any form of skepticism, given his persistent attempts to undermine the ground upon which the skeptic stands (1987: 226). But what is at stake here is not whether Wittgenstein was 'really' a Pyrrhonist (actually familiar with their writings, and so on), but whether Wittgenstein's methods and motives exhibit Pyrrhonian tendencies.
6 See Drury 1981: 97, 99.
7 See Nussbaum 1991: 521–2, 536, 538, 541.
8 See Nussbaum 1991: 527.
9 Stated otherwise 'unperturbedness' (Hookway 1990: 4) or 'freedom from disturbance' (Nussbaum 1991: 529). Pyrrho of Elis is thought to have visited India (Diogenes 1925: 475; Hankinson 1995: 58ff.), which raises interesting questions about the relationship between Pyrrhonism and Eastern philosophy.
10 See Nussbaum 1991: 538; Sextus 1996: 1:13–17.
11 See also Nussbaum 1991: 540, 545. As we will see, while the strength of treatment may alter, there remains an essential methodology of oppositional argumentation here. As such it is misleading for Sextus to claim that Pyrrhonism lacks a definitive method.
12 See Diogenes 1925: 491; Hookway 1990: 1; Nussbaum 1991: 548.

13 See Sextus 1996: 1:3–4.
14 On philosophical 'dogmatism' see Wittgenstein 1958: §131; 1994b: 72; Nietzsche 1968: §446.
15 See Nietzsche 1968: §455.
16 There remains a question as to whether she must implicitly allude to 'truth.' On a related point see Derrida 1992a: 257, 265, 288, 296–8; 1996b: 82; 1998b: 18, 26–8, 30, 44–5, 47, 63–4.
17 See Diogenes 1925: 515–17. This is not a trivial maneuver, for '[w]hen language-games change, then there is a change in concepts, and with concepts the meaning of words change' (Wittgenstein 1999: §65; see also 1990: §438). Note also Rorty's voluntarism on this matter (1999: pp. xviii–xix, xxii, 176), and passages of a more voluntaristic flavor in Wittgenstein (1979b: 98). Derrida's remarks on 'philosophical' and 'natural' language (1995a: 374) are also pertinent here.
18 See Hookway 1990: 9.
19 See also Diogenes 1925: 501–3, 507. On a similar point made by Hume against the Cartesian, see Passmore 1968: 135–6. Popkin reiterates many of these issues in relation to the epistemological crisis inaugurated by the Reformation (1979: 1–2, 13, 51). Derrida makes a similar point regarding the foundations of law (1990: 943, 1001; 2001e: 57), and the 'decision to calculate' (1990: 963) – though, as we will see in Chapter 8, this does not lead Derrida to Pyrrhonian quietism (1990: 947, 963, 971).
20 See also Diogenes 1925: 515.
21 See Nussbaum 1991: 523.
22 The reason I here avoid the word 'cause' will become clear later.
23 While the Pyrrhonist criticizes the dogmatist for opposing natural inclination, she also suggests that theoretical dogmatism is itself of natural origin (Nussbaum 1991: 530; see also 526).
24 See Nussbaum 1991: 523, 534.
25 On the similarities between the human and animal, see Sextus 1996: 1:59–79.
26 See Nussbaum 1991: 529.
27 See also Inwood and Gerson 1988: 238.
28 See Burnyeat 1983: 126.
29 See also Diogenes 1925: 513.
30 See also Nussbaum 1991: 524, 531.
31 See Sextus 1996: 1:25–30 (compare with Nietzsche 1968: §260).
32 See also Diogenes 1925: 519.
33 That 'painful exertion is not something unqualifiedly worth avoiding,' see Sextus' remarks quoted in Inwood and Gerson 1988: 238. Note also Caputo 1993: 29.
34 See Sextus 1996: 1:27–8.
35 See also Nussbaum 1991: 529.
36 See Nussbaum 1991: 527.
37 See Nussbaum 1991: 545.
38 See Nussbaum 1991: 544.
39 Even conceding this minimal necessity for belief, the Pyrrhonist could still justify himself on the aforementioned pragmatic grounds; that although a life *totally* devoid of commitment may be impossible, Pyrrhonism still offers the best way of minimizing such troublesome commitments.
40 For a summary of the ten 'modes' of Pyrrhonian argumentation see Diogenes 1925: 493–9.
41 See Popkin 1979: 63.
42 See also Diogenes 1925: 487.
43 See also Inwood and Gerson 1988: 181–2.

44 See Diogenes 1925: 484–5.
45 We should here note the quasi-performative character of the Pyrrhonist's utterances (Nussbaum 1991: 535). On a related point see Rousseau 1930: 210.
46 Nussbaum thus draws attention to the principle of non-contradiction in the Pyrrhonian method (1991: 548).
47 See Mates 1996: pp. 30–2.
48 Interestingly, Wittgenstein refers to doubt as 'a moment of hesitation' (1993: 379).
49 Doubtless even this phrase could, in specific circumstances, be intelligible (Wittgenstein 1999: §350).
50 One might say that the Pyrrhonist attempts to place herself between or outside language-games, thereby lacking 'a criterion ... that is, a basis for deciding' (Mates 1996: p. 31) sense from nonsense.
51 Or a 'standstill of reason' through which one will 'neither deny nor assert anything' (Nussbaum 1991: 528; see also Hookway 1990: 5). Nussbaum likewise refers to this as the 'paralysis' (1991: 530) of 'rational commitment' (ibid.: 547). There are correlations here between the Pyrrhonian (Sextus 1996: 1:36ff.) and phenomenological (Husserl 1982: §§7–9) *epoche*, which is unsurprising given the influence of the sixteenth-century revival of Pyrrhonism on Descartes (Popkin 1979: Chs II–X), and Husserl's Cartesian inheritance.
52 Derrida also speaks of the 'perhaps' and 'maybe,' though for him these are not synonymous (1992b: 95; 1997a: 2, 4, 13, 16–17). Of additional interest here is Derrida's claim that the 'aporia' is not 'a failure or a simple paralysis' (1993b: 32; see also 1999a: 66, 73). I will return to these points in Chapter 8.
53 The Pyrrhonist's 'being-at-a-loss' does not apply to immediate appearances, for although he 'withholds assent ... from all categorical assertions ... he is willing to say how things now seem to him to be, but on the question of how they are in fact, he takes no position' (Mates 1996: p. 31).
54 *Ataraxia* is not purposely sought, for if it became a teleological goal then it too would likely generate additional anxieties. Rather, *ataraxia* comes about 'by mere chance' (Nussbaum 1991: 530; see also 532, 541–5; Sextus 1996: 1:25–30).
55 See Burnyeat 1983; Nussbaum 1991: 551ff.
56 Indeed, the 'orientation to *ataraxia*' itself becomes quite 'natural' (Nussbaum 1991: 546; see also 528, 540).
57 See Nussbaum 1991: 554. A question already arises here as to what extent 'indifference' (Diogenes 1925: 477) and 'tolerance' are being conflated? I will return to this in Chapter 3.
58 See also Inwood and Gerson 1988: 174.
59 It was this inherent 'conservatism' that lay at the heart of the Catholic Pyrrhonian-fideism of the sixteenth and seventeenth centuries (Popkin 1979: Ch. III).
60 See Annas and Barnes 1985: 163–4, 169.
61 See Sextus 1996: 1:145–63.
62 See also Inwood and Gerson 1988: 239; Sextus 1996: 1:231.
63 See Nussbaum 1991: 531, 534.
64 See Nussbaum 1991: 535. The final part of the 'Skeptic Way' is 'instruction in arts and crafts' (Sextus 1996: 1:23–4; see also Burnyeat 1983: 126).
65 The necessity of making this qualification highlights a deeper problem; namely, that the very concepts of 'prejudice' and 'intolerance' (and their antitheses) cannot even get a foothold in a Pyrrhonian framework.
66 See Hankinson 1995: 293.
67 See Annas and Barnes 1985: 169.
68 The question of why one would or should make a 'movement toward the

other' (and not simply bask in one's unperturbedness) will be discussed in Chapters 6 and 7.
69 The same can be said of the Pyrrhonist's supposed lack of epistemic commitments.
70 See Nussbaum 1991: 528, 540, 546.
71 See Derrida 1992a: 257, 265, 288, 296–8; 1995a: 384; 1996a: 68.
72 See Sartre 1977: 48; Derrida 1992a: 195.
73 See Heidegger 1999: p. 386. Somewhat paradoxically, then, a pluralistic society would pose more problems for the Pyrrhonist than would a totalitarian dictatorship. I will return to pluralism and totalitarianism in Chapter 3.
74 See Annas and Barnes 1985: 169.
75 I use the term 'categorical' in Kant's sense (1976: 78ff.), to which I will return in Chapter 5 with reference to Wittgenstein.
76 See Rhees 1969: 171; Wittgenstein 1993: 161.
77 Both Wittgenstein (1958: §106; 1993: 183; 1994a: 74) and Freud use the metaphor of untying a knot to characterize their respective projects. Note also a certain 'entanglement' both within and between psychoanalysis and deconstruction (Derrida 1998a: 1–38).
78 On Wittgenstein's remarks on the 'trivial,' see Moore 1993: 114.
79 On Wittgenstein's fear of his work leading him 'to insanity,' see 1993: 468.
80 See Luckhardt 1991: 255–72. Neither Rhees nor Luckhardt mention Pyrrhonism.
81 See Drury 1981: 96.
82 See Drury 1981: 136; Monk 1991: 334ff.; Shusterman 1997: 21.
83 In this sense Wittgenstein maintains a highly teleological view of philosophical practice in general (and philosophical argument in particular) as he seems not to address the possibility of someone simply *enjoying* philosophical perplexity and argumentation. On the possibility and value of non-teleological argumentation, see Bennington 2000.
84 Philosophy-as-therapy is thus a profoundly 'counter-institutional institution' (Derrida 1992a: 58, see also 36; 1995a: 327–8, 346, 376; 2002f: 74–5) insofar as it both laments its own existence and dreams of its own demise.
85 See also Moore 1993: 114.
86 See Wittgenstein 1958: §93.
87 See Monk 1991: 335, 356–7. Like psychoanalysis, Wittgenstein's work stresses the importance of 'discussion' (Moore 1993: 113).
88 See Nussbaum 1991: 538, 540, 545; Sextus 1996: 3:280.
89 See Rosenzweig 1999: 55. Putnam (1999, 1–20) here likens Rosenzweig's position with Wittgenstein's.
90 See also Derrida 1998a: 3, 17.
91 Wittgenstein also speaks of one's being 'calmed' regarding what makes us 'so profoundly uneasy' (1993: 173), that the 'disorder in our concepts' can be remedied in such a way that 'certain troubles ... disappear' (at which point we reach 'complete satisfaction' (ibid.: 181–3)), and that '[o]ur object is to get rid of certain puzzles' by 'pulling ordinary grammar to bits' (1979b: 31).
92 See Wittgenstein 1958: §§25, 244, 343, 415; 1990: §§391, 540–1, 545; 1994a: 31.
93 See Wittgenstein 1996a: 61–81. On the similarities between Wittgenstein's work and Tolstoy's *Confessions,* Thompson notes their shared emphasis on: (1) the 'dissolution' of life's problems (1997: 101–7, 109, 111), (2) action over theory (ibid.: 110), and (3) the non-eschatological nature of religious belief (ibid.: 104–5). Thompson also alludes to Tolstoy's naturalistic 'nostalgia,' as does Sontag (1995: 125).
94 See also Wittgenstein 1958: §109; 1990: §690; 1999: §435.

95 See Wittgenstein 1993: 183–7.
96 See also Wittgenstein 1990: §405.
97 See also Wittgenstein's remarks on the relation between the 'instinct' to ask certain questions and what 'leads children to ask "Why?"' (Moore 1993: 114).
98 In his own commentary on Wittgenstein, Wood mistakenly suggests that it is traditional philosophy's 'attempts to make language behave in artificial ways that *generate* philosophical problems' (1990: 55, my emphasis; see also Rorty 1999: xxi–xxii).
99 Staten's deconstructive reading of Wittgenstein overlooks his naturalism (see especially Staten 1986: 75).
100 Wittgenstein suggests that our tendency toward confusion (and the mistaken belief that philosophical perplexities can be 'solved' by new discoveries and explanations) is also due to our obsession with the methods of scientific practice (1958: §230; 1969: 18).
101 This distinction pertains to our being preoccupied with words alone ('surface grammar'), rather than attending to the way words function within various human activities ('depth grammar'). I will return to this in later chapters.
102 See also Moore 1993: 114; Blanchot 1997: 238–40.
103 Thus 'philosophizing has to be as complicated as the knots it unties' (Wittgenstein 1990: §452; see also §382). Echoing Nietzsche (1977: p. 58; 1989: 209), Wittgenstein also refers to an 'entire mythology laid down in our language' (1993: 199).
104 See also Moore 1993: 109–10.
105 Note Nietzsche's remarks on the seductive nature of words and grammar (1972a: pp. 37–8; 1987: §§16–17, 19), and his accusation that philosophers fail to notice that 'concepts and words are our inheritance from ages in which thinking was very modest and unclear' (1968: §409; see also 1989: 209). Regarding Nietzsche's views on the relation between language and philosophy, see Hollingdale's remarks in Nietzsche 1972a: p. 191.
106 See Staten 1986: 77.
107 See also Wittgenstein 1993: 453. Wittgenstein provides the following examples of such an 'urge': 'What happens with the words "God" and "soul" is what happens with the word "number". Even though we give up explaining these words ostensively, by pointing, we don't give up explaining them in substantival terms. The reason people say that a number is a scratch on the blackboard is the desire to point at something' (1979b: 32), and likewise: 'we are misled if we think that [ostensive definition] is a peculiar process of christening an object which makes a word the word for an object. This is a kind of superstition' (1993: 448). He similarly refers to our 'powerful urge ... to see everything in terms of cause and effect,' which effectively means that 'we are going to apply this picture come what may' (ibid.: 375).
108 See also Moore 1993: 114.
109 See also Wittgenstein 1994a: 17.
110 Here lies the difficulty facing the Pyrrhonist when attempting to extract the vocabulary of 'belief' and 'truth' from her life.
111 See Putnam 1999: 2.
112 Just as a molecular biologist does not necessarily make a good doctor, neither does a Wittgensteinian therapist require a thorough grounding in current evolutionary theory (Wittgenstein 1996a: 69). There lies a question of 'precision' here; of whether the sort of precision required in the natural sciences would even be of *possible* use in other domains (Wittgenstein 1958: §88).
113 As will become clear in later chapters, this normativity is particularly apparent in Wittgenstein's reflections on religious belief.
114 Compare this with Diogenes 1925: 487–8.

115 See also Wittgenstein 1958: §§109, 124–8, 665; 1990: §220; 1993: 177; 1996a: 61–2; 1999: §189.
116 Although the term 'solution' sits uncomfortably alongside Wittgenstein's objective of 'dissolution,' the general point remains applicable.
117 See Nussbaum 1991: 527.
118 See Moore 1993: 113.
119 See Sluga 1996: 13. Nietzsche employs a similar metaphor (1972a: 27, n. 42).
120 See Wittgenstein 1995: 4.114–4.1212.
121 See Wittgenstein 1995: 4.46–4.4661, 6.22.
122 See Wittgenstein 1995: 4.121, 5.511, 6.13.
123 See also Diogenes 1925: 490–1.
124 See Wittgenstein 1995: 6.41–445, 6.522. As will become clear in Chapter 2, the saying/showing distinction re-emerges in *On Certainty* (Clack 1999: Chs 1–2).
125 Indeed, Wittgenstein claims that the 'point of the book is ethical,' and his concern is with the (absent) book the *Tractatus* renders impossible to write (Monk 1991: 178). I will return to this in Chapter 5.
126 Compare with Wittgenstein 1958: §§128–9, 415; 1994a: 63.
127 Compare with Wittgenstein 1958: §§89, 109.
128 See Wittgenstein 1993: 183. This is not, for example, to deny the reality of free will, but rather to acknowledge that the choices one can make are always framed within given natural and cultural horizons.
129 See Monk 1991: Chs 8–9. Wittgenstein identifies his happiest times as those spent away from philosophy (see his letter to Fouracre in Monk 1991: 494).
130 See Drury 1981: 92, 186 n. 9. This is not entirely accurate; one only has to consider his brief excursion into architecture to see his abilities in other fields (Monk 1991: 235–8). It would thus perhaps be better to say that Wittgenstein failed to find anything that captivated him so intensely as philosophy.
131 See also Burnyeat 1983: 123–4; Hookway 1990: 2; Nussbaum 1991: 539, 548.
132 See Wittgenstein 1958: §§23, 114.
133 Recalling the Pyrrhonist's emphasis on the need to bend with the vacillations of the world, what Wittgenstein effectively does in *Philosophical Investigations* is replace the methodological assumption that 'the world must fit the theory' with non-theorizing, descriptive procedures.
134 See Fogelin 1996: 34.
135 On this point, Cioffi's suggestion (1998: 155–81) that, despite appearances, Wittgenstein's anti-instrumentalist reading of Frazer ought not to be taken as wholesale is in keeping with this warning. I will return to 'Remarks on Frazer's *Golden Bough*' in Chapters 3 and 5.
136 See also Wittgenstein 1958: §§103, 115, 133, 255; 1994a: 63; Genova 1995: 33; Fogelin 1996: 34.
137 See Wittgenstein 1958: §656, p. 200.
138 See Wittgenstein 1958: §133; 1994a: 9.
139 See McGinn 1997: 25.
140 See Burnyeat 1983: 121.
141 See Derrida's remarks on the relation between the 'fragment' and 'system' (1999c: 181).
142 See Feyerabend 1988: 281.
143 See Rhees 1969: 170.
144 There is doubtless something to be said about more orthodox confessional practices and Wittgenstein's frequent use of an interrogative interlocutor in his later writings. I will return to confession in Chapter 8 with reference to Derrida.
145 See Wittgenstein's remarks on 'confession' (1994a: 18) and Derrida's remarks on the 'futurity' of confession and guilt (1997b: 19–21).

146 See Shields 1997: 55–6.
147 I will argue in Chapter 5 that it is this lack of institutional allegiance (and not, as Holland maintains, Wittgenstein's alleged incapacity to pray) that lies behind his claim: ' "I am not a religious man ..." ' (Drury 1981: 108, 117, 144, 162, 179–80). Holland attempts to address the apparent discrepancy between the previous remark and Wittgenstein's comment that 'I cannot kneel to pray because it's as though my knees were stiff' (1994a: 56). Using Taylor's 'The Faith of the Moralist' for comparison, Holland concludes that 'the point above all which differentiates Taylor's position from Wittgenstein's is that a person in Taylor's shoes gets down on his knees and prays' (1990: 28). But Holland makes no mention of the fact that upon his return from Norway Wittgenstein claimed to have there 'spent his time in prayer' (Drury 1981: 135), or that on another occasion he remarked that there was 'a sense in which' both he and Drury were 'both Christians' (ibid.: 130).
148 See Wittgenstein's remarks on being 'obsessed by a certain language form' (1979b: 98).
149 See Moore 1993: 113.
150 Although Wittgenstein criticizes Freud's essentialism (1994b: 47–8, 50) and his failure to show 'how we know *where to stop* – where is the right solution' (ibid.: 42, see also 51; 1994a: 16, 34), Wittgenstein is not unduly perturbed by Freud's attempt to develop a new 'way of thinking' that makes 'certain ways of behaving and thinking natural' for people (1994b: 45) (see also Wittgenstein's remarks on Darwin and Copernicus (1994a: 18)). But how could he object, given that – on Wittgenstein's own admission – this is precisely what *he* is attempting to do?
151 See Rhees 1969: 170.
152 See Wittgenstein 1958: p. x.
153 Although one might have to start with oneself before helping others (Wittgenstein 1994a: 44).
154 See Wittgenstein 1994a: 32, 53, 64, 86.
155 See Monk 1991: 334ff.; Pascal 1996: 34ff.; Shusterman 1997: 21.
156 See Wittgenstein 1999: §§65, 256.
157 As will become clear in Chapter 3, this emphasis on multiplicity (Wittgenstein's alleged 'pluralism') is tempered by his naturalism.
158 See Wittgenstein 1958: §§23, 97, 114; 1999: §321.
159 We should note that in §133 of *Philosophical Investigations* Wittgenstein speaks of the 'discovery' that makes *him* 'capable of stopping doing philosophy' when *he* 'wants to.'
160 See Wittgenstein 1994a: 48. In the preface to *Philosophical Investigations* Wittgenstein remarks: 'Up to a short time ago I had really given up the idea of publishing my work in my lifetime. It used, indeed, to be revived from time to time: mainly because I was obliged to learn that my results (which I had communicated in lectures, typescripts and discussions), variously misunderstood, more or less mangled or watered down, were in circulation. *This stung my vanity and I had difficulty in quieting it*' (1958: pp. ix–x, my emphasis).
161 See Wittgenstein 1958: §§105–8. As will become clear in Chapter 5, while Wittgenstein rejects the linguistic-conceptual perfectionism of his early work, he maintains a certain *ethical* perfectionism – something which is perhaps most apparent in his confession of 'sins' to (amongst others) Fania Pascal (1996: 45–50). I will return to the latter in Chapter 6.
162 See Wittgenstein 1958: §§24, 79–80, 179, 203, 304, p. 224; 1990: §17; 1999: §§348, 432.
163 See Wittgenstein 1993: 183.
164 See Wittgenstein 1958: §§108, 132, 271.

165 One must distinguish this from the biographical question regarding Wittgenstein's own – often naïve – political sympathies (Monk 1991: 178, 342–4; Pascal 1996: 55–7).
166 Nyíri focuses on the conservatism elucidated by (amongst others) Kaltenbrunner, Oakeshott, Mannheim, Mohler and Grabowsky.
167 See also Nyíri 1982: 54.
168 See also Nyíri 1982: 45.
169 See Derrida's remarks on Wittgenstein's silence and the 'mystical' foundations of law (1990: 943).
170 Phillips takes issue with this conservative reading, claiming that '[l]eaving everything where it is involves taking account of cultural turmoil as much as cultural stability' (1986: 49). But this compounds the problem, for the question is not whether the descriptive method (coupled with Wittgenstein's principle of non-interference (1958: §§126, 226)) is 'conservative' due to its *selectivity*, but whether this approach is conservative *insofar as it is descriptive*.
171 As will become clear in later chapters, Wittgenstein remained suspicious of our obsession with 'reason' and neglect of more natural 'phenomena' and behavioral 'patterns' (1993: 389).
172 See Popkin 1979: 1–17, 49, 70ff.
173 See Nielsen 1967.
174 See also Wittgenstein 1999: §559. Concerning 'lifestyles, customs and laws' Philo remarks that 'since among different people these things are not just slightly different but utterly discordant, so as to compete and conflict, necessarily the appearances experienced will differ and the judgments be at war with one another. This being so, who is so senseless and idiotic as to say steadfastly that such-and-such is just or intelligent or fine or advantageous? Whatever one person determines to be such will be nullified by someone else whose practice from childhood has been the contrary' (quoted in Annas and Barnes 1985: 155). I will return to (apparently) similar remarks in *On Certainty* in Chapters 2 and 3.
175 Regarding this alleged 'conservative' element in Wittgenstein's work, see also Jones 1986: 282; Wittgenstein 1993: 407.
176 See Wittgenstein 1958: §§126, 226. With reference to a specifically political question (the survival of the Irish language), Drury recalls Wittgenstein claim that: ' "It is always a tragic thing when a language dies. But it doesn't follow that one can do anything to stop it doing so. It is a tragic thing when the love between a man and wife is dying; but there is nothing one can do. So it is with a dying language ..." ' (Drury 1981: 152). On a related point, see Derrida 1998c: 30.
177 See Wittgenstein 1994a: 4, 27.
178 For a critique of Nyíri's 'conservative' reading, see Jones 1986; Schulte 1986.
179 Interestingly, when referring to 'training' Wittgenstein frequently employs the German word *abrichten*; a term normally associated with the 'conditioning' of animals. I thank Peter Baumann for bringing this to my attention.

2 Trusting in a world-picture

1 Parts of this chapter have appeared in Plant 2003a and 2003b.
2 See Pitkin 1993: 325; Scheman 1996: 384.
3 *On Certainty* was never intended for publication, but rather represents 'first-draft material' Wittgenstein 'did not live to excerpt and polish' (1999: p. vi). Nevertheless, I would suggest that it is precisely the 'rough edges' of this text that make it so provocative (Hudson 1986a: 123–4; Plant 2003b). Indeed, Wittgenstein's suggestion that '[o]ne could teach philosophy solely by asking

questions' (1979b: 97) seems especially pertinent when reading *On Certainty* (Bambrough 1992: 242).

4 Wittgenstein appears to substantiate Edwards's reading when he remarks: 'On all questions we discuss I have no opinion; and if I had, and it disagreed with one of your opinions, I would at once give it up for the sake of argument because it would be of no importance for our discussion' (Wittgenstein 1979b: 97). But Wittgenstein's point here is methodological; that he is not concerned with offering theoretical solutions, but rather with providing grammatical reminders concerning the actual use of words.

5 Edwards does not make this Pyrrhonian connection.

6 As I will discuss in later chapters, radically 'nonfoundationalist' interpretations of Wittgenstein underestimate the 'worries' (Gill 1974: 279) haunting *On Certainty*.

7 See Gill 1974: 282; Kober 1996: 414, 418.

8 The two classic statements of this are Moore's 'A Defence of Common Sense' (1994a) and 'Proof of an External World' (1994b). Gill plausibly suggests that there is no more 'concise statement' (1974: 279) of Wittgenstein's position in *On Certainty* than that provided in §521: 'Moore's mistake lies in this – countering the assertion that one cannot know that, by saying "I do know it".'

9 See Kober 1996: 411.

10 That Wittgenstein's Pyrrhonism is not thoroughgoing can be seen in his attitude toward belief. For while the Pyrrhonist maintains a fundamental dichotomy between natural life and the life of belief, Wittgenstein insists that reason and deliberation are derivative of natural behaviors. Moreover, while the Pyrrhonist attempts to escape the aporia of justification by *abandoning* belief, Wittgenstein's therapeutic strategy is to acknowledge the 'groundlessness' of our believing. Wittgensteinian *ataraxia* thus comes not in the renunciation of belief but in accepting that many beliefs cannot be given (and do not require) justification. I will return to these points later.

11 See also Fann 1969: 169.

12 See Malcolm 1958: 89; Wittgenstein 1990: §314. It will become clear later why this formulation is provisional.

13 See also Wittgenstein 1999: §1.

14 See Malcolm 1958: 89.

15 See Malcolm 1958: 90; Wittgenstein 1999: §9.

16 See Diogenes 1925: 481; Nussbaum 1991: 523.

17 See also Wittgenstein 1999: §475. This is in keeping with Wittgenstein's reflections on causality (1993: 371–411).

18 Although, as I will discuss later, belief is prerequisite for doubt (Wittgenstein 1999: §480).

19 See also Wittgenstein 1999: §504. There are occasions when even one's own pain is uncertain. As often happens in childhood, the mere shock of a (potentially) injurious event can be enough to temporarily make one suppose that one is 'in pain.'

20 See Gill 1974: 280; Wittgenstein 1999: §549.

21 See also Moore 1994b: 81–2.

22 See also Moore 1994a: 48.

23 See also Moore 1994a: 48; 1994b: 80–1, 83.

24 See also Moore 1994a: 48.

25 See also Moore 1994a: 48.

26 Moore also refers to the certitude of the existence of other human beings (1994a: 48, 53–4, 55) and objects in the past (1994b: 83). Note also Schutz's remarks on 'the zone of things taken for granted' (1970b: 111; see also 1974:

4–5; Husserl 1970: 110, 121–5, 127–32, 140–1, 146–9, 165; 1982: 17, 37, 132, 151).
27 See also Wittgenstein 1999: §§21, 481–2.
28 See Malcolm 1958: 88; Wittgenstein 1999: §§91, 243, 550–1.
29 See also Malcolm 1958: 92; Wittgenstein 1993: 379; 1999: §260.
30 See Wittgenstein 1999: §§47, 347, 407.
31 To put this in Derridean terms, what interests Wittgenstein here is the *iterability* of the phrase 'I know.' I will return to Derrida in Chapter 8.
32 See Wittgenstein 1999: §554. Finch calls this a 'universal context' (1975: 385).
33 That is, his 'accompanying feeling' (Wittgenstein 1999: §524) of 'subjective certainty' (ibid.: §563; see also 1958: §607).
34 See also Martin 1984: 594.
35 Moore's propositions have a peculiar 'grammatical' status that means: 'the "I" cannot be important. And ["I know"] properly means "There is no such thing as a doubt in this case" or "The expression 'I do not know' makes no sense in this case". And of course it follows from this that "I *know*" makes no sense either' (Wittgenstein 1999: §58; see also Hudson 1986a: 119).
36 See Wittgenstein 1999: §§54, 56, 87–8, 526, 653. They might be meaningful in very '*particular circumstances*' (ibid.: §423; see also §§25, 372, 387, 433, 461, 553, 622). Moore's error is therefore partly one of omission; that is, of not determining those situations in which such propositions can meaningfully be used (Malcolm 1958: 89), and this is why his propositions make Wittgenstein 'feel as if these words were like "Good morning" said to someone in the middle of a conversation' (1999: §464).
37 See also Wittgenstein 1990: §405.
38 See Malcolm 1958: 89; Wittgenstein 1999: §308. Wittgenstein remarks: 'Why is it not possible for me to doubt that I have never been on the moon? And how could I try to doubt it? First and foremost, the supposition that perhaps I have been there would strike me as *idle*. Nothing would follow from it, nothing could be explained by it. It would not tie in with anything in my life' (1999: §117). This, and other passages in both *On Certainty* and 'Lectures on Religious Belief,' echoes James's application of the principles of pragmatism to the question of religious belief (1985: 444–7).
39 See Finch 1975: 384, 394; Wittgenstein 1999: §§94, 105, 153, 204, 472.
40 The role of the imagination in *On Certainty* is ambiguous, for it remains unclear to what extent the inability to imagine circumstances in which one's fundamental beliefs would be falsified is *itself* determined by one's current 'frame of reference' (1999: §83) or 'world-picture' (ibid.: §§162, 167). What qualifies *as* a fundamental belief (or its falsification) would thus be dependent upon the imaginative capacities of specific individuals within specific communities. On the limits of imagination, see also Cavell 1979: 117–18.
41 See also Wittgenstein 1999: §§472–3, 492, 516, 558, 576–9.
42 See Hudson 1986a: 120.
43 See Wittgenstein 1999: §199.
44 See Finch 1975: 392.
45 See Gill 1974: 281.
46 See Wittgenstein 1999: §§337, 509, 672. Josipovici rightly suggests that *On Certainty* 'could equally well have been called *On Trust*' (1999: 271).
47 See Hudson 1986a: 122; Wittgenstein 1999: §§7, 115, 150, 162–7, 283, 401–2, 472–7. Schutz likewise refers to 'trust' in this regard (1964: 95, 102; 1970a: 78; 1970b: 74, 92; 1971: 228; 1974: 7, 107–8). It will become clear later how Moore's 'trivialization' parallels Wittgenstein's views on blasphemy.
48 See Wittgenstein 1999: §§141–2, 144, 446. The example of gambling has further significance for the question of religious belief, for Wittgenstein (like

Kierkegaard) not only speaks about 'risk' (1994b: 54) in this context, he also maintains that in religious discourse one does not 'talk about . . . high probability' (ibid.: 57).
49 See Gill 1974: 283–5, 290; Finch 1975: 385. As I will discuss in later chapters, Levinas makes a similar distinction between the 'Said' and its 'Saying.'
50 See Wittgenstein 1993: 397; 1999: §§7, 285, 411, 414, 427, 431.
51 See Wittgenstein 1958: §325; 1999: §§501, 524, 552. Wittgenstein remarks: 'What is the proof that I *know* something? Most certainly not my saying I know it' (1999: §487). This is not to deny that what one *says* can itself be a form of *showing* (indeed, what Moore wishes to *say* is already *shown* in his *saying anything* (ibid.: §114)). My point is rather to highlight the non-propositional (even persuasive (ibid.: §669)) nature of such instances of 'showing.' It should nevertheless be noted that Moore himself is concerned with the im/possibility of articulating this certitude 'directly' (1994a: 56–7; 1994b: 83–4).
52 See also Wittgenstein 1958: §129; Hudson 1986a: 122–3.
53 See also Wittgenstein 1958: §§109–15, 664, p. 224; 1969: 27; 1990: §690; 1993: 183–7; 1999: §§31, 435.
54 See Gill 1974: 282; Finch 1975: 389. As we will see later, this is central to Wittgenstein's distinction between 'genuine' religiosity and mere 'superstition.'
55 See Descartes 1976: 20–1, 31ff., 61.
56 See Morawetz 1978: 121; Wittgenstein 1999: §§4, 220, 323, 458, 519; Gaita 2000: 172.
57 See Gill 1974: 281.
58 See also Wittgenstein 1993: 377, 379, 381; 1999: §§354, 509, 625, 672.
59 See also Drury 1981: 114; Wittgenstein 1994a: 16; 1999: §§459, 641, 672. That 'the earth has existed for many years,' or that 'this is my hand' are not (indeed, cannot be) open to the sort of verification Moore attempts to offer (Wittgenstein 1999: §§103, 138) because '[a]ll testing, all confirmation and disconfirmation of a hypothesis takes place already within a system. And this system is not a more or less arbitrary and doubtful point of departure for all our arguments: no, it belongs to the essence of what we call argument. The system is not so much the point of departure, as the element in which arguments have their life' (ibid.: §105).
60 See Wittgenstein 1999: §§250, 307.
61 See Wittgenstein 1999: §§111, 125, 138, 150, 245, 459, 515.
62 See Wittgenstein 1999: §§341, 343, 655.
63 See Malcolm 1958: 92; Schutz 1964: 233; 1966: 119–20; 1970a: 84; 1970b: 81, 96; 1971: 7, 13; 1974: 7, 174–5, 244–5; Wittgenstein 1990: §413. As I have argued elsewhere (Plant 2003a) there are a number of important correlations between Wittgenstein and Reid's 'Common Sense' philosophy (note especially Reid's remarks on the principles of 'veracity' and 'credulity' (1997: 193–4)).
64 See Hertzberg 1988: 318; Wittgenstein 1999: §160. Wittgenstein suggests that, because foundational propositions like 'I have two hands' are 'on the same level' as propositions of arithmetic, his remarks are 'logical' rather than 'psychological' (1999: §447; see also Hudson 1986a: 121; Lagenspetz 1992: 7).
65 See Hertzberg 1988: 314.
66 See Lagenspetz 1992: 8; Wittgenstein 1999: §344.
67 See Hudson 1986b: 176. Note also Schutz's remarks on 'inheritance,' one's 'biographically determined situation,' 'predecessors,' 'contemporaries' and 'successors' (1964: 23, 25, 57–8, 59, 95, 229, 232–3; 1966: 119; 1970a: 91; 1971: 7, 15, 318; 1974: 19, 88).

68 See Wittgenstein 1999: §170.
69 See Wittgenstein 1990: §§413–16; 1999: §§170, 374, 472, 476, 509, 534, 538; Gaita 2000: 161–2. Whereas doubt is parasitic upon certitude, distrust is similarly parasitic upon trust. Thus, according to Hertzberg, although distrust is 'what happens normally in the process of growing up,' the 'distrustful person' is 'someone who has been damaged by other people.' Indeed, the 'destruction of our trust in others' is, despite its familiarity, 'a tragedy' (1988: 320).
70 See Hertzberg 1988: 309.
71 This relation of trust works both ways (Wittgenstein 1993: 383).
72 I will return to this in Chapter 8 with reference to Derrida.
73 See Hertzberg 1988: 313–14.
74 See Hertzberg 1988: 309, 316.
75 See also Hertzberg's account of this episode (1988: 309–10).
76 See Isaiah 6:8–9. In Chapters 6 and 7 I will explore why Levinas often uses the 'Here I am' in discussing intersubjectivity.
77 Hertzberg qualifies this point by claiming that, only if Isaac had 'known what was on his father's mind, and had still gone on without resisting' would *his* trust 'have been similar to his father's trust in God' (1988: 310).
78 It is this unconditionality that accounts for children's vulnerability with regard to abuses of trust (Gaita 2000: 22).
79 See Hertzberg 1988: 312.
80 As I will discuss in Chapters 6 and 7, this can be related to Levinas's remarks on the other's moral 'height' (1996a: 17, 54).
81 See also Malcolm 1958: 92.
82 See also Wittgenstein 1999: §§95, 209, 262.
83 See also Wittgenstein 1999: §§102, 105, 108, 136, 144, 185, 247, 279, 410–11.
84 Wittgenstein likewise refers to a 'hinge on which your dispute can turn' (1999: §655; see also §§341, 343), 'generally accepted axioms' (ibid.: §551), one's 'point of view' (ibid.: §92), a 'host of interdependent propositions' (ibid.: §274), the 'foundations of our language-game' (ibid.: §558; see also §§449, 614), the 'rock bottom of my convictions' or the 'foundation-walls' (ibid.: §248), one's 'fundamental attitudes' (ibid.: §238; see also §517), 'our whole way of looking at things' (ibid.: §292; see also §291), a 'nest of propositions' (ibid.: §225), one's 'principles' (ibid.: §611), and a 'mythology' (ibid.: §§95, 97). We should also note that Wittgenstein frequently speaks of dissension from such propositions in terms of madness and imbecility (ibid.: §§71, 155, 217, 257, 420, 611; see also Kober 1996: 423; Plant 2003a), and even remarks that '[t]here are cases where doubt is unreasonable, but others where it seems logically impossible. And there seems to be no clear boundary between them' (1999: §454; see also §673; Bambrough 1992: 242–3).
85 See also Wittgenstein 1999: §§475, 614.
86 See Wittgenstein 1999: §§5, 95, 105, 108, 129, 131, 162, 209, 262, 291–2, 298, 517. A related ambiguity emerges between Schutz's analyses of 'the fundamental structures of ... the life-world' and 'relative-natural world view[s]' (1974: 104). Schutz has a similarly diverse vocabulary to describe 'the natural attitude' of the 'everyday life-world' (ibid.: 243). These include 'the attitude of common sense' (ibid.: 3), a 'scheme of reference' (1971: 7; see also 13, 74, 77, 208; 1964: 233), a 'system of relevances' (1964: 236; see also 1966: 125, 130–1; 1970b: 120; 1971: 5, 227, 228, 317; 1974: 91, 243, 261), a 'network of typifications' (1964: 232), and 'the unquestioned background of the world just taken for granted' (ibid.: 234). Note also Husserl's references to the 'life world' and related concepts (1970: 108, 113, 116, 119, 121–2, 125–6, 131, 136, 138, 140, 144–5, 158–9, 164; 1982: 19–20, 33, 135–6, 138, 156).
87 See Nyíri 1982: 59.

88 Gaita suggests that it is upon the love relation (and the 'language of love') that our moral vocabulary has been 'built' (2000: p. xviii; see also pp. xix, 5).
89 A similar point is made by Wittgenstein (1999: §§599, 606, 662–3).
90 See Wittgenstein 1994b: 56. Note also Gaita's remarks on the grammar of love (2000: 24). Concerning the relationship between love and history, one might say that there is a quasi-messianic dimension to the love relation insofar as the lover inaugurates a 'new history' liberated from the ghosts of one's previous relationships (Barthes 1990: 23, 38, 174). This clearly relates to more explicitly religious matters, and, as I will discuss in Chapter 5, the conversion process Tolstoy describes.
91 See also Morawetz 1978: 134. Compare these remarks with Kolakowski's comments on tolerance (1999: 36–7).
92 Contrast Morawetz's remarks just quoted with Svensson 1981: 90–1.
93 See Bambrough 1992: 241–2.
94 Wittgenstein recognizes this potential for 'circularity' (1999: §191).
95 See Wittgenstein 1999: §134.
96 A similar example appears in Malcolm 1990: 4–5.
97 See Wittgenstein 1999: §130.
98 For a literary example of this see Wells 1988: 99–103. A more philosophical example appears in Graham's *Evil and Christian Ethics*. While conceding that his explanation of evil (by returning to a 'pre-scientific' cosmology of Satanic forces) is 'antithetical to ... naturalistic and humanistic ... thinking' (2001: 164; see also 157, 159, 219), Graham nevertheless insists that such a reorientation would do 'explanatory work that alternative [secular] conceptions cannot do' (ibid.: 192). Indeed, this pre-modern 'cosmic drama within which our moral lives are set' (ibid.: 159; see also 153) 'provides ... the best available explanation of evil, and since evil is something which cries out to be explained, we ought to believe the best explanation' (ibid.: 161). But Graham's advice that we should 'in so far as we are to be rational ... prefer better explanations to less good ones' (ibid.: 157; see also 154) begs the question. For what is also at stake here is what is to *count* as a 'better' account, 'rationality,' 'explanatory work,' and so on. Likewise, when he asserts that this cosmological-theological picture 'makes more sense of human existence' (ibid.: 229; see also 223) than secular alternatives, Graham presupposes that 'making more sense' has an obvious and homogeneous application across – or even within – world-pictures. It is hardly self-evident that, for example, any 'satisfactory explanation of why evil things happen must include reference to their intrinsic nature and not merely appeal to their causal antecedents' (ibid.: 163), for this surely depends upon the sort of account of 'explanation' one's system of reference provides. In this way Graham thus underestimates the stakes involved in shifting from a 'secular' (or even liberal Christian) to a 'pre-modern' eschatological perspective.
99 See Wittgenstein 1999: §167.
100 Which is not to deny that they may *retrospectively* be seen to falter. I will return to this qualification later.
101 See Derrida 1990: 945; 1992b: 30, 97; 1995a: 360, 393; 1995b: 77; 1996b: 82; 1998b: 3, 18, 31, 44–5, 47–8, 54, 60, 63–4; 1998c: 9, 20–1, 85; 1999a: 80; Gaita 2000: 160. I will return to Derrida in Chapter 8.
102 See Wittgenstein 1999: §141.
103 See Wittgenstein 1999: §§140, 142, 225, 274; Kober 1996: 422. This point might usefully be read alongside Heidegger's claim that 'in our natural comportment toward things we never think of a *single* thing, and whenever we seize upon it expressly for itself we are taking it *out* of a contexture to which it belongs in its real content' (1982: 162; see also 163–5).

104 That is, 'not explicitly' for '[n]o one ever taught [him this]' (Wittgenstein 1999: §§152–3).
105 See Wittgenstein 1999: §473.
106 See also Wittgenstein 1999: §101.
107 Although (again) *retrospective* acknowledgment of such 'fundamental judgments' (Wittgenstein 1999: §517, see also §152) may be possible.
108 See Wittgenstein 1999: §§279, 283.
109 See Derrida 1998: 18, 28, 44–5, 63.
110 See Tilghman 1991: 103; Wittgenstein 1999: §§7, 152, 185, 204, 217, 220, 344, 427, 524.
111 See Wittgenstein 1958: §23; 1999: §§231, 250, 672.
112 See also Wittgenstein 1990: §320; 1999: §§141, 554, 620.
113 See Malcolm 1972: 208; Wittgenstein 1999: §§110, 130. Note also Derrida's remarks on the groundlessness of law (1992a: 192, 202–5, 208).
114 It is thus false to say that philosophy *begins* with doubt (Wittgenstein 1993: 399). On a related point see Derrida's remarks on the 'pre-originary pledge' or 'faith' before any 'question' (1989: 129–30, n. 5).
115 See Wittgenstein 1999: §110. It is Wittgenstein's recurrent emphasis on a 'way of acting' that not only discloses his naturalism but also problematizes the nonfoundationalist reading of his work. As will become clear in Chapters 3 and 5, although Wittgenstein *is* nonfoundationalist if one means 'rational' foundationalism, he nevertheless emphasizes the instinctive, primitive foundations of human life.
116 See Wittgenstein 1958: p. 200; 1999: §475. In this sense there can be no meta-discourse on trust that would not thereby enact (*show*) what it aspired to elucidate (*say*). Again, I will return to this in Chapter 8 with reference to Derrida.
117 See Wittgenstein 1958: §116, p. 200; 1999: §§164, 192, 212, 370, 375, 519, 620.
118 See Wittgenstein 1999: §§495, 513, 526, 616, 619, 657.
119 Some notable exceptions include Malcolm 1972; Gill 1974: 282, 290; Martin 1984; Hudson 1986a: 127; 1986b: 175–83; Phillips 1988: 38ff.
120 This is not to say that all types of religious belief are entirely non-hypothetical (Hudson 1986b: 177).
121 See also Drury 1981: 105.
122 See Martin 1984: 608–13.
123 See Hudson 1986b: 176.
124 See Wittgenstein 1994b: 61.
125 See also Wittgenstein 1994b: 53, 55.
126 See Nietzsche 1968: §161. It would, for example, prove more difficult to demarcate so sharply between belief in the Last Judgment and the Marxist's belief in the coming Revolution.
127 See also Kierkegaard 1973: 255.
128 See Hudson 1986b: 179–80; Wittgenstein 1999: §199.
129 This is an adaptation of one of Sartre's examples (1977: 35–8). That 'it is I myself... who have to interpret the signs' is again brought out by Sartre when he comments on a 'remarkable' Jesuit, who, having experienced 'a succession of rather severe [personal] setbacks' interpreted all this 'as a sign that he was not intended for secular successes, and that only the attainments of religion, those of sanctity and of faith, were accessible to him.' But of course, this interpretation was not dictated by the phenomena themselves; '[o]ne could have drawn quite different conclusions' (ibid.: 38). We should here note that another's *suffering* constitutes one 'phenomenon' that does not require interpretation, but rather commands us *immediately* to offer help. I will expand on this in Chapters 3, 7 and 8.
130 See Wittgenstein 1958: §§5, 630; 1990: §419; 1999: §128.

216 *Notes*

131 See Wittgenstein 1958: p. 224. Should 'an irregularity in natural events ... suddenly occur' even that 'wouldn't *have* to throw me out of the saddle' (Wittgenstein 1999: §619).
132 See Kober 1996: 422.
133 It is possible that a response to such an occurrence would not involve any deliberation at all – one would instead 'obey [a] rule *blindly*' (Wittgenstein 1958: §219).
134 'For me to question my world-picture in this way is *already* for me to disown it in the face of a new conviction about how things are' (Morawetz 1978: 132). Sartre similarly remarks: 'if you seek counsel – from a priest, for example – you have selected that priest; and at bottom you already knew, more or less, what he would advise. In other words, to choose an adviser is nevertheless to commit oneself by that choice' (1977: 37).
135 See Derrida 1990: 1015; 1992a: 192, 204–5; 1998a: 9, 13. This point also relates to Derrida's remarks on the inherent 'coloniality of culture' (1998c: 24, see also 39; 2001d: 88, 102; 2002f: 57) and the 'border' (1993b: 11).
136 See Hudson 1986b: 179; Wittgenstein 1999: §472.
137 A notable example of the former appears in *On Certainty* itself, where Wittgenstein comments on the impossibility of flying to the moon (1999: §106) – a proposition that was 'in principle falsifiable,' 'has since been falsified,' and therefore 'belongs to the sand of the river bank' (Hudson 1986a: 124).
138 Elsewhere Hudson attempts to refine this by making a threefold distinction between those fundamental propositions that are: (1) 'absolutely fundamental to our entire world view,' (2) 'fundamental to a certain discipline or universe of discourse,' and (3) 'taken for granted at certain times.' He concludes: 'Fundamental propositions of these three kinds constitute a limit to thinking, though with varying degrees of exclusiveness and permanence' (1986b: 177).
139 Moreover, if we now drop the distinction between 'sand' and 'rock' and speak instead of 'fundamental propositions' *in general*, what distinguishes these from mere hypotheses – a distinction Hudson makes earlier (1986a: 120; see also 1986b: 176)?
140 See Wittgenstein 1999: §§52, 87, 203.
141 We get a sense of this when Wittgenstein remarks: 'I do not explicitly learn the propositions that stand fast for me. I can *discover them subsequently* like the axis around which a body rotates' (1999: §152, my emphasis). See also Morawetz 1978: 132–5 and Wittgenstein's allusions to 'prophesy' (1999: §§492, 652).
142 See Gaita's remarks on the 'unthinkable' and 'ruling things out of consideration' (2000: 164–6, 181, 185).
143 See Hertzberg 1988: 309–10.
144 See Hertzberg 1988: 312.
145 See Lagenspetz 1992: 19.
146 What Flew primarily objects to is the inability of the religious believer to specify falsification conditions *in advance* (1971: 14–15).
147 This often happens when extreme personal suffering undermines belief in God's infinite power and love. But again, though someone may lose their faith in such circumstances, these conditions could not be delineated *in advance*.
148 Identifying any possible 'fundamental proposition' that could *not* be taken as absolute seems problematic. The question here is therefore whether some fundamental convictions are more 'reasonable' (as rock) than others – though what criteria could govern such an assessment remains equally unclear.
149 As Kierkegaard quips, though it is 'true, as philosophers say, that life must be

understood backwards' they nevertheless 'forget ... that it must be lived forwards' (1965: 89).
150 Or a '*sacred gesture*' (Wittgenstein 1994a: 50). Although Wittgenstein alludes to stigmata in particular (1994b: 60), other possible examples include visions, miraculous healings and glossolalia.
151 See also Wittgenstein's remarks on the 'grammar of the word "God"' and specifically that '[w]hat is ridiculous or blasphemous also shows the grammar of the word' (1979b: 32).
152 Gaita makes a similar point concerning the ethical (2000: 179).
153 As Kierkegaard remarks, to possess genuine faith 'you must still have it for yourself in such a way that you ... retain it even if all others renounce it' (1973: 293; see also 1965: 185).
154 See Drury 1981: 128. Sometimes this sensitivity becomes rather perverse – as when Wittgenstein expresses his sympathy with Calvin for having 'Michael Servetus burnt for heresy' (Drury 1981: 180, see also 183). Contrast this with Helvétius's remarks on this event (1969: 47).
155 See also Kierkegaard 1973: 292.
156 See Wittgenstein 1999: §§609–12.
157 See also Kierkegaard 1973: 437.
158 One might deny that the former belief is 'really' quasi-empirical. Given both: (1) the believer's determination to 'stay in the saddle' of belief (even in the face of predictive failure), and (2) the existential risks they would take for their belief, such an individual thereby shows the truly 'religious' nature of their faith.
159 See Wittgenstein 1999: §512.
160 See Cavell 1979: 106–7.
161 See Wittgenstein 1994a: 72; 1994b: 59.
162 It is difficult to see how Wittgenstein could deny this formulation without thereby condemning generations of Christians as merely 'superstitious.' For an interesting account of the possible difference between religious and superstitious belief, see Gaita's reflections on his father's faith (1998: 174ff.).
163 See Wittgenstein 1994b: 56. Kuhn makes a number of remarks pertinent to the Wittgensteinian schema here – not least concerning the reluctance to accept falsifying data of specific scientific laws (where those laws are treated as tautologies (1996: 133) or 'quasi-analytic' (Hoyningen-Huene 1993: 211)). Compare this with Wittgenstein's suggestion that the distinction between empirical and mathematical certainties is blurred (1999: §§455, 651, 657).
164 See Wittgenstein 1994b: 54, 56, 57, 69, 70.
165 The difficulty of maintaining this distinction parallels the difficulty facing Hudson's distinction between the 'sand' and 'rock' of the 'river-bed.'
166 Many such religious groups do not recognize *themselves* as 'fundamentalists,' and in that sense this term remains pejorative. Caputo confesses how '[f]undamentalism seems almost impossible for intellectuals to understand,' for it 'looks just plain mad to those of us who fancy ourselves critical and intelligent' (2001: 94).
167 See Barrett 1998: 71.
168 See Barrett 1998: 84. The Christadelphians similarly forecast Christ's return for 1868 and 1910.
169 See Barrett 1998: 88.
170 As Wittgenstein notes, this is not to say that they are ignorant of evolutionary theory, for '*Very* intelligent and well-educated people believe in the story of creation in the Bible, while others hold it as proven false, and the grounds of the latter are well known to the former' (1999: §336).
171 See Nelson 1987: 77–8. The Christadelphians are notable on this point, given

their beliefs concerning the eschatological significance of the establishment of the State of Israel in 1948 (Barrett 1998: 76).
172 Along Derridean lines, Caputo remarks of early Christianity ('where the faithful believed the Messiah did come and take flesh' and 'concluded that the world was over') that when the world 'did not end, they set about asking and praying, when will you come *again?* For this "when will you come?" is the key to having a future' (2000: 116).
173 See Wittgenstein 1958: p. 224.
174 See Caputo 1993: 143. These terms are not necessarily synonymous, and for that reason I am using 'dogmatism' and 'sectarianism' in a rather strong sense. There is an ongoing debate here between the sort of pluralism Hick advocates and Plantinga's religious exclusivism. I will return to Hick in Chapter 3.
175 And similarly, that religion 'becomes repellent' when it attempts to 'justify' (Wittgenstein 1994a: 29) itself. In *On Certainty* Wittgenstein remarks: 'One might simply say "O, rubbish!" to someone who wanted to make objections to the propositions that are beyond doubt. That is, not reply to him but admonish him' (1999: §495). He proceeds: 'The queer thing is that even though I find it quite correct for someone to say "Rubbish!" and so brush aside the attempt to confuse him with doubts at bedrock, – nevertheless, I hold it to be incorrect if he seeks to defend himself (using, e.g., the words "I know")' (ibid.: §498).
176 See Wittgenstein 1999: §495.
177 See Matthew 24:23–4. Along with others, the Christadelphians now concede their past predictive errors and – in line with Matthew 24:36, 39, 42–4 – stress the ineffability of knowing when Christ will return (Barrett 1998: 76).
178 See Matthew 25:31–3; Mark 13:22–3. There is also a tendency to use scriptures such as Matthew 24:7–10, Luke 21:12 and John 16:18–27; 16:33 to explain why the faithful will experience profound difficulties in maintaining their belief during the 'Last Days.' This inbuilt persecution complex (something Nietzsche identifies (1968: §§173–4, 202)) is not, one suspects, peculiar to religious world-pictures.
179 Wittgenstein refers to 'unshakable' belief regarding Moore's fundamental propositions (1999: §§86, 103, 173) and religious belief (1994a: 54; 1994b: 73).
180 See Barrett 1998: 87–8.
181 Though, one should add, these only appear 'minor' *in retrospect*; prior to such predictive failures the very idea that revisions might be needed would have been significantly unthinkable, if not blasphemous.
182 See also Schutz 1964: 105; Bambrough 1992: 240–1. For this reason Graham's perplexity (2001: 41) in the face of such phenomena is itself puzzling.
183 See Bambrough 1992: 243.
184 These worries lie at the heart of Flew's 'Theology and Falsification' (1971).
185 See Gaita 2000: p. xxxii.
186 See also Wittgenstein 1999: §336.
187 This relates to Hudson's 'discipline-relative' and 'historically-relative' (1986b: 177) fundamental propositions.
188 As Kuhn and Feyerabend have argued, this picture of scientific practice is simplistic. Indeed, given Wittgenstein's remarks in *On Certainty* regarding the non-falsifiability of foundational beliefs, his own demarcation between 'science' and 'religion' thereby becomes less obvious.
189 See Wittgenstein 1999: §609.
190 See Wittgenstein 1993: 181. This point is bilateral; neither religion *nor* science requires support from the other. Having noted Wittgenstein's dislike of reli-

gious apologetics, we should also recall those remarks that extend this aversion to apologetics of any 'primitive' language-game (1958: p. 200; 1999: §475).
191 Wittgenstein's allusion to 'language-games' conflicting is unhelpful. I will therefore refer to conflicting 'world-pictures.'
192 This scenario is perhaps simplistic, for although on Wittgenstein's account one may not be able to judge one world-picture by the rules of another, this does not seem to prevent one from spotting a 'blunder' in *another's* world-picture. Moreover, for such a judgement to be possible only a fairly rudimentary grasp of these rules is required; one would not need to be a 'player.' (We should recall that, regarding religious belief, Wittgenstein himself was not in any traditional sense a 'player.') Likewise, Wittgenstein's account does not prohibit one from condemning a third party who attempts to impose the rules of their world-picture onto another's. Indeed, Wittgenstein himself must rely on these very possibilities in his own demarcation of genuine belief from pseudo-scientific superstition. I will return to the question of the 'third party' in Chapters 7 and 8 with reference to Levinas and Derrida.
193 See Wittgenstein 1958: §§22, 49.
194 See Wittgenstein 1999: §§34, 110, 164, 192, 204, 563, 625.
195 See Schutz 1964: 247.
196 On this soft case of dissensus see also Quine and Ullian 1970: 125–38; Morawetz 1978: 119. I will return to Lyotard in Chapter 3.
197 See Sextus 1996: 2:20.
198 Although I am here assuming that such 'radical difference' is a coherent notion, I will argue in Chapter 3 that to find oneself 'in conflict' with another is already to have (implicitly) acknowledged some degree of commonality. This is one way of understanding Levinas's suggestion that 'the gratuitousness of the *for-the-other*, the response of responsibility ... already lies dormant in a salutation, in the *hello*, in the *goodbye*' (1997b: 106) – or, as Derrida summarizes: 'war, hostility, even murder, *still* presuppose and thus *always* manifest [an] originary welcoming that is openness to the face' (1999b: 90). I will return to this in Chapter 7.
199 See Gill 1974: 283–4.
200 See Quine 1994: 44.
201 See Quine 1994: 45.
202 See Glock 1996: 48. While *The Structure of Scientific Revolutions* appeared in 1962, *On Certainty* was not published until 1969. Unless unpublished manuscripts of the latter were already in circulation, Wittgenstein could not have influenced Kuhn in this way. Indeed, although Kuhn cites *Philosophical Investigations* (1996: 45), he identifies Piaget, Whorf and Quine as more specific influences on his own thinking (ibid.: p. viii).
203 See Kuhn 1996: 125–6. A related point is made by Schutz on the 'selectivity' of experience (1964: 236; 1966: 125, 130–1; 1970b: 120; 1971: 5, 8, 76, 82, 227, 228, 317; 1974: 91, 243, 261). Note also Schutz's remarks on anomalies or crises of experience (1964: 96; 1966: 124; 1970a: 69, 88; 1971: 231; 1974: 12, 168–9, 171).
204 Although Kuhn indicates some important differences between the process of scientific revolution and gestalt perceptual change (1996: 85, 114–15).
205 See Kuhn 1996: 150–2, 204. Compare this with Wittgenstein 1999: §§92, 262.
206 See Kuhn 1996: 84ff.
207 See Kuhn's remarks on the customary understanding of 'progress' and his aversion to questions concerning 'what nature is really like' (1996: 206).
208 A similar point can be made concerning Wittgenstein's remark that 'one is sometimes convinced of the *correctness* of a view by its *simplicity* or *symmetry*, i.e.,

220 *Notes*

these are what induce one to go over to this point of view' (1999: §92), for if such criteria are to have any rhetorical force it must either be the case that there is *already* agreement about what constitutes 'simplicity' and 'symmetry,' or that the new criteria must simultaneously be what one is being persuaded *of.*

209 See Wittgenstein 1999: §170.
210 See Wittgenstein 1999: §§160, 283, 374, 472, 476.
211 See Sextus 1996: 2:20. For a historical contextualization of this see Popkin 1979: 1–17.
212 See Wittgenstein's allusion to 'missionaries convert[ing] natives' (1999: §612), and Kuhn's remarks on 'persuasion' and 'force' (1996: 93).
213 To this extent Feyerabend is right to emphasize the connection between science and society – although Kuhn makes similar allusions (1996: 92–4).
214 As will become clear, this is not to conflate language-games with world-pictures. Rather, language-games constitute the building blocks of world-pictures.
215 In a peculiar formulation Wittgenstein refers to 'the human language-game' (1999: §554).
216 See Phillips 1986: 5–16; Clack 1999: 78–89.
217 See Wittgenstein 1958: §71; 1990: §392.
218 See also Wittgenstein 1958: §293.
219 See also Wittgenstein 1999: §§63, 65, 256, 646.
220 See also Wittgenstein 1958: p. 188; 1999: §555.
221 See Wittgenstein 1999: §§393, 396, 554, 620.
222 Kuhn's understanding of incommensurability came to approximate this softer position (Hoyningen-Huene 1993: 218–22; Kuhn 1996: 198–207).
223 In Chapter 3 I will develop Winch's suggestions on precisely this possibility. On why moral disagreement might often seem impossible to resolve, see Winch 1987: 186.
224 See Wittgenstein 1958: §217.
225 I use this term in the Habermasian sense (Steuerman 1992: 103–7; Love 1995: 53–4; Moon 1995: 146–8). With §23 of *Philosophical Investigations* in mind, Steuerman questions Habermas's distinction between the 'strategic' and 'communicative' by noting that Wittgenstein 'stresses that giving reasons is one possible language game and not the foundation of all possible games' (Steuerman 1992: 106). But this criticism can be pushed further. For Habermas's demarcation is problematic, not merely because it is insensitive to the *multiplicity* of language-games but also because even *within* (or, more precisely, at the end of) the language-game(s) of 'reason giving' the strategic plays a crucial role (Wittgenstein 1999: §612). Thus, 'communicative action' ultimately finds itself in the realm of the 'strategic,' thereby undermining Habermas's prioritization of the former over the latter (Steuerman 1992: 105).
226 See Wittgenstein 1994b: 28.
227 See Wittgenstein 1999: §206. The rhetorical force of such an attempt lies in its implicit claim that the 'new' way of looking at things is not merely *different* but also *better* (Kuhn 1996: 203). I will return to this point later.
228 See Wittgenstein 1999: §612.
229 Kuhn refers to the internal 'circularity' of '[e]ach group [using] its own paradigm to argue in that paradigm's defence' (1996: 94).
230 To make this move would itself 'be a particular kind of substantive position, viz. extreme relativism' (Johnston 1991: 143). I will return to this in Chapter 3.
231 See Wittgenstein 1999: §512. Although Wittgenstein's overriding emphasis is

upon one's inheriting and being trained in such world-pictures, he does speak of 'decid[ing] to retain my old belief' (1999: §516).
232 See Wittgenstein 1999: §611.
233 See Morawetz 1978: 123; Wittgenstein 1999: §199. Morawetz's claim that such a move 'is not to make a grounded decision' is misleading, for it *is* a thoroughly 'grounded decision' according to *my* criteria. Taking his lead from other passages in *On Certainty*, Morawetz emphasizes that the 'concepts one uses to describe alien ways of thinking are one's own concepts; one's attitude toward truth and falsity of the beliefs of others is determined by one's own criteria for what is true' (1978: 133), and thus the suggestion that one cannot (or must not) judge an 'alien' practice is utterly misconceived (ibid.: 128). While I agree with much of Morawetz's analysis (and specifically his emphasizing the stakes involved in questioning one's own world-picture (ibid.: 132–7)), I remain unconvinced that one can so easily sidestep the relativism of *On Certainty* on these epistemic grounds – that is, without reference to moral considerations. As I will argue in Chapters 3 and 5, other of Wittgenstein's writings open the way to a more ethical challenge to relativism.
234 See Kuhn 1996: 151.
235 Kuhn similarly alludes to the 'conversion experience' that occurs in the 'transfer of allegiance from paradigm to paradigm' (1996: 151). For a more sympathetic interpretation of this aspect of Kuhn's work see Hoyningen-Huene 1993: 221, 252–8.
236 Which is not to say that silence can be adequately characterized as a mere absence or lack (Lyotard 1988: p. xii, 29; Derrida 1988a: 145–8; 2000b: 135; Levinas 1989: 487; Heidegger 1999: 208–9).
237 See Bambrough 1992: 243. Note also Derrida's remarks on 'forgiveness' (1992b: 164–8).
238 See James 1985: 209.
239 This terminology is steadily replacing previous discussion of 'cults' and 'brainwashing.' For an overview of these 'new' religions see Barker 1990: 31–40.
240 This parallels what James says of Revivalism's understanding of religious conversion (1985: 228).
241 See Wittgenstein 1999: §262.
242 This might be contrasted with the more formal recruitment procedures of Scientology, where an individual can (allegedly) 'convert' themselves (Nelson 1987: 139). From a Wittgensteinian perspective such groups would doubtless fail the criteria demanded of genuine religiosity. It is perhaps significant that the 'religious' status of Scientology has indeed been contested by a number of governments (Barker 1990: 40, n. 6).
243 See also Drury 1981: 114.
244 See Wittgenstein 1999: §609.
245 See Wittgenstein 1999: §5. One might be tempted to claim that *A*'s position is superior insofar as it can accommodate *B*'s, whereas *B*'s position cannot accommodate *A*'s (Morawetz 1978: 130–1). But this is questionable. After all, it is hardly self-evident that *B*'s position could *not* accommodate *A*'s. One's temptation to assume this simply reveals a deeper obsession with a specific, empirical-scientific account of what constitutes genuine 'accommodating.' *A* could doubtless provide a compelling account (to *her* community) of *B*'s activities. But so could *B* likely provide a compelling account (to *his* community) of *A*'s. The question here is whether cashing out 'superiority' in terms of 'accommodating' (or 'being capable of explaining') is itself the product of a specific scientific world-picture (ibid.: 124; Wittgenstein 1999: §298)? Moreover, the very notion of being able to 'embrace and include' an alien world-picture and 'say what they believe' (Morawetz 1978:

130) is itself problematic (Wittgenstein 1994b: 55). I will return to the latter in Chapter 5.
246 See Johnston 1991: 142–3; Plantinga 1998: 187–209.
247 This relates to Wittgenstein's distinction between judgements of 'relative' and 'absolute' value. I will discuss this in Chapter 5.
248 This is why Rorty simply begs the question when he asserts that 'the benefits of modern astronomy and space travel outweigh the advantages of Christian fundamentalism' (1999: p. xxv).
249 See Feyerabend 1988: 258.
250 See Plantinga 1998: 131.
251 This point can be seen as a development of Wittgenstein's remark that '[y]ou must ask yourself: what does one accept as a criterion for a medicine's helping one?' (1993: 403). The situation concerning Jehovah's Witnesses' rejection of blood transfusions is pertinent here, for even enforced transfusions frequently make the recipient feel as though *they* have committed (or at least been instrumental in) an act of blasphemy.
252 See Wittgenstein 1993: 377.
253 Even on the broadly scientific criteria of theory-simplicity (Kuhn 1996: 206), *B*'s account may prove the 'better' option (Morawetz 1978: 124).
254 To this extent Wittgenstein's claim that, through such descriptive procedures, the other will be 'convinced' (1999: §671), is questionable. Regarding *A*'s 'explaining' to *B* what she is doing – and even showing him microscopic 'evidence' in support – we should note Feyerabend's remarks on Galileo's argument with the Church concerning his telescopic findings. Feyerabend considers the Church's response to have been 'scientifically correct' and also as having 'the right social intention, viz. to protect people from the machinations of specialists' (1988: 137). One of the reasons he draws this conclusion is Galileo's failure to substantiate his findings theoretically by volunteering any cogent reason why the telescope offered 'better' observational data than the unaided eye (ibid.: 89–105, 131–8). Likewise, in my example, *B*'s coming to accept *A*'s 'evidence' does not rest on the data presented but rather on *B*'s having been trained in *A*'s world-picture. There is no reason why *B* should accept *A*'s procedures (and microscopic data in particular) as providing 'evidence' for *anything at all.*
255 Preston summarizes Feyerabend's position on the alleged superiority of Western medicine as follows: 'By the very different standards of another tradition, the "achievements" of Western science may seem piffling' (Preston 1997: 201). Presumably Preston does not mean that the achievements of Western science seem 'piffling' in the sense that they are only small achievements, but rather that they are not seen to be 'achievements' *at all.*
256 See Morawetz 1978: 128.
257 And the additional point here is that the *criterion* of 'effectiveness' is also accepted. The context of my assertions here should make it clear that I am not advocating an uncritical attitude toward Western medicine *per se.*
258 See Levinas 1988b: 158.
259 See Caputo 1993: 32–3, 54. The frequent accusation that television news betrays a deep morbidity in its preoccupation with 'bad' news is in this sense *itself* morally questionable. For it is precisely the 'disasters' that highlight our shared humanity. The same objection could be made against Rousseau's lamentations concerning the tendency of historians to focus on 'catastrophes' (1973: 107).
260 See Wittgenstein 1999: §609.
261 See also Wittgenstein 1958: §656.

3 Pluralism, justice and vulnerability

1 See Wittgenstein 1999: §9.
2 See Wittgenstein 1995: 4.121.
3 It is here worth noting the ontological wonder expressed in the *Tractatus*, 'A Lecture on Ethics' and 'On Heidegger on Being and Dread.' Interestingly, in 'A Lecture on Ethics' Wittgenstein adds that 'the right expression in language for the miracle of the existence of the world ... is the existence of language itself' (1993: 43–4). On this point see Derrida's remarks on the 'telephonic *yes* ... which recalls the origin of the universe' (1992a: 271, see also 260, 270, 273), and the givenness of language (1992b: 27, 80–1; 1998c: 40, 64, 67–8) – including any discourse *on* the nature of 'the gift' and 'giving' in general (1992b: 62, 80, 82, 90–2, 99; 1999c: 58, 66–7, 71). I return to a number of these themes in Chapter 8.
4 This is a contentious point, and, as will become clear, I favor a minimally naturalistic interpretation of such concepts.
5 See also Sextus' remarks, cited in Schopenhauer 1995: 122.
6 This relates to Winch's reflections on the need to contextualize the concepts of 'decision' (1960: 235–7), 'facts' (ibid.: 237–8), 'objective reality' (1964: 308–9, 313; 1970: 253), and the possibility of 'different rationalities' (1964: 316–18; 1960: 236). The extent to which the moral realm is *actually* fragmented in the way Feyerabend (and others) suggest is debatable (Graham 2001: 8–9).
7 Without some appeal to universal criteria Feyerabend could not justify this use of 'reasonable' and 'civilized,' for what constitutes each of these will be a matter of contention between traditions.
8 See Wittgenstein 1958: §23; 1999: §609.
9 See Feyerabend 1987: 106ff.
10 Winch likewise alludes to the mutability of scientific concepts (1960: 234). For his reflections on scientism, see 1964: 308–9, 321; 1970: 250, 253–4, 258–9.
11 See also Morris 1990: 194. Compare Feyerabend's remarks with Rousseau's advice concerning religious education (1973: 115–16).
12 Concerning Feyerabend's political agenda, see Preston 1997: 191–211.
13 A similar problem arises when Critchley asserts that 'the problem of politics is that of delineating a form of political life that will repeatedly interrupt all attempts at totalization' (1999a: 223; see also Campbell 1999: 42, 51), for even *this* imperative must thereby enact something of a 'totalizing' gesture. Much the same could be said of Derrida's claim: 'This is what must be avoided – dogmatic theses – this is a categorical imperative; dogmatism ... must be avoided at any price' (2002f: 213).
14 See Johnston 1991: 143.
15 Bernstein (1991: 222) makes a similar point regarding Lyotard.
16 Since 9/11 and the so-called 'War on Terror' the themes I will discuss in this chapter have become even more pressing. Likewise, my discussion of Levinas and Derrida in Chapter 8 (specifically on the question of 'hospitality') is especially relevant in the current political climate of anxiety about immigration.
17 I will refer primarily to *The Rainbow of Faiths* where Hick explicitly responds to his critics (1995).
18 See Hick 1995: 31. Hick suggests that his own pluralism does not claim a 'privileged vantage point' (ibid.: 49) but 'is arrived at inductively, from ground level' (ibid.: 50), and, further, that his hypothesis is 'offered as the "best explanation" ... from a religious point of view, of the facts of the history of religion' (ibid.: 51).

19 See Hick 1995: 34–7. A distinction should be made between *pluralism* and the mere recognition of *plurality* (Surin 1990: 117) – a distinction lacking in, for example, Sugden's 'informed evangelicalism' (1990: 148, see also 150–2). Pluralism, as Sugden construes it, amounts only to a certain patience and non-coerciveness regarding the non-evangelical (that is, *yet-to-be-converted*) world. Refer also to Derrida 1998b: 21–2; 1998c: 37–8; 2001a: 62–3.
20 See Hick 1995: 34.
21 See Hick 1995: 16, 125.
22 See also Caputo 2001: 20.
23 See Hick 1977: 167–84; 1995: 87.
24 The 'quasi' is important here, for although Hick alludes to Wittgenstein's employment of Jastrow's 'duck-rabbit picture' (Hick 1995: 24), he is antagonistic to Wittgenstein's (alleged) 'fideism' (Hick 1966: 237–8; 1988: 7ff).
25 See Hick 1995: 45–9.
26 See Hick 1977: 184; 1995: 121.
27 See also Hick 1995: 133.
28 Hick's political agenda is thus, like Feyerabend's, deeply voluntaristic (contrast with Wittgenstein 1999: §317).
29 There is, after all, not just 'one way of assembling the [historical] data' (Wittgenstein 1996a: 69).
30 See Hick 1995: 12.
31 See also Hick 1995: 19. Thus, 'one of the primary motivations behind [the pluralist's] adoption of a "theocentric" ... theological standpoint is precisely the desire to discredit and to undo the theological legacy' of these sorts of 'shameful' (Surin 1990: 119) practices.
32 Hick's criterion is covertly homogenizing (Surin 1990: 121–2) insofar as he claims that what 'is of central concern to each of the great world faiths' (Hick 1995: 17) is their preoccupation with 'salvation/liberation' – that is, 'of an actual change in human beings from natural self-centredness towards a recentering in the Divine' (ibid.: 18; see also Derrida 1998b: 42–3).
33 See also Surin 1990: 114.
34 Or what differentiates the 'sand' from the 'rock' (Wittgenstein 1999: §99) of the riverbed. Hick fails to give this point due attention in his explicit hope that 'different traditions ... will each gradually winnow out the aspect which entails its own superiority' (1995: 123). This desire to down-play the normativity of his work similarly manifests itself when Hick asserts that 'it is not for me to presume to tell my Muslim or Jewish or Hindu or Buddhist colleagues how to try to develop their own traditions' (assuming, of course, they were not of an exclusivist disposition), because 'in the end change has to come from within a religious tradition' (ibid.: 121).
35 See Hick 1995: 30.
36 See Wittgenstein 1994b: 61. Note also Levinas's remarks on the possibility of there being 'a place for the pre-eminent absolute of faith' (1997a: 172–3).
37 Hick also alludes to the 'implicit religious pluralism' (1995: 122) prevalent in everyday contexts.
38 See Caputo 2001: 102–3. Note also Levinas's remarks on confession (1997a: 172).
39 See Derrida 1995b: 106.
40 See also Derrida 1995a: 198–9, 386–7; 2000b: 39.
41 See Derrida 1993b: 10–11, 33; 1995b: 64; 1999a: 69–70, 81; 2000b: 51. Or, more paradoxically, one might ask: 'How can the unforgivable be forgiven? But what else can be forgiven?' (Derrida 2000b: 39).
42 This relates to my earlier discussion regarding the limits of justification, and the extent to which the possibility of reaching a 'rational' consensus depends

upon shared judgement-criteria (and thus our being trained appropriately)? See also Winch 1960: 234–5, 239.
43 See Surin's remarks on the 'homogenizing tendency' of Hick's argument that is 'obscured' by his 'loud disavowal of "exclusivism"' (Surin 1990: 125).
44 See Derrida 1995b: 61; 2000a: 405.
45 See Morris's appeal for a '"genuine pluralism"' (1990: 193) and his criticism of Western liberalism regarding its treatment of Jewish religious practice (ibid.: 179–96).
46 See Hick 1995: 31.
47 Derrida's account of 'iterability' is relevant here (1992a: 42–3, 64, 276, 304; 1995a: 175, 200, 372–3, 378, 388). I return to this in Chapter 8.
48 On Surin's reading what is paradoxical about Hick's pluralism is that it is only the religious *exclusivist* who truly recognizes the 'otherness' of the other.
49 See Surin 1990: 125–6. Caputo similarly refers to the 'mutually irreducible forms of life' (2001: 131) that constitute 'religion.'
50 See Lyotard 1985: 51–4. Lyotard claims that 'postmodern' society is characterized by its 'incredulity toward metanarratives,' for now we instead find a distribution of 'clouds of narrative language elements' and a basic 'heterogeneity' of localized 'language games' (1997a: xxiv; see also 1993: 20).
51 Lyotard is here attacking Levinas's prioritization of the ethical over other 'narratives' or 'language games' (Lyotard 1985: 60). Lyotard's criticism of Wittgenstein's alleged voluntarism (the latter's 'anthropological assumption' (Lyotard 1993: 21; see also 1985: 51; 1988: xiii; Readings 1991: 107)) is misplaced, for Lyotard is similarly at fault (1985: 61) – assuming this *is* a fault. I criticize Lyotard's position later, and return to Levinas in Chapters 6 and 7.
52 Compare with Wittgenstein's remarks on game playing (1994a: 27). Of course, at this stage Lyotard (like Hick) would have trouble accommodating the hardened religious exclusivist who wants to 'stick to [their] signified' and 'think that they are in the true.' But, as will become clear, accommodation is precisely not what Lyotard recommends. Compare also Lyotard's remarks on Parmenides and Freud (1985: 62) with Wittgenstein's remarks on Copernicus, Darwin (1994a: 18), and Freud (1994b: 51–2).
53 See Carrol 1987: 160. This emphasis on 'narrative imagination' re-emerges in *The Differend* where the vocabulary of the 'phrase' replaces that of 'language-games.' The 'phrase' now comes to represent the indubitable, simplest and 'smallest of discursive units' (Carrol 1987: 164), for '[w]hat escapes doubt is that there is at least one phrase, no matter what it is. This cannot be denied without verifying it *ideo facto. There is no phrase* is a phrase, *I lie* is a phrase' (Lyotard 1988: 65, see also xii). (Indeed, Lyotard claims that even silence is 'a phrase' (ibid.: xii, 29).) *That-there-is-a-phrase* is necessary. What remains open is how linkages *between* phrases are made (ibid.: 29). It is here, then, that 'the problem of politics' (ibid.: xiii) emerges, not least because any linkage necessarily operates at the expense of *other* linkages (ibid.: xii).
54 Compare with Wittgenstein 1999: §609.
55 See Levinas 1997b: 9.
56 See also Lyotard 1993: 20.
57 Of course, the distinction between playing *the same game differently* and playing *a different game* will itself be contentious.
58 See Carrol 1987: 159. Lyotard thus seems to rule out the possibility of totalitarianism itself forming a 'given' and legitimate region of discourse.
59 See Readings 1991: 113.
60 See Readings 1991: 118.
61 See also Lyotard 1988: 13.

62 See Graham 2001: 8.
63 But, it might be argued, one is *always already* compromised, for '[a]ll culture is originarily colonial ... Every culture institutes itself through the unilateral imposition of some "politics" of language' (Derrida 1998c: 39).
64 See also Lyotard 1985: 66–7.
65 See Lyotard 1985: 25; Readings 1991: 108.
66 See Readings 1991: 112. For Lyotard, politics is thus a necessarily experimental, a-teleological endeavor (ibid.: 124), and this is why he further claims (without a hint of pessimism (Readings 1992: 184)) that 'there is no just society' (Lyotard 1985: 25). If it were not for the fact that one can always do *more, better,* be *more just,* the very notion of justice itself would be meaningless. Any society (or individual) inclined to affirm its (or their) moral rectitude is either dangerously naive or despotic (Caputo 2000: 112, 115). As we will see in Chapters 7 and 8, both Levinas and Derrida make similar claims.
67 See also Derrida's remarks on the silencing of madness (1998a: 80–1).
68 Hick seems to think his pluralistic hypothesis constitutes a natural extension of this implicit pluralism.
69 See Hick 1995: 19.
70 See Readings 1991: 109; Lyotard 1997a: xxiv–xxv.
71 See Lyotard 1988: xiii; 1997a: 82.
72 See also Derrida 1990: 951.
73 For a rather unconvincing account of radical cultural 'otherness' regarding methods of spatialization see Shapiro 1999: 62.
74 See Readings 1992: 181–2. Note also Winch's remarks on 'magical influence' and 'causation' (1964: 320).
75 Readings insists that any notion of 'common humanity' (or 'human nature') is *by definition* totalitarian (1992: 174–6, 184, 186). I contest this claim later.
76 See Derrida 2000b: 15, 27, 135. Readings later remarks that the 'injustice perpetrated on indigenes is not a racism accidental to modernism which might be prevented by including them within a wider concept of human nature. Rather, the assumption of universal human nature, like all modernist metanarratives, lights the way to terror even as it upholds the torch of human rights' (1992: 186).
77 Here we might recall the Pyrrhonist's 'being-at-a-loss,' discussed in Chapter 1. Compare these passages with Morawetz's remarks on *On Certainty* (1978: 123).
78 See also Pitkin 1993: 325–6; Greisch 1999: 50. Note Husserl's remarks on 'empathy' (1982: 134–5; 1989: 84).
79 Although I will not pursue this here, there is doubtless a story to be told about Wittgenstein and Hume at this juncture (Clack 1999: 11–24).
80 Similarly, Werhane has misplaced 'Levinasian' reservations concerning Wittgenstein's later work – specifically his (alleged) inability to develop a 'notion of the self or of interrelationships between selves' (1995: 62).
81 See Cockburn 1990: 6, 76; Tilghman 1991: 98.
82 This passage should be contrasted with Wittgenstein's remark that others are sometimes 'a complete enigma' (that '[w]e cannot find our feet with them'), especially when entering 'a strange country with entirely strange traditions' (1958: p. 223; see also Glendinning 1998: 71). The claim that such others are a *complete* mystery is misleading. Indeed, these remarks are immediately followed by Wittgenstein's equally deceptive remark that 'If a lion could talk, we could not understand it' (ibid.). I return to the latter in Chapter 7.
83 See Wittgenstein 1990: §567.
84 Even applying the term 'colony' presupposes some minimally identifiable form of social – though not necessarily human – structure (Derrida 2000a: 405).
85 See Winch 1987: 144; Cockburn 1990: 119.

86 See also Wittgenstein 1958: §415; Tilghman 1991: 100–1; Gaita 2000: 269. A related point is made in Merleau-Ponty 1996: 353.
87 See Cockburn 1990: 77.
88 Wittgenstein also remarks: 'Only of what behaves like a human being can one say that it *has* pains' (1958: §283), and 'only of a living human being and what resembles (behaves like) a living human being can one say: it has sensations; it sees; is blind; hears; is deaf; is conscious or unconscious' (ibid.: §281, see also §360; Cockburn 1990: 66, 70; Gaita 2003: 44, 59).
89 Wittgenstein's remarks on slavery illustrate something of the disingenuousness of treating others as mere machines (1990: §§108, 528–30; see also Cavell 1979: 376; Gaita 2000: 48–9, 54–5, 68). One might say that even in 'hatred' one exhibits a certain 'form of desire' (Derrida 1995c: 47) for the other; that in my saying 'no' to the other there lies an indelible trace of a 'yes' (Derrida 1996b: 82). I return to these suggestions in Chapters 7 and 8.
90 Gaita alludes to the 'face' on a number of occasions (2000: 15, 61–2, 266–8), though fails to explain its significance. I pursue this in later chapters with reference to Levinas.
91 See Wittgenstein 1990: §220; Merleau-Ponty 1996: 351.
92 See Wittgenstein 1958: §286; Cockburn 1990: 66–7, 70–1, 77; Rose 1997: 61, 67.
93 See Wittgenstein 1990: §506.
94 Wittgenstein's allusions to the face may be surprising from a biographical perspective insofar as he is thought to have suffered from Asperger's syndrome (*Guardian Education* supplement, 20/2/01: 45).
95 See Tilghman 1991: 97–8; Gaita 2000: 270.
96 See Wittgenstein 1958: p. 179; Winch 1987: 147, 151–2; Kerr 1997: 80; Gaita 2000: 264–6.
97 Eye contact is especially significant here (Cockburn 1990: 5).
98 See Wittgenstein 1958: §537.
99 Although Husserl similarly insists that one does not make an 'inference from analogy' (1982: 111), he nevertheless maintains this general 'from-me' *structure* insofar as 'the body over there, which is … apprehended as an animate organism, must have derived this sense by an *apperceptive transfer from my animate organism*' (ibid.: 110; see also Schutz 1964: 22–4, 37; 1974: 62, 104). For a more sympathetic reading of Husserl on this point, see Derrida 1997c: 123ff.
100 See also Wittgenstein 1958: §285; Dilman 1987: 31.
101 See also Wittgenstein 1969: 162.
102 Compare this with Schopenhauer 1995: 143, 147, 148.
103 Regarding the natural priority of the human face, see Wittgenstein 1958: §§281, 283, 583.
104 See Descartes 1976: 73–4.
105 See Hume 1988: 159; Tilghman 1991: 98ff.; Gaita 2000: xxviii.
106 See Wittgenstein 1996a: 69; 1994a: 37.
107 See Wittgenstein 1994a: 4. This is perhaps akin to the sense of wonder at one's own body (ibid.: 11).
108 See Bergson 1911: 30.
109 By 'unmechanical' I do not mean random, which would itself likely generate an 'uncanny feeling.'
110 Or better, a degree of *iterability* (repetition-without-sameness (Derrida 2001d: 76; 2002d: 24)), thus allowing for the possibility of distinguishing between natural behavioral repetition and catatonia.
111 See Wittgenstein 1990: §§603–4.
112 See Bergson 1911: 32, 34. The history of film bears witness to the fact that

madness, possession and the alien are most effectively portrayed by stunted, repetitive movements, lifeless speech, limited and inapt facial expressions (ibid.: 24, 56). Of this repertoire of cinematic devices the 'fixed look' (Wittgenstein 1958: §420) stands out. On the role of the face in cinema, see Balázs 1985: 255–64.
113 See also Cockburn 1990: 119.
114 Bergson's analysis of comedy is essentially an extended meditation on this point (1911: 8–10, 16, 18, 20, 24–5, 29–34, 36–7, 43, 48, 57–9, 69, 72–3, 77, 79, 87, 101–2, 109).
115 What does change between each listening is *oneself*; one's circumstances, memories, anticipations, and so on (Derrida 2000d: 65–6). Note also Schutz's remarks on the impossibility of 'pure' repetition in social relations (1964: 115), and regarding experience in general (1970b: 118).
116 See Buber's remarks quoted in Gaita 2000: 271.
117 The sort of predictability I have in mind here is not deliberative. Rather, we *react* to the regularity of another's behavior quite naturally, and it is upon this sort of reaction that deliberation is subsequently founded. I return to this point in a moment.
118 See Mulhall 1993: 76.
119 Contrast: (1) predicting the results of a simple physics experiment, with (2) predicting that a friend will find a specific anecdote amusing. In both cases we can meaningfully speak of 'prediction' (even 'calculation'), but the type of exactness involved in each differs (Wittgenstein 1958: §§69–70, 88; 1990: §438).
120 See also Wittgenstein 1958: p. 178; 1999: §221; Winch 1987: 149. Of course, this does not ensure against illusion or deception. But, recalling *On Certainty*, the question to ask the skeptic here is why, if I cannot trust *this*, should I trust *anything* – including my powers of suspicion?
121 See Wittgenstein 1958: p. 178; 1994a: 49; Winch 1987: 140–1; Kerr 1997: 90–4.
122 See Wittgenstein 1958: §420.
123 Levinas similarly remarks that the soul 'shows itself in the non-reified face ... in expression' as the 'glimmer of someone' (2000: 12) – although, as we will see in Chapter 7, he excludes animals from this.
124 See Cockburn 1990: 6, 9; Mulhall 1993: 80.
125 See also Wittgenstein 1994b: 57; 1996a: 64.
126 See also Tilghman 1991: 115.
127 See Winch 1987: 147.
128 See Cavell 1979: 372–3; Graham 2001: 8.
129 See Gaita's remarks on different types of 'nonsense' (2003: 128–9). Interestingly, Benso has attempted to articulate a Heideggerian–Levinasian 'ethics of *things*' (2000: 59–196).
130 The same sort of question could be asked of both Shapiro's gloss on the 'absolute alterity' (1999: 63) of the other, and Molloy's claim that the other is 'beyond my ... grasp' (1999: 218).
131 See Cockburn 1990: 72. Any 'concernful' gesture toward such an object would be derivative of our responses to others. To treat a stone as if it were suffering would be to treat it *as though* it were human (Wittgenstein 1958: §§283–4). There are at least two things wrong with Connolly's remark that 'it is extremely probable that all of us today are unattuned to some modes of suffering and exclusion that will have become ethically important tomorrow after a political movement carries them across the threshold of cultural attentiveness and redefinition' (1999: 147). First, there is no necessary reason why we should *presently* think this to be a *future* possibility – and certainly no reason why we should think it 'extremely probable' (recall both Wittgenstein's

remarks in *On Certainty* concerning 'staying in the saddle' of one's world-picture, and my analysis of 'retrospection' in Chapter 2). And second, even if we concede Connolly's general point, the 'modes of suffering' to which he refers would only appear *as such* if they were not *radically* different from present forms of suffering.
132 See Winch 1987: 149; Wittgenstein 1996a: 64–71; 1999: §§475, 538, 559.
133 See also Husserl 1982: §§50–4. Wittgenstein is not denying the possibility that in exceptional circumstances one *may* reason in this way (1990: §539). For an overly rationalized account of 'empathy,' see Molloy 1999: 214–16.
134 With these passages in mind, Gaita's reticence to describe 'primitive reactions' as 'pre-linguistic' (2000: 272–3) is rather puzzling.
135 See Winch's remarks on 'truth-telling' (1960: 242–6, 250) and Wittgenstein's remarks on lying (1958: §249).
136 See also Wittgenstein 1958: p. 223. Of course, none of this is to deny that we also possess a natural capacity for violence (indeed, Wittgenstein sometimes appears overly fatalistic regarding this (Drury 1981: 131)). The point is that – contrary to philosophers like Levinas who judge 'the natural' to be *essentially* egoistic – it is *also* natural to care for others. As will become clear in Chapters 6 and 7, the problem with Levinas's anti-naturalism is that it makes any other-oriented acts seem like a 'miracle' (Greisch 1999: 51; Caputo 2001: 139).
137 See also Wittgenstein 1999: §§391–2, 458.
138 See also Cavell 1979: 110–11; Wittgenstein 1990: §391; Cockburn 1990: 76.
139 See Wittgenstein 1958: §§244, 343; Kerr 1997: 85.
140 It is not incidental that children do not generally display the same sort of curiosity ('is this suffering?') with regard to stones, carpets or iron filings.
141 Despite Tilghman's later comments (1991: 113), in emphasizing beliefs 'that "stand fast" for us' (ibid.: 104) he does not give due weight to Wittgenstein's naturalism.
142 See also Nietzsche 1992b: Essay 2, §7. Caputo makes too much of the possibility for a 'genealogy' of pain (1993: 208–9). Indeed, such a genealogy would severely problematize Caputo's forthright condemnation of 'cruelty or the causing of useless suffering' (2003: 177). In a similar vein, Foucault remarks: 'We believe in the dull constancy of instinctual life and imagine that it continues to exert its force indiscriminately in the present as it did in the past. But historical knowledge easily disintegrates this unity ... We believe, in any event, that the body obeys the exclusive laws of physiology, and that it escapes the influence of history, but this too is false. The body is molded by a great many distinct regimes ... Nothing in man – not even his body – is sufficiently stable as the basis for self-recognition or for understanding other men' (2000: 379–80; see also Derrida 2001c: 262; 2002f: 204, 210). Needless to say, I think these claims are fundamentally misguided.
143 See Caputo 1993: 196, 216. My suggestions here correlate with Winch's 'limiting notions' of 'birth, death' and 'sexual relations' (1964: 322) (categories echoed in Wittgenstein 1996a: 66–7) which 'are inescapably involved in the life of all known human societies in a way which gives us a clue where to look, if we are puzzled about the point of an alien system of institutions.' For Winch, then, 'the very notion of human life is limited by these conceptions' (1964: 322, see also 324), and in this crucial sense his position is not relativistic (ibid.: 308, 320–1; 1960: 232–3, 238, 244, 250; 1970: 249). With Winch's 'limiting notions' in mind, note also Derrida's remarks on the transcultural preoccupation with death (1993b: 24, 42–4, 60–1).
144 See Tilghman 1991: 113; Caputo 2000: 111.
145 See Winch's remarks on the necessary presuppositions for understanding another human being and/or culture (1960: 232–3; 1970: 250). Wittgen-

230 *Notes*

stein's remarks on 'agreement ... in form of life' (1958: §241) should likewise be read in this minimally naturalistic light.
146 See also Schopenhauer 1995: 139.
147 See Mates 1996: pp. 30–1.
148 I am not denying that genuine amoralism and/or 'moral blindness' are possible (Gaita 2003: 167ff.). My point is to caution against applying these categories too hastily.
149 Wittgenstein's reflections on 'free will' are interesting here, particularly his suggestion that determinism is a form of 'fatalism' (1993: 431) and signifies 'that you don't want to make [the other] responsible, or be harsh in your judgment' (ibid.: 433) ('It is the way in which we look at a case when we don't want to judge' (ibid.: 437, see also 440–1)). He proceeds in Nietzschean fashion: 'That you are inclined in this way ... is a fact of psychology' (ibid.: 433).
150 As Gaita puts it: 'morality does not serve our purposes but is the judge of them' (2003: 181).
151 See Gaita 2000: 17–27.
152 The same point is made by Levinas (1996b: 247).
153 See also Caputo 1993: 28–9. Caputo is therefore mistaken when he (along with Lyotard (1985: 60)) criticizes Levinas for prioritizing ethics above other 'language games' (Caputo 1993: 125). Indeed, Caputo himself relies upon this prioritization of the ethical when he asserts that there is 'nothing subjectivistic about obligation,' for the other's suffering 'places us under its claim' (ibid.: 31–2). This confusion can be further seen when Caputo insists (rightly in my view) that, methodologically speaking, we should not attempt to determine what constitutes the 'Good Life' but rather 'start from below, with the multiple disasters (evils) by which we are daily visited, with broken bodies and damaged lives' (ibid.: 32–3, see also Ch. 9), because the latter 'have an ominous sameness' (ibid.: 41) and thus possess the capacity for 'binding us together' (ibid.: 54). With such claims in mind it is therefore unnecessary for Caputo to deny that he is 'trying to make flesh into an ahistorical principle' (ibid.: 208). For a more concise account of this 'ethics without principles' (and all its paradoxes), see Caputo 2003.
154 See also Gaita 2000: 209, 267, 276.
155 See Caputo 1993: 31–3, 36–7. Even the most brutal writings of De Sade bear witness to this, for it is only the suffering of *others* that excites his passions.
156 See also Cavell 1979: 115; Winch 1987: 153.
157 See also Wittgenstein 1958: §217; 1999: §563.
158 Of course, the *specific* form such 'persuasion' takes will itself be a question for moral consideration. In his reading of Levinas, Nuyen fails to distinguish between 'the problem of moral motivation' (2000: 411) (that is, asking precisely '[w]hat awakens ... conscience?' (ibid.: 417) on Levinas's account) and the assumed threat the amoralist poses to morality *per se* (ibid.: 412, 416, 421).
159 See Drury 1981: 171.
160 Wittgenstein began writing 'Remarks on Frazer's *Golden Bough*' in 1931, adding notes as late as 1948. I return to this text in Chapter 5.
161 See Wittgenstein 1996a: 69, 80.
162 See also Wittgenstein 1996a: 72.
163 See Wittgenstein 1999: §559. Thus, although Wittgenstein distances himself methodologically from questions pertaining to natural history, ontologically he nevertheless remains naturalistic.
164 See Wittgenstein 1958: §§109, 126, 217, 654, 656, p. 224; 1999: §§204, 559; Nyíri 1982: 59.
165 See also Malcolm 1993: 81.

166 This relates to Wittgenstein's criticism of O'Hara in 'Lectures on Religious Belief' (1994b: 57–9) – although it is O'Hara's *theological* scientism that Wittgenstein there repudiates.
167 See Wittgenstein 1996a: 68, 72–3; 1999: §477, 538.
168 This parallels those remarks in *On Certainty* pertaining to the child's 'reacting' (1999: §538) and only much later coming to 'know' and 'doubt' (ibid.: §475).
169 See Wittgenstein 1958: §244.
170 See Wittgenstein 1958: §656; 1996a: 62; Rhees 1996: 56–7.
171 See Wittgenstein 1958: §§343, 244, 546, p. 224; 1990: §§391, 540–1, 545; 1994a: 31, 46; 1999: §505.
172 See Wittgenstein 1958: §§23, 25, 656.
173 See Wittgenstein 1996a: 63–4, 73–4.
174 See also Wittgenstein 1996a: 70, 74, 76.
175 See also Wittgenstein 1958: §206.
176 See Wittgenstein 1996a: 77.
177 See Wittgenstein 1996a: 81. As Wittgenstein remarks: 'I think it might be regarded as a basic law of natural history that wherever something in nature "has a function", "serves a purpose", the same thing can also be found in circumstances where it serves no purpose and is even "dysfunctional"' (1994a: 72).
178 See also Wittgenstein's remarks on Schubert's death (1996a: 66) and laughter (ibid.: 73). On the moral significance of humor compare Wittgenstein's reflections on the claim that 'humor was stamped out in Nazi Germany' (1994a: 78) and Gaita's remarks on Costa-Gavras's *The Confession* (Gaita 2000: 48–9).
179 See Wittgenstein 1994a: 49.
180 See Wittgenstein 1996a: 65.
181 See Wittgenstein 1993: 181; 1996a: 71; 1999: §§609–12. Wittgenstein further claims that Frazer's 'savages' understand only too well where the natural boundaries of their rituals reside, for the 'same savage, who stabs the picture of his enemy apparently in order to kill him, really builds his hut out of wood and carves his arrow skillfully and not in effigy' (1996a: 64, see also 71–4). In a similar vein Husserl remarks: 'Truth and falsity, criticism and critical comparison with evident data, are an everyday theme, playing their incessant part even in pre-scientific life' (1982: 12).
182 Although I will not pursue this correlation, my critique of Lyotard has certain parallels with Davidson's 'On the Very Idea of a Conceptual Scheme' (1984).
183 See Derrida 1993b: 41.
184 See also Wittgenstein 1958: §§283, 360.
185 See also Winch 1960: 236; 1964: 311, 317; Caputo 1993: 74, 80–1; 2000: 113. It is here worth recalling that Readings assures us that '[a]n encounter takes place, it happens, but no language is available to phrase it' (1992: 183). (Note also Derrida's remarks on Levinas's notion of the 'other' (1997c: 125–9).) My claim that an encounter with the *radically* other is a paradoxical notion correlates with Derrida's reflections on the aporia of the gift, and particularly the necessity of both donor and donee of not even recognizing (indeed, of *forgetting*) the gift *as such* (1992b: 13–14, 15, 16–17, 23, 27, 35–6, 47, 56, 91, 101, 147, 148, 171; 1995a: 209; 1995b: 29, 31, 97, 112).
186 See Surin 1990: 120.
187 See Readings 1992: 175–6.
188 See Derrida 1985: 292; 2002d: 18–19; 2002f: 102, 207; Putnam 2002: 35; Gaita 2003: 167.
189 See Derrida 2002f: 194. To re-cast this in Derridean terms (to which I will

return in Chapter 8), what worries Readings here is the *iterability* of the term 'human nature.'
190 See also Wittgenstein 1999: §§192, 563, 612.
191 See Wittgenstein 1994a: 1. Schopenhauer makes the same point regarding the loss of 'natural compassion' (1995: 149).
192 This example is from *MacIntyre Undercover*, broadcast on BBC1, 10/11/99.
193 See Gaita 2000: 178–9.
194 See Gaita 2000: 39.
195 See Gaita's remarks on his father's 'confusion' and 'bewilderment' (1998: 124–5).
196 'Auschwitz' has thus become an important signifier in our moral vocabulary (Levinas 1988b: 162; Peukert 1998: 156; Gaita 2000: 111, 141).
197 Winch is unclear on this point, for while he also alludes to 'radical disagreement' (1987: 186), in his subsequent remarks on Orwell and Ghandi he seems to imply that such a degree of conflict would be impossible (ibid.: 187–8).
198 See Davidson 1984: 184–5, 192, 197; Bambrough 1992: 247–50; Wittgenstein 1999: §156.
199 See Caputo 1993: 29, 54.
200 See Wittgenstein 1994a: 45–6. Tilghman similarly concludes that 'the human body and especially the human face [is] a moral space, that is ... the locus of the possibility of all those expressions that are at the basis of moral life' (1991: 115; see also Caputo 1993: Ch. 9; Gaita 2000: 283). I return to these points in Chapters 6 and 7.
201 One commentator remarks of the Habermasian agenda: 'If there is a universal moral community, it is constituted by a relatively narrow set of norms,' and proceeds: 'Because the forms of the good are plural and because all humans are subject to common vulnerabilities, the solidarity projected by a discourse ethics must be based largely on a vision of the "damaged life" rather than an affirmative view of the "good life"'; 'To the extent that all humans are vulnerable in similar ways, it is plausible to suppose that there are "generalizable interests" that could provide the basis for norms that would command universal assent' (Moon 1995: 152; see also Caputo 1993: 41). However, Habermas clarifies that he is primarily concerned with vulnerabilities of socialization (1983: 120–2; 1996: 196–7), not those of 'biological' (1983: 120) fragility.

4 Interlude

1 This would hold even on a differential account of meaning where the absent (excluded) terms play a constitutive role in the production of meaning.
2 Of course, we are dealing also with the practices within which words have their life (Wittgenstein 1990: 144; 1994a: 85; 1994b: 55). The point I am drawing from this passage might usefully be correlated with Heidegger's remarks on 'equipment' that becomes 'conspicuous' due to its breaking or otherwise being rendered 'unusable' (1999: 104–5).
3 Interestingly, Winch remarks that 'human beings are essentially potential critics of each other' to the point where even another's presence can constitute 'an implicit criticism' of one's 'views of life' and 'roles in life' (1987: 180, see also 146–7, 150). The Levinasian significance of such claims will become clear in Chapter 6.
4 See Handelman 1991: 195.
5 This, of course, constitutes the problem at the root of every naive contractualism. See also Levinas 2000: 164.
6 See Winch's remarks on the Good Samaritan (1987: 174) and tolerance (ibid.: 190).

7 See Winch 1987: 174; Caputo 1993: 126–7; Schopenhauer 1995: 126, 130, 138, 144; Levinas 1998a: 163; 1998b: 227.
8 As I discuss in Chapter 8, the notion of *pure* self-sacrifice is complicated on Derrida's account (1992b: 7, 10, 12, 27, 29–30, 76, 104, 123; 1993b: 38–9, 79; 1995b: 42–5). Nevertheless, he would concede that a certain *desire* for 'the impossible' remains essential to moral life (1992b: 8, 31, 36; 1999c: 59, 72).
9 See Derrida 1992a: 68; Bennington 1993: 310.

5 Wretchedness without recompense

1 This 'identification' is not primarily deliberative, but 'immediate' in the sense discussed in Chapter 3.
2 See also Caputo 1993: 120.
3 See also Derrida 1990: 927, 1015; 1997c: 117, 125.
4 It thereby constitutes both the conditions of possibility *and* impossibility of ethical responsibility: *Conditions of possibility* insofar as any relationship with the other demands such a prior identification of them *as* 'other.' *Conditions of impossibility* because this identification means that any subsequent relation will never be wholly uncontaminated by such a primary 'violence' (Derrida 1971: 328; 1992b: 12; 1997c: 132, 137–8, 140–1, 143, 152; 2002c: 135; 2002f: 298, 300; Caputo 1993: 74–5, 80–3; Levinas 2001: 51). I return to this in Chapter 8.
5 See Wittgenstein 1994b: 63, 71–2. One's having no 'clear idea' here does not necessarily mean that the utterance is absurd, but rather that one would not know how to make such an assessment (Winch 1964: 311–12, 319; 1970: 256–7).
6 See Drury 1981: 162; Wittgenstein 1994a: 48.
7 See Mates 1996: pp. 30–2.
8 See Engelmann 1967: 77.
9 See Wittgenstein 1994a: 33. Only if such dissent involved a denial of the *truth* of the believer's utterance would such a pre-understanding be assumed. As noted in Chapter 1 with reference to Pyrrhonism, such pre-understanding would not be assumed if one denied that the believer's utterance had *meaning*. It is therefore striking that Wittgenstein does not merely dismiss the believer's utterances as meaningless. One of the reasons he invests so much time in reaching a sympathetic understanding of religious concepts must be located in the fact that people *do* profess such beliefs and that these beliefs *do* play a pivotal role in their lives. While a specific belief may be 'mistaken,' how an *entire way of life* could be 'mistaken' is significantly less clear (Wittgenstein 1996a: 61).
10 For a similarly striking example see Kierkegaard 1965: 69–78.
11 See Tolstoy 1987: 66, 68. As Wittgenstein remarks: '*everything* will be different and it will be "no wonder" if you can do things that you cannot do now' (1994a: 33).
12 This is not to say that the believer is necessarily better placed to understand and represent another's *non*-belief.
13 See Phillips 1970: 69; Cavell 1979: 371–2.
14 See Wittgenstein 1993: 181; 1994b: 72.
15 See also Wittgenstein 1994b: 56, 61–2, 71; 1999: §361.
16 See also Wittgenstein 1996a: 61. Note also Winch's remarks on contradiction (1960: 234; 1964: 312, 314–15; 1970: 254, 257–8). Wittgenstein once claimed that 'many controversies about God could be settled by saying "I'm not using the word in such a sense that you can say … ", and that different religions "treat things as making sense which others treat as nonsense, and don't merely deny some proposition which another religion affirms"' (Moore 1993: 103).

17 See also Wittgenstein's distinction between secular and sacred history (1994a: 31–2; 1994b: 53–4, 56–7). This might usefully be compared with Derrida's own distinction between the 'future' and that which is 'to come' (1990: 969–71; 1992a: 37–8; 1997a: 2, 9; 1997b: 19–20, 30; 1998b: 7, 47; 1999a: 79; 2001d: 67).
18 See Wittgenstein 1994b: 61. Note also my discussion of blasphemy in Chapter 2.
19 See Wittgenstein 1958: §§109, 126. Of course, after such analysis another's professed belief may show itself to be merely hypothetical – and thus, for Wittgenstein, not 'genuinely' religious.
20 See Winch 1987: 198, 200; Wittgenstein 1994a: 85; 1994b: 55. For a similar emphasis on the primacy of action, see Tolstoy 1987: 58, 61.
21 That is, despite 'Lectures on Religious Belief' only being available to us via students' notebooks that Wittgenstein hoped would not be published (Drury 1981: 155).
22 See Drury 1981: 108.
23 See Bambrough 1992: 249.
24 Wittgenstein's metaphor of 'different planes' is in keeping with his more general spatial rhetoric (1958: p. ix, §§18, 68, 71, 76, 85, 99, 119, 203, 257, 426, 499, 525, 534).
25 See also Frazer 1993: 253.
26 See Wittgenstein 1996a: 64.
27 See Wittgenstein 1996a: 64–5. Mindful of this, it is worth noting the similarities between the existential stakes involved in religious faith Tolstoy alludes to (1987: 66, 68) and Barthes's reflections pertaining to: (1) the gratuitous 'stubbornness' of love (1990: 22, 85–6, 177, 180–2, 186), (2) the inadequacy of language when referring to, and addressing, the lover (ibid.: 35, 59, 73–4, 77–9, 147–54, 157–8, 204), (3) the lover's being 'simultaneously and contradictorily happy and wretched' (ibid.: 22, see also 62, 165, 171), and (4) love's capacity to both infuse everything with meaning and, once lost, render the world meaningless (ibid.: 23, 38–9, 75, 155, 160–1, 173–4, 189).
28 See Frazer 1993: 207, 216, 551. On this point note Derrida's own confession (1993a: 161–2, 260–3) and Barthes's discussion of the relation between the photographic image and the 'resurrection' (2000: 82) or 'return of the dead' (ibid.: 9) (and hence also to a certain 'wound,' 'mourning' (ibid.: 21; see also 79) and guilt of the survivor (ibid.: 84)). I return to 'survivor's guilt' in later chapters.
29 See Hertzberg 1988; Wittgenstein 1994a: 72; 1999: §§34, 160, 283, 509.
30 See Wittgenstein 1996a: 61, 71–2.
31 See Derrida's remarks on immortality (1993b: 55).
32 See Derrida 1990: 965; Wittgenstein 1994a: 25. Of course, I am not claiming that 'this has arisen from that,' but rather 'it could have arisen this way' (Wittgenstein 1996a: 80).
33 See Winch 1964: 322–4; Wittgenstein 1996a: 66–7; Gaita 2000: 60. Wittgenstein also suggests that the limits of imagination are determined by such phenomena (1996a: 65, 72–3, 78). Note also Derrida's remarks on 'cultures of dying' (1993b: 24, 43).
34 See also Clack 1999: 123.
35 See Clack 1999: 124.
36 Having discussed the influence of Spengler's cultural pessimism on Wittgenstein, this is how Clack's analysis proceeds (1999: 127–9). Regarding Wittgenstein's pessimism, see also Drury 1981: 128, 131; Wittgenstein 1994a: 6, 27, 71.
37 See also Derrida 1998c: 30.
38 And what is an earnest desire *for* faith if not itself fundamentally 'religious'?

Indeed, one might say that such desire is constitutive of religiosity insofar as one can never possess 'enough' faith.

39 See Wittgenstein 1994a: 48. It is perhaps through this desire to discuss religion so reverently that Wittgenstein's alleged 'fideism' must first be questioned.
40 Given what Wittgenstein says about 'staying in the saddle' of one's world-picture (1999: §§616, 619) we might ask why Frazer should be condemned for holding onto *his* world-picture (Wittgenstein 1996a: 61, 63, 65, 67–8, 71, 73–4)?
41 This can be seen in Frazer's references to sun worship rituals. For there is nothing inherently superstitious in these behaviors; it is not as though modern science has rendered such natural phenomena any less awe-inspiring (Wittgenstein 1994a: 5; 1996a: 67). Indeed, we might recall our own ritualized fascination with such phenomena, the decline of which is neither inevitable nor prerequisite for one's immersion into secular world-pictures (Winch 1987: 202–4). Note also Levinas's phenomenology of 'enjoyment' (1996c: 110ff.).
42 Frazer would have to concede this in order to assess the superiority of one over the other (Drury 1981: 134).
43 This point cuts both ways: the charge – often made from a misplaced self-deprecation by Westerners – that the West is spiritually barren, is similarly superficial. See Derrida's remarks on the 'secular' (2001b: 67).
44 See Wittgenstein 1994a: 16.
45 See Bambrough 1992: 249–50.
46 See Wittgenstein 1996a: 61.
47 While the existential complexities of (for example) Kierkegaard's troubled relationship with Regina Olsen (Kierkegaard 1965: 69–78) can only begin to be understood by virtue of our naturally shared orientation to seek companionship and sexual partners, to hope to illuminate this *specific* episode by a study of (for example) primate behavior would clearly be misguided. Wittgenstein's accusation that 'Frazer is much more savage than most of his savages, for they are not as far removed from the understanding of a spiritual matter as a twentieth-century Englishman' (1996a: 68) is not reductive in this sense. For Frazer's 'savagery' is not only not *inevitable* (he *could* be attuned to such 'spiritual matter[s]'), it is also anomalous with a genuinely 'anthropological' attitude.
48 See Wittgenstein 1994a: 78; 1996a: 80.
49 See Derrida 1995c: 3.
50 The square brackets and enclosed text are present in the translation. I have added emphasis to suggest that, although Wittgenstein can begin to identify what 'consequences' might follow from such a statement ('ethical ideas of responsibility'), he is not sure that the person who makes such a claim necessarily has these in mind.
51 Similar analyses could be offered of the lover's pronouncement 'I have always loved you' or 'I will always love you.' The 'always' here is not empirical-historical; 'I will *always* love you' does not mean that, if our relationship ends, I have thereby been proved an opportunist or disingenuous. Neither does it commit me to believing that our relationship will continue *post mortem* in some spiritual realm. The 'always' here is rather a performative pledge of commitment.
52 The square brackets and enclosed text are present in the translation.
53 Gaita's position on the religious and non-religious is interesting here. On the one hand, he claims that religious language (concerning, for example, the 'sacredness' of others) is a superior form of expression than its 'secular equivalent' (2000: 23; see also Nielsen 1967: 196). On the other hand, Gaita

not only makes much of 'non-religious' ritual (2000: 219–21) but also suggests of the 'soul' that the 'religious or metaphysical conception ... *depends* on the conception expressed in the more natural ways of speaking' (ibid.: 239, my emphasis). His point would thus seem to be twofold: (1) we should not conflate 'secular' with 'natural' ways of speaking, and (2) the religious is closer to the 'natural' than the scientific and philosophical.

54 See James 2:17–18. In response to a letter received from a pupil telling him of their conversion to Catholicism, Wittgenstein pithily remarked: '"If someone tells me he has bought the outfit of a tight-rope walker I am not impressed until I see what is done with it"' (Drury 1981: 103).

55 Regarding Tolstoy's *A Confession*, Greenwood remarks: 'What he leaves us with, in the end, is an overwhelming feeling of his need for God to exist and his sense that many among the people possess an enviable faith in the reality of that existence which he himself lacks' (1975: 121). Much the same could be said of Wittgenstein (Drury 1981: 162, 182) – indeed, Greenwood's allusion to 'envy' (a word Tolstoy himself uses (1987: 73)) goes some way toward explaining why Wittgenstein cannot adequately be described as 'agnostic.'

56 As will become clear in Chapters 6 and 7, this formulation similarly applies to Levinas's work.

57 See Wittgenstein 1994a: 86.

58 See Breton 1984: 98.

59 See also Wittgenstein's remarks on the need for one's 'soul ... to be saved,' not one's 'abstract mind' (1994a: 33), and the marginal value of 'sound doctrines' (ibid.: 5) for the religious life.

60 See Malcolm 1958: 20; Engelmann 1967: 77–8.

61 In this regard it is significant that, like Nietzsche, Wittgenstein suggests that 'even our more refined, more philosophical doubts have a foundation in instinct' (1994a: 73).

62 A reverence perhaps more obvious in Heidegger's work. Interestingly, in his own brief remarks on Heidegger, Wittgenstein again refers to 'the astonishment that anything exists' (1978: 80).

63 See also Wittgenstein 1993: 44.

64 See also Derrida's comments on his own preoccupation with negative theology (1995c: 69) and the 'impossible' more generally (1990: 981; 1995c: 81). I return to the latter in Chapter 8.

65 See Wittgenstein 1993: 40.

66 See also Picard 1948: 227.

67 As discussed in Chapter 3, the traditional is/ought distinction maintained in both the *Tractatus* and 'A Lecture on Ethics' is problematized by Wittgenstein's later phenomenology of the body. Regarding Wittgenstein's attitudinal emphasis on the ontological question, see also his remarks on belief in predestination (1994a: 30), fate (ibid.: 61) and free will (ibid.: 63).

68 See Wittgenstein 1994a: 32, 53, 61, 63; 1994b: 53–4.

69 See Phillips 1970: 44–5.

70 See Malcolm 1972: 214. This is why any alleged religious movement which does not aim at the transformation of the moral character of the convert might be referred to as 'religious' in only an attenuated sense (ibid.: 211).

71 See Wittgenstein 1958: §109.

72 See Wittgenstein 1958: §§38, 132. Note also Wittgenstein's remarks on Socrates (Drury 1981: 131) and Hegel (ibid.: 171).

73 See Wittgenstein 1994a: 41.

74 Passages like this – where Wittgenstein appears to advocate a *change* in the way we speak – clearly threaten the 'conservative' interpretation of his work discussed in Chapter 1 (Jones 1986: 282).

75 See also Moore 1993: 109–10.
76 See Wittgenstein 1969: 18.
77 See Wittgenstein 1994a: 22.
78 See Phillips 1970: 49. In response to Drury's admission that he thought of 'death as the gateway to a permanent state of mind,' Wittgenstein 'seemed disinclined to continue with this conversation' – Drury having 'the feeling that [Wittgenstein] thought what [Drury] had said was superficial' (1981: 147, see also 183). Analogously, the same might be said of confession, for this cannot be adequately understood as an exercise in personal reportage (Derrida 1993a: 16–18, 48, 56; 1995c: 38–9; 1999c: 98–9). What differentiates confession from the 'merely' autobiographical is the way the former 'has to be a part of your new life' (Wittgenstein 1994a: 18). I return to confession in Chapter 8.
79 See also Malcolm 1960: 60–1.
80 See also Pascal 1961: §255; Kierkegaard 1973: 429–30.
81 See Engelmann 1967: 74, 77, 79–80; Monk 1991: 186–8, 367–72; Pascal 1996.
82 Compare with Levinas's remark on 'the search for God' (1998a: 95).
83 See Graham 2001: 15ff.
84 I return to this question in Chapters 6 and 7 with reference to Levinas's 'religious' humanism.
85 See Engelmann 1967: 79–80. That is, Tolstoy's 'attempt to state "the religion of Christ ... purged of dogmas and mysticism."' It is also interesting that Greenwood describes Tolstoy's purpose in *A Confession* and *What I Believe* as 'not just trying to establish the correct point of view ... but also as trying to *awaken* the educated classes to a lively sense of the realities of life and death, and of the demands of the Christianity that many of them outwardly profess. Tolstoy is just as concerned with a *metanoia* or a "change of heart" as with a "correct point of view"' (Greenwood 1975: 126, see also 128–31).
86 This 'nostalgia' is not wholly unreserved in Tolstoy (1987: 77; Greenwood 1975: 120–1).
87 Warning Drury against theology, Wittgenstein remarked: 'The symbolism of Christianity is wonderful beyond words, but when people try to make a philosophical system out of it I find it disgusting' (Drury 1981: 101), and more vehemently: 'It is a dogma of the Roman Church that the existence of God can be proved by natural reason ... If I thought of God as another being like myself, outside myself, only infinitely more powerful, then I would regard it as my duty to defy him' (ibid.: 123).
88 See Tolstoy 1981: 70–1. Note Wittgenstein's reassurance to Drury on the latter's feeling of 'emptiness' at the 'ceremonies of Holy Week and Easter' (1981: 144). On a related matter, refer also to Wittgenstein's lamentation that Drury's not having 'lived a religious life' (ibid.: 179) had perhaps been due to his own baleful influence.
89 Clack is right to highlight Wittgenstein's changing attitude toward the 'peasants' admired by Tolstoy (and, not least, Wittgenstein's occasional antihumanism and anti-romanticism (Drury 1981: 128; Wittgenstein 1999: 114–15)). Nevertheless, I think that this ambiguity lies *within* Wittgenstein's Tolstoyan attitude, for Wittgenstein never unburdened himself of a deeply Tolstoyan ideal; the ambiguity lies rather in his inability to assimilate himself with such 'ordinary folk.'
90 The entire passage reads as follows: 'In the Gospels ... everything is *less pretentious*, humbler, simpler. There you find huts; in Paul a church. There all men are equal and God himself is a man; in Paul there is already something like hierarchy; honours and official positions' (Wittgenstein 1994a: 30; see also Nietzsche 1968: §167). Likewise, Wittgenstein warned Drury: 'remember the

Christian religion does not consist in saying a lot of prayers, in fact we are commanded just the opposite. If you and I are to live religious lives it must not just be that we talk a lot about religion, but that in some way our lives are different' (Drury 1981: 109). These sentiments are best illustrated in what Wittgenstein described as his 'favorite' (ibid.: 101) of Tolstoy's short stories; 'The Three Hermits' (Tolstoy 1982: 280–6; see also King 1981: 87).

91 Likewise, and as I intimated earlier, although no meaningful access to the religious can be gained except through its practical-ethical consequences, the ontological dimension of religious belief (belief *that* God exists) cannot simply be jettisoned in favor of the ethical (belief *in* God). The ontological, we might say, is *already* ethical (I return to this in later chapters with reference to Levinas).

92 Though they are always susceptible to becoming 'complete automatism' (Bergson 1911: 46, see also 44–5; Derrida 1995c: 132–3). Here again one might talk of a certain *iterability* (I return to this in Chapter 8).

93 See Wittgenstein 1994a: 30. One sees this lower level of religiosity emerge in Wittgenstein's markedly Pyrrhonian advice to Drury to 'try experiments in religion. To find out, by trying, what helps one and what doesn't' (Drury 1981: 179).

94 While in Norway Wittgenstein 'spent his time in prayer' and had also 'felt it necessary to write out a confession' (Drury 1981: 135) – the latter was eventually offered to, amongst others, Moore and Fania Pascal (ibid.: 190–218; Pascal 1996: 45–50).

95 Likewise, when Wittgenstein remarks to Drury that 'the religion of the future' will perhaps be 'without any priests or ministers,' he proceeds to suggest that 'one of the things *you and I* have to learn is that *we* have to live without the consolation of belonging to a church' (Drury 1981: 129, my emphasis).

96 Recalling my discussion of Rhees in Chapter 1, emphasizing this terminology tends to make Wittgenstein's view of philosophy look overly categorical.

97 This is most evident in Wittgenstein's 'A Lecture on Ethics.' Moreover, the notion of absolute dependence relates to what I said in Chapter 2 concerning the role of unconditional trust in *On Certainty* (indeed, both Hertzberg (1988: 309–10) and Shields (1997: 48) allude to Abraham and Isaac in this respect). See also Derrida 1995b: Chs 3–4.

98 See also Wittgenstein 1979a: 74.
99 See also Shields 1997: 65; Gaita 2000: 219–20.
100 See also Shields 1997: 70.
101 See Wittgenstein 1994a: 29, 32, 45, 53; 1994b: 56, 58.
102 See Wittgenstein's remarks on 'How God judges a man' (1994a: 86), and Derrida's comments on God not having 'to give his reasons or share anything with us' (1995b: 57).
103 As Hertzberg remarks of 'reliance' and 'trust': 'In relying on someone I as it were look down at him from above. I exercise my command of the world. I remain the judge of his actions. In trusting someone *I look up from below*' (1988: 315, my emphasis). Of course, even in Abraham's example, God did not demand what was practically *impossible* (Kierkegaard 1985: 44–6). Wittgenstein's remarks thus seem to move beyond even Abraham's example; namely, that God could demand of me not merely something I cannot justify (beyond the fact that *He* has commanded it) but something I *could not do* even if I had the *will* to do it. As will be seen in Chapter 8, Derrida's remarks on responsibility and im/possibility are pertinent here.
104 See also Phillips 1970: 68–9.
105 Interestingly, Tolstoy remarks: 'the essence of any faith consists in giving a meaning to life that will not perish with death' (1987: 68).

106 That is, in this primitive experience of bad conscience one undergoes a certain 'haunting' by the other (Levinas 1984: 63; Derrida 1993a: 260–3; 1993b: 20). I return to this in Chapter 6.
107 For a detailed analysis of the relationship between 'A Lecture on Ethics' and the *Tractatus*, see Edwards 1985: 75–101.
108 See Kant 1976: 78ff.
109 See Wittgenstein 1993: 38–9; Derrida 1995a: 273, 276.
110 See Wittgenstein 1994a: 3; 1995: 6.42; Levinas 1998a: 154.
111 See Wittgenstein 1978: 80–1.
112 See also Engelmann 1967: 74–5.
113 See also Derrida 1995c: 17–21. Wittgenstein similarly remarks that he should like to 'put an end to all the idle talk about Ethics – whether there be knowledge, whether there be values, whether the Good can be defined, etc.' (1978: 80–1).
114 See Wittgenstein 1995: 6.4–6.421.
115 In one of his more caustic moments Levinas remarks: 'Those who have worked on methodology all their lives have written many books that replace the more interesting books that they could have written. So much the worse for the philosophy that would walk in sunlight without shadows' (1998a: 89). The extent to which Wittgenstein's remarks on ethics here correspond to Levinas's own textual practice is discussed in Chapter 6.
116 This relates to what I said in Chapters 1 and 2 regarding the need for shared criteria in judgement. See also Drury's remarks concerning his first meeting Wittgenstein at the Moral Sciences Club (Drury 1981: 114).
117 See Phillips 1970: 47.
118 See Winch 1987: 176. The distinction between the 'relative' and 'absolute' is not straightforward. One might argue that 'You *ought* to want to play tennis better because your partner will then get more enjoyment out of the game, and her enjoyment is of greater ethical significance than your own contentment to play badly.' Here playing tennis is thus the *means* by which a deeper ethical obligation toward increasing the happiness of others becomes realizable.
119 In Chapter 6 I discuss Levinas's work under the rubric of the 'guilt of the survivor' with specific reference to the impact of the Holocaust on his work. On a biographical note, Wittgenstein might also have experienced something of this 'guilt' regarding the suicide of three of his brothers (Monk 1991: 11ff.). Interestingly, although Wittgenstein himself contemplated suicide many times, he nevertheless judged this to be 'the elementary sin' (1979a: 91; see also Gaita 2000: 221–2).
120 Likewise, the question 'What's the point in friendship?' is misplaced (assuming it is not really a cry of despair). There is no essential 'point' to friendship, although doubtless one can *retrospectively* identify certain benefits of having friends. The initial question erroneously assumes that there are good *reasons* upon which friendship is 'founded.' See also Derrida's remarks on 'forgiveness' (2001e: 27).
121 See also Caputo 2000: 121; 2001: 4, 12–13.
122 See Derrida 1999e: 132–3.
123 See Schopenhauer's remarks on how religion does not combat egoism but rather shifts it to 'another world' (1995: 137).
124 On the anthropological 'principle of loss,' see Bataille 1996: 116–23.
125 See also Nietzsche 1968: §§172, 246; 1992b: First Essay §§14–15. Kierkegaard remarks: 'Official preaching has falsely represented religion, Christianity, as nothing but consolation, happiness etc. And consequently doubt has the advantage of being able to say in a *superior* way: I do not wish to be made

happy by an illusion. If Christianity were truthfully presented as suffering, ever greater as one advances further in it: doubt would have been disarmed' (1965: 209). This sentiment is echoed in Wittgenstein's conversations with Drury (1981: 110). King similarly recalls Wittgenstein having claimed: '"of one thing I am certain – we are not here in order to have a good time"' (1981: 90).
126 See Derrida 1990: 953; 1996b: 86.
127 See Malcolm 1958: 52; Redpath 1990: 50; Sontag 1995: 57, 64; Pascal 1996: 32.
128 See also Drury 1981: 101, 117–18.
129 There is a correlation between this passage and Wittgenstein's own remark that: '"You can't hear God speak to someone else, you can hear him only if you are being addressed". – That is a grammatical remark"' (1990: §717). The 'grammatical' point here concerns the impossibility (at least in the Judeo-Christian tradition) of coolly witnessing God addressing an *other*, for to hear God is always to have *oneself* implicated. See also Levinas's endorsement of Halevy's suggestion that 'God speaks to each man in particular' (Levinas 1994a: 184), and Derrida's remarks on 'speak[ing] with God' (1995b: 57).
130 The sentiments of this passage are repeated a number of times in *The Bothers Karamazov*, particularly in 'From the Discourses and Sermons of Father Zossima' (Dostoyevsky 1967: 376–9).
131 See also Wittgenstein 1994a: 86.
132 See Derrida 1993b: 19–20; 1997b: 20–1; 1999: 67.
133 See Engelmann 1967: 80. Again, Wittgenstein's Jewish heritage may be relevant here (Drury 1981: 175).
134 See Glendinning 1999, 2000.
135 See Davis 1996: 129–41.
136 According to Levinas this was his 'main theme' (1999: 179; see also 2000: 12, 17).

6 Trespassing

1 Parts of the present chapter have appeared in Plant 2003c.
2 See also Derrida 1997c: 90–1. Levinas claims that ethics is 'unintelligible within being' (2000: 172).
3 See Levinas 1994a: 94.
4 See Greisch 1991: 71.
5 According to Greisch, what Levinas provides (specifically in his remarks on the 'here I am' that precedes discourse) is an 'answer to the question of the essence of language' (1991: 69), or 'the condition of possibility of all ... language games' (ibid.: 70). Greisch's remarks on 'sincerity' (ibid.: 69; see also Levinas 2000: 190–4) might usefully be read alongside Wittgenstein's reflections on trust discussed in Chapter 2.
6 By focusing on Wittgenstein's earlier 'transcendental' (Greisch 1991: 72) view of ethics, Greisch overlooks how Wittgenstein's naturalism problematizes the 'nonfoundationalist' reading. As will become clear, although Levinas denies that he is seeking 'the "transcendental foundation" of "ethical experience"' (1994a: 148; see also 2000: 200), the face of the other 'accusing' me is emphatically *not* proffered as a hypothesis. On the contrary, insofar as the 'flesh-and-blood' (Nuyen 2000: 415) face makes demands on me *immediately*, one might say that the other's face is the indisputable 'given' of Levinas's work.
7 See Handelman 1991: 258; Levinas 1992: 22; 2001: 24, 28, 81, 89; Stone 1998: 5.
8 See Levinas 1992: 98, 101; 1993: 44; 1994a: 146; 1996a: 102; 1998b: 105; 2001:

72, 133. According to Robbins (1999: 147) this citation appears at least twelve times in Levinas's work.
9 See Levinas 1999: 101.
10 See also Levinas 2000: 175.
11 For the Heideggerian–Levinasian application of these terms I will, where possible, capitalize 'Conscience' and 'Guilt.'
12 See also Levinas 1984: 51–2; 1989: 487–8; 1992: 38, 42; 1997a: 281; 2001: 141. Levinas's explicit reference to Heidegger's remarks on Guilt are extremely negative (Levinas 2001: 141). As will become clear, I believe that Levinas remains blind to the affinities between his own work and Heidegger's on this topic.
13 Caygill (2002) has recently provided a meticulous analysis of the political dimension to Levinas's work – and, not least, the influence of the Holocaust on his thinking.
14 See Heidegger 1999: 336; Derrida 1993b: 80–1; 1998b: 15; Levinas 2000: 30–1.
15 See Harries 1978: 141–2; Derrida 1993b: 45, 51, 54, 59; Heidegger 1999: 313, 317, 327–8.
16 See also Heidegger 1999: 322, 329, 334–5.
17 Ultimately, of course, Dasein is concerned with its Being-toward-death (Harries 1978: 147–8; Derrida 1993b: 28–9, 44–6, 52, 57–8, 62, 68–9; Mulhall 1996: 116–17; Levinas 2000: 48–9).
18 See Glendinning 1998: 59; Heidegger 1999: 120, 157; Levinas 2001: 57.
19 See Mulhall 1993: 109–12.
20 See Mulhall 1993: 112; 1996: 48–52.
21 See Husserl 1982: p. 92; 1989: pp. 197, 201, 206; Merleau-Ponty 1996: 347–8, 353–4; Levinas 1998b: 17.
22 See also Mulhall 1993: 115.
23 See Derrida 1993a: 64.
24 See also Macann 1992: 220.
25 See Heidegger 1999: 313, 315, 317, 319, 321–2, 334, 342–5. Heidegger remarks that 'the "they" is not something like a "universal subject" which a plurality of subjects have hovering above them,' nor is it 'the genus to which Dasein belongs' (ibid.: 166). Moreover, authentic being 'does not rest upon an exceptional condition of the subject, a condition that has been detached from the "they"; *it is rather an existentiell modification of the "they"* ... ' (ibid.: 168). In other words, Dasein cannot wholly escape the '*they-self* (ibid.: 167) for the 'they' is partly constitutive of Dasein's very being-in-the-world (ibid.: 167, 210). Nevertheless, Dasein can resist the 'stubborn dominion' (ibid.: 165) of the 'they' to a greater or lesser extent.
26 See Kellner 1992: 199.
27 See Heidegger 1999: 326. Derrida makes much of this point in his remarks on the non-programmatic nature of the 'decision' (1990: 947, 961, 963–5, 967; 1992b: 137–8, 142, 146, 162; 1993b: 16–17, 56–7; 1995a: 359; 1995b: 24, 77, 95; 1995c: 7, 59, 132–3; 1996b: 84; 1998a: 113; 1998c: 62; 1999a: 66–8, 73). I return to this in Chapter 8.
28 See also Heidegger 1982: 170–1; Derrida 1993b: 58, 67–9, 77. This deep anti-conventionalism is perhaps complicated by Heidegger's remarks on Dasein's 'loyally following in the footsteps' of its chosen 'hero' (1999: 437, see also 422; Kellner 1992: 204–5; Derrida 2002f: 110–11).
29 See also Macann 1992: 220, 224.
30 See Heidegger 1999: 192, 344.
31 See Heidegger 1999: 345–6.
32 See Macann 1992: 217–18, 221, 223.
33 See Sartre 1977: 48; Derrida 1992a: 195; 2002f: 296, 309–10.

34 See Pascal 1961: p. 157. As discussed in Chapter 1, this inescapability of choice (and hence responsibility) is precisely what the Pyrrhonist fails to recognize, for in the attempt to extricate belief and commitment from her life, she does not see that in even attempting *this* one (implicitly) commits oneself to at least the attainment of *ataraxia* – and all that may entail in the ethical-political realm. As Levinas pithily remarks: 'Even if you adopt an attitude of indifference you are obliged to adopt it!' (2001: 50).
35 This 'relatively' must, I think, be stressed because the horizon of choices open to Dasein is not unbounded. Essential to Dasein's facticity are certain 'very general facts of nature' (Wittgenstein 1958: p. 230) pertaining to 'the natural history of human beings' (ibid.: §415).
36 See Heidegger 1999: 319, 322, 340.
37 See also Harries 1978: 144.
38 See Heidegger 1999: 317, 319–20, 325, 334.
39 See Heidegger 1999: 315.
40 See Heidegger 1999: 326.
41 See Heidegger 1999: 341.
42 See Heidegger 1999: 326.
43 See Heidegger 1999: 334, 340.
44 See also Heidegger 1999: 336.
45 See Heidegger 1999: 334.
46 See also Heidegger 1999: 328, 332. Nietzsche claims that guilt originates in debt (1992b: Essay 2, §§4, 8).
47 See Heidegger 1999: 330.
48 See Heidegger 1999: 334.
49 Compare this with Levinas's remarks on apologetics (2000: 174).
50 See also Heidegger 1999: 322, 329, 334–5.
51 See Derrida 1998a: 72. Schutz makes a related point concerning the sacrificial nature of 'knowledge' (1974: 164–6, 169, 171–3, 177).
52 This point is to be understood over and above any 'inadvertent' (Levinas 1998b: 3) consequences a specific choice has. See also Derrida 1999b: 108.
53 While this might be interpreted as a radicalized rejection of the so-called 'acts and omissions' distinction, it is not reducible to such a position. This is because the traditional rejection of this distinction functions on an ontic rather than ontological level. Thus, according to Singer (1995: 224), I may be said to be responsible for (and guilty of) letting a starving man die because I choose to buy a stereo rather than give him the money. However, what this fails to take into account is how, even if I *do* give my money to the starving man (even if I give *it all*) I *necessarily* exclude the possibility of giving that money to *another* in need. No matter *how much* I do on behalf of the needy, this sacrificial structure remains in place. (Even the most severe critics of the acts and omissions distinction maintain that one's responsibilities and guilt are nevertheless restricted by what one can 'reasonably' be expected to do in such circumstances (ibid.: 207, 222–3, 225, 228).) I return to this point later with reference to Levinas and Derrida.
54 See Heidegger 1999: 325.
55 See Derrida 1990: 965.
56 See Heidegger 1999: 337–8.
57 See Heidegger 1999: 314, 343–6.
58 See Levinas 1998b: 117.
59 See Levinas 1984: 63; Derrida 1991: 18.
60 See Derrida 1995a: 380–1.
61 See Blanchot 1986: 50. Accordingly, Levinas's *Otherwise than Being* is dedicated to 'the memory of those who were closest among the six million assassinated

by the National Socialists, and of the millions on millions of all confessions and all nations, victims of the same hatred of the other man, the same anti-Semitism' (1994a: inside cover note; see also Derrida 1995a: 380–1; Putnam 2002: 33). Interestingly, Levinas also remarks: 'Everyone is a little bit Jewish' (2001: 164).

62 See also Levinas 2001: 77–8, 92, 126; Bernstein 2002: 167–83. The claim that 'everyone should act like the Nazis' is misleading. If morality is dead then there can be no 'should' about it. What Levinas ought to have said was that 'everyone *could* act like the Nazis.'

63 See Peperzak 1997: 2–3.

64 Derrida briefly alludes to 'trespassing' (1993b: 33).

65 See also Levinas 1994a: 91; 2001: 126.

66 See Derrida 1996c: 5–6; 2002a: 382–5, 390–1.

67 See Levinas 1993: 44. Elsewhere, Levinas alludes specifically to the 'Holocaust' and feeling 'oneself to be already a responsible survivor' (1999: 162), and even describes his conception of ethics in terms of 'the culpability of the survivor' (2000: 12) and 'the responsibility of the survivor' (ibid.: 17).

68 See Handelman 1991: 212. Levinas also refers to the effect of the 'extreme exposure' of the other on the "I" as being both 'like a shot fired at point-blank range' (1998a: 162), and as an 'entry into me by burglary' (1994a: 145).

69 See also Campbell 1999: 33; Levinas 2001: 53, 92, 98, 128, 225.

70 See also Levinas 1993: 48; 1998a: 169, 171, 175. Note Hofstadter's remarks on the spatial emphasis of the 'Da' of 'Dasein' (Heidegger 1982: 334–5), and Heidegger's own comments on the 'here' and 'there' of Dasein (1999: 171; see also Husserl 1982: 116–19, 123; 1989: 88, 177). Schutz likewise discusses the 'here' and 'there' (1971: 11–12, 178, 312, 315–16; 1974: 59), the 'interchangeability of standpoints' (1971: 12, 317; 1974: 60), and 'reciprocity of perspectives' (1964: 54–5; 1971: 316; 1974: 4–5, 60, 67, 85). See also Schutz's remarks on the 'here and now' of the absent other (1964: 38–9).

71 See also Levinas 1999: 22. Note Derrida's remarks on the host as hostage (1999b: 56–7). I return to this in Chapter 8.

72 See also Levinas 1992: 121; 1998b: 130, 144, 216.

73 See also Levinas 1998b: 129.

74 In a similar vein Putnam describes Levinas as a 'moral perfectionist' (2002: 36). Nuyen has recently argued that Levinas's work is best thought of as an 'ethics of pity' – this, he claims, would then enable Levinas to address 'the problem of moral motivation' (2000: 411). There is much to be said for Nuyen's naturalistic reading. However, he misses the more crucial role of existential guilt in Levinas's work – a guilt that is (to answer Nuyen's own question) what 'awakens [one's] conscience' (ibid.: 417). It is notable that Nuyen overlooks this because, in his discussion of pity he remarks both that the 'pitier feel[s] that he or she has somehow escaped the misfortune that should have been his or hers' (ibid.: 418), and that 'the feeling of pity does not just reveal the subjectivity of the I; it also puts the I in question: Why this Other and not me? Why they rather than me?' (ibid.: 420). Note also Putnam's remarks on 'sympathy' and 'understanding' in Levinas's account (2002: 38).

75 Levi's reference to the other's 'entreaty' through 'his simply being there' is particularly interesting in view of Derrida's recent remarks on Jankelevitch's work on the possibility of forgiveness after Auschwitz. Jankelevitch claims that the Jews were persecuted not for any specific reason or (perceived) offence but rather for their *very being*: 'A Jew does not have the right to be, existing is his sin' (quoted in Derrida 2001b: 43). Alluding to both Heidegger and Levinas, Derrida proceeds to suggest that this 'sin of existing' possesses

244 Notes

'a horizon of possible generality' where the 'guilt ... of being-there' is 'constitutive' (ibid.) *not only* of the Jew in Nazi Germany.

76 See also Wiesel 1981: 121–3. I will return to Levinas's own reference to Cain later.
77 On Levi's rhetoric, see Gaita 2000: 89, 152.
78 According to Levinas 'the subjectivity of the subject is persecution and martyrdom' (1994a: 146).
79 See Levi's remarks on the Nazi's coercion of nudity in the death camps (1998: 90).
80 For a more critical appraisal of Levinas's rhetoric, see Caputo 1993: 79, 82–3.
81 See Handelman 1991: 212, 272–3; Mole 1997: 148ff.
82 With this passage in mind, see Melville's short story 'Provenance of a face' (1999: 169–77).
83 See Caputo 1993: 32.
84 Although Levinas provides a number of qualifications as to what he means by this term, he is explicit that his primary concern is the other *human being* (1998a: 88; 1998b: 10). I return to this in Chapter 7.
85 See Levinas 1984: 50.
86 See Levinas 1992: 61.
87 See also Levinas 1988a: 176. Here one might also recall Exodus 33:20–3.
88 See Wittgenstein 1994a: 82.
89 See Wittgenstein 1958: p. 179.
90 See also Levinas 1996c: 66; Robbins 1999: 23–5.
91 See Levinas 1988a: 171; 1992: 57, 61; 1993: 158; 1996a: 22, 92. As will become clear later, the face is not Levinas's only route of access to the ethical (1992: 87, 117; 1993: 94, 103).
92 See also Levinas 1992: 87; 2001: 48–9, 135, 204, 208, 215.
93 See also Levinas 1992: 96; 1993: 35, 44; 1996a: 22; 1998b: 232.
94 See also Levinas 2000: 196.
94 See Handelman 1991: 209; Levinas 1992: 60; 1993: 39; 1998a: 154.
96 See Derrida 1993c: 122; 1995b: 99.
97 See Jay 1993: 555–60.
98 See Levinas 1996c: 50–1.
99 See Caputo 1993: 199–200.
100 See Levinas 1992: 75–6; Derrida 1997c: 118.
101 See also Handelman 1991: 211; Levinas 1998a: 138.
102 See Peperzak 1993: 162–3; Levinas 1996c: 295–6; Derrida 1997c: 99–100.
103 See Handelman 1991: 210.
104 See Levinas 1996c: 191; 2000: 163, 165–6.
105 See Wittgenstein 1990: §222. Of course, the ear is not entirely passive, for there is a difference between *hearing* and *listening* (a distinction Levinas sometimes understates (2000: 201)).
106 See Handelman 1991: 220. While one can be selective regarding what one chooses to *look at*, one cannot be similarly selective about what one *hears* (or smells) – though one can choose to ignore what one hears (Levinas 1996a: 54). This is why it would be better to say that for Levinas the other's face is *heard* more than it is *seen* (2000: 173).
107 See also Levinas 1998a: 170; 1998b: 145.
108 See Handelman 1991: 211; Levinas 1996a: 76; 1998b: 96, 186; Derrida 1997c: 100.
109 See Levinas 1988a: 174; Robbins 1999: 23, 57. Barthes's analysis of the photographic image – and specifically its power to awaken a sense of ontological guilt in the viewer (2000: 84) – might usefully refine Levinas's rather dismissive attitude to the face in its 'plasticity.'

110 See also Levinas 1998b: 168–9, 186.
111 See Levinas 1998b: 104; Robbins 1999: 64.
112 See also Derrida 1990: 929.
113 A qualification needs to be made here, for the 'face is not a force. It is an authority. Authority is often without force.' Likewise, on the punitive interpretation of God, Levinas proceeds: 'That is a very recent notion. On the contrary, the first form, the unforgettable form, in my opinion, is that, in the last analysis, he [God] can not do anything at all. He is not a force but an authority' (1988a: 169).
114 See Levinas 1992: 89, 86; 1998b: 108; Derrida 1997c: 104.
115 See also Levinas 1996a: 17, 54; 1998b: 105. Levinas also remarks that 'the face of the other is verticality and uprightness; it spells a relation to rectitude. The face is not in front of me ... but above me' (1984: 59).
116 See Levinas 1996c: 118–19.
117 See also Levinas 1998a: 163.
118 See Rousseau 1973: 25.
119 See Derrida 2000b: 105.
120 See also Levinas 1992: 86; 1993: 94.
121 See also Levinas 1993: 158.
122 See also Levinas 1996c: 75–6, 213.
123 See also Levinas 1993: 158; 1996a: 10, 53, 69; 1996c: 74–5, 213; 1998b: 145.
124 See Levinas 1996a: 69.
125 See Levinas 1988a: 170.
126 See also Levinas 1998a: 167. This point can be extended and applied to 'the other' more generally (as Levinas implies when remarking that 'the other is the richest and poorest of beings' (1984: 63)). For what is most distinctive and unpredictable about human beings is their capacity for both extreme vulnerability *and* resilience (Camus 1975: 12–13). Indeed, it is this unpredictability that, I would argue, constitutes the other's 'mystery' (Levinas 1992: 67–8).
127 See Caputo 1993: 32, 214; Rose 1997: 54–5; Barthes 2000: 69; Levinas 2001: 48. Even from a more physiological perspective, the face (unlike many other parts of the body) cannot be made taut to withstand violence. Indeed, this is partly why the face is a natural locus for tenderness and the trust this demands.
128 Levinas denies that his analyses refer to (or are incumbent upon) a generalized, universalizable 'subject.' Indeed, as will become clear later, he occasionally claims that his analyses apply *only to him* (1984: 67; 1992: 98–9; 1996a: 120).
129 See Levinas 1998c: 108–9. Levinas prefers the positively charged trope of being-*for*-the-other (1984: 62) to Heidegger's ethically neutral being-*with*-the-other. For a summary of Husserl's account of subjectivity, see Levinas 1998c: 82–3.
130 Levinas remarks that the other with whom he is concerned is not merely the 'neighbor' (geographically speaking) but the other who is 'very distant,' or 'the one with whom initially I have nothing in common.' He thus warns against 'the words *neighbor* and *fellow human being*' because they 'establish so many things in common ... and so many similarities'; in short, that 'we belong to the same essence' (1996a: 27; see also 2000: 138). Needless to say, I think Levinas's caution is (like Lyotard's) ultimately misplaced. As I argue in Chapter 7, Levinas clearly does prioritize humanity over animality, and in doing so relies upon the prior identification of the *genuinely* 'other' specifically with the *human* other.
131 See Levinas 1992: 60.
132 See also Robbins 1999: 4, 21.

133 See also Glendinning 1998: 7–23.
134 See Levinas 1998a: 9; Glendinning 1998: 1–6.
135 It is on this point that Levinas (1993: 24, 35, 44–5) criticizes Buber.
136 See Levinas 1998a: 164; 1998b: 186.
137 See Levinas 1992: 76; Robbins 1999: 23–4.
138 See also Derrida 1998c: 28.
139 See also Levinas 1998a: 91, 164–5, 169; 2000: 195–6, 202–3, 209; Derrida 1999b: 55–7.
140 See also Levinas 2000: 172, 202–3.
141 Likewise, Levinas remarks that the 'relationship with the Other ... puts me in question' (1996a: 52), the 'face is a visitation and a coming which *disturbs* immanence' (ibid.: 59, see also 69), and that '[o]nly the meaning of the other is irrecusable, and forbids the reclusion and reentry into the shell of the self' (1994a: 183).
142 See also Levinas 2000: 187; 2001: 50, 55.
143 See Robbins 1999: 16–19; Levinas 2000: 193. Levinas does occasionally refer to 'violence' (2000: 187) in this regard, but such allusions must be treated with caution.
144 See Derrida 1998a: 21; 1999a: 69; Levinas 2000: 152. Derrida characterizes the relation to the other as *necessarily* involving a 'preethical violence' (1997c: 125) insofar as the other must first appear (and thus be minimally assimilated to consciousness) *as* an 'other' for Levinas's ethics to get off the ground (see also Merleau-Ponty 1996: 359, 361). In reference to the need for judgement between competing responsibilities Levinas himself acknowledges that '[t]here is a certain measure of violence necessary in terms of justice' (1998b: 105; see also 2001: 167, 221; Derrida 1996a: 63; 1997b: 25, 32; 1999a: 72–3).
145 See Sartre 1993: 252ff.; Levinas 1984: 52–3. On the relationship between Sartre and Levinas, see Howells 1988.
146 This is an important point, for otherwise Levinas's frequently shocking terminology of being 'hostage' and 'persecuted' (1996a: 80–95) could be misconstrued. Nevertheless, there is a sense in which Levinas himself relies on just such a 'mythical past' in his holding justice accountable to the preoriginal ethical relation, and thereby maintaining the possibility of legitimate violence on behalf of another. I return to this in Chapter 7.
147 See also Levinas 2000: 195–6; 2001: 52, 55–6, 192, 204, 225.
148 Here one might recall Wittgenstein's cautionary remarks concerning the 'temporality' that is 'embedded in grammar' (1994a: 22).
149 See also Levinas 1996a: 17, 94.
150 See also Levinas 1996a: 144–5.
151 See also Levinas 2000: 196.
152 This gains support from Derrida's earlier remarks (1996c: 5–6; see also 2002a: 383–91). On Derrida's own preoccupation with confession see 1992a: 34–35; 1998c: 60.
153 See Levinas 1996a: 144. Aside from the Heideggerian overtones of the term 'guilt' (Levinas 1996a: 18), there is an issue of translation here, for the French *culpabilité* refers to notions of fault or blame. Levinas would want to avoid such connotations insofar as they imply more-or-less specifiable transgressions voluntarily perpetrated (1996b: 83–4; 1998a: 170; 1999: 106).
154 See Levinas 2000: 203–4.
155 See Derrida 1993b: 77; Levinas 1997a: 225.
156 See Levinas 1998a: 169–70; 1999: 179; Derrida 2001b: 26, 56. Note also Lyotard's remarks on eschatology (1997b: 96, 98).
157 See also Levinas 1999: 106; 2000: 195–6, 208–9.

Notes 247

158 See Levinas 1998a: 152, 175. As Derrida puts it, I am '*a priori* guilty' (2002a: 384).
159 See also Levinas 2000: 12, 20, 138, 161, 193, 195.
160 See also Levinas 1996c: 84.
161 See also Derrida 1993b: 19–20; 1995a: 184, 194, 286–7, 361–2; 1996b: 86; 1997b: 20–1; 2001d: 87. In this sense Levinas's remark that 'I am placed in the accusative case, in the place of the one accused – I lose all place' (2000: 161) is potentially misleading. For it is not that I have *no* place before the other but rather that I have no *rightful* place.
162 See Culler 1976: 26.
163 See Derrida 1993a: 255. Levinas did once remark that the fact that I am 'in one place in space and the other is at another place in space ... is not the alterity that distinguishes you from me. It is not because your hair is unlike mine or because you occupy another place than me – this would only be a difference of properties or of dispositions in space, a difference of attributes' (2001: 49). While I am not suggesting that the other's 'otherness' can be reduced to such 'spatial differences,' I nevertheless believe (and numerous passages in Levinas's work bear this out) that these cannot be dismissed as mere differences 'of attributes.'
164 See also Derrida 1993b: 39, 61, 76.
165 For similar remarks concerning the 'Third World' see Levinas 1999: 23, 30, 179; Derrida 2003: 121–2. Derrida rejects the suggestion that his own conception of ethics is reducible to a 'distributive justice' (2002f: 105).
166 Rousseau there refers to the 'first man who, having enclosed a piece of ground, bethought himself of saying *This is mine*' (1930: 207) – an event along with which came the notion of 'property' and 'a thousand quarrels and conflicts' (ibid.: 210), 'slavery and misery' (ibid.: 215). On such a reading Rousseau's own vocabulary of trespassing (the 'usurpations' of the rich, the injustice of 'proprietorship,' and his reminder: 'Do you not know that numbers of your fellow-creatures are starving, for want of what you have too much of?' (ibid.: 219–20)) takes on renewed significance. Interestingly, De Sade makes a similar point about 'usurpation' (1969: 173).
167 On the possible significance of Levinas's work for politics see Derrida 1999b: 20, 70–1, 78–83, 197; Critchley 1999b: 274ff. I return to this in Chapter 8.
168 Recalling Derrida's allusion to 'mourning' see Levinas's remarks on Pascal (Levinas 1999: 179).
169 See Blanchot 1995: 245; Levinas 1999: 23. In some astonishing passages Levinas says of this non-symmetrical relation that 'I am responsible for the Other without waiting for reciprocity ... Reciprocity is *his* affair' (1992: 98), and 'What I say here of course only commits me!' (ibid.: 114). I return to this later.
170 Levinas remarks that, insofar as the face of the other 'demands me, requires me, summons me' it might well be aligned with 'the word of God.' He proceeds: 'Does not God come to the mind precisely in that summons ... designating me instead in the face of the other as responsible with no possible denial, and thus, as the unique and chosen one?' (1999: 27). I return to this religious subtext in Chapter 7.
171 See Levinas 1998a: 169–71.
172 See Levinas 1997b: 70; 1999: 19–20.
173 A point contested in Bachelard 1994: 5, 7, 46, 213.
174 As Levinas summarizes: 'for a being that is always in the possible, it is impossible to be a whole' (2000: 32).
175 See Heidegger 1999: 342–3.
176 See Heidegger 1982: 171.

248 *Notes*

177 See Heidegger 1982: 297–8.
178 See also Levinas 1999: 22.
179 See Levinas 1996a: 88; 1999: 20–3; 2001: 62, 92, 97–8, 128, 132. This trespassing is a violation both against this *particular* other who faces me and, more generally, *any* present or absent other.
180 See also Derrida 2001b: 67; 2001d: 86.
181 See also Derrida 1996b: 86; 2002f: 383.
182 Bernstein is therefore in danger of oversimplifying Levinas's position when he summarizes: 'for Levinas, to acknowledge the supreme ethical imperative does not mean that we always follow it; but we *can* obey this command. Ethics presupposes saintliness not as an accomplishment, but as a value or an ideal. I can always act in such a manner as will give ethical priority to the life of the other' (Bernstein 2002: 179, see also 181).
183 See also Heidegger 1982: 298; Husserl 1989: 427. Heidegger's remarks on 'my having the responsibility for the Other's becoming endangered in his existence, led astray, or even ruined' (1999: 327) should be read with this in mind.
184 See Macann 1992: 214; Kellner 1992: 206.
185 See also Levinas 1998b: 148; 1999: 23, 28, 30. Recalling Wittgenstein's remarks on the ontological question (1994a: 85), one might say that even in its *asking the question* of Being Dasein thereby sacrifices other questions (Lyotard 1988: xii; Bennington 1993: 105; Derrida 2000b: 29). That is, in pursuing the issues of fundamental ontology Dasein must overlook the violence involved in assuming the right to do *even this* over 'feeding the hungry and clothing the naked' (Levinas 1998b: 116; see also Caputo 1993: 132) – something that problematizes all theorizing, including Levinas's own.
186 See Lyotard 1997b: 110.
187 See Levinas 1988a: 175; 2001: 134–5, 197; Derrida 1997c: 95.
188 See Levinas 1984: 63; Derrida 1995a: 381; Mole 1997: 148–9.
189 See Levinas 1992: 89; 1994a: 117; 1996a: 91, 103; 1999: 107; 2000: 138; 2001: 49.
190 See Wittgenstein 1994a: 77; 1994b: 70.
191 Notably Wittgenstein's moral perfectionism (Pascal 1996: 48).
192 See Levinas 1984: 68; 1996a: 103. On at least one occasion Levinas (like Rousseau) exalts 'the goodness of everyday life' over the failure and corruption of '[e]very [political] attempt to organize the human' (1999: 107).
193 See Levinas 1993: 148; 1997b: 43; 1998b: 18.
194 Levinas's allusion to the 'haughty priority of the A *is* A' (1998a: 174) is not, I think, an attack on logic. Rather, he is highlighting the danger of transferring the logical principle of identity into the ethical-political realm. For this would imply that 'I am I, and he is he' is the whole story.
195 Regarding the non-reasonableness of love, see Gaita 2000: 27.
196 A similar lamentation appears in Derrida's own 'confession' (1993a: 118–19, 248). See also Derrida's remarks on murder (ibid.: 297–8; 1999b: 108), and being guilty without fault (1993a: 300–2, 305).
197 See Rousseau 1953: 25–8, 37, 166.
198 See also Rousseau 1953: 176.
199 See Heidegger 1999: 328.
200 See Heidegger 1999: 327. Note also Heidegger's warning against 'idle talk' (ibid.: 213–14; Macann 1992: 218–19).
201 See Levinas 1993: 135–43; Robbins 1999: 16–19.
202 See Winch 1987: 168. Gaita defines 'remorse' as a 'haunting' (2000: 32) by – or 'pained acknowledgment' (ibid.: 34) of – one's guilt. I would assume all this in what I simply refer to as 'guilt.'
203 More recently Gaita has claimed that 'reflection on remorse takes us closer ...

to the nature of morality and of good and evil, than reflection on rules, principles, taboos and transgressions can' (2000: 32).
204 See Gaita 1991: 48; 2000: 36, 98; 2003: 163ff.
205 See Wittgenstein 1974: 169; Rhees 1981: 190–219; Monk 1991: 367–70; Malcolm 1993: 12; Pascal 1996: 45–50.
206 See Derrida 2002c: 88, 101, 103.
207 See Heidegger 1999: 312–15; Gaita 2000: 33–4, 128–9. To put this differently, there is an important disparity between the grammar of innocence and guilt, for whereas the former ultimately refers to a *public* realm (a 'we'), the latter can be radically *singular*. The problem with Heidegger's account is that while the 'they' cannot *absolve* me of my Guilt, neither can 'they' *accuse* me of it.
208 See Heidegger 1999: 323.
209 See also Derrida 2002f: 50. Likewise, Levinas refers to 'the everyday extraordinary dimension of my responsibility for other men' (2000: 185). It seems to me that the child's questions: 'Why was I born?', 'Why am I here?' and 'Why am I *me* and not *someone else*?' bear witness to the natural birth of moral consciousness (in the Levinasian sense).
210 See Derrida 1995b: 67–9, 78–9, 85–6.
211 See Drury 1981: 102; Derrida 1996c: 9–10.
212 See Schopenhauer 1918: 125; Gaita 2000: 31.
213 See Gaita 2000: 4.
214 See Nietzsche 1972a: 23; Levinas 1993: 87.
215 See Caputo 1993: 65; Derrida 2001e: 43; 2002c: 134.
216 See also Wittgenstein 1999: §§86, 103, 173.
217 See also Martin 1984: 603.
218 While Bauman notes that '"I am ready to die for the Other" is a moral statement; "He should be ready to die for me" is, blatantly, not' (1995: 51), Levinas likewise claims that, although ethics demands *self*-sacrifice, 'to say that the other has to sacrifice himself to the others would be to preach human sacrifice!' (1994a: 126). On a similar note, though here concerning theodicy, Levinas also refers to the 'scandal' of 'justifying my neighbour's suffering' – a justification that constitutes 'the source of all immorality' (1988b: 163).
219 Given my previous discussion of Heidegger and Levinas, it is interesting that Gaita should emphasize this dual character of guilt; that I am identified and positioned ('placed') in my singularity with regard to others, and that in being positioned thus I find myself ('elsewhere') unable to find relief in a common 'we.'
220 See Rousseau 1953: 17; Derrida 2002c: 132.
221 See Rousseau 1953: 31, 65, 134, 136, 176.
222 See Derrida 1992a: 42–3, 68–9; 1992c: 142–3; 1993b: 15; 1996a: 62–3; 1997b: 28–9; 1998a: 31; 1998c: 19–20; 2002c: 164.
223 See Gaita 2000: 31; Derrida 2000d: 32–3, 34, 36, 40–2, 92–4. This relates to Newton's 1662 confession where, for purposes of 'secrecy' as much as 'for speed,' he made 'a record of his private sins in Shelton's shorthand' (confessing, amongst other things, his 'breaches of the sabbath,' a 'more general impiety,' 'normal sexual pressures,' a 'bad temper,' 'casual acts of violence' a 'naughty playfulness,' '[p]eevishness,' 'stealing,' '[g]luttony' and having threatened his '"father and mother ... to burn them and the house over them"' (Hall 1996: 5–6)). Newton's use of a coded language is pertinent insofar as this 'secrecy' could likewise not be *radical*, for every code *as such* must in principle be decipherable by others (Bennington 1993: 58, 155; Derrida 1997d: 48ff.; 2000b: 65).
224 Handelman remarks that the '"force" of Levinas's argument has its source in the appeal of Levinas's own "face," Levinas in the first person as well as

250 *Notes*

Levinas the philosopher' (1991: 272–3). As Connolly notes (1999: 128–9), Caputo makes a similar move in *Against Ethics* (1993).
225 See Levinas 1987: 116, 119, 121–2; 1992: 87–8; 1993: 135–7, 140–2, 147–8, 158; 1996a: 4, 8–9, 36–8, 56, 114–15, 167.
226 See Derrida 1997c: 111.
227 See Derrida 1997c: 146. As I suggested earlier, by reading Levinas's work as a response to the questions raised by the early Wittgenstein, one sees just how necessary it becomes for the former to 'run against the boundaries of language' (Wittgenstein 1993: 44). Note Derrida's anecdotal remarks on Levinas's fear of silence (1996c: 7; see also Levinas 1998a: 99; 2000: 192).
228 See Derrida 1996c: 5–6; 1997c: 94.

7 The unreasonableness of ethics

1 Parts of the present chapter have appeared in Plant 2003d.
2 See Cockburn 1990: 11.
3 See also Levinas 2000: 137.
4 See Levinas 1984: 54; Davis 1996: 93–5.
5 See also Derrida 1984: 107–8. Although Derrida is here referring to *Totality and Infinity*, I would extend the point much further. Regarding Levinas's evocation of the Bible, see 2001: 62–3, 133, 149, 170, 243. On the emergence of a troubling ethnocentrism in Levinas's work see ibid.: 63–5, 137, 149, 170, 224, 243.
6 Levinas similarly talks of the face as a '*visitation*' (1996a: 53). Here we might also recall Wittgenstein's claim that '[e]thics, if it is anything, is supernatural and our words will only express facts' (1993: 40).
7 See Levinas 1996a: 7.
8 See Husserl 1982: §§23–9; 1989: p. 171; Levinas 1993: 93, 166, n. 3; Derrida 1997c: 123–4.
9 See Levinas 1995: 98.
10 See Caputo 1993: 79–80. Note also Hume 1988: 176.
11 Levinas's vocabulary of 'transcendence' might therefore only function as a way of drawing attention to the other's 'incalculability' (Wittgenstein 1994a: 73). Critchley's account of Levinas seems epistemological in this sense (1999a: 285), as occasionally does Derrida's (1997c: 124). I return to this later.
12 Peperzak remarks on the 'deceptively' (1993: 109) religious overtones of Levinas's work, and Kearney comments on how, for Levinas, 'God as the absolutely Other can only be encountered in and through our ethical rapport with our fellow humans' (1984: 48).
13 See Levinas 1992: 92, 105; 1993: 47, 94, 103; 1996a: 8, 25, 29, 76. Levinas also claims that love 'is commanded by the face of the other man, which is not a datum of experience and does not come from the world' (1998b: 187).
14 See Levinas 1984: 51.
15 See also Levinas 1992: 60, 92; 2000: 173, 186.
16 See also Levinas 1998a: 151.
17 See also Levinas 2000: 175.
18 See also Levinas 1994b: 14–15, 32; 1996a: 30; 2000: 180, 193–4; Peperzak 1993: 224–6.
19 See also Levinas 1999: 95; 2000: 185.
20 See Derrida 1997c: 107–9.
21 Here we might recall Malcolm's distinction between belief *that* God exists and belief *in* God – the latter being inextricably linked to 'action ... or if not, at least a bad conscience' (1972: 211).
22 See Levinas 1992: 105.

23 See Levinas 1998a: 80, 161.
24 See Husserl 1989: p. 200.
25 See Levinas 1992: 86; 1993: 44; 1996a: 60.
26 Levinas's remark that '[i]n this sense one can say that the face is not "seen"' (1992: 86; see also 1988a: 176) thus becomes less bewildering.
27 Levinas makes a similarly dismissive gesture toward the attempt to limit the meaning of the face to its cultural, socio-historical manifestations (1992: 86; 1993: 44; 1996a: 52, 53).
28 See Levinas 1992: 66–7.
29 See Caputo 1993: 75; Derrida 1997c: 90, 112, 116–17, 125, 137–8, 140–1.
30 See also Wittgenstein 1994a: 50.
31 See Shields 1997: 101.
32 See Levinas 1994a: 184.
33 See Wittgenstein 1994a: 29; 1994b: 54, 56–8, 62–3.
34 See also Levinas 1992: 87–8; 1998b: 10.
35 See Derrida 1999b: 112; 2002a: 384.
36 See Wittgenstein 1994a: 77.
37 See also Levinas 2000: 187.
38 See Malcolm 1960: 61; Wittgenstein 1969: 179. Interestingly, Levinas refers to the 'great novelty of a way of thinking in which the word God ceases orienting life by expressing the unconditional foundation of the world and cosmology, and reveals, in the face of the other man, the secret of his semantics' (1999: 96).
39 Levinas's 'here I am' does not translate easily from the French *me voici* (literally 'see-me-here'). One would, for example, employ *me voici* in circumstances where one's appearance was not expected by the other. In this sense *me voici* pertains to the occurrence of something new (a 'visitation'). As Handelman notes, what Levinas is effectively doing here is 'translating the "I think" of the rational Cartesian cogito ... into the biblical "here I am" of subjectivity and ethics' (1991: 266; see also Peperzak 1993: 25).
40 See Isaiah 6:9.
41 I will return to this in Chapter 8.
42 See Handelman 1991: 272–3.
43 See Levinas 1993: 164, n. 3.
44 See also Levinas 1992: 117; 1993: 94, 103; 1996a: 53.
45 See Levinas 1993: 44; 1996a: 9.
46 See Levinas 1988a: 169–74.
47 See Levinas 1996a: 29.
48 See also Levinas 1998a: 175.
49 See Levinas 1992: 86–7. Levinas also remarks that 'across all literature the human face speaks – or stammers, or gives itself a countenance, or struggles with its caricature,' and similarly that the 'Holy Scriptures do not signify through the dogmatic tale of their supernatural or sacred origin, but through the expression of the face of the other man that they illuminate' (ibid.: 117).
50 See Peperzak 1993: 164, n. 28.
51 See Wittgenstein 1958: p. 178; 1994a: 23, 49.
52 See also Derrida 1999b: 32, 110.
53 See also Schutz 1964: 43; 1971: 10, 314; 1974: 17, 75; Husserl 1989: pp. 171, 206.
54 See Levinas 1988a: 174.
55 See also Husserl 1982: 19, 135–6, 138, 140; 1989: 385–7; Heidegger 1999: 153–4.
56 See Levinas 1996c: 213–14; 1998b: 185. I return to this point later.

252 *Notes*

57 There *is* a sense in which for Levinas the face of the other – while not a 'private object' for me alone – does regard me in a singular way. One might say that, epistemologically, the other's face is *there-for-everyone*, but ethically it commands *only me directly*.
58 See also Levinas 2001: 50–1, 67–8, 100, 115–16, 133, 143, 165–8, 183, 193–4, 205–6, 214, 230, 246.
59 See Peperzak 1993: 167.
60 See Derrida 1999b: 60.
61 See also Levinas 1994a: 159; Derrida 1999b: 74, 79.
62 In Barthes's analysis of love, even the world of objects is prone to a certain fetishization (1990: 75, 173; see also Kundera 1998: 55, 81).
63 See also Kierkegaard 1973: 286, 288.
64 See also Levinas 1994a: 157; 1998b: 227.
65 See Levinas 1998b: 104, 195.
66 See also Derrida 1995a: 272–3; 2002f: 304–5.
67 See also Levinas 1994a: 157–8; 1998b: 205.
68 See Levinas 1998b: 103, 203–4.
69 See Caputo 1993: 118. While 'violence must be avoided as much as possible ... one cannot say that there is no legitimate violence' (Levinas 1998b: 106; see also 1999: 172).
70 This is one way of understanding Levinas's allusions to a past that is 'immemorial' (1996a: 60; 2000: 162), 'preoriginal' (1996a: 116), 'never a *now*' (ibid.: 77), or 'never present!' (1998b: 233).
71 In much the same way as 'I am *I* as if I had been chosen' (Levinas 1993: 35), so too is it *as if* the other were God, or *as if* God commands us with 'His Word in the face of the Other' (1998b: 175). God is, like Derrida's 'regulating idea of pure hospitality' (1999c: 133) (or the 'transcendental illusion of the gift' (1992b: 30; see also Caputo 1997a: 135)), only expressible in these excessive terms. 'God,' the 'Infinite' (and so on) might therefore be the *least inadequate* way of articulating the desire for the impossible central to both Levinas's and Derrida's work (Derrida 2002f: 52). I return to this in Chapter 8.
72 See Levinas 1992: 90; 1994a: 159; Derrida 1996b: 83–4; 1997a: 12; 1997b: 25, 27, 32; 1999a: 68–9.
73 Levinas read Rousseau during his incarceration as a prisoner of war.
74 See also Rousseau 1973: 44, 54.
75 See Rousseau 1930: 209.
76 See Rousseau 1973: 45. Interestingly, Rousseau chooses the life of Robinson Crusoe as his literary 'touchstone' (ibid.: 84) for the education of Emile.
77 Rousseau's remarks on compassion and pity seem less obviously naturalistic (1973: 101–5), despite the fact that he also maintains that 'justice and goodness are ... real affections of the soul enlightened by reason which have developed from our primitive affections' (ibid.: 105).
78 See also Rousseau 1930: 210, 217.
79 See Rousseau 1930: 219–21.
80 See De Sade 1969: 173–5.
81 Of course, Levinas's emphasis on 'usurpation' runs deeper insofar as the 'I' is accused of being a trespasser in its very *being-in-the-world*. Compare also Rousseau's suspicions concerning the divisive nature of property and Levinas's claim that '[t]he Other ... paralyzes possession, which he contests by his epiphany in the face' (1996c: 171). I return to this later.
82 See also Campbell 1999: 37; Molloy 1999: 232.
83 See Derrida 1995b: 69, 71; 2002e: 394–5, 416.
84 This is presumably what Levinas means by the 'excellence of democracy, whose fundamental liberalism corresponds to the ceaseless deep remorse of

Notes 253

justice ... A bad conscience of justice!' (1998b: 229–30; see also 2001: 52, 134, 136, 194, 206; Derrida 1996b: 86–7; 1999b: 76, 112, 115; 2003: 129).
85 See Levinas 1998b: 106; Nuyen 2000: 415.
86 See Rousseau 1930: 208–10.
87 See Derrida 1999a: 68–9; 1999b: 30, 33, 97.
88 See Derrida's remarks on 'perjury' (2001b: 49; 2002a: 388). Levinas is not wholly consistent on this point. Thus, for example, he laments: 'Unfortunately we are three – at least – the third always appears' (2001: 143).
89 See Levinas 1994b: 50.
90 See Derrida 1995b: 2–3, 6; 1997b: 21; 1998b: 26.
91 See also Levinas 1994b: 66.
92 See Robbins 1999: 68–9.
93 See also Derrida 1999b: 72. Compare Levinas's remarks with Wittgenstein 1994a: 77. The 'love' Levinas here has in mind is 'love without Eros ... love in which the ethical aspect dominates the passionate aspect, love without concupiscence' (1998b: 103; see also 194; 2000: 174). Gaita's notion of 'justice beyond fairness' (2000: 80–1; see also 84–5) which constitutes 'the most sublime aspect of our legal tradition' (ibid.: 11) is in keeping with Levinas's sentiments. Likewise, Gaita's insistence that guilt (and pity) cannot be adequately accounted for in consequentialist terms (that is, in terms of *actual* harm caused) is consonant with Levinasian Guilt.
94 Levinas claims that 'the fear of God is concretely my fear for my neighbor' (1993: 47), and that the ' "Here I am!" is the place through which the Infinite enters into language' (1992: 106) insofar as for 'every man, assuming responsibility for the Other is a way of testifying to the glory of the Infinite, and of being inspired' (ibid.: 113).
95 See Levinas 1998b: 110.
96 See Derrida 1995b: 84.
97 This same question arose in Chapter 5 regarding Wittgenstein's ethicalization of religious belief, and specifically his suggestion to Drury that, despite their non-belief, there was 'a sense in which' they were 'both Christians' (Drury 1981: 130). I return to this in Chapter 8 with reference to Derrida.
98 See Levinas 1998a: 176; 1998b: 103. This remark might be read alongside Barthes's allusions to the economics of love (1990: 84–5, 171, 208–9), the politics of giving (ibid.: 76–9, 85), and the narcissism of the lover (ibid.: 161, 179, 182, 199). Barthes also emphasizes a certain gratuitousness of love in both the a-teleology of the lover's discourse (ibid.: 73, 85–6) and risk of the 'I-love-you' (ibid.: 147–54).
99 See also Levinas 1987: 115; 2000: 151. Contrast this with Husserl's remarks on language and communication (1989: 202–4).
100 Although this picture of language is complicated by Austin's account of speech-acts, he nevertheless maintains the notion of performative *success* (1976: 14ff.) – which would, for Levinas, maintain even this account under the rubric of 'knowledge.' Levinas's point gains some support from Wittgenstein's warning against both the temptation to look for the '*essence* of language' (1958: §92, see also §65; 1990: §444), and that 'giving information' is what constitutes such 'essence' (1958: §356, p. 178; 1990: §160).
101 See Levinas 2000: 192.
102 This is not the contact 'in which coincidence and identification occur' (Levinas 1999: 93), but rather one's being *exposed* to another – and specifically to her 'face [which is] weighted down with a skin' (1994a: 89).
103 Note Picard's nostalgia regarding how words were 'once used' (1948: 175, 177).
104 See also Defoe 1985: 211–13.

254 *Notes*

105 Picard similarly refers to 'the creation of the word' as 'the greatest event' (1948: 100).
106 See also Levinas 2000: 164, 192. Note too Derrida's remarks on the 'promise' (1995a: 384; 1996b: 82; 1997a: 3, 11, 16; 1997b: 27, 30, 35).
107 See Handelman 1991: 223–4.
108 See Levinas 1988a: 176; 1993: 44.
109 See Levinas 1984: 60; 1988a: 172; Davis 1996: 84–5.
110 See Picard 1948: 102; Caputo 2001: 139.
111 Although I will not expand on this, the 'unreasonableness' Levinas considers to lie at the heart of ethics parallels his remarks on the persistent return of skepticism (1994a: 166–71). Briefly stated, while the propositional, constative *Said* of the skeptic's claims clearly render them refutable ('There is no truth' is patently self-contradictory), on the level of the quasi-performative *Saying* the skeptic can – and does – always return to haunt philosophy (1994a: 167–8). For a summary of this, see Critchley 1999a: 156–69.
112 Of course, Nietzsche vehemently denies that he wants to be 'pronounced holy' or 'a saint' (1992a: 96). What is interesting is his subsequent quasi-prophetic remarks on the potential significance of his own transvaluation of value: 'all the power-structures of the old society have been blown into the air – they one and all reposed on the lie: there will be wars such as there never yet have been on earth. Only after me will there be *grand politics* on earth' (ibid.: 97; see also 101; 1968: §273). Thus, Nietzsche speaks *against* saintliness in the name of *another* saintliness (Derrida 2002f: 223–5, 227).
113 See also Derrida 1999b: 61; Levinas 2001: 90, 111, 170, 183–4, 207, 218, 220.
114 See Rousseau 1930: 213–14. Indeed, according to Levinas, 'Heideggerian being-with-one-another' sounds 'like a marching together' (2001: 137).
115 See Levinas 1998b: 229–30.
116 See Gaita's remarks on loving 'better' (2000: 25–7).
117 Levinas remarks that '[t]he Desirable does not gratify my Desire but hollows it out, and somehow nourishes me with new hungers' (1996a: 52). This passage is relevant here insofar as the bad conscience inaugurated with the third party is similarly insatiable insofar as the more I do for *this* other, the more I have failed to do for *that* other. I return to Levinasian 'desire' later.
118 And also the conditions of *impossibility*, for it is precisely this excessiveness (and thus bad conscience) that prevents me from ever claiming to have 'fulfilled' my responsibilities.
119 See Levinas 1988b: 165. For Levinas's distinction between the 'moral' (or 'just') and the 'ethical' see 1988a: 171; 1992: 80–1, 90; 1996b: 237–8.
120 See also Derrida 1999b: 112, 115.
121 See also Levinas 1998c: 130–4.
122 See Levinas 1984: 62; 2001: 136, 145, 191. Levinas's characterization of Dasein in terms of a 'struggle for life' (1988a: 172) is contentious, not only because Dasein is always being-towards-*death* (indeed, given Heidegger's anti-biologism (Derrida 1988c: 165), this purported complicity between fundamental ontology and Darwinian evolution becomes additionally problematic), but also because his reading of Darwin is questionable (Darwin 1875: 97–145).
123 The implication would thus seem to be that Heidegger's Dasein is not *properly* human. Levinas's allegation is curious given that the very 'natural' relation between parent and offspring represents a paradigm case of both 'love without reward' and 'putting the other first.' I return to this later.
124 See also Picard 1948: 102–4; Levinas 1998a: 164, 171; 2001: 47.
125 See also Levinas 2001: 53, 113, 119, 132. Picard similarly remarks that 'human nature' is so 'absolutely different' from the animal that the former 'could never have come straight out of animal [nature]' (1948: 104). Indeed,

'[a]nimals seem to have dropped out of a human dream' (ibid.: 103). Compare this with Levinas 1984: 61.

126 The same ambiguity occurs when Levinas claims that 'Goodness' (though a 'childish virtue') is 'already ... the possibility of sacrifice in which the humanity of man bursts forth' (1998b: 157).

127 Neither can it be a matter of will, as this would subordinate responsibility to autonomy, and Levinas maintains that ethics calls my freedom into question (1994b: 37, 85).

128 Even if one accepts the claim that only the human can be saintly, this does not warrant Levinas's conclusion that the human 'breaks' with the natural. The advent of the human might mark an unprecedented evolutionary stage, but that does not sever the human from such natural processes (of course, given Levinas's comments on Darwinism (1984: 62; 1988a: 172), and more general suspicions concerning the notion of a 'human race' (1998a: 10), it is doubtful that he has anything 'evolutionary' in mind). I will return to some of these points.

129 Interestingly, Levinas refers to our 'natural goodness ... with respect to the other' (2001: 55).

130 See Robbins 1999: 3–4.

131 See also Levinas 1996a: 55; 1996c: 117.

132 See also Levinas 1996a: 52, 55, 76; 1996c: 117; Blanchot 1997: 53.

133 Although I return to this point later, one might object that this classification gets things precisely backwards; that *needs* are in fact what remain insatiable. See Derrida 1992b: 158; 1995a: 282.

134 See Derrida 1992b: 7, 12–13, 35, 38, 45–7, 64, 76, 91, 126, 137, 139, 147–8, 156. Of course, the very notion of a *pure* gift (or *absolute* expenditure) is itself caught up in a certain economics of return. For my giving *everything* could likewise harbor entirely teleological hopes for a 'good conscience.' Somewhat paradoxically then, sacrificing one's *life* for another may not (as Levinas occasionally suggests) be the 'ultimate' gift. On this general point see Bernasconi 1997: 258.

135 See Levinas 1992: 92; 1996a: 44–5, 76–7; 1996c: 63; Weil 1987: 86.

136 See also Derrida 2002f: 242.

137 See also Jay 1993: 558–60; Levinas 1998a: 176. There remains an ambiguity here concerning who/what touches who/what in the caress? That is, do I here touch the other, or rather touch myself *with* or *through* the other? (Derrida 1993c: 126–7, 133–4, 140). Regarding the ethics of touch, see Benso 2000: 160, 162ff.

138 See Levinas 1992: 32, 61, 67–9.

139 See Levinas's remarks on 'justice,' the 'liberal state' and his own 'utopianism' (1988a: 177–8).

140 According to Rorty, Levinas's ethics is 'pointless hype' (1996: 42). Rorty's objection is, I think, metaphilosophical; namely, that he sees no pragmatic value in even attempting an 'ethics of ethics.' But while Levinas is not concerned with offering a specific ethical-political agenda, this is not to say that (for example, on the question of moral Guilt) his work lacks 'practical consequences.' I have discussed some of these points in Plant 2003d.

141 See Rousseau 1973: 13ff. D'Holbach similarly claims that the 'compassion in man is a habitual inclination to feel more or less keenly the ills with which others are afflicted' (1969: 66) which is made possible by way of 'man's structure' (his 'faithful memory' and 'active imagination' (ibid.: 67)) – in short, his capacity to 'transfer' the pain of an other to himself. However, as I have previously argued, this deliberative notion of 'transference' (Levinas 1988a: 172) needs to be questioned.

142 See Picard 1948: 105; Levinas 2001: 47, 59, 97, 106, 183, 204, 235.
143 Levinas occasionally refers to Hobbes in this regard (1996a: 51; 1996b: 273).
144 See also De Sade 1991a: Dialogue 5; Nietzsche 1992b: Essay 2, §§5–6. De Sade's critique of the Christian 'invention' of the notion of brotherhood (a claim reiterated in his 'Dialogue entre un Prêtre et un Moribond' (1991b: 23)) is developed by Nietzsche.
145 Regarding Levinas's identification of Nietzsche with Nazism, see Bataille 1996: 192–3.
146 There is something quasi-Pyrrhonian about remarks such as this – though for Nietzsche there is no corresponding *ataraxia*. For a more striking similarity between Nietzsche and Pyrrhonism see Nietzsche 1994: pp. 71, 99.
147 For a powerful literary account of the corruption of pity, see Zweig 2000.
148 See also Nietzsche 1968: §§268, 297.
149 See Nietzsche 1968: §§266, 276, 280, 285, 296; Derrida 2001a: 33–4.
150 See also Nietzsche 1968: §327.
151 See also Nietzsche 1968: §§173–4, 200.
152 See Nietzsche 1992b: Essay 2, §§16, 19.
153 See also Nietzsche 1968: §§245–6. Compare this with Malcolm's remarks on guilt and the Judaic-Christian conception of God (1960: 60–1).
154 See also Nietzsche 1968: §176. According to Levinas fear *of* the other (which is 'fear for the self') is subordinate to fear *for* the other, and he likens the latter to the 'mother who fears for the child, or even, each of us who fears for a friend' (1998b: 117; see also 1993: 47; 2001: 124, 177). As will become clear in Chapter 8, Derrida would be more cautious here insofar as one must ask to what extent *fear-for-the-other* is also a *fear-for-oneself* (for *one's own* potential loss or mourning)?
155 In this sense traditional moralities constitute a '*sign-language of the emotions*' (Nietzsche 1987: p. 92).
156 See Nietzsche 1992b: Essay 1, §13.
157 See also Levinas 2001: 54, 250.
158 The 'judged' would here refer to the poor and vulnerable other, while the 'judgement' would designate the accusation of my being Guilty.
159 Even Derrida acknowledges that 'it is not by chance that Nietzsche could be reappropriated by Nazism' (Derrida 2002f: 221).
160 See Wittgenstein 1958: §§281, 283, 583; 1990: §506.
161 See also Levinas 1996a: 8, 73.
162 See Derrida 1993b: 35, 75–6, 78; 1995a: 268, 277–9, 284–5. Although Levinas is critical of Heidegger's concept of 'Dasein' (insofar as it prioritizes the self over the other), for both philosophers the emphasis remains squarely anthropocentric. On this feature of Heidegger's work refer to Glendinning 1998: 62–70. I return to this point later.
163 See Wittgenstein 1958: §§250, 357, 650, pp. 174, 229; 1990: §§389, 518.
164 See Glendinning 1998: 71.
165 See Wittgenstein 1958: §§283, 360.
166 See also Wittgenstein 1958: §244, p. 218; 1993: 389; 1994a: 67; 1999: §§359, 475, 538.
167 See Wittgenstein 1996a: 66–7.
168 And similarly: 'the epiphany of the Other (*Autrui*) involves a signifyingness of its own, independent of this meaning received from the world ... The nudity of a face is a bareness without any cultural ornament ... The face *enters* into our world from an absolutely foreign sphere' (Levinas 1996a: 53). On the relation between concepts, humans and animals, contrast Levinas's remarks with Gaita 2003: 60–1.
169 See Caputo 1993: 81; Derrida 1997c: 89, 107. This is not simply a matter of

bodily form, for the 'behavior one meets is *human* behavior in the first place ... One sees it and responds to it as such' (Dilman 1987: 29).
170 See Derrida 1997c: 114–16, 121–3, 125, 127, 132, 137–8, 140–1, 143. Of course, Derrida's argument is broadly phenomenological rather than naturalistic.
171 See Caputo 1993: 74–5, 80.
172 See Derrida 1997c: 125. This parallels Derrida's remarks on the necessary non-recognition of the gift (1992b: 13–17, 23, 27, 35–6, 47, 56, 91, 101, 147; 1995b: 106–7).
173 See Derrida 1997c: 112, 116–17, 125. To reiterate: this is why Derrida refers to a 'preethical violence' (ibid.: 125, 128) only upon which an ethical relation to the other is possible. That is, although this minimal recognition of the other as an other (not a thing, 'not a stone' (ibid.: 125)) constitutes a 'violence,' insofar as such an assimilation is a necessary condition for my being responsible for her, it is therefore 'preethical.'
174 See also Levinas 1996a: 7, 28, 73; 1998b: 185.
175 See Levinas 1997b: 93.
176 See also Levinas 1994a: 87, 159; Putnam 2002: 55.
177 See also Gaita 2000: 32.
178 Or what Levinas refers to as a 'miracle' (2001: 59, see also 106, 111, 113, 216–18, 250). The difficulty Levinas's anti-naturalism presents is how this singularity is to be understood given that *any* commonality enabling the (singular) face to be recognized *as such* is condemned as inherently unethical.
179 To what extent Levinas emphasizes verbal communication is contentious. Thus, Critchley argues against the charge of anthropocentrism (and against Derrida's reading of Levinas here (Critchley 1999a: 180)) that Levinas 'reserves a privileged place for non-verbal communication.' Critchley then alludes to a parallel 'non-verbal language of the skin' (ibid.: 178–9). But even if he is right to conclude that 'the original *logos* of ethics from which the experience of obligation derives can be shown to be rooted in the non-verbal' (ibid.: 181) this simply makes Levinas's neglect of the animal more bemusing.
180 See also Derrida 1992b: 139, 142, 145; Handelman 1991: 210.
181 See Handelman 1991: 223–5.
182 See also Levinas 1993: 142.
183 See Levinas 1988a: 172.
184 See also Levinas 2001: 41, 90.
185 While Winch does 'not want to deny that in some attenuated sense one could speak of allowing a dumb animal to choose and of "respecting" its choice,' he nevertheless insists that the 'sense' would be 'attenuated' (1987: 176–7). While we might concede Winch's point concerning deliberative 'choice,' there is little reason to accept this general criterion for moral worthiness. What Winch overlooks here (although he emphasizes it regarding other matters) is Wittgenstein's naturalism.
186 Interestingly, Levinas begins the essay by referring to our becoming 'vegetarian again' like Adam, and to 'the butchery that every day claims our "consecrated" mouths!' (1997a: 151).
187 See also Derrida 2002e: 388.
188 See Wittgenstein 1958: §§244, 343.
189 See also Malcolm 1986: 303; Dilman 1987: 49–50.
190 See Wittgenstein 1958: §25.
191 For an example of how Wittgenstein's remarks on animals have been misapplied, see Pinker 1994: 56. Note also Gaita 2000: 240.
192 See Glendinning 1998: 72–5.
193 See Gaita 2003: 61. Certainly one *can* become deaf to the cry of the

non-human animal – those working in abattoirs presumably do. My point is that such cases represent an erosion of a more primitive responsiveness to animals.
194 See also Levinas 1988b: 156–7. In these circumstances even the human is (albeit temporarily) 'worldless' or without a 'world-picture.'
195 Interestingly, in response to the question 'Can animals suffer?' Derrida claims that there is 'no doubt. In fact it has never left any room for doubt ... it is not even indubitable; it precedes the indubitable, it is older than it' (2002e: 397).
196 See also Wittgenstein 1993: 381, 383.
197 It is due to this that remarks such as: 'The great "experiences" of our life have properly speaking never been lived' (1987a: 68) seem enigmatic.
198 See Levinas 1995: 103, 112.
199 See Levinas 1997a: 47.
200 See also Wittgenstein 1990: §545. Although Levinas acknowledges that '[c]ompassion is ... a natural sentiment,' he qualifies this by adding 'on the part of him who was hungry once, toward the other and for the hunger of the other.' But it is only due to such a partial account of natural compassion that Levinas can then conclude that (genuine) ethical responsibility constitutes a 'break' in this 'mechanical solidarity' (2000: 173).
201 See Derrida 1997c: 89.
202 This is not entirely out of keeping with Levinas's remark that '[t]he Other comes to us not only out of context but also without mediation ... The nudity of a face is a bareness without any cultural ornament' (1996a: 53). One might therefore re-cast Levinas's dichotomy between need and desire as follows: What I *desire* is that the other's *needs* be satisfied. Though this desire is insatiable insofar as I can never legitimately assure myself that 'I have done enough,' it is nevertheless *from their basic needs* that the other's call comes to me, and *toward their basic needs* that my responsibility is first oriented (indeed, elsewhere Levinas seems to suggest precisely this (1994b: 99)).
203 See Dufourmantelle 2000: 142.
204 See also Derrida 2002e: 372–3, 378, 380, 382–3.
205 See Blanchot 1997: 50.
206 See also Levinas 1988a: 172; 1997a: 293.
207 See Rousseau 1973: 25.
208 Of course, the non-human animal may still demand justice from those capable of universalizing maxims – just as many humans (children, the severely mentally ill, and so on) make their silent demands.
209 See Glendinning 1998: 142.
210 See also Levinas 2001: 47.
211 See Rousseau 1930: 210.
212 See also Levinas 1984: 64–5.
213 See Sextus 1996: 1:75. Levinas also makes the questionable claim that 'the dog ... cannot suppress its bark' (1984: 65).
214 See also Levinas 1996a: 114. Although, as Levinas often maintains, there may be no way of separating the Saying from the Said (in the same way as there can be no ethical *facing* without an empirical face or body), clearly *some* 'Saids' are closer to the spirit of their Saying than others.
215 See Gaita's remarks on 'the love of saints' (2000: 24).
216 See Caputo 1993: 145; Derrida 1988c: 173ff.; 1990: 953; 1992b: 144, 167; 1995a: 268, 277–9; 1995b: 71; 1997c: 142–3; 1999c: 135; 2000a: 406–7; 2000c: 4; 2003: 133.
217 See also Derrida 1997d: 136; 2000a: 404–5; 2000b: 137–8; 2002d: 87. Regarding one's responsibility to those *other* others necessarily excluded by one's

being responsible to *this* other, Derrida refers to 'animals' as being 'even more other others than my fellows' (1995b: 69).
218 And specifically Derrida's own 'desire for the impossible' (1999c: 72). I return to this in Chapter 8.
219 Derrida 'refuse[s] to speak of "the animal" in general' – indeed, he does not even 'think there is such a thing as "the animal"' (2000a: 407; see also 2002c: 231; 2002e: 292, 402, 415; 2002f: 241, 308–9).
220 See Levinas 1995: 110.
221 See also Derrida 1999b: 86–8; 2002b: 7, 8; Dufourmantelle 2000: 4.
222 Levinas also refers to 'the gratuitousness of the *for-the-other*, the response of responsibility that already lies dormant in a salutation, in the *hello*, in the *goodbye*' (1997b: 106).
223 See also Derrida 1999b: 95.
224 See also Derrida 1999b: 37.
225 See also Caputo 1993: 205, 218; 1997a: 143.
226 See Derrida 2000b: 123; 2002f: 377. I explain this in Chapter 8.
227 See also Wittgenstein 1990: §542.
228 See Levinas 1994a: 75.
229 And why equate 'nature' with the 'rootedness' (Derrida 1999b: 92) Levinas problematizes in his phenomenology of the 'home'? (I return to the latter in Chapter 8). Critchley claims that Levinas provides a '*material phenomenology of subjective life*' that emphasizes the 'sentient subject of sensibility.' That is, the 'ethical relation takes place at the level of sensibility, not at the level of consciousness, and thus, in a way that recalls both Bentham's and Rousseau's criteria for ethical obligation ... it is in my pre-reflective sentient disposition towards the other's suffering that a basis for ethics and responsibility can be found' (1996: 33; see also Derrida 2002e: 395–7). While I am sympathetic to Critchley's application of Levinas, it is misleading to suggest that the latter's intentions are in any way naturalistic. As Levinas insists, the ethical relation he is describing is 'earlier than nature' or 'pre-nature' (1994a: 75).
230 See also Derrida 2001d: 111–13.
231 See Derrida 1999e: 118; 2001d: 101; 2002f: 372. I return to these themes in Chapter 8.
232 Interestingly, in her commentary on Derrida's remarks on hospitality, Dufourmantelle refers to '*the body's most archaic instinctual reactions* [which] *are caught up in an encounter* [with the other]' (2000: 26–8; see also Caputo 1997a: 143). These are what I want to encompass under 'the natural.'

8 Contaminations

1 Parts of the present chapter have appeared in Plant 2003c.
2 That is, beyond the methodological correlations between deconstruction and Wittgenstein's later philosophy (Staten 1986).
3 See Derrida 1999c: 57. In a discussion with Ricoeur in 1971 Derrida claims that his interest is with 'a type of questioning which has not yet coincided with the need for ethics' (1992c: 159). However, the beginnings of the so-called 'ethical turn' in Derrida's work can be identified as early as 'Violence and Metaphysics' where a certain rhetoric of hospitality emerges (1997c: 152–3; see also Bernstein 1991: 172–229).
4 According to Critchley, Derrida's recent work represents a '*quasi-phenomenological ... description and analysis of particular phenomena.*' That is, Derrida is 'concerned with the particular *qua* particular ... with the grain and enigmatic detail of everyday life' (Critchley 1996: 32). Of course, what also 'regulates' Derrida's analyses of the gift, hospitality (and so on) is 'what is inscribed' in

the 'heritage' of these concepts 'in a number of traditions' (Derrida 2001b: 53).
5 See Critchley 1999a.
6 Dooley (1999, 2001) has recently attempted to show the fundamental disparity between Derrida and Levinas. I have criticized this in Plant 2003c.
7 Derrida himself alludes to this section of *Totality and Infinity* in 'A Word of Welcome' (1999b: 16, 21), although he there focuses on Levinas's discussion of the 'feminine.' For other analyses of 'home' (and related concepts), see Bollnow 1967; Dovey 1978; Seamon 1979; Seamon and Mugerauer 1985: Bird *et al.* 1993; Bachelard 1994; Benjamin 1995; Ingold 2000.
8 See also Bachelard 1994: 47, 51; Levinas 1994b: 107.
9 See Bachelard 1994: 5–7, 66; Levinas 1996c: 162.
10 See Harries's somewhat disparaging remarks on the 'mobile home' (1998: 144–8).
11 See also Levinas 1996c: 156.
12 See also Heidegger 1994: 351.
13 See Levinas 1996c: 157.
14 See also Peperzak 1993: 157–8.
15 For Levinas this would presumably include the domestication of animals. For a critique of Levinas's claim that 'things' are 'faceless,' see Benso 2000.
16 See also Levinas 1996c: 171; 1998b: 17.
17 See also Heidegger 1999: 156–7.
18 See Levinas 1996c: 162; Heidegger 1999: 99–100.
19 See Husserl 1989: pp. 31, 88, 177.
20 See also Derrida 1993b: 20; Levinas 1984: 63.
21 See also Derrida 1999b: 111; 2001a: 84–5.
22 See Levinas 1996c: 153.
23 See Levinas 1996c: 158.
24 See Derrida 1992b: 10–11; 1995a: 282; 1999b: 99.
25 See also Derrida 1999b: 55; 2000b: 109; 2000c: 3.
26 See also Derrida 1999b: 46, 92.
27 See also Derrida 1996b: 84–5; 1997a: 13–14; 1999a: 81.
28 See Levinas 1992: 66–7.
29 See also Derrida 1997e: 17; 1998c: 68; 2001a: 21. Schutz also refers to the 'stranger' (1964: 91–105; 1970b: 87–8), and the concept of 'home' (1964: 106–19; 1970b: 82).
30 Thus perhaps revealing a 'complicity of theology and metaphysics' (Derrida 1997c: 108–9) in Derrida's own work. See also Derrida 1995b: 108–9; 1999c: 57.
31 See Derrida 1999c: 75–6.
32 See Derrida 1988e: 593; 1992b: 122–3, 147; 1997a: 3, 4, 7; 1998b: 17; 2003: 90, 91–2. Note also Gaita's remarks on 'conversation and Otherness' (1998: 73).
33 See also Derrida 1990: 971; 1992b: 95; 2002c: 159; 2003: 118.
34 Clearly, the other often does *not* surprise me, and in that sense even the 'perhaps' cannot be reduced 'to the modalities of being and certainty.' In short, the 'perhaps' necessarily entails that the other might *not* surprise me in the least. See Wittgenstein's remarks on the 'surprise' (1994a: 45).
35 See also Wittgenstein 1990: §525.
36 See also Husserl 1982: p. 114; Tilghman 1991: 100.
37 See Derrida 1999c: 77; 2000c: 14, 17 n. 17; 2001d: 98; 2002a: 360–2. Levinas refers to the other (and specifically the face) in terms of a 'visitation' (1996a: 53–4, 59; see also Derrida 1999b: 62–3).
38 See Derrida 1995c: 14. However, the openness of the latter is of a restricted kind, for most often an invitation to 'Come whenever' does not mean at *any*

time. The sort of genuinely open invitation I have in mind therefore relates to Derrida's notion of 'pure' hospitality.
39 Recalling my discussion of Hertzberg in Chapter 2, the invitation could thus be said to parallel the relation of *reliance*, whereas the visitation (as will become clear shortly) parallels the relation of *trust*.
40 See Derrida 1995c: 14.
41 See Derrida 1993b: 10–11.
42 See Derrida 1992b: 7; 1995a: 355; 1999b: 99. Again, the 'interruption' of the other is a term Levinas uses (1996a: 69).
43 See Derrida 2000b: 25. Derrida also claims that – by contrast – the genuine gift permits no such signature (1992b: 148, 171).
44 See also Derrida 1992b: 126; 2000b: 55; Caputo 1997a: 110–11.
45 See Derrida 1998c: 28; 2000c: 4–5. On 'giving time' to others refer to Derrida 1992b: 28.
46 See also Derrida 1999b: 45.
47 See also Levinas 1984: 63; Derrida 1997e: 14; 2003: 95. This is why Derrida remains suspicious of the notion of 'tolerance' (2003: 127–9).
48 See Kant 1976: 79; Derrida 1998c: 67.
49 See Derrida 1999c: 72.
50 See also Derrida 1992b: 7, 12–13, 35, 76, 91, 147, 156; 1997e: 18–19; 2001a: 34, 56; 2001e: 44, 48–51, 55. Regarding the aporia of the gift, compare Christ's warning: 'when you do some act of charity, do not let your left hand know what your right is doing' (Matthew 6:3–4) with Derrida's claim that 'like a gift confession must be from the unconscious' (1993a: 233). I discuss this in Plant 2004a.
51 Although this cannot be an *absolute* surprise, for otherwise 'that would make it impossible to recognize the surprise *as* a surprise.' Indeed, we would not even know 'that anything was happening at all' (Caputo 1993: 74; see also 2000: 113).
52 See Derrida 1993b: 33–4; 1997e: 17; 2000c: 8, 10; 2001a: 83; 2002a: 361, 372, 381. Again, this 'surprise' relates to Derrida's reflections on the gift (1992b: 122–3, 147).
53 See Matthew 24:36, 39, 42–51; Derrida 1997e: 22–4; 2001a: 31; 2002d: 14; 2002f: 94–6; Smith 1998.
54 See also Derrida 1993b: 33; 2001e: 22–3; 2002d: 12, 17; Caputo 2000: 113.
55 See also Luke 14:12–13. Contrast with 2 John 9–11. While Derrida acknowledges that all this is 'politically unacceptable' insofar as 'every nation-state is constituted by the control of its border' (2002f: 100, see also 115), he nevertheless maintains that 'a politics that does not maintain a reference to this principle of unconditional hospitality is a politics that loses its reference to justice' (ibid.: 101).
56 See also Derrida 1992b: 15–16, 82; 1993b: 11; 2000a: 353.
57 See also Derrida 1992b: 9, 35, 45–6, 55; 2002a: 362; Gaita 2000: 105–6. Note Derrida's remarks on the 'madness' of the gift (1992b: 9, 35, 45–6, 55).
58 See Derrida 1995a: 198; 1995b: 68; 1997a: 10; 1997b: 23, 28–9; 1998b: 31; 1998c: 62; 1999a: 70–1; 1999c: 72; 2001d: 68–9; 2002d: 11, 22, 79–81.
59 See Derrida 1997d: 112; 1998c: 14; 1999b: 35. On this point note also Derrida's memories of the Algerian war (1995a: 120).
60 See Baier 1986: 235; Derrida 2000b: 61, 125. Indeed, vulnerability is prerequisite for love and friendship *in general*, and this is why Levinas insists that the exposed, mortal 'body is the very condition of giving, with all that giving costs ... [giving] implies a body, because to give to the ultimate degree is to give bread taken from one's own mouth' (2000: 188; see also 1994a: 77).
61 See also Derrida 1992b: 12, 53–4, 64; 1995a: 387, 392; 1995c: 143; 1997a:

12–13, 16–17; 1997b: 28–9; 2000a: 352; 2002a: 402; 2003: 101; Bennington 2000a: 341, 348. Freud and Nietzsche are notable in this regard insofar as each 'shows himself *hospitable* to madness' (Derrida 1998a: 104); that is, insofar as each attempts a 'dialogue with madness *itself*' (ibid.: 83; see also 2002f: 217).
62 See Derrida 1999a: 70.
63 See Derrida 1992b: 12, 53–4, 62–4; Gaita 2000: 26–7.
64 See also Wittgenstein 1994a: 8; Levinas 1999: 101; Derrida 2000b: 25, 81–2; 2002c: 134.
65 See also Derrida 1995a: 198, 387; 1999c: 132–3; 2002f: 106, 108, 179, 238. The force of this 'must' is descriptive; radical evil is *of necessity* a possibility that haunts *every* event, even the most 'ethical.'
66 Despite these passages, for Bachelard the home remains essentially a shelter for 'day-dreaming' (1994: 6), where one's 'being' is first 'well-being' (ibid.: 12).
67 The 'threshold,' Lang remarks, is 'where I hospitably receive others into my personal domain ... My history is present at the portal and is preserved in the benign lingering or haunting presence of the people who have passed through this gateway' (1985: 207). In the light of our discussion, Lang's observation requires two qualifications. First, if the threshold (and 'home' more generally) is 'haunted,' it is not only by the 'people who have passed through,' but also the *other* others who have not been granted hospitality. The 'haunting presence' Lang rightly identifies cannot be restricted to those who have *actually* visited, for 'the other' as *possible* guest similarly troubles the home. Likewise, Lang's conjunction of 'benign lingering' and 'haunting presence' tends to imply that only the hospitable guest truly 'haunts' the threshold. But hauntings are not always 'benign,' for even the most amiable of guests must (*qua* guest) harbor the *possibility* of ingratitude, violence or evil. Moreover, even if the guest turns out to have been wholly peaceable, during their sojourn *other* other's have been denied *their* 'place in the sun' and thereby suffered a certain violence.
68 See Derrida 1990: 929; Kearney 1993; Baker 1995: 97–116.
69 Similarly hazardous moments appear in Derrida's remarks on Heidegger's 'silence' (Derrida 1988a: 145–8). This should be qualified, however, for Derrida is not necessarily suggesting that a world in which evil (and thus also good) *was not possible* would be 'worse' than *this* world.
70 Not to mention Derrida's preoccupation with confession (1992a: 34–5; 1993a: 160).
71 See Derrida 2000a: 402.
72 Even of those who believe (in a quasi-empirical way) in immortality, this point would still apply to their present 'earthly' existence. The structural law of iterability is not undermined by immortality (only here the figure of *actual* death would not represent iterability's most radical form of 'absence'). See Derrida's remarks on the immortality of language (2000a: 402–3), to which I will return.
73 See Derrida 1995b: 91.
74 See Levinas 2000: 21.
75 See also 2 Peter 3:10; Revelation 16:15.
76 See Derrida 1993b: 4, 26, 49, 65. Although '[d]*eath carries off what it touches*' and in that sense '*it precisely does not "visit"*' (Dufourmantelle 2000: 148–50).
77 See Derrida 1993b: 165, 206–7; 2001a: 23.
78 See Derrida 1993b: 51.
79 See Kierkegaard 1973: 103.
80 As such they are also always potentially inappropriate for the tragedy of the

deathbed scene (Rousseau 1953: 86; see also Derrida 2002c: 95), or, as in Wittgenstein's case, simply puzzling with respect to the life they bring to a close (Monk 1991: 579). In this respect every signature aspires to the finality of the last word of the deathbed (Bennington 1993: 157). Note also Montaigne's remarks on 'this last scene' which is 'judge of all the rest' (1958: 35).
81 See Derrida 2002c: 100.
82 By implication, this relation of independence necessitates caution regarding the notion of a wholly authoritative source or 'author.'
83 Obviously, this is not to deny that one's words *are* frequently lost or forgotten. The claim that language is 'immortal' is a structural point.
84 See Wittgenstein 1958: §§269-75.
85 See also Glendinning 1998: 107-27.
86 By means of this fiction I am deliberately attempting to constrain Derrida's suggestion that 'language *is*, in its structure, "immortal" ' (2000a: 402).
87 This scenario could be developed to encompass speech and non-linguistic 'marks.'
88 See Derrida 1992c: 142-3.
89 Indeed, Derrida responds to a skeptical interlocutor: 'show me a mark which cannot be iterated' (1992c: 155).
90 See Wittgenstein 1999: §337.
91 See Bennington 1993: 49, 52, 148.
92 See also Derrida 1988e: 593; 1993a: 191; 1996e: 186; 2000d: 45; 2001a: 88; 2002a: 382-4. The pre-performative 'Yes' Derrida refers to is at least a 'Yes, here I am *surviving.*'
93 Derrida criticizes one commentator for translating iterability into a 'thesis on our mortality,' when in fact it is a structural point: 'that for a sentence such as "I am dead" to *be* a sentence ... it has to be implied that I may be absent and that it can continue to function' (2000a: 400). After all, when Derrida speaks of 'death' it is 'just a figure to refer to this absence, to refer to the structural conditions of possibility for the sentence to be performed ... Thus, it is not a thesis about death' (ibid.: 401). While this point is well taken (not least because the law of iterability would still hold were one 'immortal' (2000a: 401)), given that death (in the usual sense of the word) is the most radical form of such 'absence,' Derrida's criticism is somewhat unjust.
94 Even the 'proper name' suffers this differential guilt (Bennington 1993: 105).
95 See Levinas 1999: 22-3, 32.
96 See Levinas 1994a: 91; Derrida 1996c: 5-6.
97 Confessional practice embodies certain features of the 'literary institution' – notably, the latter's right to 'say everything' (Derrida 1992a: 37; 2000d: 28). Here we might, for example, note the inherent risks of both offering (Rousseau 1953: 25, 31, 65, 84, 114-15, 134, 136) *and* receiving (Monk 1991: 368; Pascal 1996: 45-6, 49-50) a confession, and the status of the confessee as 'visitor' (thereby requiring a certain 'hospitality' of the confessor). Note also Levinas's remarks on the perils of forgiveness (1994b: 13-29).
98 See also Derrida 2001b: 56; 2001e: 29; 2002e: 389-90.
99 See also Derrida 2001b: 22.
100 See also Derrida 1997a: 10; 1997b: 20; 2000b: 83; 2000c: 8.
101 See Derrida 1997b: 20.
102 See Derrida 1998b: 23.
103 See Derrida 1997e: 22; 1998b: 18, 44-5, 47, 63-4; 1999a: 80, 82; 2001c: 254.
104 See also Derrida 1992b: 122-3; 2000a: 353; 2001d: 64-5, 99. These are '*quasi-transcendental*' (Bennington 2000b: 41) insofar as they constitute both the conditions of possibility *and* impossibility.
105 At least, not in any 'ordinary' sense. This does not contradict my claim

(in Chapter 7) that such things happen 'all the time.' For here we must demarcate between: (1) their 'happening' as known and intended consequences of one's actions, and (2) their 'happening' without intention or recognition (where one could only have a certain *faith* that they 'happen').
106 See Bennington 1993: 42–64.
107 See Derrida 1971: 309.
108 See also Derrida 1971: 324; 1998a: 31.
109 See Austin 1976: 9, 22, 104–5. According to Derrida, while Austin recognizes the structural possibility of such 'failures,' he trivializes them by appealing to 'ordinary language' and 'extenuating circumstances' (Derrida 1971: 323–5).
110 See also Derrida 1997d: 129.
111 See also Derrida 1992a: 68–9; Bennington 1993: 58.
112 See also Derrida 1997d: 117; 2001a: 72–3. For a synopsis of Derrida's reading of Austin, see Derrida 1992c: 154ff.; Glendinning 2000: 320ff. On a related point see also Levinas's remarks on phenomenology (1998c: 93).
113 See Derrida 1971: 321.
114 See Derrida 1993a: 12; 1995a: 175, 200, 372–3; 1995c: 143; 1996a: 62–3; 1997b: 28–9.
115 Even if all signs did *as a matter of fact* pass with total success, this would not undermine the structural point Derrida is making.
116 See Wittgenstein 1999: §178.
117 See Bennington 1993: 310; Derrida 1997d: 119.
118 While dogs (for example) may not be able to 'simulate pain' (Wittgenstein 1958: §250), I remain unconvinced that they are incapable of pretense more generally. Certainly many primates are capable of sophisticated types of deception.
119 See Wittgenstein 1990: §389.
120 See also Bennington 1993: 85–6; Wittgenstein 1995b: 80.
121 See Derrida 1971: 322–5.
122 See also Derrida 1997d: 89–90, 131.
123 See Derrida 1971: 310, 324–5, 327; 1995c: 143; Glendinning 2000: 328.
124 See also Dufourmantelle 2000: 136; Glendinning 2000: 330.
125 See Hertzberg 1988: 309; Lagenspetz 1992: 6, 8; Derrida 1997e: 22; 1998b: 18, 64; 1999a: 80; Ricoeur 1999: 17.
126 See Derrida 1971: 328; 1990a: 945; 1992b: 98; 1996b: 82; 1997e: 22; 1998b: 44, 63–4; 1998c: 9, 20–1. Compare Derrida's remarks on the 'believe me' and 'promise' (1996b: 82) with Winch 1960: 250.
127 See Derrida 1993a: 43, 51, 127; 1998c: 22.
128 See Derrida 1993a: 127.
129 Interestingly, Derrida describes himself as 'the last of the eschatologists' (1993a: 75; see also 1999e: 156–7, 165–7).
130 See also Wittgenstein 1990: §573.
131 See also Wittgenstein 1999: §§310, 329; Winch 1960: 242–4, 246.
132 See Derrida 1995a: 383–4; 1997e: 23.
133 See Wittgenstein 1958: §§8, 19–21, 60, 86, 143, 630.
134 See Baier 1986: 233–4; Bok 1989: 31; Wittgenstein 1999: §509.
135 Contrast Winch's point with Panaccio's remarks in Derrida 1992c: 147.
136 See also Winch 1960: 245–6; Derrida 2001a: 10.
137 See Wittgenstein 1999: §559.
138 See also Baier 1986: 233.
139 Derrida would doubtless question this as sounding suspiciously like an 'originary presence' (Culler 1987: 102ff.). On a related point, Wittgenstein's remarks on the relationship between '"primitive" ... *pre-linguistic*' (1990: §541) and linguistic behavior (that the latter 'is merely an auxiliary to, and

further extension of' (ibid.: §545) the former), would also seem to call for deconstructive analysis. Here one might recall Derrida's work on Rousseau in *Of Grammatology*, and specifically: (1) Rousseau's phonocentric characterization of writing as a 'supplement' to speech (Derrida 1998d: 141ff.; Norris 1987: 97–141; 1991: 32–41; Howells 1999: 43–60), and (2) his nostalgia for pre-social or 'primitive' (Norris 1987: 104) human expression. The question that emerges here is whether a deconstructive reading of Wittgenstein would reveal a similar phonocentrism at work? But Wittgenstein's position cannot be phonocentric in the sense Rousseau's perhaps is, for what Wittgenstein emphasizes is the *continuity* between pre-linguistic and linguistic behavior (1990: §545). As such, the hierarchical opposition between the primitive (natural) and linguistic (cultural) that Rousseau posits – and which feeds his nostalgia for the former – is effectively ruled out for Wittgenstein.

140 Of course, as Derrida notes, this notion of 'truth' is not 'truth in a theoretical sense' insofar as 'giving a false testimony' (2000a: 383) is here inscribed as a necessary possibility (2000d: 27–8, 29–31, 49, 72, 75; 2002c: 173). Note also Gaita's numerous references to 'confessional' writers (2000: 187–258).
141 See Hertzberg 1988: 309, 313.
142 See Baier 1986: 241–6; Hertzberg 1988: 318; Wittgenstein 1993: 377, 379, 381, 383, 385, 397, 399; 1999: §§115, 160, 341, 354. Bok thus notes how normally '[l]ying requires a *reason*, while truth-telling does not' (1989: 22).
143 From such passages one might build common ground between Derrida and Gadamer. I here have in mind their (almost) meeting in 1981, and specifically Derrida's suspicions concerning Gadamer's reference to the necessity of 'good will' in conversation (Wood 1990: 118–31). Likewise, Ricoeur's remarks on the necessity for sincerity in 'all the language games which can be considered acts of discourse' (and that '[a]ll the ways of being committed are marked by prior ethical structures. We don't know an ethically neutral world' (1992: 147)), seem consonant with Derrida's recent work.
144 See also Derrida 2001d: 97; 2001e: 16–17; 2002a: 362, 364.
145 See Derrida's remarks on the 'pledge' in 1989b: 129–30, n. 5.
146 This qualification is important, for, as discussed in Chapter 2, one can only doubt *x* on the grounds of *not* doubting many other things (Wittgenstein 1999: §§115, 160, 341, 450, 519).
147 See Glendinning 2000: 319, 327–31. Winch similarly claims that one can only 'mean what [one] says' if it is also possible to '*not* mean what [one] says' (1960: 248).
148 See also Derrida 1997e: 22–3; 2000b: 67.
149 Winch's reflections on the primacy of 'truth-telling' (that 'to act in the context of a social institution is always to commit oneself in some way for the future' (1960: 250)) parallel Derrida's emphasis on the pre-performative 'yes,' 'promise' and 'believe me' (1992a: 38, 70, 74, 257, 265, 272, 276, 279, 288–9, 294, 296–305; 1995a: 171–2, 261, 268, 382–4; 1996a: 68; 1996b: 82; 1996c: 3; 1997a: 16; 1997b: 28, 35; 1998b: 18, 26–8, 30, 44–5, 47, 63–4; 1998c: 21–2, 66–8, 93 n. 11; 1999a: 82; 2002f: 33–4, 247).
150 See Austin 1976: 25–52.
151 See Derrida 1997d: 122, 135; 1999b: 89. Compare also Derrida's remarks on the 'police' (1997d: 132–4, 138) with Wittgenstein's remarks on drawing a 'boundary' (1958: §499).
152 See Derrida 1995b: 67–71; 1996d: 215; 2000b: 55; 2001b: 49.
153 See Derrida 1992b: 64, 137–8, 142, 146, 162; 1995b: 107, 111–12; 1995c, 74, 133; 1996b: 86; 1997e: 48; 1999b: 48.
154 See Derrida 1995b: 71.
155 Derrida thus resists equating 'violence' with 'evil' (2001a: 90; see also 2002f: 80).

266 Notes

156 See also Derrida 1992b: 12; 2001b: 22.
157 See Hill 1997: 179–80; Derrida 2000b: 53–4, 59–61. Note also Levinas's remarks on 'wronging the third one' (1998b: 19).
158 On Derrida's account of friendship see Bennington 2000b: 110–27.
159 See Weil 1987: 88; Derrida 1997d: 112.
160 See also Derrida 2000b: 147–8; 2001a: 17; 2001e: 44–5.
161 See Gaita 2000: 7.
162 Blanchot suggests that the question 'Who is the other?' *already* perpetrates a violence insofar as it implies 'a nature ... or an essential trait.' Nevertheless, he later concedes that while this point 'must be recalled' such a 'precaution is somewhat ludicrous' (1997: 70; see also Derrida 2001e: 23). I take Blanchot's point to be in line with Derrida's; that such questions have to be asked, discriminations must be made (and so on) for ethics to get off the ground.
163 Moreover, in order to be hospitable and 'open my home' (Levinas 1996c: 171) to the other, I must thereby have a 'home' of some description (Derrida 1992b: 126; 2000c: 14). Indeed, recalling my previous remarks on Levinas's phenomenology of home, part of the tragedy of human destitution might be said to lie not only in the other's being without a 'private domain' (1996c: 152) in which to 'withdraw from the elements' (ibid.: 153) but also in their being denied the gift of *giving* hospitality (Derrida 1999b: 41–2).
164 See also Derrida 2001d: 87, 101, 107; 2002f: 92; 2003: 115.
165 See also Levinas 1988a: 177–8; Derrida 2001d: 98.
166 'It is necessary to do the impossible. If there is hospitality, the impossible must be done' (Derrida 2000c: 14).
167 See Wittgenstein 1994a: 77.
168 See Wittgenstein 1994a: 31.
169 See Derrida 1997e: 21–2.
170 See Derrida 1998a: 37.
171 See also Derrida 1990: 981; 1995c: 43, 81; 1998c: 9; 1999c: 60; 2001e: 31–3, 37–9.
172 See also Derrida 1992b: 8, 31; 1997b: 30; 1999c: 77.
173 See also Derrida 1997d: 116; 2002f: 31; 2003: 134.
174 See also Wittgenstein's remarks on genuine ritual (1994a: 8). Although I will not pursue this, there is doubtless much to be said regarding Derrida's account of the 'decision' and Wittgenstein's remarks on 'rule following.' One wonders, for example, whether Wittgenstein's notion of following a 'rule *blindly*' (1958: §219) complicates Derrida's account of the 'programmatic' decision? (note, however, Derrida's suspicion of the term 'blind' in this context (2002f: 231–2)).
175 See also Winch 1987: 179; Derrida 1999b: 116; 2002f: 229, 231–2; 2003: 118.
176 See also Derrida 1997b: 23; 2001b: 62; 2001d: 63.
177 Winch makes some closely related points regarding 'judgment' and 'risk' (1979: 60–2) in his critique of Apel.
178 See also Derrida 1995b: 24, 77; 1997a: 10; 1997b: 20, 34; 1997d: 148; 1998a: 113; 1999c: 133–4.
179 The minimal naturalism I have been defending does not undermine Derrida's account of the decision. Rather, all meaningful talk of 'decision' can only occur *within* certain natural boundaries. My decision to attend to the suffering of x rather than y is conditioned by x and y first being the sort of thing one *could* 'attend to' in this way. As such, when Wittgenstein claims that 'it is a primitive reaction to tend, to treat, the part that hurts when someone else is in pain; and *not merely* when oneself is' (1990: §540 my emphasis) this is not a refutation of the possibility (or necessity for) deliberation.
180 See Derrida 1990a: 963; 1997c: 133; 1999c: 133–4.

181 See also Derrida 1990: 967; 1997e: 117; 1999a: 67; 1999b: 117; 2000a: 383, 416; 2002f: 181, 200, 372; Caputo 1997a: 138.
182 See also Derrida 1990a: 965; 2001d: 103.
183 See also Derrida 1995b: 25; 2001a: 22; 2002f: 13–14.
184 Here we might recall Heidegger's remarks on the 'they' discussed in Chapter 6 (there is also more than a little Nietzchean suspicion of 'morality' in Derrida's work). See Bernstein 1991: 215.
185 See Derrida 1990a: 965; 1997d: 135.
186 See Derrida 1990a: 965.
187 See Levinas 1996c: 157, 170–4.
188 See Levinas 1998b: 20–1.
189 See also Derrida 2001a: 89.
190 See Derrida 1995b: 67–8, 70–1.
191 See Derrida 1995a: 272–3.
192 There is an internal peculiarity about the very notion of 'randomness' here insofar as any genuine randomness must necessarily be inscribed with the possibility of order. That is to say, there is a tendency to misconstrue randomness as that which *defies a rule*, whereas genuine randomness could manifest itself as complete order.
193 See Derrida 1990a: 961; 1996b: 83–4. In any case, there would here be a *decision* to act chaotically (just as one may decide not to decide about a specific matter) that would not *itself* be of the order of the 'chaotic.'
194 See Derrida 1988b: 594; 1995a: 272–3, 359; 1996d: 223; 1999a: 66; 2001a: 61.
195 To be anti-rational is to take a distinctive (subversive) stance toward rationality, and thus to recognize – albeit tacitly – the rule of reason itself.
196 See also Derrida 1995b: 95.
197 See Derrida 1999b: 112–13, 115. Note also Derrida's remarks on 'the rule of translation' (1997f: 233).
198 As Pascal remarks concerning the 'wager' on God's existence: 'you must bet. There is no option; you have [already] embarked on the business' (1961: p. 157). On the 'wager' and the 'incalculable,' see Derrida 2001a: 13.
199 See Derrida 1992a: 298.
200 See Derrida 1992a: 297, 299; Levinas 2001: 47, 59, 211–12. Derrida makes a similar claim about 'messianicity' (1999d: 253–5).
201 See Derrida 1992a: 257, 265, 270, 288, 296–9, 302; 2002f: 314.
202 See Derrida 1988a: 148; Plant 2001.
203 See Kellner 1992: 207; Heidegger 1999: p. 342.
204 See Derrida 1995a: 286–7. Not least because it is always possible to speak 'in order not to say anything' (Derrida 1995b: 76).
205 See Derrida 1989a: 837; 1992b: 16, 142, 148; 1995c: 16–17.
206 See also Derrida 1999a: 67–9; 2002f: 195.
207 See Derrida 1997b: 23.
208 See Derrida 1997e: 17.
209 A curious parallel emerges here with Moore's moral intuitionism, and specifically his account of the naturalistic fallacy. Moore argues that the 'Good' is indefinable insofar as it is not a 'composite' concept. That is: 'there is no meaning in saying that pleasure is good, unless good is something different from pleasure' (1948: 14). Moreover, 'whatever definition [of Good] be offered, it may be always asked, with significance, of the complex so defined, whether it is itself good' (ibid.: 15). With this in mind one might therefore note Derrida's claim that justice is undeconstructible (1997b: 27; 2001d: 87; 2002f: 104–5), and his suspicion of anyone's claiming to have acted 'justly' (1990: 935, 947, 949, 961–3, 967; 2001d: 87).
210 I thus take Caputo's remark that Derrida provokes us to think of 'obligation

268 *Notes*

without ... the deadening weight of guilt' (1997a: 149) to be potentially misleading. See Caputo's more recent remarks on ethics and 'bad conscience' (2000: 116).
211 See also Levinas 1998b: 114.
212 See also Levinas 1988a: 177.
213 See Levinas 1999: 170.
214 See Levinas 1999: 105; Derrida 2001a: 21–2. Although Derrida's account of literature is complex, a few general observations seem pertinent here. Derrida claims that '[w]hat we call literature ... implies that license is given to the writer to say everything he wants to or everything he can, while remaining shielded, safe from all censorship, be it religious or political' (1992a: 37; see also 1993a: 210; 1995a: 346; 1995c: 28; 1996b: 80). This 'promise' (1992a: 39) and 'power' to 'say everything' (ibid.: 37) is inseparable from those ethical-political questions pertaining to 'democracy ... human rights' and 'freedom of expression' (1996b: 80; see also 1995a: 10, 86, 213–14; 1995c: 15; 1997b: 31–2; 1999a: 67, 70). And this cardinal verbosity enables the literary establishment (and perhaps philosophy also (Derrida 1995a: 219, 327–8, 376–7)) to call its own institutionality into question, thus demarcating itself as a 'counter-institutional institution' (1992a: 58, see also 36, 72, 346). In other words, it is precisely literature's incessant desire to question the 'rules' (ibid.: 37) of its own institutionality that constitutes its ethical-political power. Of course, there could be no such transgression were there not some relatively determinate and regulated institution in the first place – Derrida (like Levinas) is not 'against' institutions *per se* (Derrida 1997d: 132–3, 141; 1997e: 12, 16–17, 21, 27). Nevertheless, the curious nature of the literary institution is constituted by this reflexive ability to call *itself* into question and thus, one might say, bear witness to a certain bad conscience.
215 See Levinas 1998a: 97; 2001: 98; Derrida 2001a: 20.
216 See also Levinas 1993: 44; 1998a: 93; 1999: 30.
217 See Levinas 1988a: 172–3; 1998b: 227.
218 See Caputo 1997b: 288ff. Note also Caputo's more recent remarks on his own (apparent) atheism (2001: 32).
219 See also Derrida 1995b: 6; 1999c: 73.
220 See Derrida 1998c: 41.
221 See also Derrida 2001a: 20; 2002c: 111–12, 140, 166, 189; 2002f: 27.
222 See Scanlon 1999: 224. Derrida's allusion to the 'absolutely universal' here (something Levinas also refers to (1988a: 177; 1994b: 15)) constitutes a direct challenge to those who judge his thinking to be essentially skeptical or relativistic (Derrida 2001a: 63–4).
223 As does the possibility of 'love without reward' (Levinas 1988a: 176; see also Derrida 1999b: 72).
224 With reference to §559 of *On Certainty,* Culler remarks that a Derridean might here object 'that one can never be quite certain who is playing [a language-game], or playing "seriously"' (1987: 130–1). This seems to me to rely too heavily on a quasi-communitarian reading of Wittgenstein that, as I have argued, neglects his underlying naturalism.

Bibliography

Annas, J. and Barnes, J. (eds) (1985) *The Modes of Skepticism: Ancient Texts and Modern Interpretations*, Cambridge, UK: Cambridge University Press.
Austin, J.L. (1976) *How To Do Things With Words*, Oxford: Oxford University Press.
Bachelard, G. (1994) *The Poetics of Space*, trans. M. Jolas, Boston, Mass.: Beacon Press.
Baier, A. (1986) 'Trust and Antitrust,' *Ethics* 96 (January): 231–60.
Baker, P. (1995) *Deconstruction and the Ethical Turn*, Gainesville, Fla.: University Press of Florida.
Balázs, B. (1985) 'The Close-Up' and 'The Face of Man,' in G. Mast and M. Cohen (eds) *Film Theory and Criticism: Introductory Readings*, Oxford: Oxford University Press, 255–64.
Bambrough, R. (1992) 'Fools and Heretics,' in P. Griffiths (ed.) *Wittgenstein: Centenary Essays*, Cambridge, UK: Cambridge University Press, 239–50.
Barker, E. (1990) 'New Lines in the Supra-market: How Much Can We Buy?,' in I. Hamnett (ed.) *Religious Pluralism and Unbelief: Studies Critical and Comparative*, London and New York: Routledge, 31–42.
Barrett, D.V. (1998) *Sects, 'Cults' & Alternative Religions: A World Survey and Sourcebook*, London: Blandford.
Barron, A. (1992) 'Lyotard and the Problem of Justice,' in A. Benjamin (ed.) *Judging Lyotard*, London and New York: Routledge, 26–42.
Barthes, R. (1990) *A Lover's Discourse: Fragments*, trans. R. Howard, Harmondsworth: Penguin.
—— (2000) *Camera Lucida*, trans. R. Howard, London: Vintage.
Bataille, G. (1996) *Visions of Excess: Selected Writings, 1927–1939*, trans. and ed. A. Stoekl *et al.*, Theory and History of Literature, 14, Minneapolis: University of Minnesota Press.
Baudelaire, C. (1996) *The Poems in Prose* (Vol. II) and *La Fanfarlo*, trans. and ed. F. Scarfe, London: Anvil Press Poetry.
Bauman, Z. (1995) *Postmodern Ethics*, Oxford: Basil Blackwell.
Benjamin, D.N. (ed.) (1995) *The Home: Words, Interpretations, Meanings, and Environments*, USA/Hong Kong/Singapore/Sidney: Avebury.
Bennington, G. (1988) *Lyotard: Writing the Event*, Manchester: Manchester University Press.
—— (1993) 'Derridabase,' in G. Bennington and J. Derrida, *Jacques Derrida*, Chicago and London: University of Chicago Press.
—— (2000a) 'For the Sake of Argument (Up to a Point),' in *Arguing with Derrida*, *Ratio* (new series), XIII, 4 (December): 332–54.

270 Bibliography

Bennington, G. (2000b) *Interrupting Derrida*, London and New York: Routledge.
Benso, S. (2000) *The Face of Things: A Different Side of Ethics*, Albany: State University of New York Press.
Bergson, H. (1911) *Laughter: An Essay on the Meaning of the Comic*, trans. C. Brereton and F. Rothwell, London: Macmillan.
Bernasconi, R. (1997) 'What Goes Around Comes Around: Derrida and Levinas in the Economy of the Gift and the Gift of Genealogy,' in A.D. Schrift (ed.) *The Logic of the Gift: Toward an Ethic of Generosity*, London and New York: Routledge, 256–73.
Bernstein, R.J. (1991) *The New Constellation: The Ethical-Political Horizons of Modernity/Postmodernity*, Oxford: Polity Press.
—— (2002) *Radical Evil: A Philosophical Investigation*, Oxford: Polity Press.
Bird, J. *et al.* (eds) (1993) *Mapping the Futures: Local Cultures, Global Change*, London and New York: Routledge.
Blanchot, M. (1986) 'Our Clandestine Companion,' in R.A. Cohen (ed.) *Face to Face with Levinas*, New York: State University of New York Press, 41–50.
—— (1995) *The Blanchot Reader*, M. Holland (ed.) Oxford: Basil Blackwell.
—— (1997) *The Infinite Conversation*, trans. S. Hanson, Theory and History of Literature, 82, Minneapolis and London: University of Minnesota Press.
Bloor, D. (1983) *Wittgenstein: A Social Theory of Knowledge*, London: Macmillan.
Bok, S. (1989) *Lying: Moral Choice in Public and Private Life*, New York: Vintage.
Bollnow, O.F. (1967) 'Lived-Space,' in N. Lawrence and D. O'Connor (eds) *Readings in Existential Phenomenology*, Englewood Cliffs, N.J.: Prentice-Hall, 178–86.
Breton, S. (1984) 'Being, God and the Poetics of Relation,' in R. Kearney, *Dialogues with Contemporary Continental Thinkers: The Phenomenological Heritage*, Manchester: Manchester University Press, 90–104.
Burnyeat, M.F. (1983) 'Can the Skeptic Live His Skepticism?,' in M. Burnyeat (ed.) *The Skeptical Tradition*, Berkeley: University of California Press, 117–48.
Cage, J. (1968) *A Year from Monday: Lectures and Writings*, London: Calder and Boyars.
Campbell, D. (1999) 'The Deterritorialization of Responsibility: Levinas, Derrida, and Ethics after the End of Philosophy,' in D. Campbell and M.J. Shapiro (eds) *Moral Spaces: Rethinking Ethics and World Politics*, Minneapolis: University of Minnesota Press, 29–56.
Campbell, D. and Shapiro, M.J. (eds) (1999) *Moral Spaces: Rethinking Ethics and World Politics*, Minneapolis: University of Minnesota Press.
Camus, A. (1975) *The Myth of Sisyphus*, trans. J. O'Brien, Harmondsworth: Penguin.
Caputo, J.D. (1993) *Against Ethics: Contributions to a Poetics of Obligation with Constant Reference to Deconstruction*, Bloomington and Indianapolis: Indiana University Press.
—— (1997a) 'Commentary,' in J.D. Caputo (ed.) *Deconstruction in a Nutshell: A Conversation with Jacques Derrida*, New York: Fordham University Press, 31–202.
—— (1997b) *The Prayers and Tears of Jacques Derrida: Religion without Religion*, Bloomington and Indianapolis: Indiana University Press.
—— (2000) 'The End of Ethics,' in H. Lafollette (ed.) *The Blackwell Guide to Ethical Theory*, Oxford: Basil Blackwell, 111–28.
—— (2001) *On Religion*, London and New York: Routledge.
—— (2003) 'Against Principles: A Sketch of an Ethics without Ethics,' in E. Wyschogrod and G.P. McKenny (eds) *The Ethical*, Oxford: Basil Blackwell, 169–80.

Carrol, D. (1987) *Paraesthetics: Foucault, Lyotard, Derrida*, London: Methuen.
Cavell, S. (1979) *The Claim of Reason: Wittgenstein, Skepticism, Morality, and Tragedy*, Oxford: Clarendon Press.
Caygill, H. (2002) *Levinas & the Political*, London and New York: Routledge.
Cioffi, F. (1998) *Wittgenstein on Freud and Frazer*, Cambridge UK: Cambridge University Press.
Clack, B.R. (1999) *An Introduction to Wittgenstein's Philosophy of Religion*, Edinburgh: Edinburgh University Press.
Cockburn, D. (1990) *Other Human Beings*, Basingstoke: Macmillan.
Connolly, W.E. (1999) 'Suffering, Justice, and the Politics of Becoming,' in D. Campbell and M.J. Shapiro (eds) *Moral Spaces: Rethinking Ethics and World Politics*, Minneapolis: University of Minnesota Press, 125–53.
Critchley, S. (1996) 'Deconstruction and Pragmatism – Is Derrida a Private Ironist or a Public Liberal?,' in C. Mouffe (ed.) *Deconstruction and Pragmatism*, London and New York: Routledge, 19–40.
—— (1999a) *The Ethics of Deconstruction: Derrida and Levinas*, Edinburgh: Edinburgh University Press.
—— (1999b) *Ethics–Politics–Subjectivity: Essays on Derrida, Levinas and Contemporary French Thought*, London and New York: Verso.
Culler, J. (1976) *Saussure*, Glasgow: Fontana/Collins.
—— (1987) *On Deconstruction: Theory and Criticism after Structuralism*, London and New York: Routledge.
Darwin, C. (1875) *The Descent of Man, and Selection in Relation to Sex*, London: John Murray.
Davidson, D. (1984) 'On the Very Idea of a Conceptual Scheme,' in *Inquiries into Truth and Interpretation*, Oxford: Clarendon Press, 183–98.
Davis, C. (1996) *Levinas: An Introduction*, Oxford: Polity Press.
Defoe, D. (1985) *The Life and Adventures of Robinson Crusoe*, Harmondsworth: Penguin.
Derrida, J. (1971) 'Signature Event Context,' in (1982) *Margins of Philosophy*, trans. A. Bass, Brighton: Harvester Press, 309–30.
—— (1982) *Positions*, trans. A. Bass, London: Athlone Press.
—— (1984) 'Deconstruction and the Other,' in R. Kearney, *Dialogues with Contemporary Continental Thinkers: The Phenomenological Heritage*, Manchester: Manchester University Press, 107–26.
—— (1985) 'Racism's Last Word,' trans. P. Kamuf, *Critical Inquiry* 12 (Autumn): 290–9.
—— (1988a) 'Heidegger's Silence,' trans. J. Neugroschel, in G. Neske and E. Kettering (eds) (1990) *Martin Heidegger and National Socialism*, New York: Paragon House, 145–8.
—— (1988b) 'Like the Sound of the Sea Deep within a Shell: Paul De Man's War,' trans. P. Kamuf, *Critical Inquiry* 14 (Spring): 590–652.
—— (1988c) '*Geschlecht* II: Heidegger's Hand,' in J. Sallis (ed.) *Deconstruction and Philosophy: The Texts of Jacques Derrida*, Chicago and London: University of Chicago Press, 161–96.
—— (1989a) 'Biodegradables: Seven Diary Fragments,' trans. P. Kamuf, *Critical Inquiry* 15 (Summer): 812–73.
—— (1989b) *Of Spirit: Heidegger and the Question*, trans. G. Bennington and R. Bowlby, Chicago: University of Chicago Press.

Derrida, J. (1990) 'Force of Law: The "Mystical Foundation of Authority",' trans. M. Quaintance, *Cardozo Law Review* 11, Nos 5–6, 921–1045.

—— (1991) 'At This Very Moment In This Work Here I Am,' trans. R. Berezdivin, in R. Bernasconi and S. Critchley (eds) *Re-Reading Levinas*, Bloomington and Indianapolis: Indiana University Press, 11–48.

—— (1992a) *Acts of Literature*, D. Attridge (ed.) London and New York: Routledge.

—— (1992b) *Given Time: I. Counterfeit Money*, trans. P. Kamuf, Chicago and London: University of Chicago Press.

—— (1992c) 'Philosophy and Communication: Round-table Discussion Between Ricoeur and Derrida,' trans. L. Lawlor, in L. Lawlor, *Imagination and Chance: The Difference Between the Thought of Ricoeur and Derrida*, Albany: State University of New York Press, 131–63.

—— (1993a) 'Circumfession,' trans. G. Bennington, in G. Bennington and J. Derrida, *Jacques Derrida*, Chicago and London: University of Chicago Press.

—— (1993b) *Aporias*, trans. T. Dutoit, Stanford, Calif.: Stanford University Press.

—— (1993c) '*Le toucher*: Touch/To Touch Him,' *Paragraph*, Vol. 16, No. 2 (July): 122–57.

—— (1995a) *Points . . . Interviews, 1974–1994*, trans. P. Kamuf *et al.*, E. Weber (ed.), Stanford, Calif.: Stanford University Press.

—— (1995b) *The Gift of Death*, trans. D. Wills, Chicago and London: University of Chicago Press.

—— (1995c) *On the Name*, trans. D. Wood *et al.*, T. Dutoit (ed.), Stanford, Calif.: Stanford University Press.

—— (1996a) *Archive Fever: A Freudian Impression*, trans. E. Prenowitz, Chicago and London: University of Chicago Press.

—— (1996b) 'Remarks on Deconstruction and Pragmatism,' trans. S. Critchley, in C. Mouffe (ed.) *Deconstruction and Pragmatism*, London and New York: Routledge, 77–88.

—— (1996c) 'Adieu,' trans. P.A. Brault and M. Naas, *Critical Inquiry* 23 (Autumn): 1–10.

—— (1996d) '*As If* I Were Dead: An Interview with Jacques Derrida,' in J. Brannigan, R. Robbins and J. Wolfreys (eds) *Applying: To Derrida*, Basingstoke: Macmillan, 212–26.

—— (1996e) 'By Force of Mourning,' trans. P.A. Brault and M. Naas, *Critical Inquiry* 22 (Winter): 171–92.

—— (1997a) 'Perhaps or Maybe' (interview with A.G. Düttmann), in J. Dronsfield and N. Midgley (eds) *Responsibilities of Deconstruction, Warwick Journal of Philosophy* 6 (Summer): 1–18.

—— (1997b) 'On Responsibility' (interview with J. Dronsfield and others), in J. Dronsfield and N. Midgley (eds) *Responsibilities of Deconstruction, Warwick Journal of Philosophy* 6 (Summer): 19–35.

—— (1997c) 'Violence and Metaphysics: An Essay on the Thought of Emmanuel Levinas,' trans. A. Bass, in *Writing and Difference*, London and New York: Routledge, 79–153.

—— (1997d) *Limited Inc.* (trans. various), Evanston, Ill.: Northwestern University Press.

—— (1997e) 'The Villanova Roundtable: A Conversation with Jacques Derrida,' in J.D. Caputo (ed.) *Deconstruction in a Nutshell: A Conversation with Jacques Derrida*, New York: Fordham University Press, 3–28.

—— (1997f) *Politics of Friendship*, trans. G. Collins, London: Verso.

—— (1998a) *Resistances of Psychoanalysis*, trans. P. Kamuf *et al.*, Stanford, Calif.: Stanford University Press.

—— (1998b) 'Faith and Knowledge: the Two Sources of "Religion" at the Limits of Reason Alone,' trans. S. Weber, in J. Derrida and G. Vattimo (eds) *Religion*, Oxford: Polity Press, 1–78.

—— (1998c) *Monolinguism of the Other; or, The Prosthesis of Origin*, trans. P. Mensah, Stanford, Calif.: Stanford University Press.

—— (1998d) *Of Grammatology*, trans. G.C. Spivak, London: Johns Hopkins University Press.

—— (1999a) 'Hospitality, Justice and Responsibility: A Dialogue with Jacques Derrida,' in R. Kearney and M. Dooley (eds) *Questioning Ethics: Contemporary Debates in Philosophy*, London and New York: Routledge, 65–83.

—— (1999b) 'A Word of Welcome,' trans. P.A. Brault and M. Naas, in *Adieu: To Emmanuel Levinas*, Stanford, Calif.: Stanford University Press, 15–152.

—— (1999c) Various remarks in J.D. Caputo and M.J. Scanlon (eds) *God, the Gift and Postmodernism*, Bloomington and Indianapolis: Indiana University Press.

—— (1999d) 'Marx & Sons,' in M. Sprinker (ed.) *Ghostly Demarcations: A Symposium on Jacques Derrida's* Spectres of Marx, London: Verso, 213–69.

—— (1999e) 'On a Newly Arisen Apocalyptic Tone in Philosophy,' trans. J. Leavey Jr., in *Raising the Tone of Philosophy: Late Essays by Immanuel Kant, Transformative Critique by Jacques Derrida*, Baltimore, Md.: Johns Hopkins University Press, 117–71.

—— (2000a) Various remarks in *Arguing with Derrida*, *Ratio* (new series), XIII 4 (December).

—— (2000b) 'Foreigner Question' and 'Step of Hospitality/No Hospitality,' in J. Derrida and A. Dufourmantelle, *Of Hospitality: Anne Dufourmantelle Invites Jacques Derrida to Respond*, trans. R. Bowlby, Stanford, Calif.: Stanford University Press.

—— (2000c) 'Hostipitality,' trans. B. Stocker and F. Morlock, *Angelaki* Vol. 5, No. 3 (December): 3–18.

—— (2000d) (with M. Blanchot) *The Instant of My Death/Demeure: Fiction and Testimony*, trans. E. Rottenberg, Stanford, Calif.: Stanford University Press.

—— (2001a) 'I Have a Taste for the Secret,' in J. Derrida and M. Ferraris, *A Taste for the Secret*, trans. G. Donis, G. Donis and D. Webb (eds), Oxford: Polity Press, 1–92.

—— (2001b) Various remarks in J.D. Caputo, M. Dooley and M.J. Scanlon (eds) *Questioning God*, Bloomington and Indianapolis: Indiana University Press.

—— (2001c) 'A Roundtable Discussion with Jacques Derrida,' in L. Simmons and H. Worth (eds) *Derrida Downunder*, Palmerston North, New Zealand: Dunmore Press, 249–63.

—— (2001d) Various remarks in P. Patton and T. Smith (eds) *Deconstruction Engaged: The Sydney Seminars*, Sydney: Power Publications.

—— (2001e) *On Cosmopolitanism and Forgiveness*, trans. M. Dooley and R. Kearney, London and New York: Routledge.

—— (2002a) 'Hostipitality,' trans. and ed. G. Anidjar, in *Acts of Religion*, London and New York: Routledge, 358–420.

—— (2002b) *Ethics, Institutions, and the Right to Philosophy*, trans. and ed. P.P. Trifonas, New York and Oxford: Rowman and Littlefield.

274 Bibliography

Derrida, J. (2002c) *Without Alibi*, trans. and ed. P. Kamuf, Stanford, Calif.: Stanford University Press.

—— (2002d) (with B. Stiegler) *Echographies of Television: Filmed Interviews*, trans. J. Bajorek, Cambridge, UK: Polity Press.

—— (2002e) 'The Animal That Therefore I Am (More to Follow),' trans. D. Wills, *Critical Inquiry* 28 (Winter): 369–418.

—— (2002f) *Negotiations: Interventions and Interviews 1971–2001*, trans. and ed. E. Rottenberg, Stanford, Calif,: Stanford University Press.

—— (2003) 'Autoimmunity: Real and Symbolic Suicides – A Dialogue with Jacques Derrida,' in G. Borradori, *Philosophy in a Time of Terror: Dialogues with Jürgen Habermas and Jacques Derrida*, Chicago and London: University of Chicago Press, 85–136.

Descartes, R. (1976) *Philosophical Writings*, trans. E. Anscombe and P.T. Geach, Middlesex: Nelson's University Paperbacks, Open University.

De Vries, H. (1999) *Philosophy and the Turn to Religion*, Baltimore, Md and London: Johns Hopkins University Press.

Dilman, I. (1987) *Love and Human Separateness*, Oxford: Basil Blackwell.

Diogenes, L. (1925) *Lives of the Eminent Philosophers*, trans. R.D. Hicks, London: Heinemann.

Dooley, M. (1999) 'The Politics of Exodus: Derrida, Kierkegaard, and Levinas on "Hospitality",' in R.L. Perkins (ed.) *International Kierkegaard Commentary: Works of Love*, Macon, Ga.: Mercer University Press, 167–92.

—— (2001) 'The Civic Religion of Social Hope: A Response to Simon Critchley,' in *Philosophy and Social Criticism*, Vol. 27, No. 5: 35–58.

Dostoyevsky, F. (1967) *The Brothers Karamazov I*, trans. D. Magarshack, Harmondsworth: Penguin.

Dovey, K. (1978) 'Home: An Ordering Principle in Space,' *Landscape*, Vol. 22, No. 2: 27–30.

Drury, M. (1981) 'Some Notes on Conversations with Wittgenstein' and 'Conversations with Wittgenstein,' in R. Rhees (ed.) *Ludwig Wittgenstein: Personal Recollections*, Oxford: Basil Blackwell, 91–189.

Dufourmantelle, A. (2000) 'Invitation,' in J. Derrida and A. Dufourmantelle, *Of Hospitality: Anne Dufourmantelle Invites Jacques Derrida to Respond*, trans. R. Bowlby, Stanford, Calif.: Stanford University Press.

Edwards, J.C. (1985) *Ethics Without Philosophy: Wittgenstein and the Moral Life*, Oxford: Basil Blackwell.

Engelmann, P. (1967) *Letters from Ludwig Wittgenstein, with a Memoir*, B.F. McGuinness (ed.), Oxford: Basil Blackwell.

Fann, K.T. (1969) *Wittgenstein's Conception of Philosophy*, Oxford: Basil Blackwell.

Feyerabend, P. (1987) *Science in a Free Society*, London: Verso.

—— (1988) *Against Method*, London: Verso.

Finch, H.R. (1975) 'Wittgenstein's Last Word: Ordinary Certainty,' *International Philosophical Quarterly* 15: 383–95.

Flew, A. (1971) 'Theology and Falsification: A Symposium' (with R.M. Hare and B. Mitchell), in B. Mitchell (ed.) *The Philosophy of Religion*, Oxford: Oxford University Press, 13–22.

Fogelin, R.J. (1986) 'Wittgenstein and Classical Skepticism,' in S. Shanker (ed.) *Ludwig Wittgenstein: Critical Assessments* (Vol. II), London: Croom Helm, 163–75.

—— (1987) *Wittgenstein*, London and New York: Routledge.

—— (1996) 'Wittgenstein's Critique of Philosophy,' in H. Sluga and D.G. Stern (eds) *The Cambridge Companion to Wittgenstein*, Cambridge, UK: Cambridge University Press, 34–58.
Foucault, M. (2000) *Aesthetics: Essential Works of Foucault 1954–1984* (Vol. 2), London: Penguin.
Frazer, J. (1993) *The Golden Bough: A Study in Magic and Religion*, Ware, Herts: Wordsworth.
Gaita, R. (1991) *Good and Evil: An Absolute Conception*, Basingstoke: Macmillan.
—— (1998) *Romulus, My Father*, London: Headline Book Publishing.
—— (2000) *A Common Humanity: Thinking about Love and Truth and Justice*, London and New York: Routledge.
—— (2003) *The Philosopher's Dog*, London and New York: Routledge.
Garver, N. and Lee, S.C. (1994) *Derrida & Wittgenstein*, Philadelphia: Temple University Press.
Gellner, E. (1993) *Postmodernism, Reason and Religion*, London and New York: Routledge.
Genova, J. (1995) *Wittgenstein: A Way of Seeing*, London and New York: Routledge.
Gill, J. (1974) 'Saying and Showing: Radical Themes in Wittgenstein's *On Certainty*,' *Religious Studies*, Vol. 10, No. 3 (September): 279–90.
Glendinning, S. (1998) *On Being With Others: Heidegger–Derrida–Wittgenstein*, London and New York: Routledge.
—— (1999) 'The Ethics of Exclusion: Incorporating the Continent,' in R. Kearney and M. Dooley (eds) *Questioning Ethics: Contemporary Debates in Philosophy*, London and New York: Routledge, 120–31.
—— (2000) 'Inheriting "Philosophy": The Case of Austin and Derrida Revisited,' in *Arguing with Derrida, Ratio* (new series) XIII 4 (December): 307–31.
Glock, H.J. (1996) *A Wittgenstein Dictionary*, Oxford: Basil Blackwell.
Graham, G. (2001) *Evil and Christian Ethics*, Cambridge, UK: Cambridge University Press.
Greenwood, E.B. (1975) *Tolstoy: The Comprehensive Vision*, London: J.M. Dent and Sons.
Greisch, J. (1991) 'The Face and Reading: Immediacy and Mediation,' in R. Bernasconi and S. Critchley (eds) *Re-Reading Levinas*, Bloomington and Indianapolis: Indiana University Press, 67–82.
—— (1999) 'Ethics and Lifeworlds,' in R. Kearney and M. Dooley (eds) *Questioning Ethics: Contemporary Debates in Philosophy*, London and New York: Routledge, 44–61.
Habermas, J. (1983) *Philosophical–Political Profiles*, trans. F.G. Lawrence, London: Heinemann.
—— (1996) *The Habermas Reader*, W. Outhwaite (ed.), Cambridge, UK: Polity Press.
Hall, R.A. (1996) *Isaac Newton: Adventurer in Thought*, Cambridge, UK: Cambridge University Press.
Handelman, S.A. (1991) *Fragments of Redemption: Jewish Thought & Literary Theory in Benjamin, Scholem, & Levinas*, Bloomington and Indianapolis: Indiana University Press.
Hankinson, R.J. (1995) *The Skeptics*, London and New York: Routledge.
Hardwick, C.S. (1971) *Language Learning in Wittgenstein's Later Philosophy*, The Hague: Mouton.
Harries, K. (1978) 'Death and Utopia: Towards a Critique of the Ethics of

Satisfaction,' in J. Sallis (ed.) *Radical Phenomenology: Essays in Honor of Martin Heidegger*, Atlantic Highlands, N.J.: Humanities Press, 138–52.
—— (1998) *The Ethical Function of Architecture*, Cambridge, Mass.: MIT Press.
Harvey, I.E. (1986) *Derrida and the Economy of Différence*, Bloomington: Indiana University Press.
Heidegger, M. (1961) *An Introduction to Metaphysics*, trans. R. Manheim, New York: Anchor.
—— (1982) *The Basic Problems of Phenomenology*, trans. A. Hofstadter, Indianapolis: Indiana University Press.
—— (1994) *Basic Writings*, trans. various, D.F. Krell (ed.), London and New York: Routledge.
—— (1999) *Being and Time*, trans. J. Macquarrie and E. Robinson, Oxford: Basil Blackwell.
Heller, J. (1961) *Catch-22*, London: Corgi.
Helvétius, C.A. (1969) 'On Man' (excerpt from *De L'Homme*), in L.G. Crocker (ed.) *The Age of Enlightenment*, New York: Harper and Row, 45–7.
Hertzberg, L. (1988) 'On the Attitude of Trust,' *Inquiry* 31: 307–22.
Hick, J. (ed.) (1966) *Faith and the Philosophers*, New York: St Martin's Press.
—— (1977) 'Jesus and the World Religions,' in J. Hick (ed.) *The Myth of God Incarnate*, London: SCM Press, 167–85.
—— (1988) *God and the Universe of Faiths: Essays in the Philosophy of Religion*, Basingstoke: Macmillan.
—— (1995) *The Rainbow of Faiths: Critical Dialogues on Religious Pluralism*, London: SCM Press.
Hill, L. (1997) *Blanchot: Extreme Contemporary*, London and New York: Routledge.
D'Holbach, P.H.D. (1969) 'Universal Morality, or the Duties of Man Founded on His Nature' (excerpt from *La Morale Universelle*), in L.G. Crocker (ed.) *The Age of Enlightenment*, New York: Harper and Row, 66–8.
Holland, R.F. (1990) 'Not Bending the Knee,' *Philosophical Investigations* Vol. 13, No. 1 (January): 18–30.
Hookway, C. (1990) *Skepticism*, London and New York: Routledge.
Howells, C. (1988) 'Sartre and Levinas,' in R. Bernasconi and D. Wood (eds) *The Provocation of Levinas: Rethinking the Other*, London and New York: Routledge, 91–9.
—— (1999) *Derrida: Deconstruction from Phenomenology to Ethics*, Oxford: Polity Press.
Hoyningen-Huene, P. (1993) *Reconstructing Scientific Revolutions: Thomas S. Kuhn's Philosophy of Science*, trans. A.T. Levine, Chicago: University of Chicago Press.
Hudson, W.D. (1986a) 'Wittgenstein on Fundamental Propositions,' in S. Shanker (ed.) *Ludwig Wittgenstein: Critical Assessments* (Vol. IV), London: Croom Helm, 116–28.
—— (1986b) 'The Light Wittgenstein Sheds on Religion,' in S. Shanker (ed.) *Ludwig Wittgenstein: Critical Assessments* (Vol. IV), London: Croom Helm, 167–84.
Hume, D. (1988) *Enquiries Concerning Human Understanding and Concerning the Principles of Morals* (rev. P.H. Nidditch), Oxford: Clarendon Press.
Husserl, E. (1970) *The Crisis of European Sciences and Transcendental Phenomenology: An Introduction to Phenomenological Philosophy*, trans. D. Carr, Evanston, Ill.: Northwestern University Press.
—— (1982) *Cartesian Meditations: An Introduction to Phenomenology*, trans. D. Cairns, The Hague: Martinus Nijhoff.

—— (1989) *Ideas Pertaining to a Pure Phenomenology and to a Phenomenological Philosophy (Second Book: Studies in the Phenomenology of Constitution)*, trans. R. Rojcewicz and A. Schuwer, Dordrecht: Kluwer Academic Publishers.

Ingold, T. (2000) *The Perception of the Environment: Essays in Livelihood, Dwelling and Skill*, Oxford: Basil Blackwell.

Inwood, B. and Gerson, L.P. (trans.) (1988) *Hellenistic Philosophy: Introductory Readings*, Indianapolis, Ind./Cambridge, Mass.: Hackett.

James, W. (1985) *The Varieties of Religious Experience: A Study in Human Nature*, Harmondsworth: Penguin.

Jay, M. (1993) *Downcast Eyes: The Denigration of Vision in Twentieth-Century French Thought*, Berkeley: University of California Press.

Johnston, P. (1991) *Wittgenstein and Moral Philosophy*, London and New York: Routledge.

Jones, K. (1986) 'Is Wittgenstein a Conservative Philosopher?,' *Philosophical Investigations* Vol. 9, No. 4 (October): 274–87.

Josipovici, G. (1999) *On Trust: Art and The Temptations of Suspicion*, New Haven, Conn: Yale University Press.

Kant, I. (1976) 'Groundwork of the Metaphysic of Morals,' trans. H.J. Paton, in H.J. Paton, *The Moral Law: Kant's Groundwork of the Metaphysic of Morals*, London: Hutchinson and Co., 53–123.

Kearney, R. (1984) *Dialogues with Contemporary Continental Thinkers: The Phenomenological Heritage*, Manchester: Manchester University Press.

—— (1993) 'Derrida's Ethical Re-Turn,' in G.B. Madison (ed.) *Working Through Derrida*, Evanston, Ill.: Northwestern University Press, 28–50.

Kellner, D. (1992) 'Authenticity and Heidegger's Challenge to Ethical Theory,' in C. Macann (ed.) *Martin Heidegger: Critical Assessments* (Vol. IV), London and New York: Routledge, 198–213.

Kerr, F. (1997) *Theology after Wittgenstein*, London: SPCK.

Kierkegaard, S. (1965) 'The Journals,' trans. and ed. A. Dru, in *The Journals of Kierkegaard 1834–1854*, London and Glasgow: Fontana, 39–254.

—— (1973) *A Kierkegaard Anthology*, R. Bretall (ed.) Princeton, N.J.: Princeton University Press.

—— (1985) *Fear and Trembling*, trans. A. Hannay, Harmondsworth: Penguin.

King, J. (1981) 'Recollections of Wittgenstein,' in R. Rhees (ed.) *Ludwig Wittgenstein: Personal Recollections*, Oxford: Basil Blackwell, 83–90.

Kober, M. (1996) 'Certainties of a World-picture: The Epistemological Investigations of *On Certainty*,' in H. Sluga and D.G. Stern (eds) *The Cambridge Companion to Wittgenstein*, Cambridge, UK: Cambridge University Press, 411–41.

Kolakowski, L. (1999) *Freedom, Fame, Lying and Betrayal: Essays on Everyday Life*, trans. A. Kolakowski, Harmondsworth: Penguin.

Kuhn, T. (1996) *The Structure of Scientific Revolutions*, Chicago and London: The University of Chicago Press.

Kundera, M. (1998) *Identity*, trans. L. Asher, London and Boston: Faber and Faber.

Lagenspetz, O. (1992) 'Legitimacy and Trust,' *Philosophical Investigations* Vol. 15, No. 1 (January): 1–21.

Lang, R. (1985) 'The Dwelling Door: Towards a Phenomenology of Transition,' in D. Seamon and R. Mugerauer (eds) *Dwelling, Place and Environment: Towards a Phenomenology of Person and World*, Dordrecht/Boston/Lancaster: Martinus Nijhoff, 201–13.

Levi, P. (1996) *If This is a Man/The Truce*, trans. S. Woolf, London: Vintage.
—— (1998) *The Drowned and the Saved*, trans. R. Rosenthal, London: Abacus.
Levinas, E. (1984) 'Ethics of the Infinite,' in R. Kearney, *Dialogues with Contemporary Continental Thinkers: The Phenomenological Heritage*, Manchester: Manchester University Press, 49–69.
—— (1987) *Collected Philosophical Papers*, trans. A. Lingis, Dordrecht: Martinus Nijhoff Publishers.
—— (1988a) 'The Paradox of Morality: An Interview with Emmanuel Levinas,' trans. A. Benjamin and T. Wright, in R. Bernasconi and D. Wood (eds) *The Provocation of Levinas: Rethinking the Other*, London and New York: Routledge, 168–80.
—— (1988b) 'Useless Suffering,' trans. R. Cohen, in R. Bernasconi and D. Wood (eds) *The Provocation of Levinas: Rethinking the Other*, London and New York: Routledge, 156–80.
—— (1989) 'As if Consenting to Horror,' trans. P. Wissing, *Critical Inquiry* 15 (Winter): 485–8.
—— (1992) *Ethics and Infinity: Conversations with Philippe Nemo*, trans. R.A. Cohen, Pittsburgh: Duquesne University Press.
—— (1993) *Outside the Subject*, trans. M.B. Smith, London: Athlone Press.
—— (1994a) *Otherwise Than Being Or Beyond Essence*, trans. A. Lingis, Dordrecht: Kluwer Academic Publishers.
—— (1994b) *Nine Talmudic Readings*, trans. A. Aronowicz, Bloomington and Indianapolis: Indiana University Press.
—— (1995) 'Philosophy and the Idea of the Infinite,' in A. Peperzak, *To The Other: An Introduction to the Philosophy of Emmanuel Levinas*, Indiana: Purdue University Press, 88–119.
—— (1996a) *Basic Philosophical Writings*, A. Peperzak *et al.* (eds), Bloomington and Indianapolis: Indiana University Press.
—— (1996b) *The Levinas Reader*, S. Hand (ed.), Oxford: Basil Blackwell.
—— (1996c) *Totality and Infinity: An Essay on Exteriority*, trans. A. Lingis, Pittsburgh: Duquesne University Press.
—— (1996d) *Proper Names*, trans. M.B. Smith, London: Athlone Press.
—— (1997a) *Difficult Freedom: Essays on Judaism*, trans. S. Hand, Baltimore, Md.: Johns Hopkins University Press.
—— (1997b) *Time and the Other*, trans. R.A. Cohen, Pittsburgh: Duquesne University Press.
—— (1998a) *Of God Who Comes To Mind*, trans. B. Bergo, Stanford, Calif.: Stanford University Press.
—— (1998b) *Entre Nous: Thinking-of-the-Other*, trans. M.B. Smith and B. Harshav, New York: Columbia University Press.
—— (1998c) *Discovering Existence with Husserl*, trans. R.A. Cohen and M.B. Smith, Evanston, Ill.: Northwestern University Press.
—— (1999) *Alterity & Transcendence*, trans. M.B. Smith, London: Athlone Press.
—— (2000) *God, Death, and Time*, trans. B. Bergo, Stanford, Calif.: Stanford University Press.
—— (2001) *Is It Righteous To Be? Interviews with Emmanuel Levinas*, J. Robbins (ed.), Stanford, Calif.: Stanford University Press.
Llewelyn, J. (1991) *The Middle Voice of Ecological Conscience: A Chiasmic Reading of Responsibility in the Neighborhood of Levinas, Heidegger and Others*, London: Macmillan.

—— (2002) *Appositions of Jacques Derrida and Emmanuel Levinas*, Bloomington and Indianapolis: Indiana University Press.

Love, N.S. (1995) 'What's Left of Marx?,' in S.K. White (ed.) *The Cambridge Companion to Habermas*, Cambridge, UK: Cambridge University Press:, 46–66.

Luckhardt, C.G. (1991) 'Philosophy in the *Big Typescript*,' in J. Hintikka (ed.) *Wittgenstein in Florida* (Proceedings of the Colloquium on the Philosophy of Ludwig Wittgenstein, Florida State University, 7–8 August 1989), Dordrecht/Boston/London: Kluwer Academic Publishers, 255–72.

Lyotard, J.F. (1985) *Just Gaming*, trans. W. Giodzich, Manchester: Manchester University Press.

—— (1988) *The Differend: Phrases in Dispute*, trans. G. Abbeele, Manchester: Manchester University Press.

—— (1993) *Political Writings*, trans. B. Readings and K.P. Geiman, London: University College London Press.

—— (1997a) *The Postmodern Condition: A Report on Knowledge*, trans. G. Bennington and B. Massumi, Manchester: Manchester University Press.

—— (1997b) *Postmodern Fables*, trans. G. Abbeele, Minneapolis: University of Minnesota Press.

Macann, C. (1992) 'Who is Dasein? Towards an Ethics of Authenticity,' in C. Macann (ed.) *Martin Heidegger: Critical Assessments* (Vol. IV), London and New York: Routledge, 214–46.

Malcolm, N. (1958) *Ludwig Wittgenstein: A Memoir*, London: Open University Press.

—— (1960) 'Anselm's Ontological Arguments,' *The Philosophical Review*, Vol. LXIX: 41–62.

—— (1972) 'The Groundlessness of Belief,' in *Thought and Knowledge: Essays by Norman Malcolm*, Ithaca, N.Y.: Cornell University Press, 199–216.

—— (1986) 'Wittgenstein: The Relation of Language to Instinctive Behavior,' in S. Shanker (ed.) *Ludwig Wittgenstein: Critical Assessments* (Vol. II), London: Croom Helm, 303–18.

—— (1990) 'On "Ceasing to Exist",' in R. Gaita (ed.) *Value and Understanding: Essays for Peter Winch*, London and New York: Routledge, 1–12.

—— (1993) *Wittgenstein: A Religious Point of View?*, P. Winch (ed.), London and New York: Routledge.

Martin, D. (1984) '*On Certainty* and Religious Belief,' *Religious Studies*, Vol. 20, No. 4 (December): 593–613.

Mates, B. (trans., introduction and commentary) (1996) *The Skeptic Way: Sextus Empiricus's* Outlines of Pyrrhonism, Oxford: Oxford University Press.

McGinn, M. (1997) *Wittgenstein and the* Philosophical Investigations, London and New York: Routledge.

Melville, P. (1999) *The Migration of Ghosts*, London: Bloomsbury.

Merleau-Ponty, M. (1996) *Phenomenology of Perception*, trans. C. Smith, London and New York: Routledge.

Mole, G.D. (1997) *Lévinas, Blanchot, Jabès: Figures of Estrangement*, Gainesville, Fla.: University Press of Florida.

Molloy, P. (1999) 'Face-to-Face with the Dead Man: Ethical Responsibility, State-Sanctioned Killing, and Empathetic Impossibility,' in D. Campbell and M.J. Shapiro (eds) *Moral Spaces: Rethinking Ethics and World Politics*, Minneapolis and London: University of Minnesota Press, 211–37.

Monk, R. (1991) *Ludwig Wittgenstein: The Duty of Genius*, London: Vintage.

Bibliography

Montaigne, M. (1958) *Essays*, trans. J.M. Cohen, Harmondsworth: Penguin.
Moon, D. (1995) 'Practical Discourse and Communicative Ethics,' in S.K. White (ed.) *The Cambridge Companion to Habermas*, Cambridge, UK: Cambridge University Press, 143–64.
Moore, G.E. (1948) *Principia Ethica*, Cambridge, UK: Cambridge University Press.
—— (1993) 'Wittgenstein's Lectures in 1930–33,' in L. Wittgenstein, *Philosophical Occasions 1912–1951*, J. Klagge and A. Nordmann (eds), Indianapolis, Ind./Cambridge, Mass.: Hackett, 46–114.
—— (1994a) 'A Defence of Common Sense,' in R. Ammerman (ed.) *Classics of Analytic Philosophy*, Indianapolis, Ind./Cambridge, Mass.: Hackett, 47–67.
—— (1994b) 'Proof of an External World,' in R. Ammerman (ed.) *Classics of Analytic Philosophy*, Indianapolis, Ind./Cambridge, Mass.: Hackett, 68–84.
Morawetz, T. (1978) *Wittgenstein and Knowledge: The Importance of* On Certainty, Amherst: University of Massachusetts Press.
Morris, P. (1990) 'Judaism and Pluralism: The Price of Religious Freedom,' in I. Hamnett (ed.) *Religious Pluralism and Unbelief: Studies Critical and Comparative*, London and New York: Routledge, 179–201.
Mulhall, S. (1993) *On Being in the World: Wittgenstein and Heidegger on Seeing Aspects*, London and New York: Routledge.
—— (1996) *Heidegger and* Being and Time, London and New York: Routledge.
Nelson, G.K. (1987) *Cults, New Religions and Religious Creativity*, London and New York: Routledge.
Nielsen, K. (1967) 'Wittgensteinian Fideism,' *Philosophy: The Journal of the Royal Institute of Philosophy*, Vol. XLII, No. 161 (July): 191–209.
Nietzsche, F. (1968) *The Will to Power*, trans. W. Kaufmann and R.J. Hollingdale, W. Kaufmann (ed.), New York: Vintage.
—— (1972a) *Twilight of the Idols* and *The Anti-Christ*, trans. R.J. Hollingdale, Harmondsworth: Penguin.
—— (1972b) *Thus Spoke Zarathustra: A Book for Everyone and No One*, trans. R.J. Hollingdale, Harmondsworth: Penguin.
—— (1977) *A Nietzsche Reader*, trans. R.J. Hollingdale, London: Penguin.
—— (1987) *Beyond Good and Evil*, trans. R.J. Hollingdale, Harmondsworth: Penguin.
—— (1989) 'On the Origin of Language,' in *Friedrich Nietzsche on Rhetoric and Language*, trans. and eds S.L. Gilman, C. Blair and D.J. Parent, New York and Oxford: Oxford University Press, 209–12.
—— (1992a) *Ecco Homo: How One Becomes What One Is*, trans. R.J. Hollingdale, London: Penguin.
—— (1992b) *On the Genealogy of Morality*, trans. C. Diethe, K. Ansell-Pearson (ed.), Cambridge, UK: Cambridge University Press.
—— (1994) *Human, All Too Human*, trans. M. Faber and S. Lehmann, London: Penguin.
Norris, C. (1987) *Derrida*, London: Fontana Press.
—— (1991) *Deconstruction: Theory and Practice*, London and New York: Routledge.
Nussbaum, M. (1991) 'Skeptic Purgatives: Therapeutic Arguments in Ancient Skepticism,' *Journal of the History of Philosophy*, Vol. 29, No. 4 (October): 521–57.
Nuyen, A.T. (2000) 'Lévinas and the Ethics of Pity,' *International Philosophical Quarterly*, Vol. XL, No. 4, Issue No. 160 (December): 411–21.

Nyíri, J.C. (1982) 'Wittgenstein's Later Work in Relation to Conservatism,' in B. McGuinness (ed.) *Wittgenstein and His Times*, Oxford: Basil Blackwell, 44–68.
Pascal, B. (1961) *The Pensées*, trans. J.M. Cohen, Harmondsworth: Penguin.
Pascal, F. (1996) 'Wittgenstein: A Personal Memoir,' in C.G. Luckhardt (ed.) *Wittgenstein: Sources and Perspectives*, Bristol: Thoemmes Press, 23–60.
Passmore, J. (1968) *Hume's Intentions*, London: Duckworth.
Patrick, M. (1997) *Derrida, Responsibility and Politics*, Aldershot, Ashgate: Athenaeum Press.
Peperzak, A. (1993) *To the Other: An Introduction to the Philosophy of Emmanuel Levinas*, Indiana: Purdue University Press.
—— (1997) *Beyond: The Philosophy of Emmanuel Levinas*, Evanston, Ill.: Northwestern University Press.
Peukert, H. (1998) 'Unconditional Responsibility for the Other: The Holocaust and the Thinking of Emmanuel Levinas,' trans. F.S. Gardiner, in A. Milchman and A. Rosenberg (eds) *Postmodernism and the Holocaust*, Amsterdam/Atlanta, Ga.: Rodopi, 155–65.
Phillips, D.Z. (1970) *Death and Immortality*, London and Basingstoke: Macmillan, St Martin's Press.
—— (1986) *Belief, Change and Forms of Life*, Atlantic Highlands, N.J.: Humanities Press International.
—— (1988) *Faith After Foundationalism*, London and New York: Routledge.
Picard, M. (1948) *The World of Silence*, trans. S. Goodman, London: Harvill Press.
Pinker, S. (1994) *The Language Instinct: The New Science of Language and Mind*, London: Lane.
Pitkin, H.F. (1993) *Wittgenstein and Justice: On the Significance of Ludwig Wittgenstein for Social and Political Thought*, Berkeley, Los Angeles, London: University of California Press.
Plant, B. (2001) 'On Heidegger's Silence,' *Philosophical Writings*, Nos. 15–16 (Spring): 3–21.
—— (2003a) 'Our Natural Constitution: Wolterstorff on Reid and Wittgenstein,' in *Journal of Scottish Philosophy*, Vol. 1, No. 2 (Autumn): 157–70.
—— (2003b) 'Blasphemy, Dogmatism and Injustice: The Rough Edges of *On Certainty*,' in *International Journal for Philosophy of Religion*, Vol. 54, No. 2 (October): 101–35.
—— (2003c) 'Doing Justice to the Derrida-Levinas Connection: A Response to Mark Dooley,' in *Philosophy and Social Criticism*, Vol. 29, No. 4 (July): 427–50.
—— (2003d) 'Ethics without Exit: Levinas and Murdoch,' in *Philosophy and Literature*, Vol. 27, No. 2 (October): 456–70.
—— (2004a) 'Christ's Autonomous Hand: Simulations on the Madness of Giving,' in *Modern Theology*, Vol. 20, No. 4 (October): 547–66.
—— (2004b) 'The End(s) of Philosophy: Rhetoric, Therapy and Wittgenstein's Pyrrhonism,' in *Philosophical Investigations*, Vol. 27, No. 3 (July): 222–57.
Plantinga, A. (1998) *The Analytic Theist: An Alvin Plantinga Reader*, Grand Rapids, Mich.: W.B. Eerdmans Publishing.
Popkin, R.H. (1979) *The History of Skepticism from Erasmus to Spinoza*, Berkeley, Los Angeles, London: University of California Press.
Preston, J. (1997) *Feyerabend: Philosophy, Science and Society*, Oxford: Polity Press.
Putnam, H. (1999) Introduction, in F. Rosenzweig, *Understanding the Sick and the*

282 Bibliography

Healthy: A View of World, Man, and God, trans. N. Glatzer, Cambridge, Mass. and London: Harvard University Press, 1–20.

—— (2002) 'Levinas and Judaism,' in S. Critchley and R. Bernasconi (eds) *The Cambridge Companion to Levinas*, Cambridge, UK: Cambridge University Press, 33–62.

Quine, W.V.O. (1994) *From a Logical Point of View: Nine Logico-Philosophical Essays*, Cambridge, Mass. and London: Harvard University Press.

—— (with J.S. Ullian) (1970) *The Web of Belief*, New York: Random House.

Readings, B. (1991) *Introducing Lyotard: Art and Politics*, London and New York: Routledge.

—— (1992) 'Pagans, Perverts or Primitives? Experimental Justice in the Empire of Capital,' in A. Benjamin (ed.) *Judging Lyotard*, London and New York: Routledge, 168–91.

Redpath, T. (1990) *Ludwig Wittgenstein: A Student's Memoir*, London: Duckworth.

Reid, T. (1997) *An Inquiry into the Human Mind: On the Principles of Common Sense*, D.R. Brookes (ed.), Edinburgh: Edinburgh University Press.

Rhees, R. (1969) *Without Answers*, London and New York: Routledge.

—— (1981) 'Postscript,' in R. Rhees (ed.) *Ludwig Wittgenstein: Personal Recollections*, Oxford: Basil Blackwell, 190–231.

—— (1996) *Discussions of Wittgenstein*, Bristol: Thoemmes Press.

Ricoeur, P. (1992) 'Philosophy and Communication: Round-table Discussion Between Ricoeur and Derrida,' trans. L. Lawlor, in L. Lawlor, *Imagination and Chance: The Difference Between the Thought of Ricoeur and Derrida*, Albany: State University of New York Press, 131–63.

—— (1999) 'Imagination, Testimony and Trust,' in R. Kearney and M. Dooley (eds) *Questioning Ethics: Contemporary Debates in Philosophy*, London and New York: Routledge, 12–17.

Robbins, J. (1999) *Altered Reading: Levinas and Literature*, Chicago and London: University of Chicago Press.

Rorty, R. (1996) 'Response to Simon Critchley,' in C. Mouffe (ed.) *Deconstruction and Pragmatism*, London and New York: Routledge, 41–6.

—— (1999) *Philosophy and Social Hope*, London: Penguin.

Rose, G. (1997) *Love's Work*, London: Vintage.

Rosenzweig, F. (1999) *Understanding the Sick and the Healthy: A View of World, Man, and God*, trans. N. Glatzer, Cambridge, Mass. and London: Harvard University Press.

Rousseau, J.-J. (1930) *The Social Contract & Discourses*, trans. G.D.H. Cole, London and Toronto: J.M. Dent and Sons.

—— (1953) *The Confessions*, trans. J.M. Cohen, London: Penguin.

—— (1973) (excerpts from) *Emile*, trans. W. Boyd, in W. Boyd (ed.) *Emile For Today*, London: Heinemann.

Sade, D.A.F. (1969) (excerpt from) *Juliette, or the Prosperities of Vice*, trans. L.G. Crocker, in L.G. Crocker (ed.) *The Age of Enlightenment*, New York: Harper and Row, 172–6.

—— (1991a) *Philosophy in the Boudoir*, trans. M. Bodroghy, London: Creation Press.

—— (1991b) *The Passionate Philosopher: A Marquis de Sade Reader*, M. Crosland (ed.), London: Owen.

Sartre, J.-P. (1977) *Existentialism and Humanism*, trans. P. Mairet, London: Methuen.

—— (1993) *Being and Nothingness: An Essay on Phenomenological Ontology*, trans. H.E. Barnes, London and New York: Routledge.
Scanlon, M.J. (1999) 'A Deconstruction of Religion: On Derrida and Rahner,' in J.D. Caputo and M.J. Scanlon (eds) *God, the Gift, and Postmodernism*, Bloomington and Indianapolis: Indiana University Press, 223–8.
Scheman, N. (1996) 'Forms of Life: Mapping the Rough Ground,' in H. Sluga and D.G. Stern (eds) *The Cambridge Companion to Wittgenstein*, Cambridge, UK: Cambridge University Press, 383–410.
Schopenhauer, A. (1918) *On Human Nature: Essays (Partly Posthumous) in Ethics and Politics*, trans. T.B. Saunders, London: Allen and Unwin.
—— (1995) *On The Basis of Morality*, trans. E.F.J. Payne, Oxford: Berghahn.
Schulte, J. (1986) 'Wittgenstein and Conservatism,' in S. Shanker (ed.) *Ludwig Wittgenstein: Critical Assessments* (Vol. IV), London: Croom Helm, 60–9.
Schutz, A. (1964) *Collected Papers II: Studies in Social Theory*, A. Brodersen (ed.), The Hague: Martinus Nijhoff.
—— (1966) *Collected Papers III: Studies in Phenomenological Philosophy*, I. Schutz (ed.), The Hague: Martinus Nijhoff.
—— (1970a) *Reflections on the Problem of Relevance*, R.M. Zaner (ed.), New Haven, Conn. and London: Yale University Press.
—— (1970b) *On Phenomenology and Social Relations: Selected Writings*, H.R. Wagner (ed.), Chicago and London: University of Chicago Press.
—— (1971) *Collected Papers I: The Problem of Social Reality*, M. Natanson (ed.), The Hague: Martinus Nijhoff.
—— (with T. Luckmann) (1974) *The Structures of the Life-World*, trans. R.M. Zaner and H.T. Engelhardt, Jr., London: Heinemann.
Seamon, D. (1979) *The Geography of the Lifeworld: Movement, Rest and Encounter*, London: Croom Helm.
Seamon, D. and Mugerauer, R. (eds) (1985) *Dwelling, Place and Environment: Towards a Phenomenology of Person and World*, Dordrecht/Boston/Lancaster: Martinus Nijhoff.
Sextus Empiricus (1996) 'Outlines of Pyrrhonism,' trans. B. Mates, in B. Mates, *The Skeptic Way: Sextus Empiricus's* Outlines of Pyrrhonism, Oxford: Oxford University Press, 88–217.
Shapiro, M.J. (1999) 'The Ethics of Encounter: Unreading, Unmapping the Imperium,' in D. Campbell and M.J. Shapiro (eds) *Moral Spaces: Rethinking Ethics and World Politics*, Minneapolis: University of Minnesota Press, 57–91.
Shields, P.R. (1997) *Logic and Sin in the Writings of Ludwig Wittgenstein*, Chicago and London: University of Chicago Press.
Shusterman, R. (1997) *Practicing Philosophy: Pragmatism and the Philosophical Life*, New York: Routledge.
Singer, P. (1995) *Practical Ethics*, Cambridge, UK: Cambridge University Press.
Sluga, H. (1996) 'Ludwig Wittgenstein: Life and Work An introduction,' in H. Sluga and D.G. Stern (eds) *The Cambridge Companion to Wittgenstein*, Cambridge, UK: Cambridge University Press, 1–33.
Smart, N. (1971) 'Conversation with Ninian Smart: Philosophy and Religion,' in B. Magee, *Modern British Philosophy*, London: Secker and Warburg, 166–77.
Smith, J.K.A. (1998) 'Determined Violence: Derrida's Structural Religion,' *The Journal of Religion*, Vol. 78: 197–212.

284 Bibliography

Sontag, F. (1995) *Wittgenstein and the Mystical: Philosophy as an Ascetic Practice*, Atlanta, Ga.: Scholars Press.
Staten, H. (1986) *Wittgenstein and Derrida*, Lincoln and London: University of Nebraska Press.
Steuerman, E. (1992) 'Habermas vs Lyotard: Modernity vs Postmodernity?,' in A. Benjamin (ed.) *Judging Lyotard*, London and New York: Routledge, 99–118.
Stone, I.F. (1998) *Reading Levinas/Reading Talmud: An Introduction*, Philadelphia and Jerusalem: The Jewish Publication Society.
Sugden, C. (1990) 'Evangelicals and Religious Pluralism,' in I. Hamnett (ed.) *Religious Pluralism and Unbelief: Studies Critical and Comparative*, London and New York: Routledge, 148–65.
Surin, K. (1990) 'Towards a "Materialist" Critique of Religious Pluralism: An Examination of the Discourse of John Hick and Wilfred Cantwell Smith,' in I. Hamnett (ed.) *Religious Pluralism and Unbelief: Studies Critical and Comparative*, London and New York: Routledge, 114–29.
Svensson, G. (1981) *On Doubting the Reality of Reality: Moore and Wittgenstein on Skeptical Doubts*, Stockholm: Almqvist and Wiksell International.
Thompson, C. (1997) 'Wittgenstein, Tolstoy and the Meaning of Life,' *Philosophical Investigations*, Vol. 20, No. 2 (April): 97–116.
Tilghman, B.R. (1991) *Wittgenstein, Ethics and Aesthetics: The View from Eternity*, New York: State University of New York Press.
Tolstoy, L. (1982) *The Raid and Other Stories*, trans. L. and A. Maude, Oxford: Oxford University Press.
—— (1987) *A Confession and Other Religious Writings*, trans. J. Kentish, London: Penguin.
Trigg, R. (1999) *Ideas of Human Nature: An Historical Introduction*, Oxford: Basil Blackwell.
Ward, G. (1998) *Barth, Derrida and the Language of Theology*, Cambridge, UK: Cambridge University Press.
Weil, S. (1987) *Gravity and Grace*, trans. E. Craufurd, London: ARC Paperbacks.
Wells, H.G. (1988) *The Time Machine*, London: Everyman's Library, J.M. Dent and Sons.
Werhane, P.H. (1995) 'Levinas's Ethics: A Normative Perspective without Metaethical Constraints,' in A.T. Peperzak (ed.) *Ethics as First Philosophy: The Significance of Emmanuel Levinas for Philosophy, Literature and Religion*, London and New York: Routledge, 59–67.
Wheeler III, S.C. (2000) *Deconstruction as Analytic Philosophy*, Stanford, Calif.: Stanford University Press.
Wiesel, E. (1981) *Night*, trans. S. Rodway, Harmondsworth: Penguin.
Williams, B. (1973) *Morality: An Introduction to Ethics*, Harmondsworth: Penguin.
Winch, P. (1960) 'Nature and Convention,' *Proceedings of the Aristotelian Society*, Vol. 20: 231–52.
—— (1964) 'Understanding a Primitive Society,' *American Philosophical Quarterly*, Vol. 1, No. 4 (October): 307–24.
—— (1970) 'Comment,' in R. Borger and F. Cioffi (eds) *Explanation in the Behavioral Sciences*, Cambridge, UK: Cambridge University Press, 249–69.
—— (1979) 'Apel's "Transcendental Pragmatics",' in S.C. Brown (ed.) *Philosophical Disputes in the Social Sciences*, Chichester: Harvester Press, 51–73.
—— (1987) *Trying to Make Sense*, Oxford: Basil Blackwell.

Wittgenstein, L. (1958) *Philosophical Investigations*, trans. G.E.M. Anscombe, Oxford: Basil Blackwell.
—— (1969) *The Blue and Brown Books*, Oxford: Basil Blackwell.
—— (1974) *Letters to Russell, Keynes and Moore*, G.H. von Wright and B.F. McGuinness (eds), Oxford: Basil Blackwell.
—— (1978) 'On Heidegger on Being and Dread,' trans. M. Murray, in M. Murray (ed.) *Heidegger and Modern Philosophy: Critical Essays*, New Haven, Conn. and London: Yale University Press, 80–1.
—— (1979a) *Notebooks 1914–1916*, trans. G.E.M. Anscombe, G.H. von Wright and G.E.M. Anscombe (eds), Oxford: Basil Blackwell.
—— (1979b) *Wittgenstein's Lectures, Cambridge 1932–35* (from the Notes of A. Ambrose and M. Macdonald), A. Ambrose (ed.), Oxford: Basil Blackwell.
—— (1990) *Zettel*, trans. G.E.M. Anscombe, G.E.M. Anscombe and G.H. von Wright (eds), Oxford: Basil Blackwell.
—— (1993) *Philosophical Occasions 1912–1951*, J. Klagge and A. Nordmann (eds), Indianapolis, Ind./Cambridge, Mass.: Hackett.
—— (1994a) *Culture and Value*, trans. P. Winch, G.H. von Wright (ed.), Oxford: Basil Blackwell.
—— (1994b) *Lectures and Conversations on Aesthetics, Psychology and Religious Belief*, C. Barrett (ed.) Oxford: Basil Blackwell.
—— (1995) *Tractatus Logico-Philosophicus*, trans. D.F. Pears and B.F. McGuinness, London and New York: Routledge.
—— (1996a) 'Remarks on Frazer's *Golden Bough*,' trans. J. Beversluis, in C.G. Luckhardt (ed.) *Wittgenstein: Sources and Perspectives*, Bristol: Thoemmes Press, 61–81.
—— (1996b) 'Letters to Ludwig von Ficker,' trans. B. Gillette (A. Janik, ed.), in C.G. Luckhardt (ed.) *Wittgenstein: Sources and Perspectives*, Bristol: Thoemmes Press, 82–98.
—— (1999) *On Certainty*, trans. G.E.M. Anscombe and D. Paul, G.E.M. Anscombe and G.H. von Wright (eds), Oxford: Basil Blackwell.
Wood, D. (1990) *Philosophy at the Limit*, London: Unwin Hyman.
Zweig, S. (2000) *Beware of Pity*, trans. P. and T. Blewitt, London: Pushkin Press.

All biblical quotations are from *The New English Bible*, Oxford and Cambridge University Press, 1970.

Index

Aboriginal people 79–80, 95, 226n76
Abraham 47–8, 53, 55
acts/omissions 242n53
agnosticism 17, 103
altruism 167, 169
amoralism 88, 230n148
Analytical philosophy 10–11
animals: children 171; Derrida 178, 179; ethics 9; face 177; humanity 169–70, 174–6, 189; Winch 257n185; *see also* non-humanity
anthropocentrism 177–8, 257n179
anti-humanism 162–3
anti-naturalism 8–9, 148–9, 166, 173–4, 178, 200, 257n178
anti-skepticism 42–3, 51–2
anti-terrorism measures 223n16
ataraxia: belief 16; Pyrrhonian Skepticism 13–15, 17, 49, 62, 96, 140; reason 18; Sextus 4, 14, 15–16, 28, 43, 202n9; suffering 16–17; undecidability 193–4; Wittgenstein 32, 210n10
atheism 101, 107, 196, 197
Austin, J.L. 188–9, 191, 253n99
authenticity 124–5, 139
automata 83–4

Bachelard, G. 122, 185
Baudelaire, C. 1, 135, 174
Bauman, Z. 249n218
being-at-a-loss 18, 204n53
belief: *ataraxia* 16; conflicting xiii, 98; foundational 54; grounds for 51; Last Judgement 52–3; Moore 64; *On Certainty* xiii, 66–8; Pyrrhonian Skepticism 206n110, 210n10; stubbornness 59; suffering 216n147; superstition 58, 217n152; trust 110; Wittgenstein 59, 102–3, 210n10, 233n9; world-pictures 53, 59; *see also* religious belief
believers/non-believers 104–5, 106
Bernstein, R.J. 10, 248n182
blame 246n153
Blanchot, M. 266n162
blasphemy 56, 57, 121, 222n251
Bloor, D. 38, 40, 42, 46, 70
Bobby, the dog 171, 172, 175–6
body 83, 85–6, 131, 232n200; *see also* face
Buber, Martin 123

Cage, John viii

Cain 130, 141, 174
can/ought 115, 119
Caputo, J.D.: atheism 196; bad conscience 130; Derrida 180; disasters 69, 222n259; fundamentalism 217n166; Levinas 130, 180, 230n153; pain 87, 229n142; religion 41
Cartesian method 46
Cavell, S. 41
children: animality 171; education 98; learning 47, 50; moral consciousness 249n209; suffering 88, 172, 229n140; vulnerability 175
Christadelphians 58, 217n168, 218n171
Christianity: altruism 167; conversion 107, 221n235; enlightenment 73; fundamentalism 57–8, 74, 75, 217n166; Hick 74–5; Kierkegaard 239–40n125; Nietzsche 168; Tolstoy 114; Wittgenstein 112, 238n90
cinematic devices 228n112
Clack, B.R. 106, 107, 237n89
clothing example 124
commonality 80–1, 92, 176
compassion 156, 255n141
confession: Derrida 188, 261n50, 263n97; guilt 143–4; Levinas 152; Newton 249n223; Tolstoy 106; Wittgenstein 143–4, 207n144, 238n94
conscience: bad 113, 129–30, 144, 167, 192, 195, 200; good 3, 88, 121, 144, 182, 193–4; guilt 123, 125–8; haunting 106; Levinas 7, 137; public 126
conservatism: fideism 204n59; Nyíri 37–8, 46; *On Certainty* 70, 97; Phillips 209n170
contamination 98, 192
Continental philosophy 9–11
conversion 107, 221n235
creationism 217n170
Critchley, S. 158, 223n13, 257n179, 259n4

Darwinism 168
Dasein: authenticity 139; Heidegger 123–8, 134, 138–9, 241n25, 254n123; Levinas 254n122
death 186, 187–8, 237n78
decision-making 194–5, 266n179
Defoe, Daniel: *Robinson Crusoe* 141–2, 144–5, 160–1, 171, 181–2
democracy 252–3n84; relativistic 71, 72–3
Derrida, Jacques xii–xiii, 70; animals 178, 179; Baudelaire 174; Caputo 180; 'Circumfession' 196; confession 261n50, 263n97188; decision-making 194–5, 266n179; dogmatism

223n13; *Ethics, Institutions and the Right to Philosophy* 12; face 152–3; gift-giving 165, 185–6; *The Gift of Death* 139; God 111, 197; guilt 136, 140; hospitality 178, 179, 180–1, 183–4, 192, 200; *Of Hospitality* 180; hostage/host 183; iterability 177–8, 187, 188–9, 225n47, 262n72, 263n93; justice 196; Levinas 2–3, 8, 149–50, 177–8; literature 268n214; love/tolerance 96; *Negotiations* 101; other 10, 170; plurality 77; religion 197–8; skepticism 188; survivor's guilt 129; truth 28; violence 192
Descartes, René 46, 83
desire for other 165–6, 182, 254n117
differences 3–7, 75–6, 80, 92, 95
Diogenes 15, 16
disasters 69, 222n259
disfigurement 82–3
dissensus 4, 71, 78, 79
dogmatism 218n174; Derrida 223n13; Pyrrhonian Skepticism 17; religion 58; Sextus 43; skepticism 19; Wittgenstein 41, 104
Dostoyevsky, Fyodor: *The Brothers Karamazov* 120–1, 123, 144; *Crime and Punishment* 120
doubt 18, 43, 44–5, 51–2
Drury. M. 12–13, 106, 107, 113, 136, 209n176, 237n78

education 65, 98
Edwards, J.C. 42, 210n4
Enlightenment 80, 166
epistemology 99
equipollence 17, 18, 19, 32
ethical approach xiii, 2, 131–2
ethical/political factors 18–21, 41
ethics: animals 9; epistemology 99; guilt 121; language 122–3, 171; naturalism 8–9; *On Certainty* 81; *Philosophical Investigations* 82; politics 18–21; predator 166; reason 9, 173–4; religion 6–7, 158, 159–60; responsibility 109, 233n4; skepticism 254n111; social relations 99–100; subjectivity 2, 135; supernatural 116–17, 196; Winch 232n3; world-book 116–17
evil 184–5, 191, 214n98
evolution, theory of 217n170
expression, facial 84–5, 134

face: animality 177; body 131; Derrida 152–3; disfigurement 82–3; ethical approach 131–2; expression 84–5, 134; God 150–1; language 132, 153; Levinas 7, 9, 131–5, 149, 151–3, 245n113, 251n49; other 132, 134, 153–4, 219n198, 247n170, 258n202; 'Thou shalt not kill' 137–8; visitation 250n6; vulnerability 174; Wittgenstein 83
faith: crisis of 53, 107; *Culture and Value* 56; Kierkegaard 217n153; Levinas 159–60, 179; love 56; sacrifice 104; trust 47, 56; world-pictures 198
Feyerabend, P. 71–3, 77, 222n254
von Ficker, Ludwig 117
fideism 5, 63, 106, 197, 199, 224n24
Fogelin, R.J. 202n5
forgiveness 243–4n75
Frazer, James 91–3, 106, 108, 231n181; *see also* Wittgenstein, 'Remarks on Frazer's *Golden Bough*'

free will 230n149
Freud, Sigmund 208n150
fundamentalism 57–8, 74, 75, 217n166

Gadamer, H.G. 265n143
Gaita, R. 96, 143, 144–5, 227n90, 235–6n53, 248–9n203, 249n219
Galileo 222n254
generosity, pure 192
Genesis 47, 58, 141
gift-giving 119, 165, 185–6, 191–2
God 53, 115, 151; Derrida 111, 197; face 150–1; Hick 74; Levinas 149, 150, 151, 159–60; Malcolm 250n21; Nazism 128–9; Tolstoy 103–4, 110, 113; Wittgenstein 109, 110–11, 115, 206n107, 240n129
goodness 96, 119
Graham, G. 214n98
grammar, surface/depth 105, 206n101
Greisch, J. 6, 70, 81–2, 101, 240n5, 240n6
guilt: confession 143–4; conscience 123, 125–8; Derrida 136, 140; ethics 121; Gaita 249n219; Heidegger 102, 140, 141, 241n12; innocence 249n207; Levinas 1, 102, 120–1, 123, 136, 140, 141, 147, 164, 187, 199–200; *On Certainty* 81; punishment 167; radical singularity 143, 145–6, 147; responsibility 116, 120–1, 143, 195; shame 196; suffering 145; survivor 7, 8, 129, 130–1, 141–2, 187–8; value judgements 117–19; Wittgenstein 119, 123

Habermas, J. 232n201
Harvey, I.E. 133
haunting 128, 182, 194
Heidegger, Martin: Auschwitz 195; *Being and Time* 8, 123–7; clothing example 124; Dasein 123–8, 134, 138–9, 241n25, 254n123; good conscience 144; guilt 102, 140, 141, 241n12; hesitancy 18; Levinas 7–8, 129–30, 139–40; ontology 7–8, 163; sacrifice 127; silence 262n69
Heller, Joseph 20, 37
Helvétius, C.A. 166
Hertzberg, L. 48, 54, 55, 175, 213n77, 238n103
Herzog, Werner 79–81
Hick, J.: Christianity 74–5; God 74; religion 77; religious exclusivism 78–9; religious pluralism 71, 73–4, 75, 76, 81, 223n18
history 214n90, 234n17
D'Holbach, P.H.D. 255n141
holiness 162, 196, 254n112; *see also* saintliness
Holland, R.F. 208n147
Holocaust 128
home 18, 2, 186, 259n229
hospitality: Derrida 178, 179, 180–1, 183–4, 192, 200, 262n67, 266n163; evil 191; language 262n67; Levinas 178, 266n163; radical indifference 192; refuge 181–2; third party 191–2; trespassing 185–6; trust 190–1; vulnerability 183–5
host 183
hostage 130–1, 183, 246n146
house keys analogy 49–50
Hudson, W.D. 50, 54–5, 216n138
human behavior 183, 264–5n139
human nature 169, 254–5n125
humanism 161–2, 162–3, 177

humans: Aboriginal peoples 95; animals 169–70, 170–1, 174–5, 174–6, 189; automata 83–4; body 86; commonality 80–1, 92; disasters 222n259; face 132, 153; Levinas 170–1; lost 94–5; non-humanity 82; sacred objects 80
humour 231n178
Husserl, Edmund 81–2, 85, 149, 153

ideal 31
imagination 211n40
immorality 121
immortality 262n72; responsibility 6–7; *Tractatus Logico-Philosophicus* 102–3; Wittgenstein 109, 112, 115, 120
imperatives: categorical 116, 133, 223n13; hypothetical 116; 'Thou shalt not kill' 137–8, 151, 174
impossible 193, 216n137
indifference 88, 192
innocence 249n207
instinct-actions 93
inter-personal relations 82–3, 164–5
intersubjectivity 131, 170–1, 178, 183–4
invitation 183–4
Isaac 47–8, 55, 213n77
iterability 177–8, 187, 188–9, 225n47, 262n72, 263n93

James, William 66
Jehovah's Witnesses 57–8, 222n251
1 John 53
2 John 261n55
judgement 60, 62; *see also* value judgements
just society 72
justice: Aboriginal people 226n76; Derrida 196; Levinas 154–5; Lyotard 77–8; Nietzsche 166; *Certainty* 62; Schopenhauer 70

Kant, Immanuel 116, 178
Kellner, D. 124–5, 142
Kierkegaard, S. 53; Christianity 239–40n125; faith 197, 217n153; life 216–17n149; Olsen 235n47
kiss as ritual 114
knowledge 43, 44–5, 48, 51–2, 189
Kolakowski, L. 41
Kuhn, T. 60; conversion 221n235; *The Structure of Scientific Revolutions* 61–2, 219n202

ladder metaphor 28–9
land ownership 79–80
Lang, R. 262n67
language: ethics 122–3, 171; face 151, 160; Irish 209n176; last words 186; Levinas 2, 122–3, 160–1, 171–2; meanings 32–3, 117; mortality/immortality 187; Nietzsche 206n105; ontology 223n3; ordinary 27, 142, 189; *Philosophical Investigations* 90–1; predictability 84; responsibility 129; social relations 160–1; translatability 133–4; Wittgenstein 4, 23, 26–7, 31–3, 90–1, 96–7, 172
language acquisition 98–9, 172
language-games: Lyotard 79; *On Certainty* 38, 63–4; primitive 86; social relations 63–4; trust 189–90; Wittgenstein 3–5, 38–9, 44, 46, 48, 71, 101, 173–4, 203n17

Last Judgement 52–3, 57, 58, 104, 110
learning 47, 50–2, 57, 81
Levi, P. 130–1, 243–4n75
Levinas, Emmanuel 136, 239n115; anti-naturalism 8–9, 148–9, 166, 173–4, 178, 200, 257n178; Caputo 130, 180, 230n153; confession 152; conscience 137; Dasein 254n122; Derrida 2–3, 8, 149–50, 177–8; desire for other 165–6, 182, 254n117; face 7, 9, 131–5, 149, 151–3, 245n113, 251n49; faith 159–60, 179; God 149, 150, 151, 159–60; guilt 1, 102, 120–1, 123, 136, 140, 141, 147, 164, 187, 199–200; Heidegger 7–8, 129–30, 139–40; home 181–2, 259n229; hospitality 266n163178; humanism 162–3, 177; humans/animals 170; justice 154–5; language 2, 122–3, 160–1, 171–2; love 253n93; 'Meaning and Sense' 98–9; *Nine Talmudic Readings* 180; other 10, 140–1, 149–50, 157–8, 161–2, 165, 170, 245n130; *Otherwise than Being* 152, 157; religion/ethics 7, 159–60; responsibility 138, 146–7, 148; Rousseau 156–7; saintliness 119, 162, 163–4, 177, 255n128; subjectivity 1–2, 70, 128, 135; survivor's guilt 129, 187–8; 'Thou shalt not kill' 137–8, 174; *Totality and Infinity* 200
literature 263n97, 268n214
Logical Positivism 111
love: as analogy 48–9; faith 56; history 214n90; intimacy 182; Levinas 253n93; performative 235n51; social relations 167–8, 154–5; tolerance 96; vulnerability 261n60
Luke's Gospel 261n55
Lyotard, J.F. 77–9, 225n50; differences 92, 95; *The Differend* 78–9, 225n53; dissensus 4, 71, 78, 79; paganism 77, 81; politics 226n66; radical pluralism 101–2, 108

Malcolm, N. 109, 110–13, 120, 250n21
Martin, D. 54
Marx, Werner 81–2
Messiah 184, 186
mining companies 79–80
Monk, R. 120
Montaigne, M. 122
Moore, G.E. 46; belief 64; common sense 43; hinged learning 47, 57, 81; knowledge 44–5, 51; moral intuitionism 267n209; other 210–11n26; propositions 112, 191, 211n35
moral community 88–9
moral consciousness 249n209
moral intuitionism 267n209
moral philosophy 142
morality 137, 167, 168–9
Morawetz, T. 49, 221n233
mortality 187
mourning 137, 157

natural realm 27–8, 39–40, 98, 163
naturalism: ethics 8–9; Nietzsche 166–7; Pyrrhonian Skepticism 25, 39; Wittgenstein 5, 10, 42, 89, 100, 105, 108, 173, 190, 199, 215n115, 230n163, 268n224
Nazism 128–9
negative theology 117
Nelson, G.K. 66
New Religious Movements 66

Newton, Sir Isaac 249n223
Nietzsche, Friedrich: Christianity 168; Darwinism 168; *On the Genealogy of Morality* 101; holiness 254n112; justice 166; language 206n105; morality 167, 168–9; naturalism 166–7; *Thus Spake Zarathustra* 122
non-believers 104–5
non-commitment 21
non-humanity 9, 82, 87, 228–9n131, 258n208; *see also* animals
Nussbaum, M. 15, 16, 18–19, 25
Nuyen, A.T. 88, 230n158, 243n74
Nyíri, J.C. 37, 38–9, 40, 42, 46, 70

On Certainty (Wittgenstein) 51–2, 209–10n3; belief xiii, 66–8; conservatism 70, 97; ethics 81; imagination 211n40; irreconcilable principles 32; judgement 60; justice 62; knowledge/doubt 44–5, 48, 189; language-games 38, 63–4; quasi-communitarianism 42, 43–4; reason/persuasion 4, 32; religious belief 52; science/religion 218n188; skepticism 42–3; trust 175, 189
ontology 7–8, 111–12, 163, 223n3, 248n185
ordinary language philosophy 27, 142
original sin 114–15, 136–7, 195
other 86, 101–2, 256n168; Derrida 10, 170; desire 165–6, 182, 254n117; differences 75–6; face 132, 134, 153–4, 219n198, 247n170, 258n202; fear of 256n154; Levinas 10, 140–1, 149–50, 157–8, 161–2, 165, 170, 245n130; Lyotard 78; Moore 210–11n26; openness to 184; responsibility 136, 137; sacrifice 139–40; self-presence 134–5; space 247n163; suffering 174; violence 102; world-pictures 99, 219n192, 221n245

paganism 77, 81, 94–5
pain 87, 88, 210n19, 227n88, 229n142; *see also* suffering
Pascal, Blaise 1, 130
Pascal, Fania 143–4, 208n161
persuasion xiii, 4, 17–18, 34, 64, 145
Phillips, D.Z. 209n170
Philo 209n174
Philosophical Investigations (Wittgenstein): ethics 82; humans/animals 170, 189; ideal 31; language 90–1; language-games 63–4; nature 90; philosophical practices 24, 207n133; preface 33
philosophical practice: Levinas 239n115; Wittgenstein 21–3, 24, 35, 205n83
physics 59, 163
Picard, M. 150, 172, 176, 254–5n125
pluralism: Hick 73–4, 76, 223n18; plurality 224n19; radical 101–2, 108; relativistic 71–2; religious 71, 73–4, 75, 76, 81, 223n18; universality 76
plurality 70–1, 77, 224n19
politics/ethics 18–21, 226n66
postmodernism 225n50
predators 166
predictions 58–9
principles: foundational 189, 191; hinged 213n84; reconciliation of 32, 59, 63–4, 65, 68; unifying 82; world-pictures 59–60
prophets, false 53

Putnam, H. 243n74
Pyrrho of Elis 202n9
Pyrrhonian Skepticism 207n133; *ataraxia* 13–15, 17, 49, 62, 96, 140; 'being-at-a-loss' 18, 204n53; belief 206n110, 210n10; ethical/political implications 18–21; liberation 96, 97–8, 203n39; naturalism 25, 39; persuasion 17–18; therapeutic techniques 13–14, 24; truth 14, 18; Wittgenstein 4, 13, 35–6, 202n5

quasi-communitarianism 41, 43–4
Quine, W.V.O. 60–1

randomness 267n192
Readings, B. 79–81, 80, 87, 94; radical pluralism 101–2, 108
reason: *ataraxia* 18; consensus 224–5n42; ethics 9, 173–4; persuasion xiii, 4, 34, 64, 145; Rousseau 12
Redpath, T. 120
refuge 181–2
relativism 42, 71–2, 239n118
reliance 48, 55, 238n103
religion: Caputo 41; conversion 66; Derrida 197–8; dogmatism 58; ethical approach 2; ethics 6–7, 158, 159–60; faith 197–8; Frazer 91–2; fundamentalism 74; Hick 77; Levinas 7, 159–60; predictions 58–9; responsibility 7; ritual 91–2, 108; superstition 5–6; Wittgenstein 5–6, 33–4, 106; *see also* confession; faith
religiosity 55–6, 107–8, 113, 150, 199
religious belief 41, 56, 57, 217n152; *On Certainty* 52; Wittgenstein 105–6, 107, 113–14, 115, 158
religious exclusivism 78–9
remorse 120, 195
responsibility: ethics 109, 233n4; guilt 116, 120–1, 143, 195; immortality 6–7; language 129; Levinas 138, 146–7, 148; moral 143; other 136, 137; religion 7; sacrifice 156–7; unconditional 115–16
Rhees, R. 21–2, 33, 34
ritual: Frazer 231n181; instinct 93; non-religious 236n53; religious 91–2, 108; Wittgenstein 114, 266n174
river-bed metaphor 54–5, 216n139, 224n34
river-blindness analogy 67–8
Robbins, J. 123
Robinson Crusoe (Defoe) 141–2, 144–5, 160–1, 171, 181–2
Rorty, Richard 203n17, 222n248, 255n140
Rousseau, J.-J. 265n139; *The Confessions* 142, 146; *A Discourse on the Origin of Inequality* 138, 156; and Levinas 156–7; property 247n166; reason 12

sacrifice: Abraham 47–8, 53, 55; faith 104; Heidegger 127; other 139–40; responsibility 156–7; self-sacrifice 99, 164, 167; Wittgenstein 148
De Sade, D.A.F. 166, 230n155
saintliness 8–9, 119, 162, 163–4, 177, 255n128
Sartre, J.-P. 215n129, 216n134
Schilndler's List (Speilberg) 143
Schopenhauer, A. 70, 94, 148, 192

science 61–2, 218n188, 220n213
scientism 108, 163
sectarianism 218n174
selfishness 167
Seventh-day Adventists 57–8
Sextus Empiricus: *ataraxia* 4, 14, 15–16, 28, 43; dogmatism 43; natural realm 27–8; *see also* Pyrrhonian Skepticism
Shields, P.R. 34, 114–15
sign 189
silence 29, 221n236, 262n69
skepticism 41; anti-skepticism 42–3, 51–2; Derrida 188; dogmatism 19; ethics 254n111
Smart, N. 5, 6
social conformity 37, 124–5
social prejudices 19, 20
social relations: differences 4; ethics 99–100; language 160–1; language-games 63–4; love 154–5, 167–8; Rousseau 156; trust 4–5, 190
society: primitive/modern 108; science 220n213
space, other 247n163
speech-act theory 191, 253n99
Speilberg, Steven 143
stubbornness 59, 61–2
subjectivity 1–2, 70, 128, 135
suffering: *ataraxia* 16–17; belief 216n147; children 88, 172, 229n140; commonality 176; guilt 145; inevitability 25; non-humanity 87, 228–9n131; other 174; pain 88, 210n19, 227n88; primitive reaction 86–7; trivialized 68–9; Wittgenstein 82, 172
supernatural ethics 116–17, 196
superstition 5–6, 58, 217n152
Surin, K. 76–7, 81, 86, 101–2, 108
survivor's guilt 7, 8, 129, 130–1, 141–2, 187–8

tennis-playing analogy 117–18
testimony 151–2, 190
therapeutic techniques: *Culture and Value* 24; ethical-political factors 41; Pyrrhonian Skepticism 13–14, 24; Sextus 4, 70, 96; Wittgenstein 4, 70, 96, 199
1 Thessalonians 186
third party 154–5, 157, 191–2; *see also* other
'Thou shalt not kill' 137–8, 151, 174
Tolstoy, Leo: Christianity 114; confession 106; *A Confession* 103–4, 110, 205n93, 236n55, 237n85; God 103–4, 110, 113
totalitarianism 71–3, 78
Tractatus Logico-Philosophicus (Wittgenstein): completion of 31; immortality 102–3; and 'A Lecture of Ethics' 116, 122–3; negative theology 117; propositions 28–9; saying/showing 45–6; silence 196
tradition 71–3, 77
transcendence 250n11
trespassing 129, 147, 183, 185–6
Trigg, R. 173
trust: Abraham and Isaac 47–8; belief 110; dissipation of 50; faith 47, 56; foundational principles 189; Hertzberg 54; hospitality 190–1; language-games 189–90; learning 47, 50–1; *On Certainty* 175, 189; primitive 50, 175; reliance 48, 55, 238n103; social relations 4–5, 190; vulnerability 69

truth 14, 18, 28, 41, 44
truth-telling 265n149

undecidability 193–4
universality 48, 76, 133, 162
unperturbedness *see ataraxia*
unpredictability 183

value judgements 116, 117–19, 239n118
violence: Derrida 192; natural capacity for 229n136; other 102; preethical 102, 246n144; third party 154; vulnerability 134
le visage 133–4
visitation 183–5, 250n6, 251n39
voluntarism 72
vulnerability: children 175; commonality 176; face 174; home 186; hospitality 183–5; love 261n60; trust 69; violence 134

Where the Green Ants Dream (Herzog) 79–81
Winch, P.: animals 257n185; community 88–9; contradiction 233n16; ethics 101; humans 232n3; truth-telling 265n149
Wittgenstein, Ludwig 12–13, 30–1; *ataraxia* 32, 210n10; belief 59, 102–3, 210n10, 233n9; believers/non-believers 104–5, 106; body 83, 85–6, 131, 232n200; Christianity 112, 238n90; confession 143–4, 238n94; differences 3–7; face 83; forms of life 3, 71; frame of reference 48; free will 230n149; God 109, 110–11, 115, 206n107, 240n129; guilt 119, 123; humour 231n178; immortality 109, 112, 115, 120; language 4, 23, 26–7, 31–3, 90–1, 96–7, 172; language-games 3–5, 38–9, 44, 46, 48, 71, 101, 173–4, 203n17; learning 50; 'A Lecture on Ethics' 111, 116, 122–3, 193; 'Lectures on Aesthetics' 34; 'Lectures on Religious Belief' 52, 55, 57, 59, 97, 102, 105, 119; natural realm 27–8, 39–40, 98, 163; naturalism 5, 10, 42, 89, 100, 105, 108, 173, 190, 199, 215n115, 230n163, 268n224; non-philosophical life 25, 96–7, 208n159; normativity 72, 112, 206n113; philosophical practice 21–3, 24, 35, 205n83; publishing work 208n160; Pyrrhonian Skepticism 4, 13, 35–6, 202n5; religion 5–6, 33–4, 106; religiosity 55–6, 107–8, 199; religious belief 105–6, 107, 113–14, 115, 158; 'Remarks on Frazer's *Golden Bough*' 5, 59, 89, 90–3, 97, 105–6, 107; ritual 114, 266n174; sacrifice 148; suffering 82, 172; therapeutic techniques 4, 36, 70, 96, 199; truth 28; universality 48; *Zettel* 25, 35, 98, 132; *see also Culture and Value; On Certainty; Philosophical Investigations; Tractatus Logico-Philosophicus;* world-pictures
world-pictures: belief 53, 59; conflicting 67–8; excluded items 98; faith 198; haunting 194; language 3, 50; other 99, 219n192, 221n245; principles 59–60
world-book 116–17
wretchedness 113, 120, 199

Zweig, Stefan viii, 148

Printed in the United Kingdom
by Lightning Source UK Ltd.
125836UK00001B/127-129/A